Approaching Historical Sources in their Contexts

In *Approaching Historical Sources in their Contexts*, twelve academics examine how space, time and performance interact to co-create context for source analysis.

The chapters cover 2000 years and stretch across the Americas and Europe. They are grouped into three themes, with the first four exploring aspects of movement within and around an environment: buildings, the tension between habitat and tourist landscape, cemeteries and war memorials. Three chapters look at different aspects of performance: masque and opera in which performance is (re)constructed from several media, radio and television. The final group of chapters consider objects and material culture in which both spatial placement and performance influence how they might be read as historical sources: archaeological finds and their digital management, the display of objects in heritage locations, clothing, photograph albums and scrapbooks. Supported by a range of case studies, the contributors embed lessons and methodological approaches within their chapters that can be adapted and adopted by those working with similar sources, offering students both a theoretical and practical demonstration of how to analyse sources within their contexts.

Drawing out common threads to help those wishing to illuminate their own historical investigation, this book encourages a broad and inclusive approach to the physical and social contexts of historical evidence for those undertaking source analysis.

Sarah Barber is Senior Lecturer in History at Lancaster University, UK. She publishes widely on early modern Britain, Ireland and the colonial Americas. Her recent work reconfigures colonialism, decolonising the writing of colonial encounter, such as in the monograph, *The Disputatious Caribbean* (2014). Recovering the voices of the silent and silenced spurs her work to expand historical source material.

Corinna M. Peniston-Bird is Senior Lecturer in Gender and Cultural History at Lancaster University, UK. She works on experiences and cultural memories of war, focussing largely on the World Wars. Her interests lie in the disruptive, the excluded and the marginalised and the sources which allow historians that focus. Her recent publications have explored British memorials, wartime cinema and the significance of wartime memories of bananas.

The Routledge Guides to Using Historical Sources

How does the historian approach primary sources? How do interpretations differ? How can such sources be used to write history?

The *Routledge Guides to Using Historical Sources* series introduces students to different sources and illustrates how historians use them. Titles in the series offer a broad spectrum of primary sources and, using specific examples, examine the historical context of these sources and the different approaches that can be used to interpret them.

Reading Russian Sources
A Student's Guide to Text and Visual Sources from Russian History
Edited by George Gilbert

History and Economic Life
A Student's Guide to approaching Economic and Social History sources
Edited by Georg Christ and Philipp R. Roessner

Approaching Historical Sources in their Contexts
Space, Time and Performance
Edited by Sarah Barber and Corinna M. Peniston-Bird

Reading Primary Sources
The Interpretation of Texts from Nineteenth and Twentieth Century History, 2nd edition
Edited by Miriam Dobson and Benjamin Ziemann

Sources for the History of Emotions
A Guide
Edited by Katie Barclay, Sharon Crozier-De Rosa, and Peter N. Stearns

For more information about this series, please visit: https://www.routledge.com/Routledge-Guides-to-Using-Historical-Sources/book-series/RGHS

Approaching Historical Sources in their Contexts

Space, Time and Performance

Edited by Sarah Barber and
Corinna M. Peniston-Bird

Routledge
Taylor & Francis Group
LONDON AND NEW YORK

First published 2020
by Routledge
2 Park Square, Milton Park, Abingdon, Oxon OX14 4RN

and by Routledge
52 Vanderbilt Avenue, New York, NY 10017

Routledge is an imprint of the Taylor & Francis Group, an informa business

© 2020 selection and editorial matter, Sarah Barber and Corinna M. Peniston-Bird; individual chapters, the contributors

The right of Sarah Barber and Corinna M. Peniston-Bird to be identified as the authors of the editorial material, and of the authors for their individual chapters, has been asserted in accordance with sections 77 and 78 of the Copyright, Designs and Patents Act 1988.

All rights reserved. No part of this book may be reprinted or reproduced or utilised in any form or by any electronic, mechanical, or other means, now known or hereafter invented, including photocopying and recording, or in any information storage or retrieval system, without permission in writing from the publishers.

Trademark notice: Product or corporate names may be trademarks or registered trademarks, and are used only for identification and explanation without intent to infringe.

British Library Cataloguing-in-Publication Data
A catalogue record for this book is available from the British Library

Library of Congress Cataloging-in-Publication Data
Names: Barber, Sarah, editor. | Peniston-Bird, C. M., editor.
Title: Approaching historical sources in their contexts : space, time and performance / edited by Sarah Barber and Corinna M. Peniston-Bird.
Description: New York : Routledge, 2020. | Series: Routledge guides to using historical sources | Includes bibliographical references and index.
Identifiers: LCCN 2019056999 (print) | LCCN 2019057000 (ebook)
Subjects: LCSH: History—Methodology. | History—Sources. | History—Study and teaching. | Historiography.
Classification: LCC D16 .A63 2020 (print) | LCC D16 (ebook) | DDC 907.1—dc23
LC record available at https://lccn.loc.gov/2019056999
LC ebook record available at https://lccn.loc.gov/2019057000

ISBN: 978-0-8153-6480-1 (hbk)
ISBN: 978-0-8153-6481-8 (pbk)
ISBN: 978-1-351-10657-3 (ebk)

Typeset in Times New Roman
by Apex CoVantage, LLC

**This collection is dedicated to
Sandra and Madeleine**

Contents

List of figures ix
List of contributors xi
Acknowledgements xvi

Introduction 1
SARAH BARBER AND CORINNA M. PENISTON-BIRD

1 **Building: constructing identities** 10
SARAH BARBER

2 **Landscape: consuming natural places** 32
MARK C. J. STODDART AND CHRISTINE KNOTT

3 **Cemeteries: tracing sepulchral cultures** 48
FELIX ROBIN SCHULZ

4 **War memorials: associative meanings** 65
CORINNA M. PENISTON-BIRD

5 **Masque and opera: staging performance** 87
ANDREW PINNOCK

6 **Radio: listening to the airwaves** 113
TONY STOLLER

7 **Television: capturing performance** 131
PHILIP KISZELY

8 **Digital surrogates: archaeological materialities** 147
ADAM RABINOWITZ

9	**Objects: dynamics of display**	166
	SARAH ANN ROBIN	
10	**Clothing: reading what was worn**	182
	LAURA R. PRIETO	
11	**Photo albums: autobiographical narrations**	207
	CORD PAGENSTECHER	
12	**Scrapbooks: a proliferation of meaning**	224
	ELOISE MOSS	

Index 242

Figures

1.1 Topographical map of the Sierra Crestellina: reproduced from *Restauación de las Ruinas y Rehabilitación como Centro Cultural de la Iglesia del Castillo de Casares* — 13
1.2 The village of Casares as depicted in the cadastral map prepared between 1756 and 1759, known as the Ensenada Cadastre. The castle and church are seen overlooking the hill — 15
1.3 Photograph of the restored steps up to the west door — 24
1.4 The east façade before (around 2001) and after (2012) the restoration, shown in a page from Restauación de las Ruinas — 25
1.5 Photograph of the interior of the Blas Infante Cultural Centre showing part of the quotation from Blas Infante — 25
1.6 Photograph of the interior of the Blas Infante Cultural Centre showing part of the exhibition of ideas for an Andalusian flag — 26
3.1 The family tomb of Franz Schlobach — 53
3.2 Friedrich Schultz's Chapel and Mortuary Building — 59
3.3 The gravestone of the Borsch Family — 61
4.1 The memorial to the Home Front in St Michael's Cathedral, Coventry — 66
4.2 St Michael's Cathedral, Coventry, the view of the exposed interior looking away from the memorial — 67
4.3 The memorial to African and Caribbean Service Personnel, London — 70
4.4 The memorial to The Women of World War II (John Mills, London, 2005) — 75
4.5 Instructions at the 9/11 Memorial Plaza — 79
4.6 Visitors around the Stelae, Berlin — 80
5.1 The Banqueting House, Whitehall. Designed by Inigo Jones for James I (1619); the backdrop for Charles I's execution in 1649 — 93
5.2 The Choir Screen, Winchester Cathedral (Inigo Jones, 1637–1638), with life-size bronze statues of James I (left) and Charles I (right). Engraving in Samuel Gale, *The History and Antiquities of the Cathedral Church of Winchester* (1715) — 94

x *Figures*

5.3	A display of garter regalia. Engraving by Wenceslaus Hollar, in Elias Ashmole, *The Institution, Laws and Ceremonies of the Most Noble Order of the Garter* (1672)	100
5.4	Garter Knights processing to St George's Hall, Windsor, for their annual feast. Charles II walks behind them under a canopy. Engraving by Hollar in Ashmole, *The Institution, Laws and Ceremonies*	101
8.1	Screen capture of a search in the Peripleo browser for coins from Antioch	151
8.2	Screen capture of search results in Open Context for records marked 'coin' including a value for 'origin place'	154
8.3	Screen capture of the spatial distribution of results of a PAS search for coins minted at Antioch	157
8.4	Scanned image of page 60 of notebook 101, from the 1928 excavations in Corinth	160
10.1	Nurse in uniform, Liverpool, England, *c.*1870–1890	189
10.2	Swimsuit (*c.*1920). Asbury Mills, New York (manufacturer), Annette Kellerman (designer)	190
10.3	Mary Schenck Woolman, *A Sewing Course,* 1901. Gift of Barbara White Haddad 1992.076.12	192
10.4	Mary Richardson Walker's lace mitts and fan Manuscripts, Archives, and Special Collections, Washington State University Libraries, Pullman, WA.	194
11.1	Album page of a Berlin couple with photographs of the Großglockner-Hochalpenstraße, 1967	212
11.2	'Ostlager, Zomer 1943'. Page from Dutch forced laborer Aart M.'s album	215
11.3	'Een gezellig zitje'. Dutch forced laborers, including Aart M. (2nd from left), on a Sunday in the barrack camp, summer 1944	216
11.4	'Ready to go!!! Everything polished once more'. Album page about the start of holiday travel 1965	220
12.1	WENSLEY/3/2, Scrapbook with News Cuttings (1930–1947), p. 46	226
12.2	WENSLEY/3/1, Scrapbook with News Cuttings (*c.*1891–1929), p. 20	231
12.3	WENSLEY/3/1, back cover	235

Contributors

Sarah Barber is Senior Lecturer in History at Lancaster University. Her interests range widely throughout the early modern period in particular, with her current research focussing on the first century of American colonisation and the transmission of ideas to-and-fro across the Atlantic. She also has extensive interests in European and British early modern history and is the author of three monographs on the English Revolution and the Caribbean: the latest of which, *Disputatious Caribbean: The West Indies in the Seventeenth Century*, was published in 2014. She has developed the techniques explored in *History Beyond the Text* (2009) to create a series of methodological and theoretical ways to approach 'irrecoverable', anonymous or hidden histories and to give weight to the narratives of those who are usually excluded because they were not the (written) recorders of their own histories.

Philip Kiszely is Director of Student Education in the School of Performance and Cultural Industries at the University of Leeds. His research explores cities and notions of urban and regional experience in the late 20th century and focusses on popular culture. He is the author of the award-nominated *Hollywood Through Private Eyes* (2006) and is founding co-editor of the international peer-reviewed journal *Punk & Post-Punk*. A tireless 'Madchester' reveller during the late 1980s and early 1990s, he is currently researching that scene.

Christine Knott is a doctoral student in Sociology at Memorial University. Her current research focus includes an intersectional political ecological approach to investigations of rural fishing communities and employment changes in the industry, including the need for temporary foreign workers.

Eloise Moss is Lecturer in Modern British History at the University of Manchester. Her expertise is in histories of crime, gender and urban culture, and she has previously published work on the scrapbooks of famous interwar detective Frederick Porter Wensley for the journal *Social History*. In 2019, her first book, *Night Raiders: Burglary and the Making of Modern Urban Life in London, 1860–1968*, was published with Oxford University Press. Eloise is currently focussing on developing a second monograph project on the history of hotels in 20th-century Britain, under the working title 'Hotelympus: A History of Power and Pampering in Modern Britain'.

xii *Contributors*

Cord Pagenstecher is a historian at the Center for Digital Systems of the Freie Universität Berlin, with a particular interest in visual and oral history, forced labour in Nazi Germany and tourism research. He has worked with Berlin History Workshop (since 1989), Ravensbrück Memorial Museum (1998–2000) and the Berlin office for compensation of Nazi victims (2001–2007). He currently oversees the online archive 'Forced Labor 1939–1945. Memory and History' and its digital learning applications. Select publications include 'Interviews als Quellen der Geschlechtergeschichte', the online archive 'Zwangsarbeit 1939–1945', and the 'Visual History Archive der USC Shoah Foundation', in: Bothe, Alina/Brüning, Christina Isabel (eds.): *Geschlecht und Erinnern im digitalen Zeitalter. Neue Perspektiven auf ZeitzeugInnenarchive*, Berlin: Lit Verlag 2015, 41–67 (with Doris Tausendfreund); and 'Der bundesdeutsche Tourismus. Ansätze zu einer Visual History: Urlaubsprospekte, Reiseführer, Fotoalben, 1950–1990, Hamburg, 2. ed. 2012; Reisekataloge und Urlaubsalben. Zur Visual History des touristischen Blicks', in: Gerhard Paul (ed.), *Visual History. Ein Studienbuch*, Göttingen 2006, 169–87.

Corinna M. Peniston-Bird is Senior Lecturer in Cultural History in the Department of History at Lancaster University, with a particular interest in pedagogy in the discipline. Since 1998, her research and teaching has centred on gender dynamics in Britain in the Second World War, with an emphasis on the relationship between memories and cultural representations. Previous publications on commemoration include 'The people's war in personal testimony and bronze: sorority and the memorial to The Women of World War II' In: Lucy Noakes and Juliette Pattinson (eds.) *British cultural memory and the Second World War*. (London: Bloomsbury Academic, 2013) pp. 67–87; 'All in it together and backs to the wall': relating patriotism and the people's war in the 21st century', *Oral History*. Autumn, 2012, pp. 69–80; and the co-edited special issue: with Wendy Ugolini, *Journal of War and Culture Studies* 'Silenced Mourning;' (2014). She has also co-edited three collections: with Emma Vickers, *Gender and the Second World War: Lessons of War* (Basingstoke, Hampshire: Palgrave Macmillan, 2016); with Sarah Barber, *History Beyond the Text: A Student's Guide to Approaching Alternative Sources*. (London: Routledge, 2008); with Gerard DeGroot, *A Soldier and a Woman: Sexual Integration in the Military* (Harlow: Pearson Education, 2000).

Andrew Pinnock is Professor in the University of Southampton's Music Department, a Purcell Society editor and administrator (Honorary Secretary from 2008 to 2014), one of the UK's most influential Purcell opera scholars and – improbably– a prize-winning cultural economist. He worked in the Arts Council's Music Department for 13 years, making public policy before taking an academic post and starting to research it. Previous publications include '*Deus ex machina*: A royal witness to the court origin of Purcell's Dido and Aeneas,' *Early Music*, 40, 2012, 265–278; and 'A double vision of Albion: allegorical re-alignments in the Dryden-Purcell semi-opera King Arthur,' *Restoration: Studies in English Literary Culture, 1660–1700*, 34, 2010, 55–81.

Contributors xiii

Laura R. Prieto (BA, Wellesley College; AM, PhD, Brown University) is Professor of History and of Women's and Gender Studies at Simmons College in Boston. Her ongoing research pays particular attention to visual culture in analysing gender, race and imperialism during the era of the Spanish-American War. Harvard University Press published her book, *At Home in the Studio: The Professionalization of Women Artists in America*, in 2001. Her most recent scholarship includes a series of essays on American and Filipina women at Protestant missions in Mindanao, published in *Women in Transnational History* (Routledge, 2016), *Paradoxes of Domesticity: Christian Missionaries and Women in Asia and the Pacific* (Australia National University Press, 2014) and *Competing Kingdoms: Women, Nation, Mission and American Empire* (Duke University Press, 2010). Another article, '"A Delicate Subject": Clemencia López, Civilized Womanhood, and the Politics of Anti-Imperialism,' appeared in the *Journal of the Gilded Age and Progressive Era* in April 2013. Prieto also created an online project on 19th-century women sculptors, abolition and women's rights for *Women and Social Movements in the United States*. She held the Ruth R. and Alyson R. Miller Fellowship at the Massachusetts Historical Society in 2010–2011 and served as the Vice-President and President of the New England Historical Association in 2008–2009 and 2009–2010, respectively. She teaches a wide range of courses in American history, gender history and methodology.

Adam Rabinowitz is Associate Professor in the Department of Classics and Assistant Director of the Institute of Classical Archaeology at The University of Texas at Austin. He holds his PhD (2004) from the Interdepartmental Program in Classical Art and Archaeology at the University of Michigan, where he wrote a dissertation on the role of communal wine-drinking in political and social interactions in the colonial Greek world. He was a 2002 Fellow of the American Academy in Rome and a field archaeologist with 25 years of archaeological field experience at Greek, Roman and Byzantine sites in Italy, England, Israel, Tunisia and Ukraine. His archaeological research focusses on daily life, domestic architecture, commensal practices and the lived experience of culture contact. He has also published on more historical questions of political organisation and competition in the early Greek world. He has a longstanding interest in the use of digital platforms for archaeological documentation and publication, which began during his work at the Roman site of Cosa in the 1990s and intensified in the course of excavations in the South Region of the Greek, Roman and Byzantine site of Chersonesos in Crimea in the mid-2000s.

He is also involved in several digital humanities projects related to the linking and visualisation of information about the Classical past, including Pleiades (http://pleiades.stoa.org), a spatial gazetteer of ancient places; GeoDia (http://geodia.laits.utexas.edu), an interactive spatial timeline of Mediterranean archaeology; Hestia2 (http://hestia.open.ac.uk/), a narrative time-map of the Histories of Herodotus; and PeriodO (http://perio.do), a gazetteer of scholarly definitions of archaeological, historical and art-historical periods funded by the National Endowment for the Humanities and the Institute of Museum and Library Services.

Sarah Ann Robin was awarded her doctorate on love and material culture in the early modern period in 2016. She has taught at the University of Manchester and currently works as a Learning Developer at Lancaster University. She specialises in the early modern period, with particular interest in the 17th century. She works with material culture to illuminate history and has a specific interest and focus on the history of emotions. She liaised with many curators and trust employees in order to complete her doctorate. Her publications include 'Male Choice and Desire: Material Offerings in Seventeenth-Century England' in *Cultural and Social History* (2019), D.O.I. 10.1080/14780038.2019.1640021; 'Jewels of the Flesh: The Corporeal Relationship between Jewellery and the Body in the Early-Modern Period' in *Jewellery History Today*, (May, 2015), 23, pp. 6–7; and 'The Public and Private Realms in the Seventeenth-Century: A Parameter of Wood and Fabric' in *The Luminary: Sleepless Beds*, (June, 2013), 3, pp. 62–73. She has presented papers at numerous institutions, including the University of Western Australia, The Institute of Historical Research and Cambridge University.

Felix Robin Schulz is Senior Lecturer in Modern European History with an interest in the contemporary history of the German-speaking countries, with a particular focus on sepulchral cultures, regional and national memorialisation, as well as the link between landscape and identity. His first monograph (Berghahn, 2013) explores East German sepulchral culture (*i.e.*, cemeteries and their design, organisation of disposal, burial ceremonies, cremation, *etc.*) in the second half of the 20th century. Schulz has also published on the Alps and the relationship between spaces, places and identities in a diverse European cultural landscape. Currently he is working on GDR thanatology, the lithurgy and staging of official and quasi-official funerals as well as the evolution of undertaking in Germany as a modern profession.

Mark C. J. Stoddart is Associate Professor in the Department of Sociology at Memorial University in St. John's, Newfoundland and Labrador, Canada. His research interests include environmental sociology; social movements; tourism, sport and recreation; and communications and culture. His recent research examines how nature-based tourism is reconfiguring relationships between rural coastal communities and environments in Atlantic Canada. He is also engaged in ongoing research on the eco-politics of climate change in Canada, with a focus on the relationship between climate change media narratives and policy networks. He is the author of the book, *Making Meaning out of Mountains: The Political Ecology of Skiing* (UBC Press). His work has appeared or is forthcoming in *Global Environmental Change, Environmental Politics, Nature & Culture, Organization & Environment, Mobilities, Society & Natural Resources, International Review for the Sociology of Sport, Social Movement Studies* and *Human Ecology Review*.

Tony Stoller CBE is Visiting Professor of Media History in the Media and Communications Faculty at Bournemouth University. In 2010, he published *Sounds of Your Life: The History of Independent Radio in the* UK, the definitive study of this medium. He has recently completed a PhD, researching classical music on UK radio between 1945 and 1995. His current research interests include broadcasting regulation, music choice on radio during the Second World War and the nature of listening to classical music radio. He began his professional career in newspapers and radio regulation before running the Independent Local Radio station in Reading, Radio 210. He was appointed Chief Executive of The Radio Authority – the regulatory body for all non-BBC radio – in 1995 and subsequently helped to set up the new communications regulator, Ofcom. He is currently Chair of the Joseph Rowntree Foundation and of the Joseph Rowntree Housing Trust and the editor of the Quaker publication *The Friends Quarterly*.

Acknowledgements

The authors and editors would like to thank the following libraries, archives and institutes for granting permission for the reproduction of the following images:

    For Figure 1.2, Archivo Histórico Provincial de Granada.
    For Figure 3.1, SLUB/Deutsche Fotothek/Straube, Stefan.
    For Figure 5.1, The British Library Board.
    For Figure 5.2, Special Collections, Hartley Library, University of Southampton.
    For Figure 5.3, The Chapter of Worcester Cathedral (UK).
    For Figure 5.4, Sherborne School Archives (UK).
    For Figure 10.1, The Wellcome Collection, London, England. CC BY.
    For Figure 10.2, National Gallery of Victoria, Melbourne.
    For Figure 10.3, the RISD Museum, Providence, Rhode Island, USA.
    For Figure 10.4, Washington State University Libraries, Pullman, WA. Photograph by James Seckington.
    For Figures 11.1 and 11.4, the Historical Archive on Tourism.
    For Figures 11.2 and 11.3, Archive Berlin History Workshop.
    For Figures 12.1, 12.2 and 12.3, Bishopsgate Library and Archives.

Introduction

Sarah Barber and Corinna M. Peniston-Bird

In this era of 'shuffle', the art of album sequencing no longer determines the listening experience. As Brian R, challenges, 'just imagine, for example, how different Pink Floyd's *Dark Side of the Moon* would feel if it began with the upbeat, sleazy funk tune "Money" rather than the slightly disturbing, crawling, melancholy "Speak to Me/Breathe"'.[1] Kirsty McColl famously determined the running order on U2's 1987 album, *The Joshua Tree*; as Bono described in a subsequent interview, 'Your hope for your album is that it will always be greater than the sum of its parts. It wasn't happening for *The Joshua Tree* and she came in and she organized it and it worked as an old-fashioned album: a beginning, middle and end'.[2] But we increasingly perceive the world out of context, or at least, out of its original context: most students have seen the Mona Lisa (Leonardo da Vinci, 1503), but they have not viewed it. The inspiration for this collection is the challenge that this potential disjuncture between spatial and temporal contexts poses for historians, and the continued need to develop methodologies that bear both contexts in mind and engage with genres of primary source, both traditional (such as architecture) and modern (for example, digital).

'Context' encompasses the manifold – from physical to temporal: the surroundings or environment, preambles and consequences – which together serve to determine, identify or clarify meaning. The twelve contributions in this collection explore the relationship between temporal and physical context through studies of space and performance, each offering a (varying) blend of methodology and case study. Each study shows how historical sources need to be read within a specific context or contexts through which meaning is co-created. The source may have been created with that context in mind (from memorials to theatre productions) or they can seldom today be viewed outside of that context (objects in historic houses (Robin); old photographs in family photo albums (Pagenstecher)). The chapters are grouped into three broader themes: the built and natural environment; performance in context; and the artefact in context and each concludes with a brief list of recommended further reading.[3] What follows is a brief outline of some of the theoretical and methodological themes that emerge from the contributions.

Space and time

Merriman and Jones argue,

> it is precisely the multiplicitous and heterogeneous nature of space and spatiality – as abstract and concrete, produced and producing, imagined and materialized, structured and lived, relational, relative and absolute – which lends the concept a powerful functionality that appeals to many geographers and thinkers in the social sciences and humanities.[4]

Awareness of temporality adds further fluidity to bear in mind as one navigates through historical space. The spatial and the temporal 'are integral to one another', 'distinct' but 'co-implicated'.[5] Along with the revolution in cultural studies that produced the 'cultural turn' and the 'literary turn', there was also a 'geographical turn'. Often expressed as 'cultural geography', but rarely as 'historical geography' or 'geographical history'; nevertheless, geographers after the cultural-turn cited history everywhere.[6]

The founding editor of the *Journal of Social History*, referring to the goals of history teaching, identified as the fundamental difference between History and other cognate disciplines the former's 'concern for change' and other social sciences' analysis of 'patterns of static generalizations': 'the historical laboratory [is] the only available source of evidence about change'.[7] Historians were under fire for being shackled by evidence, data, 'facts' leaving them unable to conceptualise, hypothesise or think abstractly. They were bad at theory: worse, they were disdainful. Historians could always fall back on the phrase 'history is an empirical discipline'.[8] History is the only discipline that deals exclusively with the past. We might explore whether the past is comparable with the present and we sometimes declare the value of our discipline to be its capacity to predict future human behaviour. We might want to say that humanity has scarcely changed at all. We nevertheless construct narratives about the past and explore the impact of the passage of time in a variety of spaces, and as such, are looking for, or at, change. Historians cannot embed themselves in past time but can experience the data-relics of past time. They cannot experience interactions with space as those in the past experienced them but can sometimes revisit a location (as they can a source) in the present.

In *Historical Sources in Spatial Contexts* we investigate the tension between the fixity of evidence and the fluidity of time and space to explore how historical writing can engage with the mutability of contexts. A key theme is the contextual space in which the historian might meet evidence. The spatial context in which a garment was created is different from the many occasions on which it was worn (Prieto). We could say the same of a moveable object (Robin). In the chapters by Cord Pagenstecher and Eloise Moss on photograph albums and scrap books respectively, the spatial context of the original experience or source has been reframed through the random or considered placing and editing of photographs or ephemera once displayed in an album. If we were to extend our analysis to the archival document, a piece in the hand of a known person often also contains the time, day, date and location of its creation. It seems to anchor itself in the spatial context of creation and even if it subsequently moves through both time and space, retains its original creative context. However, thousands of documents are brought together in personal collections, in complete deposits or as partial fragments in archives, some with and some without a geographical link to their creation/creator. The development of digital media, such a boon to scholars in terms of searches, conservation, curating, dissemination and impact, is also challenging. It enables more direct and immediate connections between a source and its viewer. This must be welcomed, and our discipline is immensely richer for it. However, we must be aware of the steps that have been omitted, or seem to have been omitted, in creating that direct relationship. When spatial sources can be so easily presented to the eyes and ears of viewers and listeners, what have they lost in not being able to see (or touch) an object in situ, in their finding-location, location of preservation, or in relation to other sources at the same location? On the other hand, Adam Rabinowitz notes, digital archives enable users to make other juxtapositions. What is the relationship, for example, in the case of archaeological findings, audience and heritage if experienced vicariously in a different context? The cinema was a highly directive spatial medium channelling the audience-gaze: seeing footage on the small screen makes the audience mobile. As the twentieth century progressed, radio signal-origins became increasingly mobile and the relationship between the community gathered around the one radio (or later television) to receive a unique broadcast, became increasingly complex. Multiple broadcasters, some themselves mobile, broadcast at different frequencies and wave-lengths of increasing impermanence to a fluid audience with boom-box, transistor, mobile-phone, ear-buds and so on. Digital libraries enable us to preserve historic sounds but require us to work harder to keep context in mind and to recreate that vital step of placing the source back into its historic context. It also challenges us as scholars to show how and why we have the skills to interpret that historic context, when potentially we have democratised access to historical sources. Indeed, Rabinowitz's study of the language of digitisation indicates that the seeming immediacy of the wider audience's access to historical knowledge is now mediated by even more specialist scholarly interventions which remain as meta-data, hidden from an audience.

A recurring theme of this volume is the performance that mediates the space between subject and object. We find both definitions of the term exhibited in different chapters: performance in the sense of performing a task or performance as presenting entertainment. Different locations and genres of motifs could be brought together in order to create a performance, be it musical, theatrical, dance, pageant or all together in a multimedia performance (Pinnock, Stoller). Sometimes the space within which the display is taking place influences the performance itself, such as a musician broadcast on radio, or appearing on television, consciously or unconsciously recorded. Walking through and around a cemetery is a performative use of space, as is leafing through an album. In his chapter, Philip Kiszely was drawn to the idea of symbolic space, as well as Mick Jagger's performativity in a live broadcast interview (*contra* the familiar stage persona). He re-narrates 'bottom-up processes of social mobility' through the filter of the television: appearances on the set; the democratising effect of the TV set in everybody's living room; and the process whereby what constituted public mores were changed but also the Establishment drew outsiders into its recreated space. Other chapters tacitly embed performance: indigenous or tourist experience of place (Stoddard/Knott, Barber), personal or visitor experience of sites (Peniston-Bird, Schulz).

In a heritage space, historians must gauge their own reaction to the history displayed within sites devoted to, say, faith, war, drama or domesticity. As Mark Stoddart and Christine Knott suggest, both heritage workers and websites mediate the space for visitors. And those sites may have attracted generations of visitors: how do we recover their performances and question the relationship between history and heritage? Given centuries'-long consumption of a site, can we create a history of the gaze? Should the guardians of heritage (and who are they?) aim to arrest changing performativity across and around a site at a particular moment in history? What is the historian's role in record, conservation, preservation and restoration? A thread running through many chapters explores how historians grapple with the contextual understanding and associations which past and present audiences bring to a site, both unique and shared. Many of our sources require performative space more literally: the wearing of clothing can be a performance of display, of disguise or of status and role (uniforms, for example, prefigure performance; theatrical costumes define it). We have drawn attention before to the different types of performative viewing required of a film shown at a cinema, to its broadcast on television or as a digital stream.[9]

'Locus' and 'line'

Andrew Pinnock made this reference to the relationship between time and space in his contribution:

> To make sense of post-Restoration masque and opera we need to recognize it as the product of a particular moment (three crucial years really, 1683–5), working round the human frailties of a particular monarch. Jacobean/Caroline masque scholarship can't be lifted and shifted into the Carolean period. Spatial contexts are highly distinctive in other words. When spatial contexts disappear (as Charles II's sumptuously baroque Windsor interiors have disappeared), so the artworks tied to them originally lose much of their meaning. Since the masques and operas I've written about were attempts to intervene in history, to reinforce the restored Stuart hegemony, the loss of their spatial contexts robs us of useful bits of "real" history – reconstructable, but absolutely not self-evident. The fundamental lesson, I guess, is assume nothing about spatial context (especially not irrelevance!). Be curious about it. Research it![10]

In fields of scholarship in which time and space are mutable and contexts constantly shifting, the scholar needs to find the locus, a particular position or place, effective or perceived. *Wired* referred to record-labels as having 'always been the center of gravity in the industry – the locus of power, ideas, and money', for example.[11] Pinnock's chapter references several media – architecture, art, drama/pageant, music/song, statuary/memorial, and more – but he draws together temporal and spatial loci from within intersecting, fluid lines. Historians are familiar with time-lines. Pinnock has focused in on an historical period of short duration and further, within that, identified the final three years of the (English/British) reign of Charles II Stuart. His spatial context is less easily 'fixed', and therefore he has reconstructed recurring motifs (his loci) from art-sources, musical sources and spaces of performance.

In chapter one, a building is the specifically fixed locus, punctuating a very long timeline, but intersected by myriad 'lines of sight': from multiple locations towards the building; from the building in 360° view lines; and by different viewers or users of the building in different historical contexts. Memorials are fixed-point loci is spatial terms, designed to commemorate fixed-point temporal loci, but the source-points are assailed by a huge array of interpretations changing from person to person and across time. The same might be said of the cemetery. In other types of source, such as objects or garments, the source itself is also (potentially) mobile, although it may come to 'reside' temporarily at a fixed point (for display or storage, for example). Sarah Ann Robin therefore likens the different layers of connection between curators, owners, trustees, researchers, public, viewers and so on as intersecting lines, passing through both time and space, to create a 'web'. A similar web is implied in Laura R. Prieto's chapter, with the additions that pieces of clothing can be adapted over time, and that the 'origin-focus' may no longer exist but must be recreated through other source-types. Both Pinnock and Prieto expose a requirement to join-up fragmentary references from multiple contexts: the historian's research is a spatial context in itself.

In *History Beyond the Text* we explored a 'tri-partite' means to recover any aspect of human communication.[12] We contextualised its use in the philosophy of language – speaker, iteration and listener/hearer – and referenced performance: performer, audience and performance. Performance theorists have also noted a binary interplay between performer and audience, which collapses when this is not two separate witnesses to a 'work of art' but a performance that is an 'event' and the performance itself an actor with transformative power.[13] If at least one of the three elements is consigned to past time, neatly encapsulating our understanding of communication within this creative triangle is further distorted. We are seeking to track the inter-relationship of the three parts through both time and space in which each or all of the three elements may be moving through time and/or space. We could further argue that whereas the focus of *History Beyond the Text* was on the creator and the object of creation, *Historical Sources in Spatial Contexts* shifts the emphasis onto the 'consumer'.

The gaze (in) therefore articulates elements of performance in the maker's process of construction, the reception of that which is constructed (and its change over time). The gaze (out) can be embedded within the object of construction, as for example, with dramatic performers or the wearer of clothes. In the case of coins minted in ancient Antioch (Rabinowitz) the gaze in identifies the motif of the object(s) itself while the gaze out is created by the web of digital links through which its significance is rendered to an audience. 'The gaze' is a phrase with its own circular history. Used as a noun, it is now considered obsolete in ordinary usage, but described that which was stared at rather than the person who stared. Thus Shakespeare's poetry rhapsodised, 'the louely gaze where euery eye doth dwell'.[14] Used to mean a steady and intent look, the word has a longer pedigree. In the 1970s, however, 'gaze' gained in popularity as the anglicisation of the French *regard* translated from Lacan's *Quatre Concepts Fondamentaux de la Psychanalyse*, published in France in 1973. For Lacan:

> [i]n our relation to things, in so far as this relation is constituted by the way of vision, and ordered in the figures of representation, something slips, passes, is transmitted, from stage to stage, and is always to some degree eluded in it – that is what we call the gaze.[15]

It was a term adopted rapidly within several branches of cultural studies, particularly fields in which determining the relationship between subject and object was key. Which element of the cultural 'circuit' is active ('to see'), passive ('to make oneself seen') or reflexive ('to see oneself' – self-awareness, consciousness)? Thus, in second-wave feminism, the term was valuable in identifying and nullifying perceptions of misogynist voyeurism inherent in the male gaze (and the objectification of women); and has been a useful analytical tool in queer theory and in developing a (de)colonised discourse of the 'white gaze'.[16]

While not overtly considered within this volume, the concept of the gaze is now forever present. Wherever we are encouraged to think visually – and the articles in this volume expect this, even when other senses take precedence – there is an opportunity to consider how perceptions might inform interpretation and analysis.[17] Spatial awareness is a key component in assessing the physical space between subject and object that informs the gaze. Therefore, several scholars have explored the role of the gaze in tourism and heritage.[18] The tourist gaze is an element within perceptions of a continuously repurposed ancient building (Barber); the development of heritage sites (Stoddart and Knott); the visitor to a cemetery (Schulz) or the site(s) of historical objects (Robin, Prieto, Peniston-Bird, Rabinowitz). Someone appearing on television is in the most obvious way the object of the viewers' gaze (Kiszely), as is any performance (Pinnock).

The historian as actor

The studies presented here require readers to be agile in tracing analytical threads and greater reflexivity from the historian, first in interpreting the sources and second as the creator of history/ies. In interpreting the sources, the historian adds their own 'gaze', and in many of the chapters presented here, this is literal: the authors have illustrated their subjects with images that they have created and have placed themselves in the position of audience, consumer and visitor. The reader is therefore reliant on the author's perspective and the author has been more overt and open than is often the case within historical writing, in blurring the role of the scholar as the objective, dispassionate and distanced observer.[19] Spatial and performative histories require us to imagine, virtually reconstruct and physically recreate past, 'lost' perspectives. Some of our contributors have placed themselves in the audience by physically entering the space under discussion; others have reconstructed the space and the actors within it from outside. Both have recreated an historical path for other readers to follow. Therefore, each study requires the reader to factor into their interpretation 'what is it that individual historians have brought to their analyses, offering an interpretation of their source, which may not be mine'? The gaze itself may be fluid and change over time or within each chapter.

Our triangle of cultural interpretation containing Creator, Receptor and Creation perhaps needs amendment in light of these studies. Cultural production as a triangular relationship is, in part, drawn from performance theory, but theatre also instigated the discussion of the audience as participator that might be helpful in thinking of the sources in *Historical Sources in Spatial Contexts*. Theatre, particularly Western theatre from the Renaissance onwards, due to the increasing use of illusion in productions, began to talk about an invisible 'fourth wall', through which the audience could see, but actors 'pretend' they cannot. 'Breaking the fourth wall' describes any way in which the audience is drawn in to be more explicitly embedded within the creation. One way of seeing the chapters in this book would be to add The Historian, turning the cultural triangle into a square in which the historian is sometimes connecting with the cultural creator, sometimes with the source, sometimes with the audience, embedding the historian within the creation of culture. Most historians, when pressed, can reflect that they became interested in pursuing knowledge because that enquiry in some way spoke to them in a personal sense.

In the case of some of the contributions here, the self-reflexivity of the historian is overt: two examples would be the chapters of Robin and Moss. Eloise Moss makes reference to the similarities between photograph albums and scrapbooks and Cord Pagenstecher, while less overtly present, is nevertheless an identifiable interpreter of the source. Why should such overt presence be more visible and necessary with the sources in the final section of this book? One is because the chapters deal with objects, either in themselves or because the source – the photograph album and the scrapbook – becomes an object. The second reason is because that object can only be assessed within its context, and thus the commentator has to see the objects in situ or the items that make up the contextual object within their location. The same, but to a lesser extent, could be said of the earliest chapters of this book. Buildings, monuments and specific sites all benefit from being seen by the commentator in their context. Doing so often sparks our initial interest and seeing something in context often changes our opinion of it (Peniston-Bird), suggests new connections, or in the case of a performance allows us the opportunity to re-imagine how a spatial context probably looked (Pinnock, Stoddard/Knott).

8 *Sarah Barber and Corinna M. Peniston-Bird*

The scholarly obligation to authenticity – or at least the obligation to strive towards authenticity – remains at the heart of this enquiry. *Historical Sources in Spatial Contexts* should be viewed as a series of essays; attempts to follow (guide? lead?) case studies through mutable and mutating contexts. While the contributions are culturally specific, the aim is to explore and expand the methodologies by which historians within any cultural framework can remain true to their discipline and to past peoples while announcing history's importance to the present and the future.

Notes

1 https://jbonamassa.com/the-lost-art-of-album-sequencing/, last accessed 09.04.19. A character in 'Fishermen's Friends' (C. Foggin, Powder Keg Pictures; Fred Films, 2019) decries the fact that modern listeners no longer know the pleasures of having the full LP experience.
2 C. Bishop, *Kirsty: The Life and Songs of Kirsty MacColl (Television Documentary)*, *BBC, 2001*. Event occurs at 23:32, cited on Wikipedia, https://en.wikipedia.org/wiki/The_Joshua_Tree, last accessed 09.04.19.
3 The contributors are drawn from Europe and North America and will use different spelling and grammatical conventions. On the whole, the editors have remained true to the author's original usage.
4 P. Merriman and M. Jones, 'Introduction', in Merriman et al. (eds), 'Space and spatiality in theory', *Dialogues in Human Geography*, 2.1, 2012, pp. 3–22, p. 4.
5 D. Massey, *For Space*, London: Sage Publications Ltd, 2006, p. 47, p. 55, p. 56; S. Chew, '"A kind of pursuit": On Boey Kim Cheng's poetry', in A. Mui Cheng Poon and A. Whitehead (eds), *Singapore Literature and Culture: Current Directions in Local and Global Contexts*, New York: Routledge, 2017, p. 49.
6 J. S. Duncan, N. C. Johnson, and R. H. Schein (eds), *A Companion to Cultural Geography*, Oxford: Blackwell, 2004.
7 P. N. Stearns, 'Some comments on social history', *Journal of Social History*, 1.1, 1967, 3; P. N. Stearns, 'Goals in history teaching', in J. F. Voss and M. Carretero (eds), *Learning and Reasoning in History*, London and Portland, OR: Woborn Press, 1998, pp. 261–93, p. 261.
8 R. J. Evans, *In Defence of History*, new edn., London: Granta, 2001, p. 217; Stearns, 'Goals', p. 288; A. R. Heinze, 'But Is It History? "World of Our Fathers" as a Historized Text', *American Jewish History*, 88.4, 2000, 495–510; J. H. Zammito, 'Ankersmit's postmodern historiography: The hyperbole of "opacity"', *History and Theory*, 37.3, 1988, 330–46; E. Kleinberg, 'Back to where we've never been: Heidegger, Levinas, and Derrida on tradition and history', *History and Theory*, 51.4, 2012, 114–35; J. H. Zammito, 'Are we being theoretical yet? The New Historicism, the New Philosophy of History, and "practicing historians"', review article, *Journal of Modern History*, 65.4, 1993, 783–814.
9 S. Barber and C. M. Peniston-Bird (eds), *History Beyond the Text: A Student's Guide to Approaching Alternative Sources*, London: Routledge, 2009.
10 A. Pinnock to S. Barber and C. M. Peniston-Bird, email, 24.04.19.
11 *Wired*, September 2006, 178/2.
12 Barber and Peniston-Bird (eds), *History Beyond the Text*, pp. 5–8, 17.
13 D. Newton, 'Performativity and the performer-audience relationship: Shifting perspectives and collapsing binaries', *The SOAS Journal of Postgraduate Research*, 7, 2014, 3–13, p. 3.
14 William Shakespeare, *Shake-speares sonnets*, London: G. Eld for T[homas] T[horpe], 1609, Sonnet v, sig.B^v.

15 J. Lacan, *The Four Fundamental Concepts of Psycho-analysis*, ed. J. Miller, London: Hogarth Press, 1977, vi, 73.
16 K. G. Drummond, 'The queering of Swan Lake. A new male gaze for the performance of sexual desire', *Journal of Homosexuality*, 45.2–4, 2003, 235–55; A. Baron, 'Masculinity, the embodied male worker, and the Historian's gaze', *International Labor and Working-Class History*, 69.1, 2006, 153–60.
17 H. Wickstead, 'The Uber Archaeologist: Art, GIS and the male gaze revisited', *Journal of Social Archaeology*, 9.2, 2009, 249–71; bell hooks, 'The oppositional gaze: Black female spectators', in A. Jones (ed.), *The Feminism and Visual Culture Reader*, New York: Routledge, 2003, pp. 94–105; P. Simons, 'Women in frames: The gaze, the eye, the profile in Renaissance portraiture', *History Workshop Journal*, 25.1, 1988, 4–30; C. Anderson Gayle, 'China in the Japanese radical gaze, 1945–1955', *Modern Asian Studies*, 43.5, 2009, 1255–86.
18 K. Hollinshead, '"White" gaze, "red" people – shadow visions: The disidentification of "Indians" in cultural tourism', *Leisure Studies*, 11.1, 1992, 43–64.
19 T. Hunt, 'Whose truth? Objective truth and a challenge for History', *Criminal Law Forum*, 15, 2004, 193–8; R. Brilliant, 'How an Art Historian connects art objects and information', *Library Trends*, 37.2, 1988, 120–9; G. Kitson Clark, *The Critical Historian*, London: Routledge, 1967.

1 Building
Constructing identities

Sarah Barber

This chapter explores the historico-spatial context of a single building over eight centuries. The building, in the village of Casares, in the southern Spanish province of Andalusia, was reimagined in the late twentieth century, and 'the council has given Casares a prime cultural space, because of its location, its significance for heritage over eight hundred years and because modernisation has greatly widened its cultural possibilities [to include] exhibitions, meetings, music concerts and theatre'.[1] Casares, a mountain village within the Sierra Crestellina, overlooking the Rio Genal, is just south of the better-known Serranía de Ronda and its 'white villages', a popular tourist destination. From Casares it is possible to see across the Andalusian mountain ranges, down to the sea and Gibraltar, towards Africa.[2] The building in question was at one time a Moorish fortification; taken by Christians and converted into the *Antigua Iglesia Mayor de la Encarnación*, in which capacity it served the community until the Spanish Civil War. The building remained in the hands of the Diocese of Málaga but was unusable, and in 1988, it was handed to the local council (*Ayuntamiento*). In 1998, a five-year restoration project began. The building was inaugurated in 2010 as the Centro Cultural Blas Infante, to mark the 125th anniversary of the birth in Casares of the so-called 'father of Andalusian nationalism', who saw in the province the positive mix of Hispanic and Arab, Christian and Moorish influences.[3] The building thus carries a weight of cultural and historical baggage, affected by its position within a national polity and a regional polity, the terrain, a repeated and re-imagined cultural position, its service to communities past, present and projected into the future, part of a conversation between public and private usage, and between individuals and institutions invested in the building's status.

The many strategies deployed in analysing this site here invariably revolve around the relationship between time and space. Geographers have explored a 'spatial turn', which paralleled cultural and literary equivalents.[4] Particularly, historical geographers have sought to claw back the perception that spatial considerations should be secondary to temporal ones. Adapted from textual studies, the notion of a palimpsest seems appropriate: that there is one element in stasis, onto which is successively written and overwritten different identities and adaptations. It would even seem fitting to explore theories of agency: can an inanimate object be considered to have effect, and must the agency always be ascribed to those who design, build, see or use a building? The relationship between spaces is important across a number of different angles. The building remains fixed, but its location is often vital to its contextual understanding, and radiating from its fixed point are a number of vantages: either from the building out into the locale or from the locality to the building. Buildings have both an interior and an exterior space; the relationship between the two is also important for context, forming a series of vantages from the perspective of users of the building. These are complicated further by the function the building was/is designed to perform, its putative users and whether its function was designed for public use, private use or both. All of these variables may change over time.[5]

What results is a complex web of variables: some geographical, some historical. All could be expressed as lines between two points: connecting people, locations, events, viewpoints, narratives and so on. As an historian, it may be possible to create a straightforward – literally straight and forward-moving – linear narrative by positioning a building as an actor or bystander in history. But not all of our narratives are so straightforwardly linear, and so the question remains whether an attempt is made to run all of the narratives in parallel, and is this possible without completely confusing the reader of this history? Or, is each narrative created distinctively and do readers make their own decisions about how (and whether) the narratives fit together, which runs the risk that readers are able to select those narratives with which they engage. Is this a problem? Both readers and writers of history are thus prepared to abandon the linear narrative. For the historian in particular this is problematic: so much of the historiography of the past fifty years has not just counselled against ahistoricity, but maintained it to be a Bad Thing, to be avoided at all costs.[6]

The building across time

Let us begin then, with the kind of narrative that can be created to tell the story of our building across time. There is evidence of Roman occupation in the area, exploiting the sulphurous waters and building the *Baños de la Hedionda*: the lore that Julius Caesar had been cured by the waters, ordered the baths and that a village grew up adjacent, says the emperor gave his name to the settlement. Alternatively, Casares could be from the Arabic word for fortress, *al-Qasr*. The 'Moors' invaded the Iberian Peninsula from the south and east – a Muslim mixture of Berber, Arab and Levantine peoples – under the Umayyid Caliphate in the early eighth century. The territory was taken back by the forces of Pedro, king of Castile and León (1350–1369), but in 1361, Pedro signed the Pact of Casares, by which the settlement passed back to the deposed Muslim ruler, the sultan of Granada, Mohammad V.[7] The earliest written reference to Casares was by Lisan ad-Din ibn al-Khatib (1313–1375), a vizier of the sultan, who referred to a village which formed a defensive stronghold on the Nasrid's southwestern border. Al-Khatib's full name was Muhammad ibn Abd Allah ibn Said ibn Ali bin Ahmad al-Salmani, born at Loja, near Granada in Spain, but he died in Fez, the subject of an execution, ostensibly for heresy and atheism, but probably as a victim of political machinations within the Nasrid kingdoms of Granada. His greatest historical work was his autobiographical *al-Ihata fi akhbar Gharnata* (1369).[8] During the wave of reconquest launched by the Catholic Kings, Ferdinand and Isabella, the kingdom of Granada was the last part of the Iberian peninsula to fall, and it was the campaign of May 1485, in which the nearby town of Ronda was taken, which led to the capitulation of Casares. In a process known as *encomienda* and *repartimiento*, the captured territory was parcelled to Castilian knights (*encomienda*); first, Sancho de Saravia, and in 1491 to his kinsman, Rodrigo Ponce de León, Duke of Cádiz and Count of Arcos.[9] Old Christians began to repopulate the conquered areas, and the Moorish population was relocated (*repartimiento*) or fled to the mountains. There was some pressure on Muslims to convert to Christianity, and those who did so, however nominally, were known as 'Moriscos', but there continued to be regional resistance to the new regime and the third Duke of Arcos, also Rodrigo Ponce de León, accepted the surrender of rebel Moriscos in Casares who had continued to battle in the War of the Alpujarras. The municipality of Casares stretched from the village to the coast at the River Manilva, at the very southwestern border of the province of Málaga with that of Cádiz. Casares and Manilva gained a separate autonomy in 1795, and Casares retains a proud tradition of having been the only town, with the exception of Cádiz, which successfully repelled the French forces during the Peninsula War (1813).[10]

In the narrative of our particular building, we can pinpoint a specific time within the linear historical record: with the conquest of Granada complete, the process of both Hispanising and Catholicising Spain dominated peninsula history in the sixteenth century. Buildings which had been created for specific purposes by Islamic/Moorish settlers could, rather than being razed and replaced, be repurposed and refaced. Castles and mosques became churches and hermitages. In Casares, its 'new' church celebrated the theology of the word made flesh (*Iglesia de la Encarnación*). These Catholic churches had to make a point about the importance of the Christian message and root the institutions, so rather than being dedicated to particular saints, they reflected areas of theological principle, the most common being Conception and Incarnation. The church was literally the embodiment of the Christian God in Casares. As part of the zealous conversion campaigns of the new Archbishop of Seville, Diego de Daza, the decision to build the church was made in 1505. Despite Daza's fall two years later, in part brought about because his cruelty towards the converts brought disgrace on the Christian religion, the project of the church at Casares was confirmed in 1510 by a Bull of Pope Julius II. Nevertheless, building it was slow, and it continued to require major repairs into the eighteenth century.[11]

The historical record does not give us much information about the structures that were created at the top of the escarpment, although the terrain and position of the settlement were dependent on and shaped by location, best seen in topographic representation [Figure 1.1]. The official account of the restoration work speculates about the lack of documentary evidence about the building: a prolonged period of disuse had relegated it in the minds of historians on top of

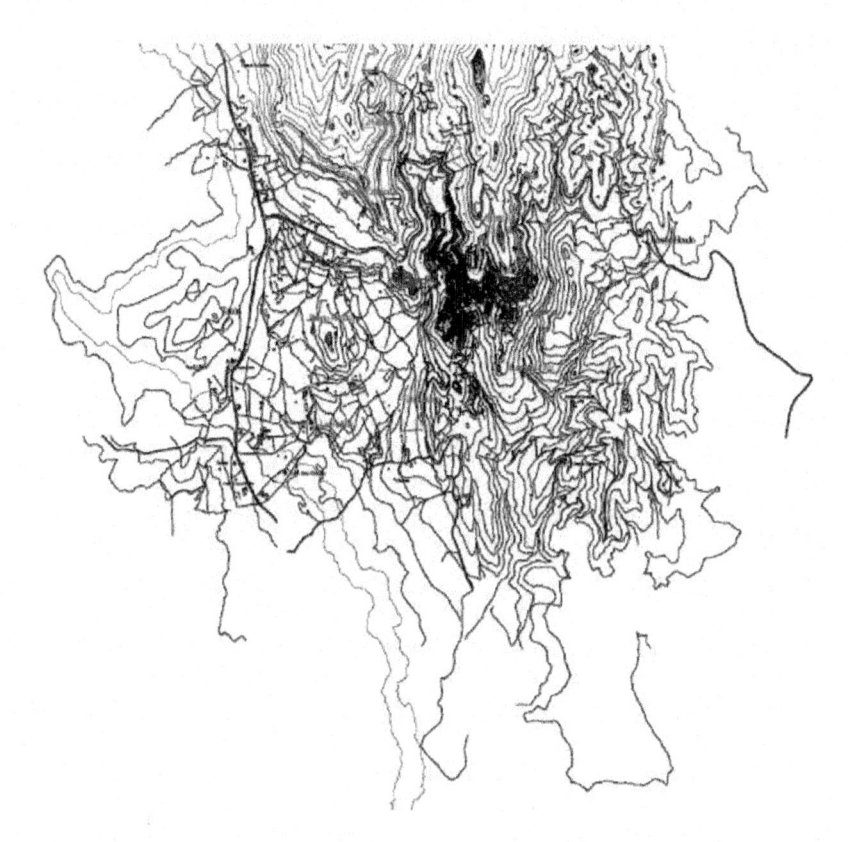

Figure 1.1 Topographical map of the Sierra Crestellina: reproduced from *Restauación de las Ruinas y Rehabilitación como Centro Cultural de la Iglesia del Castillo de Casares*.

Source: Courtesy of Rafael Juan Gómez Martin.

already thin municipal archives. The height of Casares, some 435 metres above sea level, but only 10 kilometres from the coast, made it an ideal site of settlement if defensive vistas and somewhere protected from attack was required. It also, however, shaped the historico-cultural narrative. Within the mountain-top site was both a fortress and a place of religious practice:

> [t]he church at Casares is therefore the result of a complex process dating, we suppose, from before Arab rule; its use always as a place in which the congregation could take refuge behind a secure and dominating enclosure. With the new Arab culture, the same space was reused by building another place of worship conforming to the incoming ethos; after the expulsion of the Arabs, this temple was rebuilt, conserving parts of the previous ones.[12]

The official booklet created to describe the work undertaken on this building appropriates the security of a date that can be attributed precisely to control a fluid developmental process. The Church of the Incarnation was founded in 1505, and this is the 'ruin' which is/was to be 'repurposed' (*rehabilitación*) as a cultural centre. Strictly speaking, this is the case: within the complex of masonry that sits atop Casares, it is the structure that formerly functioned as the church which now forms the cultural centre, with other stonework left as ruins. The remains of the Moorish fortress are separate. However, it establishes the space by disaggregating a point at which time and space can be divorced from fluid and shifting temporal and spatial acculturation processes.

The building in its location: Casares

The 'description' of the building operates in a different register from that of its 'history'. In order to try to reconcile the different religious uses of walls which saw service for Christian and Muslim worship and for military and civilian purposes, the building is usually described as the 'nave': the main section of a church which must be contextualised within Christian-Hispanic/Islamic-Arab contestation and acculturation, is situated within the style and cultural experience of Gothic-Mudéjar. The architectural definition, however, concedes an earlier starting point than the Reconquest church of 1505: noting it was built on an old mosque, within the Arab castle and the overall title of the project is the restoration of the 'Castle church'.[13] There is further research to be done into the attitude of the Catholic Church in releasing and deconsecrating church buildings, especially those where consecration reflected such fundamental pillars of the faith.[14] The Church may see the ruins as a testimony of its resistance to tyranny or its universality and endurance, or as a reminder of a shameful period of its past.[15] A fluid architectural and spatial context is cut across by a specific linear history of construction, although 'construction' is also a term open to discussion.

In the eighteenth century Casares was a village (until achieving *villa* status) within the province of Granada.[16] Thanks to the great cadastral survey, initiated by decree of Fernando VI (10 October 1749), geographers and historians have considerable information about settlements in Spain. The aim was to shift tax revenues from provincial control to a 'Single Contribution' to the state. Between 1750 and 1754, under the auspices of the Marques de la Ensenada, every place was ordered to compile details of population, jurisdiction, land-use and so on. Included within each return was a plan and some sketches of locations.[17] Question three asked what form the settlement took, marking the boundaries at the cardinal compass points and in Casares, this produced the image at Figure 1.2. Despite the cadastral survey being widely admired throughout Europe for its scope, rigour and progressive Enlightenment thinking, the single tax was not implemented. Nevertheless, it provides another precise point within our knowledge-line: prior to the cadastre there was no list of place-names in Spain, national map or census data; after the cadastre, this view of Casares would be destroyed during the Peninsula Wars. It noted everybody, across nearly 15,000 locations, irrespective of status, and thus chipped away at the stratified Spanish social framework. Busying themselves in the localities were a quartermaster, royal clerk, lawyer, constable and a geometrician, who would measure the boundaries of the settlement, and along with surveyors and local expertise compile verified information about every building, domestic and public. The quartermaster sent notification to each mayor, which would be read publicly. Everyone then had a fixed time in which to declare their interest in a place, their family, residency, property, income and liabilities.[18]

As far as perceptions and representations of our building are concerned, there are some interesting points to make about the Ensenada Cadastre. The first is that Casares was already quite a populous place, with nearly 100 dwellings depicted.

Figure 1.2 The village of Casares as depicted in the cadastral map prepared between 1756 and 1759, known as the Ensenada Cadastre. The castle and church are seen overlooking the hill.

Source: Courtesy of the Archivo Histórico Provincial de Granada.

However, in comparison with places elsewhere in the region, with smaller populations, there is little evidence of building for economic purposes. The image is presented – albeit distorted because of the flattened perspective – looking uphill from northeast to southwest. Although this may have been expedient – looking downhill being more difficult to represent – the aim of the perspective and viewpoint is to foreground not the parish church but the convent of San Francisco. The journey up the hill from the convent to *Encarnación* at the top is represented by two horizontal levels. At the extreme south-east is a crenellated tower which is no longer standing. The arches beside it are thought to represent a well. There is a larger, two-storey crenellated tower at the other side with nearby towers curving down the rock-face. The church in question is represented at the top and centre of the image but of lesser focus than the convent. But it is possible to make out the minaret and what would be the main door abutting the ruined tower of a house.[19] However, the vane is atop a larger domed tower which dominates the church and seems to contain the bell, which is different from the usual pattern in which the minaret was the obvious site for a bell-tower. This may have been the original of what was, at the time of the restoration, a shorter hexagonal chapel. There is no evidence of Mujedar style in the exterior.[20]

Although the building is therefore described as one of the 'Gothic-Mudéjar churches, constructed after the Reconquest', that period of reconquest was defined as 1505 to 1572, when on the latter date, a mason from the nearby town of Ronda was called to put a roof onto the church. 'At this time', according to the 'History' section of the project report, 'the Gothic building with three naves was defined, with the characteristic proportions of the period: the relationship between the main nave and the aisles and with the height and breadth of the perimeter walls and the rectangular presbytery': the 'Description' section mirrors this, drawing attention to typical Gothic-Mudéjar parishes in which the buildings were supported by perimeter walls and arches, creating an open interior space (*permeable el espacio interior*).[21] Here, historical function and structure meet contemporary intent for function and structure, or maybe determine contemporary function and structure. The nave is a large, relatively open, rectangular space with thick walls, that with additional load-bearing structures would create an open space suitable for public theatre, exhibitions and events. An argument could be convincingly made that this is the theological function of a Christian place of worship; a space in which all of the congregation (and maybe even the population) can meet together with common purpose to reflect on their shared identity.

The project, however, was refleshing an exposed skeleton, some of which pre-dated the *Iglesia de la Encarnación,* the form and function of which provided a foundational point for the contemporary structure. The naves ran east-west, over thirty meters, meaning that the view in the cadastre was of the side of the building. Another, older wall, running in a direction different from the naves had been exposed, which was tentatively attributed to the *qiblah* of the pre-existent mosque (described as the mosque of the Arab castle), by which the faithful determined the direction of Mecca; and there were remnants of a large arch within the side walls which could also have been part of the mosque or predate the Arab invasion;

part of the earlier Visigothic site. There is no indication how far back before the Moorish conquest the arch may have dated, the period of the Visigoths spanning the Christian conversion of the peninsula. The brick tower is described as the 'Bell Tower', although it does not appear to have been used as such in the mid-eighteenth century. It is also described as Mudéjar.[22]

Interpretations: Blas Infante Pérez de Vargas

The church remained in regular use until the mid-nineteenth century. The project to convert the former *Iglesia de la Encarnación* into a usable contemporary space was named after Blas Infante Pérez de Vargas. His birth, in Casares, provides another sharp and precise stop to the fluidity of our lines of time and space. His birth was at eleven in the morning, at 51 Calle Carrera, on 5 July 1885.[23] He was at school in Archidona (Málaga), some 150 kilometres away, then in Cabra (Córdoba), and finally in the city of Málaga. He returned briefly to Casares to assist his father, who was a municipal court clerk before taking a law degree at the University of Granada. He subsequently took exams for the civil service and at the age of twenty-five, took up the position of notary in the village of Cantillana, close to the River Guadalquivir to the northeast of the city of Seville.

Blas Infante was a follower of the American political economist, Henry George, who gave his name to a movement promoting a view of propriety in which production was owned by the person who produced, whereas the land on which it had been produced and the natural resources associated with that land – its economic value – rightly remained held in common. The foundational statement of Georgism was *Progress and Poverty*, published in 1879, the notorious aspect of which was a land value tax, but it indicted the cyclical nature of industrial capitalism as a whole in which while technology produced huge wealth, considerable populations were consigned to living in poverty.[24] In May 1913, the first of what would become a series of meetings of the International Union for Land-Value Taxation and Free Trade was held in the spectacular gorge town of Ronda, fifty kilometres north of Casares, where the movement 'entered the field of practical politics'.[25] Blas Infante spoke in Ronda, rallying delegates against privilege and articulating his belief that Andalusia, far from being the dusty peasant land of the south, was the most fertile and productive region of Spain. Later that same year, a Royal Decree seemed to herald the possibility of a Spain of the regions, although only Catalonia succeeded in uniting four provinces into a regional administration.[26] Blas Infante became a prolific pamphleteer in the journal *Bética*, founded in November 1913, and started to create his vision of 'The Andalusian ideal' (ultimately *andalucismo*), which he subsequently published as a book of the same name.[27] The idea of the *Centro Andaluz* was born in 1916, the first in Seville, and in 1918 the *Congreso Andaluz*, again meeting in Ronda, adopted Andalusian symbols: an anthem (hymn), motto – 'Andalusia for itself, for Spain and humanity' – and a flag; three horizontal bands of green-white-green (*la bandera blanquiverde*), which to Blas Infante represented the green of Andalusia's land, with the white villages of the kind he knew in the Serranía de Ronda cutting across the mountain-side. His distinctive national ideal was made up of the collective individual ideals of each Spaniard living the ideal life; that which maximised the personality and qualities within everyone for the sake of 'Progress'.[28] But inclusivity and universality lay at the heart of Blas Infante's vision of community, so the maximisation of the personality of Andalusia consisted of illuminating difference in the melting pot of different cultures (*razas*) which historically had shaped the region. He traced Andalusians from Cro-Magnon man, through the Greeks and Romans and then the Berbers, at which point:

> political tyranny expelled thousands of Andalusians (Jews and Moriscos) from the homeland and [there was] a barbarous econo-judicial regime. This produces oppression and misery, redistributing a great proportion of Andalusian soil to proud warriors and vain magnates, who unlike Arab nobles, were incapable of turning their swords into ploughshares, and could only keep their lands inactive or collect rent from those they had colonised.
> In that environment of death and tyranny, a slab is placed over the spirit of Andalusia which crushes its eagerness for vital originality and heterodoxy.[29]

Blas Infante's philosophy tied history and geography together. He did not deny the fluidity or complexity of either and both, but their inextricability was what constituted that which was typically Andalusian.

When Miguel Primo de Rivera came to power, during the Restoration Period (1923 to his death in 1930), the *Centros* were closed down and Blas Infante retired to the coast. But he became active again from 1931, during the period of the Second Republic, becoming a notary in Coria del Río, and opened a law firm in nearby Seville. He designed and built his own house in Coria del Río, the *Casa de la Alegría* (or '*El Castillo de don Blas*' to the locals). His creation is predominantly Moorish: it has bare brick walls, Romanesque arched windows and door, and most characteristically, the 'crenellations' of his 'castle' are the stepped merlons of Maghrebi architecture. In 1933, the preliminaries were put in place for a 'Statute of Andalusia', passed by an Assembly in Seville on 5 July 1936. Less than two weeks later, civil war broke out. Blas Infante was arrested by the Falangists on 2 August, and during the night of 10/11 August he and two other detainees were taken onto the road to Carmona and shot.[30]

Interpreting heritage: bifurcating historical lines

According to the project report, the *Iglesia de la Encarnación*, 'the building being renovated was in a ruinous condition since 1931'. This does not mean that it was not one of the churches sustaining bomb-damage during the Spanish Civil War. Nevertheless, the popular perception is that the war put pay to the church functioning as a place of Christian worship:

> during the Spanish Civil War (1936–1939), Casares endured more than its fair share of damage. The Church of the Incarnation, built in 1505, was badly

Building 19

disfigured and is no longer in use, and all that remains of the ancient Hermitage is a dome-topped alcove, and the ruins of three walls blemished by bullet holes.[31]

Despite the closer proximity of the war to our own day, the sources required by historians to determine the 'truth' of events are either not available to us or their authority is flawed. Two – possibly three – further lines of geo-historicity have been set up. One concerns the relationship between anglophone perceptions of Spain (and not only from the time of the Civil War to the present), and the second, the changing perceptions which Spaniards have of their own history and its presentation, particularly since the Civil War.

Ties between Britain and Spain were already strong, if not always friendly. Gibraltar became a point of contention at its cessation to Britain in 1713, by the Treaty of Utrecht, which ended the War of Spanish Succession, and there was a constant 'new row, accompanied by the old insults'.[32] Casares is proud of its record of withstanding Napoleon's armies during the Peninsular Wars, but the allied forces fighting in Spain were largely British. The impetus for the worldwide Georgist movement came from the US. The romantic image of partisans fighting fascism has to be weighed against the declarations of neutrality made by UK and US governments (along with other European states), concerned to halt the influence of communism: Britain allowed Franco to set up a signals base on Gibraltar and to fly over its airspace when taking Army of Africa troops to Seville.[33] The Irish National Corporate Party sent volunteers – 'Blueshirts'. Fighting for the Republicans therefore involved (romanticised?) individual statements of anti-establishment volunteering. Among the 32,000 foreign volunteers were the American 'Lincoln' and Canadian Mackenzie-Papineau Battalions. George Orwell and Ernest Hemingway wrote about their Spanish experiences.[34] Hemingway's writings are particularly close to the bone in this respect, since one of the more traumatic incidents from *For Whom the Bell Tolls* was 'Pilar's thirty-page narrative of the revolutionary terror at Ronda', late in 1936, when the town's leading men were flayed into the gorge (*El Tajo*), and although Hemingway subsequently revealed that he had fabricated the incident, 'death by tajo' stories persisted in 'a professional literature on a certain period of Spanish history'.[35]

General Franco was still in power when the British started to return in numbers to Spain. Spain had remained economically depressed by the effects of the war itself and its international isolation, but restrictions started to be lifted in the 1950s, and affordable foreign travel started to bring visitors to the Costa del Sol, leading to rapid urbanisation.[36] A combination of temperatures attractive to northern Europeans, the low cost of living, the juxtaposition of 'quaint' but shabby fishing villages with new English-speaking businesses, and the absence of planning regulations in the Franco era made it an attractive opportunity for Britons to travel abroad. The area became both an aspirational haven and a source of ridicule: raffia donkeys and flamenco dolls, and everyone could recite verbatim the Monty Python sketch in which

> when you get to Malaga airport everybody's swallowing "enterovioform" and queuing for the toilets and queuing for the armed customs officers, and

queuing for the bloody bus. . . . And . . . you finally get to the half-built Algerian ruin called the Hotel del Sol . . . and meanwhile the bloody Guardia are busy arresting sixteen-year-olds for kissing in the streets and shooting anyone under nineteen who doesn't like Franco.[37]

Between the 1970s and the turn of the century, building continued apace, but now in the form of areas of suburban developments (*urbanizaciones*), often in terraces of postmodern 'white village' design though generally restricted to the coastal side of the *Autopista del Sol*, while further inland, tourists and emigrants who fancied a more 'authentic' slice of Andalusian life, could escape the 'over-development' of the coastal zones. Sociologists have drawn attention to the creation of 'dual societies' in Spain: space is devoted either to production or leisure and divided disproportionately between age-groups and nationalities.[38] In terms of our lines of geographical and historical knowledge about place, we could see this as a series of bifurcations; perhaps a fraying of the cords which characterise the ways in which human beings make sense of their identity through time and space.

At the same time, with the end of the Franco era, Spanish society embraced liberalisation. With the new freedoms has come an investigation of its recent past and a rediscovery (or reinterpretation?) of its longer-term history. There had been a similar 'hiatus of time' during the Franco era. In the nineteenth century there had been a series of attempts to protect and encourage Spanish culture which had culminated in the Second Republic's Law of 13 May 1933 promoting artistic and archaeological heritage, leading to explorations of ethnography and the concept of 'cultural assets' (*bienes culturales*).[39] In 1985, the *Ley del Patrimonio Histórico Español* founded the *Instituto de Conservación y Restauración de Bienes Culturales*, and with it a catalogue of cultural assets, such as the town of Casares (Historic Site) and its Arab castle (Monument).[40] Following initial studies in 1980, the first project was prepared for the regional arm of the Ministry of Culture in 1989 and, after further delays, the project benefitted from the injection of interest created by the *Autopista del Sol* motorway. In 1998, moves to recognise regional autonomy, creating the *Junta de Andalucía*, local commitment (*Ayuntamiento de Casares*) and global awareness, in the form of the World Monuments Fund (Spain), created the economic will to advance the project as

> an example of the tenacity of a town, of administrations working together and above all, of an exercise in the reconciliation of historical memory and the recent past, healing old wounds with the recovery of the ruins of a building, in a practical exercise in the conservation of heritage as a factor in economic, cultural and social development in the twenty-first century.[41]

In the course of the restoration project, Spain's politicians argued over the degree to which the Socialist Party's Law of Historic Memory, passed in October 2007, would heal or re-open the wounds of Spain's past, officially condemning the Franco dictatorship and enabling victims of the regime to seek information, redress and limited compensation.[42]

The construction company chosen was Hermanos Campano S.L. which, while remaining a family company, had in itself undergone a trajectory, from its foundation in the 1960s in storage and construction, to the injection in the next generation of a 'social purpose', specialising in restoration and reconstruction, while in the twenty-first century it moved into building for leisure and tourism.[43] The chief architect was Rafael Juan Gómez Martín, a native of Málaga, born in 1953. A self-defined specialist in 'restoration and recovery' (*'Restauración y Rehabilitación'*), he had worked for the Ministry of Culture on castles and walls, and then for the *Junta de Andalucía* on the restoration and maintenance of Málaga Cathedral. The *Ayuntamiento* was most involved in obtaining the building from the Diocese of Málaga, in order to convert a religious building to a civil one, but otherwise Gómez Martín had a relatively unobstructed hand to interpret the building's development; his limitation subscribed by finance and the lack of technical expertise on the part of the local administration. Gómez Martín was asked about the potential influences of six historico-geographical factors:

> The Moorish heritage?
> The structure of a mosque?
> The history as a church?
> The location in Casares?
> The Civil War destruction?
> The legacy of Blas Infante?

and his response was telling:

> In our design, we took account of all pre-existing conditions and the location of the castle and its use as a mosque and a Mudéjar church, as well as the ruined building. In the end, for a municipality so small, it was the figure and legacy of Blas Infante which was politically decisive in making the decision to have a cultural centre of this size in this place.[44]

Nevertheless, he side-stepped the question of how far the link to or ideas of Blas Infante had influenced his work. Blas Infante had been taught in schools since the fall of Franco, but 1975 would have been after the architect's schooling had ended, and (presumably referring to before 1975) he was known 'underground' as the father of *andalucismo* and author of *Ideal Andaluz*.

Knowing context: ontologies

Returning then to the lines which connect our particular building with its contexts, we could refer to them as linear ontologies: the ways in which perceptions come into being. We could create an historical ontology; most conventionally one which passes through time in a straight line from a point of origin to the present. We could explain the history of the building as how the Centro Cultural Blas Infante came into being. Spatially, we can locate the building within its terrain, and we can construct a series of viewpoints, or vistas, which take advantage of the building's location: across to Gibraltar and the sea; for many miles across the mountains; down the escarpment in all directions. Within these planes of perception there are several places at which the one explains and provides context for the other. Its mountain-top position makes a good defensive point and sanctuary, either as a predominantly Moorish or a Christian community. Paradoxically, however, one might say that the proximity of heaven and an isolated position were ways of separating the individual from the earthly community beneath. The creation of Christian hermitages on the sites of former Moorish fortifications partly reflected this need for isolation, as did the tendency of the Catholic Church to take advantage of the locations of churches at the summits of steep inclines to position the Stations of the Cross along the route to the top. A series of heritage routes has been created around Spain, most of which, particularly those in mountainous regions, take advantage of viewpoints, at which one can park a vehicle and look out and down across an expanse.

In a further tension between the architecture and history, the project, rather than being one of construction, is dependent on, determined by and brought about by destruction. Within the historical timeline it is points of contest and change which punctuate the narrative – Visigoth to Moor, Moor to Christian, Andalusian to Castilian, Muslim to Catholic, Catholic to Muslim, ecclesiastical to civil, use to disuse. The building is 'natural' because its mountain-top position is symbolic of its functions, but the perception of it which comes through its official descriptions is of an (artificial) construct of humankind. It comes into its own as a constructed lookout which enables one to appreciate the nature of the terrain. In terms of the architect's ability to change the use of the building and to situate its utility in the present, one must think ahistorically. The starting point of the building's *reconstruction* is 1931, and this is also the point at which, in terms of a building, we are permitted by ruination to see and explore its history, with its previous walls and arches exposed, and the opportunity for archaeology (not taken). At the point at which the building becomes without function, it becomes a site of romance and emotion. Thus, the building as ruin is twice in the project outline described as Ruskinian: after 1931,

> there was no use for this building, nature having appropriated it; with figs and shrubs growing inside it, which gave it a Ruskinian air and a certain romantic charm (so well reflected in the drawings of late nineteenth-century English travellers to the South of Spain) and contrasting delicate moulding with the stark edges of the walls.[45]

Consequently, the official report of the construction project, describing the history of the building, gives disproportionate weight to elements which might be considered negative. The construction of the building is described as a 'long process' with frequent repairs and abandonment. In times of peace the community abandoned the shelter of the castle and the hill was depopulated, only to return in times of danger, in a cycle, which was another phase of the process of almost total destruction of both the church and much of the adjacent village during the Civil War, and the consequent abandonment of this area; while the activity moved to the lower town where there was better access.

The agency of the building was reflected in its 'pathologies': cracks, fissures, tears in the plaster and the ingress of moisture.

Trying to establish intention and perception is similarly ahistoric: interpreting the motives of those responsible for the decisions to restore the building to active use, and those who might use the building or view it; a difference between private and public motivations; and internal and external perceptions. The architect, present at the (re)dedication of the building in 2012 confessed that the occasion was 'quite emotional', and while the materials, construction and use of space could have been bettered, he considers the basic philosophy sound, and is 'modestly satisfied' with the final result.[46] From the perspective of an historian, one might say that there are lines of sight which seem to preserve as much of the medieval and Renaissance aspect of the building as possible [Figure 1.3]; others which are less successful in combining the historical and the practical but which give an allusion to Blas Infante [Figure 1.4]; and others which (in what may be a fanciful interpretation) appear to echo the bands of the Andalusian flag, the white villages across the mountain sides and even the lines of modern white *urbanizaciones* [Figure 1.5], certainly when viewed with an interior exhibition about Blas Infante and prototype designs for the flag [Figure 1.6].

The exhibits speak to a local – or at least Spanish audience – with echoes of an Andalusian past and an Andalusian identity: literature, dance and the objects of a rural past.[47] The words of poet José Manuel Caballero Bonald, which accompanied (in 2013) the designs for the flag, speak of not needing to articulate patriotic sentiment, for 'all Andalusians already fully recognise the affirmation of popular sovereignty which is mobilised by the call of the white and the green'. The space of the exhibition hall and the theatre and film projection room provide an opportunity to revive local and regional culture; flamenco in particular.[48] But there are no statistics kept about use or visitor numbers. What percentage of the visitors to the building are local and of those who live locally, how many are Andalusians? With internet and social media it is possible to gain quite extensive knowledge of a place without having experienced its physicality.[49] Is it necessary to have been raised in a place and at a time before elements had to be 'revived', 'restored' or 'reconstructed' to appreciate the relationship between time and space? For Blas Infante, Casares 'invoke[d] (*conjurar*) a harmonious life, in free rhythm . . . expressed in the numerous voices of Christians, which newly revealed their essential (*irreductible*) soul in Moorish flamenco songs'. Now it is a popular tourist destination and many rental apartments, holiday homes, second homes and retirement homes are lived in by those who have moved from cooler northern climes. In the wake of the economic collapse in southern Europe, the Ministry for Development (*Ministerio de Formento*) calculated that fifteen percent of Spain's empty properties were in Andalusia, and in areas along the Costa del Sol that remain popular with foreign investors, they could continue to be sold to foreign buyers.[50] It did not go

Figure 1.3 Photograph of the restored steps up to the west door
Source: Photograph by Sarah Barber, 3 April 2013.

unnoticed by the authors of *Restauración de las Ruinas y Rehabilitación como Centro Cultural de la Iglesia del Castillo de Casares* that the majority of remarks made about the site are about the magnificent vista obtained by looking *away* from the building. As Blas Infante had it in *Fundamentos de Andalucía*: 'Life is no more than the ideal realised, and the thought of that ideal being realised'.[51]

Figure 1.4 The east façade before (around 2001) and after (2012) the restoration, shown in a page from Restauación de las Ruinas

Source: Courtesy of Rafael Juan Gómez Martin.

Figure 1.5 Photograph of the interior of the Blas Infante Cultural Centre showing part of the quotation from Blas Infante

Source: Photograph by Sarah Barber, 3 April 2013.

Figure 1.6 Photograph of the interior of the Blas Infante Cultural Centre showing part of the exhibition of ideas for an Andalusian flag

Source: Photograph by Sarah Barber, 3 April 2013.

Notes

1 'Con la puesta en valor de este edificio, el Ayuntamiento dota al pueblo de Casares de un espacio cultural privilegiado, tanto por su situación, por su significado al ser una herencia con más de ocho siglos, asi como por su moderno equipamiento que abre un abanico extenso de posibilidades culturales. Exposiciones, congresos, espectáculos musicales y teatrales': https://andaluciarustica.com/casares-centro-cultural-blas-infante.htm, last accessed 24.06.18.
2 There is a small tower on the coast, with the characteristic square formation which sets it out as a Moorish fortress, on top of which was constructed a sixteenth-century defence on the orders of Carlos I in 1528. It is known locally as *Torre del Salto de la Mora* (The tower of the 'Arab' woman's leap) but is more formally known as *Torre de la Sal* as the Duke of Arcos created salt flats in the vicinity. Until the 1950s, it was a small barracks of the Guardia Civil. It was extensively restored in 2010. It forms almost a miniature parallel to the building at the centre of this study.
3 There have been many studies of the negative effect of Islam and the Moorish heritage on perceptions of Spain; see: I. Burshatin, 'The Moor in the text: Metaphor, emblem, and silence', *Critical Inquiry*, 12.1, 1985, 98–118.
4 S. Grgas, 'Notes on the spatial turn', *SKDR*, 2.2, 2012; S. Kern, *The Culture of Time and Space, 1880–1918*, Cambridge, MA: Harvard University Press, 1983; H. Nowotny, *Time: The Modern and Postmodern Experience*, Cambridge: Polity Press, 2005; E. Soja, *Seeking Spatial Justice*, Minneapolis, MN: University of Minnesota Press, 2010;

B. Warf and S. Arias, *The Spatial Turn: Interdisciplinary Perspectives*, London: Routledge, 2009.
5 F. Sánchez Pérez, 'El espacio y sus símbolos: Antropología de la casa andaluza', *Reis: Revista Española de Investigaciones Sociológicas*, 52, 1990, 47–64; O. Lucía Molano, 'Identidad cultural: un concepto que evoluciona', *Revista Opera*, 7, 2007, 69–84.
6 See: J. Dangler, 'Edging toward Iberia', *Diacritics*, 36.3/4, 2006, 12–26: who uses the dual theories of the frontier and associations to try to avoid imposing modern definitions of society and ethnicity to ten centuries of Iberian history.
7 The king was known by the names Pedro the Cruel and Pedro the Just. The distinction does not particularly refer to attitudes towards either Muslims or Jews but derived from civil war within the Spanish Christian kingdoms.
8 Rendered as *The complete Source on the History of Granada*, it is not available in an English translation.
9 Isabella created the Duchy of Arcos in 1493 as a reward for Rodrigo. This process of repartition among different incoming lords was replicated and subsequently much better known in the Spanish conquest of the Americas.
10 It is telling that there is a festival in Casares to commemorate this piece of highly localised history that does not make it into the histories of the war. It takes place in the first week in August. J. de la Pisa, 'Napoleon's nightmare: Guerrilla warfare in Spain (1808–1814). The French arm's failed counterinsurgency effort', Unpublished MA thesis, MA in Military Studies, Marine Corps University, Quantico, Virginia, USA, 2011; C. H. Gifford, *The Life of the Most Noble Arthur Duke of Wellington*, London, 1817, 2 vols, ii, p. 224.
11 *Restauración de las Ruinas y Rehabilitación como Centro cultural de la Iglesia del Castillo de Casares*, Hispania Nostra: Defensa y Promoción de Patrimonio Cultural y so Entorno/Fundación Banco Santander, n.d. [after 2013], n.p., 50pp.
12 *Restauración de las Ruinas*, 'Historia': 'La iglesia de Casares es pues un resultado de un proceso complejo cuyo origen podemos suponerlo anterior a la dominación árabe; su uso ha sido siempre de congregación de una población que se refugia en un recinto protegido y dominante. Posteriormente una nueva cultura, la árabe, reutiliza el mismo espacio y conforme a unas nuevas reglas edifica otro templo; tras la expulsión de los árabes, vuelve a constituirse este templo conservando parte de los anteriores'.
13 'Descripción', *Restauración de las Ruinas*.
14 C. Kiley, 'Convert! The adaptive reuse of churches', Unpublished Masters thesis in MSc Real Estate Development and City Planning, Massachusetts Institute of Technology, 2004. Kiley's subject is the USA, but he includes a small section on 'Deconsecrating sacred space' (p. 66) which counsels the developer to honour 'the previous sacred use of the space . . . with respect to the next user of the building, who may or may nor value (and may well even discount) the fact that their new office, home or center is a former church'. In Casares there is the added complication that the building had not been used for a sacred purpose for some years.
15 F. Lannon, *Privilege, Persecution, and Prophecy: The Catholic Church in Spain, 1875–1975*, Oxford: Oxford University Press on Demand, 1987.
16 It is now in the southwestern corner of the modern province of Málaga, abutting the province of Cádiz.
17 A digitised version of a copy is held by the Archivos General de Simancas (AGS) (which appears to be minus the plan of Casares): AGS, CE/RG/L285. The illustration consulted here is that from the Archivo Histórico Provincial de Granada. I am grateful to Concepción Camarero-Bullón a geographer at the Universidad Autónoma de Madrid for her help in reconstructing the Casares cadastre. Concepción Camarero-Bullón, 'The cadastre in 18th century in Spain', International Federation of Surveyors (FIG) Working Week paper, 2003.
18 C. Camarero-Bullón, 'La cartografía del Catastro de Ensenada', *Estudios Geográficos*, 231, 1998, 245–84; A. Ferrer Rodríguez and A. González Arcas, *Las Medidas de Tierra*

en Andalucía según las Respuestas Generales del Catastro de Ensenada, Madrid: Centro de Gestión Catastral y Cooperación Tributaria/Tabapress, 1996; R. J. P. Kain and E. Baigent, *The Cadastral Map in the Service of the State*, London: University of Chicago Press, 1992; L. Mannori (ed.), 'Kataster und moderner Staat in Italien, Spanien und Frankreich (18Jh.)', *Jahrbuch für Europäische Verwaltungsgeschichte*, 13, Baden-Baden: Nomos Verlagsgesellschaft, 2001; B. G. Peters, T. Erkkilä, and P. von Maravić, *Public Administration: Research Strategies, Concepts, and Methods*, London: Routledge, 2015.

19 C. Gonzalbes Cravioto, 'Las fortificaiones medievales de Casares', in *Casares: 200 Milliones de Años de Historia*, Málaga: Ayuntamiento de Casares/ Centro de Edicciónes de Diputación de Málaga, CEDMA, 2006, pp. 357–69.

20 The modern remains included the chapel of La Virgen del Rosario del Campo, which was constructed to the height of the roof of the nave but was octagonal rather than hexagonal.

21 'Descripción' and 'Historia', *Restauración de las Ruinas*.

22 Even the word 'Mudéjar' reflects the difficulties of terminology. In architecture, Mudéjar refers to building and decoration in a Moorish style but from a post-Moorish Christian period, whereas the term comes from the Arabic *mudajjan* meaning 'permitted to remain' and therefore refers to the Moorish people themselves, albeit permitted to remain because they had converted to Christianity.

23 However, different tourist information sites give a different number to this building. This building is now a small museum and tourist information office. Its situation in terms of the village is towards the northern outskirts, beyond the fountain of Carlos III in what is now the commercial heart. A rather grander museum connected to Blas Infante is in Coria del Río, near Seville. This information is important to understanding and interpreting the building/project that is the subject of this chapter, but is here relegated to an endnote in order not to introduce too early information that may influence readers' judgement.

24 H. George, *Progress and Poverty: An Inquiry into the Cause of Industrial Depressions and of Increase of Want with Increase of Wealth: The Remedy*, New York, 1879. In June 1894, a North American journal was started, *Land & Liberty*: 'The monthly journal for land-value taxation, free trade and personal freedom'.

25 F. W. Garrison, 'The case for single-tax', *The Atlantic*, December 1913.

26 *Real Decreto sobre Mancomunidades*, 18 December 1913.

27 Blas Infante Pérez, *Ideal Andaluz* (1915), reissued Sevilla: Centro des Estudios Andaluces, 2010. See: p. 101 for reference to the Ronda conference.

28 Infante Pérez, *Ideal Andaluz*, p. 71.

29 Ibid., p. 42: '[La otra causa es] la tiranía política [que] expulsa a millares de andaluces (judíos y moriscos) del suelo de la Patria y un bárbaro régimen económico jurídico; que produce la opresión y la miseria, repartiendo el solar andaluz en grandes porciones entre orgullosos guerreros y vanos magnates, incapaces de trocar la espada por el arado, como los nobles árabes, ni de hacer otra cosa que mantener sus tierras en inacción o cobrar las rentas a sus colonos. El genio andaluz tiene puesta una losa que aplasta sus pruritos de vital originalidad, heterodoxa en aquel ambiente de muerte y tiranía'. J. Zamostny, 'Islam and Andalusian nationalism: Historical interpretations for independence', paper presented to 'The Arab World' seminar, McDaniel College, 2007, www.yumpu.com/en/document/view/14300275/islam-and-andalusian-nationalism-historical-mcdaniel-college, last accessed 19.08.18.

30 There is a memorial to Blas Infante at the point of his assassination, called 'El kilómetro 4' on the *Carretera de Sevilla a Carmona* and regular commemorations throughout the year: 28 February, Andalusia Day. P.B., 'El kilómetro 4 de la carretera a Carmona, el homenaje a Blas Infante', *sevillaciudad*, 27 February 2015, last accessed 17.08.18; J. Cejudo, 'Todos los partidos parlamentarios, en el homenaje a Blas Infante en el 80 aniversario de su fusilamiento', *ABCandalucía*, 10 August 2016, last accessed 17.08.18.

There is some disagreement about the time and therefore the date of the assassination. The official tourist-office literature of the *Casa Natal Blas Infante*, Casares, gives 11.00 pm on 10 August.
31 'HOT Attractions – Casares – Cradle of Andalucía', *Viva. HOT Properties Magazine*, 58, 2006; 'Church of La Encarnacion', Casares, tripadvisor, United Kingdom, www.tripadvisor.co.uk/Attraction_Review-g1055348-d3372359-Reviews-Church_of_La_Encarnacion-Casares_Costa_del_Sol_Province_of_Malaga_Andalucia.html, reviews between 03.08.12 and 04.01.18, last accessed 17.08.18.
32 Under licence from the Council of State, *Tratado de Paz, A Justado entre las Coronas de España, y de Inglaterra, en Utrech* (Madrid, 1713); P. Reynolds, 'Gibraltar and other empire leftovers', *BBC News*, 3 August 2004 (over a visit by the UK Defence Secretary to Gibraltar to mark the 300th anniversary of Britain taking the rock, and also noting that Gibraltar got its name – *Jebel Tariq* – from the name of its Moorish conqueror in the eighth century), http://news.bbc.co.uk/1/hi/world/europe/3528268.stm, last accessed 17.08.18.
33 During the Civil War, Casares was part of the Southern Region, which encompassed all of Andalusia and the province of Badajoz. The Archivo Histórico del Ejército del Aire does have records of bombings during the war, but these are filed chronologically, and, therefore, unless one already knows the precise date of a bombing, these are difficult to trace. My thanks to the archivist Eloy Blanco González.
34 G. Orwell, *Homage to Catalonia*, London: Secker and Warburg, 1938.
35 E. Hemingway, *For Whom the Bell Tolls* (chapter ten), New York: Charles Scribner's Sons, 1940, pp. 96–130; H. Thomas, *The Spanish Civil War*, London: Penguin Books, 1965, p. 274; R. Buckley, 'The facts in Hemingway's *For whom the Bell Tolls*', *The Hemingway Review*, 17.1, 1997, 49–57; J. Corbin, 'Truth and myth in history: An example from the Spanish Civil War', *The Journal of Interdisciplinary History*, 25.4, 1995, 609–25, p. 611; I. Takayoshi, 'The ages of war: Liberal gullibility, Soviet intervention, and the end of the Popular Front', *Representations*, 115.1, 2011, 102–29, p. 118; S. Holgun, '"National Spain invites you": Battlefield tourism during the Spanish Civil War', *The American Historical Review*, 110.5, 2005, 1399–426.
36 J. Pollard and R. Dominguez Rodriguez, 'Unconstrained Growth: The Development of a Spanish Resort', *Geography*, 80.1, 1995, 33–44. Their study centred on Torremolinos.
37 'Travel Agent Sketch', Monty Python's Flying Circus, first performed BBC, 16 November 1972; 'Overland to the World', *The Brand New Monty Python Papperbok*, London: Methuen, 1973, n.p.
38 A. Mantecón, R. Huete, and T. Mazón, 'Las urbanizaciones "europeas". Una investigación sobre las neuvas sociedades duales en el Mediterráneo', *Scripta Nova: Revista Electrónica de Geografía y Ciencias Sociales*, xiii.301, 2009; A. Izquierdo and R. Martínez, 'La inmigración de extranjeros y el envejecimiento de la población', in A. de Miguel (ed.), *Los mayores Activos*, Madrid: Luyis Garral, 2001, pp. 227–52; R. King, T. Warnes, and A. Williams, *Sunset Lives: British Retirement Migration to the Mediterranean*, Oxford: Berg, 2000.
39 D. Ruiz de Lacanal Ruiz-Mateos, 'El Instituto de Conservación y Restauración de Bienes Culturales y la formación del conservador-restaurador', *Boletín Informativo de Instituto Andaluz del Patrimonio Histórico*, 1985, 38–45.
40 'Protección del Patrimonio', *Restauración de las Ruinas*. The 'Arab castle' is BIC (Monument): (RI)-51-0008035-00000, and the town of Casares is BIC (Historic Site) (RI)-53-0000215-00000. M. Teresa Péres Cano, 'Reflexiones sobre los BIC conjuntos históricos: la Sierra de Cádiz', *Revista PH89 Bienes, Paisajes e Itinerarios*, 89, 2016, 34–47; G. Canclini Néstor, 'Los usos sociales del Patrimonio Cultural', in E. Floescano (ed.), *El Patrimonio Cultural de México*, México: Fondo de Cultura Económica, 1993, pp. 41–61.
41 'Justificaión de la propuesta de candidatura y de categoría', *Restauración de las Ruinas*: 'ejemplo de la tenacidad de un pueblo, de concierto entre administraciones y

sobre todo de un ejercicio de conciliación con la memoria histórica del pasado reciente, cerrando viejas heridas con la restauración de las ruinas de un edificio, en un ejercicio práctico de CONSERVACIÓN DEL PATRIMONIO como factor de desarrollo económico, cultural y social, en el siglo XXI'.

42 E. Nash, 'Spanish "memory law" reopens deep wounds of Franco era', *Independent*, London, 10 October 2007.
43 Hermanos Campano SL are based in Ardales in the province of Málaga: www.hermanoscampano.com/la_empresa.html, last accessed 17.08.18. The rooms of the Apartamentos Ardales, built by the company in their home town, are decorated with enlarged photographs of local ancient monuments as feature walls.
44 Sarah Barber, questions to Rafael Juan Gómez Martín, 26 June 2018; Rafael J. Gómez Martín, 'Comentarios al cuestionario de la restauracion de la Iglesia del Castillo de Casares (Málaga)', Málaga, 14 July 2018. I am very grateful to Dr Gómez Martín for his help over several years in researching this chapter. He and his co-architect, T. Martínez Auladell, were approved as early as 1988, but they could not begin work until 2003. The 'Cession of Ecclesiastical Property Agreement' with the Diocese of Málaga was signed on 26 November 2001.
45 *Restauración de las Ruinas*: '[Consecuentemente] no existía ningún uso en este edificio, habiéndose adueñado la naturaleza del mismo; en su interior habían crecido higueras y matorrales, lo que le daba en cierta medida un aspecto ruskiniano y un cierto *encanto romántico* (cuyo ambiente tan bien reflejaban en sus dibujos los viajeros ingleses que recorrieron al final del siglo XIX el sur de España) contrastando con el delicado trazado de sus molduras y con los remates descarnados de los muros.' T. McFarland, *Romanticism and the Forms of Ruin: Wordsworth, Coleridge, the Modalities of Fragmentation*, Princeton, NJ: Princeton University Press, 1981; P. W. Silver, *Ruin and Restitution: Reinterpreting Romanticism in Spain*, Nashville, TN: Vanderbilt University Press, 1997.
46 R. Gómez Martín 'Comentarios al Cuestionario', in response to my questions 'Were you present at the re-dedication in 2010?' (this was corrected to 2012 by Gómez Martín) and 'What are your thoughts about the building looking back nearly ten years? Are you happy with the result?'.
47 C. Mignon, 'Paysanneries d'Andalousie', *Annales de Géographie*, 524, 1985, 480–4; M. Daumas, 'L'évolution récente des structures agraires en Espagne', *Annales de Géographie*, 542, 1988, 419–43.
48 B. Infante Pérez de Vargas, *Orígenes de lo Flamenco y secreto del Cante jondo*, Sevilla: Fundación Blas Infante, 1980; J. F. Balbuena Pantoja, 'El fandango de Casares', in J. Cenizo Jiménez and E. J. Gallardo-Saborido (eds), *Presumes que eres la Ciencia: Estudios sobre el Flamenco*, Sevilla: Libros con Duende, 2015, pp. 170–87; Y. Aoyama, 'Artists, tourists, and the State: Cultural tourism and the Flamenco industry in Andalusia, Spain', *International Journal of Urban and Regional Research*, 33.1, 2009, 80–104.
49 J. L. Caro, A. Luque, and B. Zayas, 'Aplicaciones tecnológicas para la promoción de los recursos turísticos culturales', in *XVI Congreso Nacional de Tecnologías de la Información Geográfica*, Madrid: AGE, 2014, pp. 938–46.
50 Source, Ministerio de Formento, 2011, www.fomento.gob.es/. The total number of empty properties in Spain in 2011 was calculated at 676,038. J. Cazorla, 'Cambios y diferencias en la Andalucía de los noventa', *Reis: Revista Española de Investigaciones Sociológicas*, 85, 1999, 27–45.
51 'La vida no es más que el ideal realizado y el pensamiento de este ideal realizándose'.

Further reading

Bafna, Sonit, 'The imaginative function of architecture: A clarification of some conceptual issues', *Proceedings of the Eighth International Space Syntax Symposium*, Santiago de Chile: PUC, 8117.1-8117.19, 2012.

Hillier, Bill, 'Space and spatiality: What the built environment needs from social theory', *Building Research & Information*, 36.3, 2008, 216–30.

King, Anthony D. (ed.), *Buildings and Society: Essays on the Social Development of the Built Environment*, London: Routledge and Kegan Paul, 1980.

Newton, M. T., 'Andalusia: The long road to autonomy', *Journal of Area Studies*, series 1, 3.6, 1982, 27–32.

Singley, Paulette, *How to Read Architecture: An Introduction to Interpreting the Built Environment*, Abingdon: Routledge, 2019.

Stallaert, Christine, 'Translation and conversion as interconnected "modes": A multidisciplinary approach to the study of ethnicity and nationalism in Iberian cultures', in Joan Ramon Resina (ed.), *Iberian Modalities: A Relational Approach to the Study of Culture in the Iberian Peninsula*, Liverpool: Liverpool University Press, 2013, pp. 109–28.

2 Landscape

Consuming natural places

Mark C. J. Stoddart and Christine Knott

Battle Harbour National Historic District is dedicated to preserving the buildings and material artefacts of Battle Harbour, a remote fishing community on Battle Island in the Labrador Straits, situated between the island of Newfoundland and the mainland of Labrador.[1] It exemplifies Baldacchino's description of cold water island tourism destinations, which 'have harsh as well as pristine and fragile natural environments, characterized by wide open spaces and low populations at best. They become contexts for an exceptional and expensive form of vigorous, outdoor, adventure or cultural tourism.'[2] Our analysis of Battle Harbour offers methodological and theoretical insights that are relevant for researchers interested in historical tourism and how the latter is used as an option for economic revival by communities that have experienced boom and bust cycles or are experiencing employment and population decline.

Along with the Red Bay UNESCO World Heritage Site, which documents the history of Basque whaling, Battle Harbour is one of the keystone tourism attractors in the Labrador Straits region. As Cooke notes, in her analysis of history-oriented tourism in Dawson City, Yukon, the creation of national historic sites is a 'process of symbolification, or encoding national-cultural guiding fictions and allowing them to congeal in place.'[3] Battle Harbour is also part of NunatuKavut southern Inuit traditional territory.[4] However, the 'national-cultural guiding fictions' that 'congeal in place' at Battle Harbour are those of colonial settler exploration, settlement, natural resource extraction, and survival in a sub-Arctic environment.

Historic narratives are not only produced through the preservation and display of material artefacts, which Zhu describes as the search for 'objective authenticity' in heritage tourism.[5] Rather, tourism involves relational processes of 'ordering,' which Franklin describes as follows:

> Tourism is a social activity, yes, but, it cannot be reduced to the social because it is relationally linked to a wide variety of objects, machines, systems, texts, non-humans, bureaucracies, times and so on, without which it would not happen and could not have become what it has.[6]

We draw on the case of Battle Harbour to demonstrate how historical narratives of community resilience in a remote place are produced through relationships among the landscape, the built environment and material artefacts, interactions between tourists and site employees, and digital media.

The narrative that is presented to tourists at this historic site can be divided into three distinct phases. First, Battle Harbour is defined as the former unofficial capital of the Labrador cod fishery.[7] At its height, Battle Harbour had a small permanent population but was a hub for a substantial seasonal migratory population centered on the fishery. During this time, it was also a regional service hub, with a police station and school, as well as one of the first (and few) hospitals and wireless communication towers in the province beyond the capital city of St. John's.

Second, there is a story of community decline. During the provincial government's resettlement program of the 1960s, the permanent population of Battle Harbour was relocated off the island to nearby communities in the St. Lewis Inlet, such as Mary's Harbour. While seasonal migration to the island for cod fishing continued for a while, this ceased with the cod fishery collapse and province-wide moratorium of 1992, which many consider among the worst ecological disasters in Canadian history.[8]

Third, there is a story of community rebuilding through the related projects of historic preservation and tourism. This commenced shortly after the 1990s' cod moratorium, with National Historic Site status granted in 1996.[9] The narrative of the reconstruction of Battle Harbour as a heritage tourism destination is similar to a broader pattern seen in Newfoundland and Labrador in the post-moratorium era, where tourism is viewed as a potential lifeline and means of economic diversification for rural coastal communities, wherein claims to the authenticity and historicity of these 'outport' communities is reimagined as a key tourism attractor.[10] While there are still no year-round residents of Battle Harbour, the transformation of the community into a historic site and tourism destination has maintained seasonal flows of employees, visitors, and area residents who maintain summer homes on the island (many of whom are members of previously resettled families).

We approach Battle Harbour through a 'tourism mobilities' theoretical framework.[11] This approach conceptualizes tourism places as local communities and environments as hubs that are linked to global networks of mobilities of visitors through socio-technological networks of airplane and car travel.[12] This perspective further asserts that tourism is a form of performance that engages visitors as well as members of host communities.[13] At the same time, it foregrounds the importance of physical places, technologies and objects for shaping tourism performances.[14] Finally, in addition to the mobilities of tourists, the tourism mobilities perspective also emphasizes the importance of what Urry and Larsen call the 'imaginative geographies' of tourism, or the images and discourses about tourism destinations that circulate through communication networks of tourism media and tourist-produced media.[15] In a sense, tourism destinations are also mobile, as media images and discourse circulate through media networks to potential visitors.

Working from a tourism mobilities standpoint, Battle Harbour National Historic District provides a valuable example of how historical narratives are coproduced through the coming together of embodied performances of tourists and hosts, landscape, the built environment, material culture, mobility networks and digital media. Battle Harbour demonstrates how history and place are deeply intertwined, where historic narratives for tourists are inseparable from the built environment and the landscape of the Labrador Straits.

Methods

A tourism mobilities approach to Battle Harbour is attentive to the performances of tourists and hosts, social-technological mobility systems, natural and built environments, and objects that structure tourism as a practice and connect local tourism places to global networks of travel.[16] This approach aligns well with John Law's notion that multiple method approaches are valuable for generating research accounts that better convey the complexity and 'messiness' of social-technological-environmental relationships.[17] Law's argument for multiple methods, or what we call being 'methodologically omnivorous,' is different from traditional social science notions of triangulation. Rather, Law asserts that multiple methods help us better grasp the multiple facets of complex social fields and relationships rather than approaching a singular point of truth.

Working from this standpoint, the Battle Harbour project included field observation, interviews and web-based textual analysis, or 'netnography,'[18] which serve as the foundation for the present analysis. This project also involved a telephone survey of residents of the surrounding St. Lewis Inlet communities about the impacts of the site on community social-economic wellbeing. The survey results are reported elsewhere and are not the focus of this chapter.[19] However, it provided useful information on community-member attitudes about the Battle Harbour site, which informed the subsequent field research.

Field research at the site was carried out over six days at the Battle Harbour National Historic District in August 2013. This provided an opportunity to conduct formal and informal semi-structured interviews with key informants working at Battle Harbour. Interview questions focused on: participants' personal experience of involvement with Battle Harbour; the messages the site conveys to visitors about local history, culture, and the environment; experiences of interacting with tourists, the cultural and social benefits of the Battle Harbour site for the surrounding communities, and participants' views of heritage tourism in relation to issues of environmental sustainability and economic diversification for the region.

Field notes were also written throughout each day at the site, interspersed with repeated observation in the formal guided tours at the site. Notes focused on how the themes and images were used throughout exhibitions and tours at the site to define local culture, history, and the environment for visitors. Notes also focused on how visitors interact with the site and employees. Field notes were also based on informal conversations with tourists about the features that draw visitors to the site, whether they are repeat, or first-time visitors to the site; the main messages they take from the site about regional history, culture, and the environment; social interactions with site-workers and members of the surrounding communities; and challenges or barriers experienced while travelling to and visiting the site. Mealtimes at Battle Harbour were particularly valuable, as they are structured as social occasions that encourage visitors to meet and interact with each other, providing opportunities to engage directly in conversation with site visitors, and to observe visitors' conversations with each other about the site.

In addition, a 'mobile methods' dimension was added to the field research in order to gain insight into the tourist mobilities required to reach Battle Harbour.[20] Field notes were written 'on the move' during travel between St. John's (the capital city of Newfoundland and Labrador) and Battle Harbour. Battle Harbour is a remote tourism destination, and for most visitors reaching it involves a multi-stage trip that includes travel by airplane, car, and ferry. Field research travel to the site involved an eleven-hour drive from St. John's across the island of Newfoundland to the Labrador Straits ferry terminal, followed by an overnight stop-over, then an early morning 90-minute ferry crossing to Labrador. This was followed by another three hour drive up the Labrador coastal highway (much of which is a gravel road), then a short 30-minute walk-on ferry from the town of Mary's Harbour to the Battle Harbour National Historic District.

Written field notes were also complemented by taking photos throughout the field research. These photos served as prompts for recollection as jotted handwritten notes were fleshed out and typed up at the end of each day. The field note photos (150 in total) were also included in the project analysis file as data sources in their own right.

Another phase of the project involved analyses of publicly accessible social media content related to the Battle Harbour Historic District. Using Small and Harris' terminology, 'netnography' refers to treating the internet as a field research site and carrying out observation and analysis of web content.[21] This analysis was carried out by the second author during September 2013 using a series of keyword and hashtag searches of Facebook, Twitter and YouTube. An advantage of this method is that it is low cost, as it can be done anywhere and does not require travel to field sites. As such, this approach may be particularly valuable for researchers or students working with limited time or fieldwork resources.

Note-taking and analysis was guided by a field note protocol, which focused the observation and analysis on dominant themes conveyed through text, images, or video about Battle Harbour and the local environment, wildlife, history and culture. Notes also focused on the following: which modes of interaction with the site and coastal environment were positioned as appropriate or inappropriate; whether positive or negative economic, social, or environmental impacts of tourism were discussed; whether environmental issues were explicitly discussed and whether the language of sustainability was invoked; how human subjects were represented in terms of social markers such as gender, race and ethnicity, and economic class; connections between Battle Harbour and the surrounding communities of the St. Lewis Inlet; connections between Battle Harbour and broader mobility networks of car, airplane, or ferry travel. Notes also focused on who appeared to be the intended audience, web links to other content, as well as signs of active audience engagement with digital media related to Battle Harbour. The analysis of Battle Harbour digital media incorporated content from six distinct

Facebook pages, 85 Twitter hits, and 32 YouTube videos. This included content produced by the Battle Harbour Historic District (for example, the official Facebook page) as well as content produced by tourists.

All of the interview transcripts, field notes, photos and netnography notes were imported to NVIVO software for qualitative research, which was used to facilitate project management and data analysis for the various components of the project. All of the project materials were manually coded using a semi-structured, 'abductive' approach that uses a theoretically derived, pre-defined coding scheme but evolves to reflect emerging themes and shifting understandings of the data.[22] Top level coding categories included: animals, the coastal environment, culture and identity, environmental issues, mobility networks, modes of interaction with the environment, sustainability discourse, and tourism and social-economic development. Each of these top-level categories served as an umbrella for several more precise second-level categories. For example, within the top-level category for culture and identity, second-level coding categories included arts, food and drink as cultural performance, history as a tourism attractor, outports (rural Newfoundland and Labrador fishing villages) as sites of history and authenticity, and outports as communities in decline. Data analysis proceeded by reviewing and comparing material within and across coding categories. Visual diagramming was also used to make connections across coding categories.

The social-environmental landscape of Battle Harbour

The most obvious and explicit role of Battle Harbour is to protect the material history of the region by preserving historic buildings, fishing infrastructure, such as the wharf and fishing stages, and the artefacts of the Labrador fishery. Around the wharf and village are several life-sized cut outs of black and white figures shown engaged in different elements of traditional fisheries work, dressed in historic clothing. These appear to be historic photos blown to life-size and cut out, standing in display to give an impression of what the wharf and village looked like when it was primarily a site of fishing work. The site also protects other historically significant objects, including an early Marconi wireless transmission tower (the first in the region), as well as artefacts of Robert Peary's 1908–1909 polar expedition. The Peary expedition stopped at Battle Harbour on the return from the Arctic to make use of the community's communication facilities and this connection to the colonial history of Arctic exploration is also woven into the narrative of the site's historical significance. Battle Harbour serves as a museum that displays the material heritage associated with a way of life that was transformed by the resettlement program and by the cod fishing moratorium. While Battle Harbour organizes space and objects to create a historical narrative that is specific to this community and place, similar processes are at play in other communities that use tourism to reconstruct the historical significance of extractive industries for present-day visitors.

The protection of the material history of the site, the buildings, wharf, and infrastructure of the cod fishery, is a key attractor for many visitors to the site. On one level, this historical value is interpreted in terms of a general sense of history associated with the type of rural, Newfoundland and Labrador outport community of which Battle Harbour is but one example and which can be found in coastal communities across the province and is not specific to Battle Harbour as a place. At another level, however, the historical value of the site is related to the specificity of the place and its role as a key hub for the Labrador cod fishery and its status as an 'unofficial capital' of Labrador, as displayed through the buildings, communication infrastructure of the Marconi wireless transmission tower, and material artefacts preserved by the Historic District that make this space distinct from other outport communities.

The meaning of the historic site is also produced in relation to the surrounding landscape and animal inhabitants of the Labrador Straits. Battle Island, and the harbor and wharf, are defined as particularly well-suited and welcoming social-ecological spaces within the 'harsh' environment of the surrounding Labrador Straits for fishing boats and the wharf. Similarly, the presence of particular wildlife species is central to the historical narrative constructed at the site. Cod, visitors are told, were the main attractor to this site, structuring centuries of seasonal migration and permanent settlement on the island. Conversely, the 1990s decline of cod populations is positioned as the final key event in a narrative of community decline and out-migration. As visitors are informed on site tours, the development of the cod fishery on Battle Harbour emerged and grew through a series of technological innovations, from long-lining to cod traps and gill nets. On one group tour, the discussion turns to overfishing and the eventual closure of the fishery, with a narrative emerging from the interaction between guide and tourists that technological change combined with human greed to lead to the fisheries collapse and moratorium.

Other animal species are also woven into the historic narrative and visitors' tourist experience. A significant portion of the exhibition at the site is devoted to the history and artefacts of the local seal fishery, which was an important source of income and sustenance for the community, especially during the winter. The northern and remote character of the island is also reinforced by tour guides' stories of the occasional polar bear coming to the island. While not as central to the historic narrative, tourists' stories about their experience on the island often invoke the pleasure of seeing whales or dolphins near the island, which is a frequent occurrence from the ferry between Mary's Harbour and Battle Harbour.

A second key part of the history of Battle Harbour is the resettlement of the community in the 1960s, with its continuing role as a seasonal hub until the cod fishing moratorium in 1992, and its re-development as a historic site. Battle Harbour is a resettled community that has become partially re-inhabited as a summer community (primarily by families with long-term connections to the island) through the project of historical preservation. The ability to experience Battle Harbour as a resettled community that has been re-developed through tourism and historical preservation is another dimension of the tourism performance that effectively communicates history as visitors walk the island's footpaths (there are no roads or cars on the island) through the island's treeless, tundra-like maritime barrens ecology. As they walk the island, visitors are moved through a landscape of abandoned buildings, including homes, schoolhouse, church, and the police outpost, that have been restored through heritage carpentry, as well as the structures of the cod fishery (such as fishing stages, flakes and salt stores), and an abandoned cemetery. This illustrates how historical tourism sites can produce new forms of mobility for visitors as they recreate experiences of movement through these places.

Alongside the historic value of Battle Harbour, the other main quality of the site that attracts visitors is the opportunity to experience the natural environment of the region, which is seen as appealing because it is remote and rugged but also peaceful and 'magical.' The latter is a term that was used by several visitors and site-workers during the field research. At the same time, another key narrative that is communicated to visitors through the site is that traditional life in the community of Battle Harbour required a high degree of creativity and resilience in order to live within a challenging natural environment. For example, the island's geography is largely treeless, requiring travel to obtain firewood. There is also limited freshwater on the island, and the ponds that would have historically been used for drinking water would freeze during the long winters. As such, visitors learn that Battle Harbour residents would have travelled from their community to other islands or the mainland by boat, or by dog-sled (and later by Skidoo), across sea ice to gather firewood and fresh water. Again, we see the importance for visitors of experiencing the history of the region in relation to the natural environment of the Labrador Straits. Throughout the historic site are interpretive signs that signal repeatedly to visitors the intimate connections between the Labrador cod populations that drew settlers and migrant fishers to the harsh landscape of the Labrador Straits and the specific geography of Battle Island as a relatively safe harbour that provided the social-ecological context for a fishing-based community to emerge.

The ability to experience history in (a) place is part of what makes Battle Harbour unique and successful from the perspective of visitors and site-workers. However, doing history in place also produces challenges to maintaining the infrastructure and material history of the site. As pointed out by many informants during field research, the restoration of the historic site, which began in 1993, was a major undertaking, involving a great deal of time, labor, and resources. During the field research, concerns were repeatedly expressed about the ability to adequately maintain the restoration work within existing resources. The wharf, in particular, is in need of repair because the rough conditions of wind, waves and sea ice in the Labrador Straits take a significant toll. Similarly, there are concerns about the conditions under which historical artefacts are being stored. Many objects are kept in historic buildings without temperature or humidity control systems in order to protect their perceived 'objective authenticity.'[23] The creation of objective authenticity at the site might be altered or lost if the artefacts were removed and kept in a museum away from Battle Harbour. One of the challenges of doing history in place, then, is maintaining the integrity of historic architecture and artefacts in a place that is characterized by a challenging climate. Here, we also see how the pursuit of objective authenticity in place may have unintended consequences, as artefacts from the site may be afforded better long-term protection if they were kept in a more modern (but less objectively authentic) building for storage and display.

Furthermore, there is a tension between preserving the sense of objective authenticity of the site and the desire of many visitors for modern amenities. For example, while the accommodations on the site offer an experiential approximation of what it might have felt like on Battle Harbour before resettlement, there is a strong sense that most tourists would prefer to have modernized, private washrooms instead of the rustic, shared facilities that are currently in place. At the time of the field research, new accommodations were being built, and older accommodations were being renovated to bring them into line with tourists' expectations for comfort, while maintaining the appearance of historicity. Following Zhu, this shows how tourism authenticity is a relational and affective construct.[24] Here, we see how tourism site managers try to navigate the balance between creating a sense of authenticity as a historic site while also relying on the comfort of modern technologies and architecture to ensure financial viability as a tourism operation. This dynamic is not unique to Battle Harbour but is a tension that must be navigated by site managers and workers across a variety of historic tourism sites.

Tourist and host performance

Battle Harbour is valued as a site for protecting the material history of the Labrador Straits within the landscape of Battle Island and the Labrador Straits. From a tourism performance perspective, it also plays an important role in providing a space for the performance of intangible heritage by site-workers in interaction with visitors. The embodied performance of history in place takes three distinct forms. First, many of the staff at Battle Harbour were trained in heritage carpentry. Heritage carpentry has been practiced over the past 20 years through the initial project of building restoration but also through ongoing site maintenance and the development of new projects. Those who have been trained in heritage carpentry have also passed on their training and skills to new employees over the years. Ongoing restoration of buildings at the site is carried out in sight of visitors, and visitors are able to watch or photograph heritage carpentry as it is performed.

Second, the tours of the site are guided by staff with long-term personal connections and family histories at Battle Harbour, most of whom also work in other jobs on the site. Rather than performing from script, as is often the case at tourist sites, tour guides bring a storytelling dimension to the tours, which skillfully integrate personal stories with the material culture of the site. The guided tours are led by long-term members of the community who have family ties to Battle Harbour and who continue to live in the area. The guided tours are informed by the personal experiences of the tour guides, as well as providing opportunities to move through historic buildings and view material artefacts.

Third, cooking at Battle Harbour can also be considered a form of intangible heritage that has been developed through additional training. The menu is based on traditional Newfoundland and Labrador food. It has been further developed through recent additional training with a visiting chef. Furthermore, there are often opportunities for visitors to join kitchen staff for short cooking workshops. This approach to local cuisine appears to be paying off, as many visitors comment that the food at Battle Harbour is among the best they have experienced throughout rural Newfoundland and Labrador.

Of the staff at Battle Harbour, several are from communities in the immediate surrounding area, while others are from the broader Labrador Straits region. For several workers at the site, the connection between Battle Harbour and the surrounding communities is an especially important dimension of performing history for tourists. According to several staff members, work at Battle Harbour has allowed them to remain embedded in their communities, rather than to leave the region for work, thereby making some contribution to the viability of the St. Lewis Inlet communities. These intimate connections between the Battle Harbour site, as a material space, and the members of the local communities who actively participate in working with tourists and making the site run are a particularly valued form of connection between Battle Harbour, as a historic site, and its surrounding communities. At the same time, the labor of doing historic tourism at Battle Harbour is also gendered, with the work of heritage carpentry performed by men and the work of running the kitchen and managing the tourist shop performed by women. As such, the performance of historic tourism also re-enacts and solidifies narratives of the gendered division of labor in traditional outport communities.

The field research component of the project also provides insight into impacts of the ways in which history is co-performed through tourist interactions with site-workers. The opportunity to connect with new people came up repeatedly as one of the benefits of working at the site. The experience of interacting with tourists is often described as an exchange, with tourism workers and visitors learning from each other. Other benefits of tourist-community interaction identified were that tourists bring ideas to help improve business practices at the site, that interacting with tourists provides local community members the opportunity to learn about places that visitors come from, and that interaction with tourists provides a framework for sharing local culture and history.

Similarly, from many tourists' perspectives, a key part of experiencing Battle Harbour is the opportunity to learn about the history and culture of the place through social interaction with community members who not only work at the site, but have lived here and have family ties to this community. There is also a collective dimension to the Battle Harbour experience, where social interaction among visitors is structured through shared dining tables and dining times, providing a set space and time for experiences and stories about the site, as well as stories about travel through Newfoundland and Labrador in general. This is complemented by opportunities for visitors to take workshops and learn about local food from cooking staff. This collective dimension is also cultivated through group tours of the buildings and artefacts preserved at the site, which are led by staff with personal experience of living on the island. The tours are often quite conversational, with visitors frequently asking questions of the guides, who draw on their personal experience to shape their narratives in response to the interests of particular tour groups. The Battle Harbour Historic District provides community members with the setting to share stories of growing up in the area and to embody their history in this place for visitors.

In addition to providing a space for protecting the material culture and intangible heritage of Battle Harbour, another key dimension of the Battle Harbour experience is in providing tourists an immersive and interactive experience of being in a resettled community. The resettlement of Battle Harbour during the 1960s is a key part of the storytelling of the tour and in the exhibition displays. The last year-round residents left in 1968, after the last teacher left and the school closed. Battle Harbour then served as a seasonal fishing village until the cod fishing moratorium in 1992. At that point, several buildings were donated to the Battle Harbour Historic Trust and restoration work began in 1993. Battle Harbour is a resettled community. However, through redevelopment as a historic site and tourist destination, it has been re-settled as a seasonal community. Local community engagement with tourism has protected against the decline and collapse typical of other resettled communities throughout Newfoundland and Labrador, while also promoting the protection and performance of history within the natural and built environment of the historic site.

Battle Harbour is also within the traditional territory of the NunatuKavut southern Inuit.[25] NunatuKavut Community Council members live throughout the St. Lewis Inlet communities around Battle Harbour. However, the narratives enacted at Battle Harbour focus primarily on histories of European settlement, community, and labor on this small island. Little attention is given to NunatuKavut history in the region, or to relationships between European settlers and NunatuKavut communities through this site. The marginalization of NunatuKavut from the historical narrative of the region generally works to enact Battle Harbour as a colonized landscape. At the same time, interviews and field research indicates that people who work at the site include those who identify as Indigenous and European. The colonial historical narrative of Battle Harbour is unsettled by prominent displays of the Labrador flag at the site, which is often described by site-workers to tourists. The Labrador flag contains three horizontal bands of white, green and blue, which represent the physical environment of snow, forest and water. It also features a three-tined spruce bough, which represents the three founding peoples of Labrador: Inuit, Innu, and Europeans. In narrating the symbolism of the Labrador flag to tourists, which inverts the usual tendency in Canada to homogenize Indigenous groups, site-workers complicate the otherwise normalized narratives of colonial exploration, settlement, and resource extraction.

Battle Harbour and extra-local mobility networks

From a tourism mobilities perspective, the local landscape of Battle Harbour can be thought of as a hub, or nodal point, in broader networks of tourism mobility that rely on car, ferry, and airplane travel.[26] These mobility routes are, in a sense, socio-technological extensions of the landscape of Battle Harbour that inform the ways in which visitors experience Battle Harbour as a historic tourism site. During field research at the site, we often heard visitors talk about how they incorporated their time at Battle Harbour into a larger travel route that often included Red Bay (a UNESCO site in the Labrador Straits, which commemorates early Basque whaling communities) and L'Anse aux Meadows (a UNESCO site on the Northern Peninsula of Newfoundland island, which commemorates Viking settlement in the region) as other key historic sites in the province. Many visitors to Battle Harbour were also either on their way to or from Gros Morne National Park, which also has UNESCO status due to its unique geology. This illustrates that many tourists experience Battle Harbour as a localized place that is interpreted within a larger route of key historic sites and natural environments in western Newfoundland and the Labrador Straits. A typical pattern is for visitors to stay one to two nights at Battle Harbour, and to use it as a key destination on a larger tour of Newfoundland and Labrador, which also typically includes time spent at Red Bay, L'Anse aux Meadows, and Gros Morne as other key places to experience the history and landscapes of the region.

Battle Harbour is a remote tourist destination. It is typical of other cold water island tourism destinations, where 'most visitors come to cold water islands on small vessels or on small planes after long haul flights that deter all but the strong-willed and affluent.'[27] Getting to Battle Harbour requires a significant amount of travel time by highway and then by two ferries (the Labrador Straits ferry and the boat from Mary's Harbour to Battle Harbour). Currently, tourists to Battle Harbour need to be highly motivated and committed to visiting the site, otherwise it will be missed. During field research, tourists and site-workers particularly noted the poor state of the gravel road from Red Bay to Mary's Harbour, which repeatedly came up as a major deterrent to tourist travel to Battle Harbour. For many visitors, Battle Harbour is also experienced as part of driving a large circle that includes travelling between Quebec and Labrador via the rugged and remote Labrador Highway, the challenges of which came up frequently over meals at Battle Harbour.

Imagined tourism: digitally mediated performance of place

Battle Harbour presents history though its intimate relationship to place, including both the built and natural environments of Battle Island and the Labrador Straits. The performance of history, as intangible heritage, also relies on the co-performances of tourists and site-workers within this remote environment. Creating history in place, however, also relies on making links between the localized performances, material artefacts and environment of Battle Harbour, and extra-local networks of tourism mobility involving ferry, car, and airplane travel. Making these links also relies on a different kind of tourism performance through various media, including websites, social media, travel articles, and guide-books, which engage potential visitors in the 'media-mediated' virtual tourism that helps provoke and structure tourism mobility.[28] Drawing tourists to local historic sites depends on achieving accolades through global communication networks such as Facebook or Trip Advisor, which help draw flows of visitors to local historic sites.

We examined social media related to Battle Harbour, with a particular focus on Facebook, YouTube and Twitter, to look at how Battle Harbour is de-localized and circulated through these digitally mediated tourism performances. There are two main Facebook pages dedicated to Battle Harbour. First, the Battle Harbour Historic Trust Inc. Facebook page (created 7 July 2011) promotes the Battle Harbour Heritage Properties. The page posts information aimed at tourists including pictures of Battle Harbour, weather conditions, news stories relevant to Battle Harbour (including plans to improve the Trans-Labrador Highway), and festival dates, as well as pictures and information on accommodation, rates, and meals. While the site is directed at tourists, people do not appear often on this page. When they do appear, they are background subjects, while the dominant images are of local landscapes, buildings, wildlife, and icebergs. Animals are featured prominently on this page and appear to signify that wildlife sightings are a common part of the Newfoundland and Labrador tourism experience. Whales (orcas, humpbacks, and belugas), foxes, seals, and a hawk are all depicted on the page. Photos are mostly taken in the months when the weather is sunny and it looks to be summer, late spring, or fall. There is also a link to a video showcasing a particularly large iceberg that passed near the historic site. At the time it was analyzed (September 2013), this Facebook page had 184 'likes,' which was the main form of audience engagement with the page.

The second main Facebook page dedicated to the site was only a few months old (created 26 June 2013) at the time of analysis. Similar in name and content, the Battle Harbour Historic Trust page visualizes the landscape, buildings, and tourist accommodation at the national historic site. It differs from the Historic Trust Inc. page, however, in that it contains fewer photos and comments, with more of a focus on people and food and less of a focus on wildlife and icebergs. While the Battle Harbour Historic Trust Inc. page is more obviously oriented towards tourists, this page appears to be more oriented towards providing a digital community for people who work or live seasonally at the site, as well as providing space for imagined tourism. The dominant photo on this page is a scenic image of the village and harbour at sunset, with smoke rising from chimneys and windows lit up from the inside working to create the sense of a small town during the evening hours. The profile picture also includes an image of the logo for the Battle Harbour Historic Trust, which incorporates a drawn image of a split cod fillet, which references the site's embodiment of the history of the Labrador cod fishery. Several of the remaining photos consist of images of historic buildings and food, including photos of food being prepared and the communal dining hall. This page depicts Battle Harbour as a place of beautiful landscapes and seascapes, icebergs, and boats. This page had 197 'likes' as of 12 September 2013, indicating that neither Facebook page has had an especially high level of active audience engagement for these digitally mediated performances.

Of the social media applications, YouTube is the best used as a site for previous tourists to circulate their own content related to Battle Harbour and to connect their embodied mobility to the site to digital communication networks of imagined tourism. At the time of searching, there were 32 YouTube videos that focused either on tourists' experience of visiting or getting to Battle Harbour or that were posted by regional tourism companies, as well as several re-postings of videos. Overall these videos showcase Battle Harbour as a historic village with opportunities to view whales and icebergs. The videos also routinely depict stunning landscapes, seascapes, and sunsets. While the main focus was mostly on being on the island or its surrounding seascape, there was also attention to multimodal travel to and from the site by planes and ferries. By contrast with the Facebook pages for Battle Harbour, which appear to have relatively low levels of user engagement, some of these YouTube videos have high levels of user engagement, with the highest ('Iceberg Collapsing off Battle Harbour, Labrador') receiving 631,965 views.

In contrast with Facebook and YouTube, Twitter was not particularly well-used as a social media venue for performing and promoting Battle Harbour to potential visitors. A variety of keyword search strategies turned up only a few hits each. Most of the Twitter content was tied to the @battleharbour account, which had 56 hits at the time the search was conducted. The majority of tweets were from tourism-related businesses, or from the Battle Harbour Historic Trust, often promoting content that was linked on the Facebook page. Individual posts to Twitter which were included also came from previous tourists who posted photos form their visit, and several of the tweets consisted of re-tweets of the same image or links to YouTube videos. Of the images on Twitter, one was from the Battle Harbour website, which had been re-tweeted several times, five were images of the outside village, one was of a woodstove inside one of the houses in Battle Harbour, one was of the coastline, and the rest were of icebergs. In particular, images of an iceberg island named Petermann Ice Island, seen near Battle Harbour, was the focus of many re-tweets, photos, and videos.

As noted previously, for many of those who work at Battle Harbour and live in the surrounding region, the poor quality of the Labrador Highway is viewed as the main challenge to connecting this place to broader networks of tourism mobility. However, while many of the tourists who make it to the site also talk about the challenges of the road, another key theme that comes up repeatedly is a lack of media visibility and online information about Battle Harbour as a tourism destination, which would allow tourists to better plan their travel routes and visit. Visitors talk about the relatively low digital media visibility of the site which is consistent with our analysis of web 2.0 content, which suggests that – other than YouTube – digital networks of imagined tourism do not appear to be used to their full potential as a form of imagined tourism that can help mobilize potential tourists to travel to the site in person. Visitors to the site appear to learn about Battle Harbour primarily through word of mouth from others who have travelled to this site, or through online information. Several visitors, however, commented on the lack of promotion or media visibility for Battle Harbour, which can create barriers to drawing visitors to this place, as the internet is now among the first avenues for information and travel planning for many people. Visitors also expressed that they had difficulties getting reliable information about the site, as well as difficulties navigating their travel and accommodation arrangements by telephone or e-mail.

Many potential visitors are unlikely to persist in repeatedly calling and e-mailing for information or making bookings, so the lack of a reliable system for communicating with potential visitors throughout the year is a significant challenge for connecting the local place of Battle Harbour to extra-local networks of tourism mobility and ensuring the viability of the site as a historic tourism destination.

Conclusion

Using a combination of methodologies, including field observation, interviews, and 'netnography,' allows us to better understand how the Battle Harbour National Historic District draws on the relationality of objects and buildings with the physical environment and animals to produce a historical tourism narrative about the Labrador cod fishery and its decline, the resettlement of the community, and its restoration as a place of historic significance.[29] Battle Harbour is within NunatuKavut southern Inuit traditional territory, and the NunatuKavut Community Council is active in the St. Lewis Inlet communities around Battle Harbour.[30] Yet, the dominant historical narrative is of colonial mobility, settlement, and resource extraction. Enacting this historic narrative at Battle Harbour relies on relationships between the localized space of Battle Island and the Labrador Straits, the embodied performances of tourists and hosts, and digitally mediated forms of imagined tourism that connect this local place to extra-local networks of tourism mobility. In tracing the connections between history, place, tourism performance, and digital media, we also demonstrate the utility of John Law's argument for multiple methodologies – or being methodologically omnivorous. Going beyond our specific case study, this is a valuable approach for creating research accounts that better account for the relational complexity among tourism hosts and visitors, the natural and built environment, and digital media that goes into making history in place.[31]

This case study also demonstrates the utility of the tourism mobilities and tourism performance perspectives for better understanding how historical tourism is produced in ways that link local communities and environments to extra-local networks of communication and tourism mobility.[32] In the case of Battle Harbour, the relationality of tourism workers, architecture, objects and the local environment appears to be working well and producing a rich experience for visitors at the historic site. By contrast, there appear to be greater challenges to navigating relationships between the local historic site and extra-local mobility networks and digital media networks. In comparison with the local social-technological-environmental space of Battle Harbour, these extra-local mobility and communication networks are more difficult for actors at the periphery of these networks to influence and control. This finding suggests another line of inquiry for future research on historic sites: How do historic site workers and managers navigate the competing demands of local historical preservation, on one hand, and requirements to connect with extra-local tourism flows and communication networks?

Going beyond the specifics of Battle Harbour, our analysis shows that those who wish to use historical tourism as a form of development for rural or remote communities need to be strategic in thinking about forms of multiscale planning and governance that can help communities navigate the links between the immediate places where historical tourism is done and the larger-scale mobility and communication networks that can draw in potential visitors. Our methodological approach also offers a model for others interested in investigating how historic tourism sites are used to respond to boom and bust cycles, economic decline, or community relocation, as well as place-making and community revival. Further research on historical reconstructions of place would benefit from the tourism mobility framework and the multiple method approach we have outlined in this chapter.

Acknowledgments

Valuable feedback was provided throughout the development of this research by Howard Ramos, Douglas House, Gordon Slade, and Mandy Applin. Research assistance was provided by David Chafe. We would like to thank Brian Beaton for his comments on an earlier version of this paper. Financial support this project was provided by The Harris Centre Applied Research Fund. Work on this paper was supported by a Fogo Island Fellowship.

Notes

1 M. Applin, *Strategic Analysis and Sustainability Planning*, Battle Harbour, NL: Battle Harbour Historic Trust Inc., 2010.
2 G. Baldacchino, 'Warm versus cold water island tourism: A review of policy implications', *Island Studies Journal*, 1.2, 2006, 186.
3 L. Cooke, 'North takes place in Dawson City, Yukon, Canada', in D. Jorgensen and S. Sörlin (eds), *Northscapes: History, Technology, and the Making of Northern Environments*, Vancouver: UBC Press, 2013, p. 234.
4 NunatuKavut, 'Who we are', *NunatuKavut: Our Ancient Land*, 2016, https://nunatukavut.ca/about/who-we-are/, last accessed 29.09.19.
5 Y. Zhu, 'Performing heritage: Rethinking authenticity in tourism', *Annals of Tourism Research*, 39.3, 2012, 1495–513.
6 A. Franklin, 'Tourism as an ordering: Towards a new ontology of tourism', *Tourist Studies*, 4.3, 2004, 279.
7 Applin, *Strategic Analysis*.
8 D. Bavington, *Managed Annihilation: An Unnatural History of the Newfoundland Cod Collapse*, Vancouver: UBC Press, 2010.
9 Applin, *Strategic Analysis*.
10 J. Overton, '"A Future in the Past"? Tourism development, outport archaeology, and the politics of deindustrialization in Newfoundland and Labrador in the 1990s', *Urban History Review*, 35.2, 2007, 60–74; G. L. Pocius, *A Place to Belong: Community Order and Everyday Space in Calvert, Newfoundland*, Athens, GA: University of Georgia Press, 2000.
11 M. Sheller and J. Urry, 'The New Mobilities paradigm', *Environment and Planning A: Economy and Space*, 38, 2006, 207–26.
12 E. H. Huijbens and K. Benediktsson, 'Practising Highland heterotopias: Automobility in the interior of Iceland', *Mobilities*, 2.1, 2007, 143–65; C. Lassen, 'Aeromobility and work', *Environment and Planning A: Economy and Space*, 38, 2006, 301–12.

13 J. O. Bærenholdt, M. Haldrup, and J. Urry, *Performing Tourist Places*, Aldershot: Ashgate Publishing, 2004; Zhu, 'Performing Heritage'.
14 J. Urry and J. Larsen, *The Tourist Gaze 3.0* (1st edn. 1990), Los Angeles, CA: Sage Publishing, 2011.
15 N. B. Salazar, *Envisioning Eden: Mobilizing Imaginaries in Tourism and Beyond*, Oxford: Berghahn, 2010; Urry and Larsen, *Tourist Gaze*, p. 116.
16 Urry and Larsen, *Tourist Gaze*.
17 J. Law, *After Method: Mess in Social Science Research*, London and New York: Routledge, 2004.
18 J. Small and C. Harris, 'Crying babies on planes: Aeromobility and parenting', *Annals of Tourism Research*, 48.C, 2014, 27–41.
19 H. Ramos, M. C. J. Stoddard, and D. Chafe, 'Assessing the tangible and intangible benefits of tourism: Perceptions of economic, social, and cultural impacts in Labrador's Battle Harbour Historic District', *Island Studies Journal*, 11.1, 2016, 209–26.
20 P. Merriman, 'Rethinking mobile methods', *Mobilities*, 9.2, 2014, 167–87.
21 Small and Harris, 'Crying babies on planes', p. 30.
22 D. L. Morgan, 'Paradigms lost and pragmatism regained: Methodological implications of combining qualitative and quantitative methods', *Journal of Mixed Methods Research*, 1.1, 2007, 48–76.
23 Zhu, 'Performing Heritage', p. 1496.
24 Ibid.
25 NunatuKavut, 'Our Ancient Land', https://nunatukavut.ca/, last accessed 29.09.19.
26 Sheller and Urry, 'The New Mobilities paradigm'; Urry and Larsen, *The Tourist Gaze*.
27 Baldacchino, 'Warm verses cold water island', p. 188.
28 Salazar, *Envisioning Eden*; Urry and Larsen, *The Tourist Gaze*, p. 116.
29 Small and Harris, 'Crying babies on planes.'
30 NunatuKavut, 'Our Ancient Land'.
31 Law, *After Method*.
32 Bærenholdt, Haldrup, and Urry, *Performing Tourist Places*; Salazar, *Envisioning Eden*; Sheller and Urry, 'The New Mobilities paradigm'; Urry and Larsen, *The Tourist Gaze*.

Further reading

Bærenholdt, Jørgen Ole, Michael Haldrup, Jonas Larsen, and John Urry, *Performing Tourist Places*, Aldershot: Ashgate Publishing, 2004.
Cooke, Lisa, 'North takes place in Dawson City, Yukon, Canada', in Dolly Jorgensen and Sverker Sörlin (eds), *Northscapes: History, Technology, and the Making of Northern Environments*, Vancouver: UBC Press, 2013, pp. 223–46.
Law, John, *After Method: Mess in Social Science Research*, London and New York: Routledge, 2004.
Merriman, Peter, 'Rethinking mobile methods', *Mobilities*, 9.2, 2014, 167–87.
Salazar, Noel B., *Envisioning Eden: Mobilizing Imaginaries in Tourism and Beyond*, Oxford: Berghahn Books, 2010.
Sheller, Mimi and John Urry, 'The New Mobilities paradigm', *Environment and Planning A: Economy and Space*, 38, 2006, 207–26.

3 Cemeteries
Tracing sepulchral cultures

Felix Robin Schulz

Death is a certainty for us as human beings, and thus there is the practical need for the disposal of the dead. Indeed, what happens after the death of a human being reveals much about a given society, since in response to mortality, complex systems have come into play. In consequence, different sepulchral cultures emerge over time and perpetually change. They have never remained static and therefore afford the historian the opportunity for close description and analysis. Societies and cultures have put a lot of thought and effort into establishing the ways in which they mourn, commemorate, and bury their dead. These can and should be interpreted. Archaeologists have done this as a matter of fact, since burial sites are a staple of archaeology.[1] Historians, however, have been slower, and the milestone regarding understanding historical attitudes towards death has long been the work of Philippe Ariès. In 1974, Ariès began to posit the question of historical changes in the relationship between one's idea of oneself and one's idea of death. He tried to explain what he saw as change over a lengthy timescale, from a matter-of-fact acceptance of death towards a more tense relationship full of drama, fear, and – towards the middle and end of the twentieth century – taboo and repression.[2]

The idea of the marginalisation of death has been ascribed to the interplay of factors of modernity such as rationalisation, medicalisation, secularisation, and individualisation, as well as the powerful force of professionals, such as funeral directors, cemetery directors, and health officials, taking control.[3] Yet, while each and every one of these forces, as we will see, had a tremendous impact, the overall idea of a marginalisation of death needs to be understood in a much more nuanced way. This was done most powerfully in 1994 by Tony Walter when he pointed out that death not only remained a visible presence which people discussed and that responses to death were perpetually evolving.[4] While some elements of death became less common practice (such as the laying out of the corpse in the family's home) others, such as the availability of hospice places and palliative care, became more widely discussed. It is evident that grief, mourning, rituals, and above all the cemetery have not lost much of their presence.[5] What follows concentrates on one of the most ubiquitous aspects of the rich tapestry of death: the modern cemetery – understood here as a designated and enclosed space set aside specifically for the burial of the dead. The cemetery has developed into the central location of death and commemoration and the aim of this chapter is to introduce various ways of unlocking what these sites can tell us about the histories of various sepulchral cultures.[6] Some of the historical overview given here is by necessity reductionist, for the developments described have not been uniform – major differences existed and still persist between different countries and regions and even within them. However, rather than weakening the analytical framework, this heterogeneity strengthens it, since on the one hand it broadens the comparative framework from looking merely at the differences between countries to analysing on a much more granular level and on the other it is precisely this diversity which allows for so much analysis.[7]

Cemeteries reveal much of both the local and the wider picture; gravestones and public sculptures can tell us individual stories but can also be read for diverse aspects such as prevalent aesthetics, social and religious attitudes, economic realities, and changing political and ideological ideals. It should be noted that changes in sepulchral culture play out in a nonlinear and staggered way, so it is important to distinguish between the *avant-garde* and the widespread, as well as between more rapidly changing urban and more sedate rural settings. Yet one should also not forget cemeteries large and small are by definition transitory landscapes, subject to both intransigent and incessant change. Even if gravestones can remain for centuries, inscriptions fade, and points of references once widespread and clear become obscure. Add to this the fact that decay and vegetation can change a site dramatically and it is clear that engaging with the cemetery as a historical source thus necessitates an immersive approach. Simon Schama famously referred to this approach in 1995 as engaging with a sense of place through the archive of the feet.[8] This means merely looking at maps and even photographs will only take the historian so far, for a complete analysis requires understanding by walking and allowing time to take in the space and employ one's senses and imagination (even if that is inherently dangerous since this is deeply subjective). To analyse a cemetery thus marries the documentary approach of more traditional historical methods with the more visceral experience of place.

However, the complexities do not end there. Cemeteries are not only transitory, they are also living cultural landscapes, meaning they have been used by people for very different purposes ranging from dog walking to mourning. It is in this field that the historiography is threadbare, especially when we compare this dearth of historical knowledge with pioneering work in the social sciences unlocking the many motivations for using cemeteries.[9] This should not deter us from trying to understand not only the place but how the different usages of the cemetery have been seen by different interest groups in the past. The last obstacle is that we need to understand both the complete picture of a cemetery as well as the different building blocks that make up the whole. This means engaging with a plethora of elements from location, layout and design elements via the architecture of the central buildings and memorials to decoding specific sections and individual graves, headstones, and inscriptions. Hence, besides looking at wider historical developments, this chapter will turn to look at particular case studies in order to demonstrate the unlocking of such complexities, and one in particular: the *Sennefriedhof,* in Bielefeld, Germany.

The emergence of the modern cemetery is related to the twin stories of urbanisation and economic growth leading to industrialisation.[10] In the first instance, in Europe the emergence of the cemetery is the story of the disappearance of the inner city burial around the parish church. While the rural churchyard often remained, in cities and towns it was gradually replaced by the cemetery adjacent to but outside of the city wall, and in the next logical step, new cemeteries were moved further to the outskirts. In October 1518, the decision to stop all funerals within the city walls taken by the council of the rich southern imperial city of Nuremberg, in the aftermath of two plague epidemics (1505 and 1508), as well as in the light of inadequate and overcrowded burial space, resulted in the city's decision to convert one outlying village churchyard into a cemetery and to build one new one entirely. This new cemetery was not a churchyard but a modern cemetery, since it was not to be dominated by a church but by a smaller chapel – denoting that this place of worship was not a parish church. All these decisions were controversial, since it moved the location of burial away from the parish churches and away from the life of the city itself. The cemeteries were opened a year later in 1519, no burials took place in the city after 1520, and the chapel was finally consecrated in 1521.[11] The practical needs of cities in terms of improved public hygiene began to drive future developments outside the city walls and were given further impetus by war and epidemics. This means the location of the cemetery itself can reveal the age of the cemetery but needs to be understood in the context of the location's history.

Nuremberg was at the forefront of this gradual change in the early modern period that started in the cities of Northern Italy and spread from there. The second central and gradual change was the change in the importance of the location of the burial space itself within the new cemeteries. The strongest expression of this can be found in adoption of the *Camposanto* design in the sixteenth century devised in Pisa as early as 1278. This design was dominated by prestigious walled niches running the full outside circumference of the cemetery and two central crossing axes serving as the main thoroughfares, linking the four sections of the cemetery. In these cemeteries, being adjacent to the wall or near the centre reflected the ability of the families of the deceased to afford specific locations and the necessary coffins and the location was thus reflective of both material and social standing. This new trend was, again, not universally popular; public resistance against the new when it comes to sepulchral change has regularly been profound. Therefore, it was the allure of finer social stratification that initially drove the move to remove burial places to the outskirts. It was precisely the emergence of an urban middle class that altered patterns of behaviour such as linking the commemoration of the dead to a specific location rather than to the act of holding a memorial mass.[12] These two spatial changes, the cemetery itself and where individual graves were located, were further amplified by the theological divide that enveloped Europe with the Reformation and led to the emergence of clearly designated Protestant and Catholic cemeteries in the early modern period. The Reformation altered the perception of death, since it was Luther in particular who painted death as the long sleep and thus introduced the idea of the resting place. This further strengthened the commemorative link to the site of burial and the wider introduction of named gravestones for those who could afford them.

The second stage in the evolution of the modern cemetery was triggered when the state intensified the attempt to wrest control of the cemetery from the churches and reform sepulchral culture along rational thinking towards the end of the eighteenth century. Driven by the ideas of the Enlightenment, Joseph II of Austria enacted an important, even if only partially successful, set of burial reforms between 1782 and 1785, which sought to remove the control of the Catholic Church over secular matters. In a series of stages, he imposed rules that set minimum standards such as depth of burial, removed the new cemeteries to the periphery of the town centres, and tried to establish civic authorities to oversee cemeteries.[13] The ideas behind the Josephian reforms were emulated across large parts of Europe and beyond in the subsequent decades. These reforms were often more successful when they were carefully introduced in the spirit of compromise and consultation by local authorities, which reinforced the disparate nature of sepulchral culture across Europe.[14] Additionally, municipal buildings such as mortuaries slowly became more central to the lawful conduct of burials. Interwoven with this wresting of control was the fact that cities gained administrative and planning control over cemeteries.

Emblematic of this triumph over the Church was the opening of Père Lachaise in 1804. Under the guidance of the prefect for the department, Paris saw not only the Napoleonic triumph of a 60-year struggle of the French cemetery reform movement, it also saw the opening of the first European garden cemetery. A space that was deliberately designed to be pleasingly Arcadian and represented what the historian Thomas Laqueur lamented was 'a genuinely new kind of space for the dead in the heart of Europe'; Père Lachaise became 'the mother house of the new religion of memory and history, its Cluny Abbey and its Disneyland.'[15] This rather harsh comment on the strongly formative nature of some cemeteries such as Père Lachaise or Mount Auburn outside Boston in Massachusetts (1831) emphasises the significance of key sites for the formation of popular taste as well as the enormous attraction some sites can have even two centuries on.[16] However, it should not undermine the realisation that Père Lachaise represented a radical departure in the design of cemeteries after 1804. Far from a mere marginalisation of the burial of the dead, we also have to observe the tremendous level of concentration as evident in the vast cemeteries of cities such as Vienna and Chicago or a little earlier London (its magnificent seven new cemeteries were opened between 1832–41). The comparison between the *Zentralfriedhof*'s strict geometric design (1863–74) and Rosehill cemetery's more meandering lines (1859–64) indicate more differences in taste: Rosehill clearly takes up the ideas of Mount Auburn, namely paths that are gently set into the landscape, while the *Zentralfriedhof* is clearly designed around its central municipal buildings, with the main avenues leading from them to the corners of the cemetery. Yet beneath the surface both share overarching developments: the urban dead were being buried according to stricter rules in groups or fields inside carefully designed and park-like areas that had good transport links to but were removed from the everyday throng of the urban centres. However, the key aspect was that, unlike in Nuremberg, these new cemeteries were updated churchyards where individual graves were set within carefully curated and cultivated flora. Planning meant that the individual sections and fields were separated by small and large pathways. What remained the same was that many a grave, tomb, or mausoleum was marked by ornate gravestones or edifices telling of the taste, wealth, and cultivation of the owner's family. Thus, these nineteenth-century developments left historians ever more material to analyse in forms of magnificent vistas, ornate tombs, and elaborate public buildings.

When one enters the fascinating time capsule that is Leipzig's largest cemetery, the *Südfriedhof* (opened in 1886) – here it is important to note that the postwar divide of Germany marginalised Leipzig to a certain extent thus preserving the *fin de siècle* elements of the 80 hectare site much better than elsewhere – one does not notice Otto Wittenberg's main design concept. The city's park planner had conceived of the main thoroughfares of the cemetery to be in the shape of a lime tree leaf in reference to the etymological origins of Leipzig. Walking through the main gate. One's attention is drawn straight to the impressive crematorium and double chapel (opened in 1909). When one then turns right after a few hundred metres and enters section 2, on a prominent spot, not too far from the main avenue, one encounters the family tomb of Franz Schlobach [Figure 3.1]. In the mid-nineteenth century, the industrialist had opened a sawmill in Böhlitz-Ehrenberg, a western borough of Leipzig, and slowly built it into a large company specialising in veneers. His fruits of industry ultimately allowed his relatives to commission a large and elaborate family tomb on his death in 1907. The tomb, made from a hard grey stone and metal work, is framed on either side by two large stone recesses in the back with adjacent pillars of medium height. On top of each stands a putti, holding a cornucopia representing wealth, and to the front, two rotund stone vases mark the forward edge of the tomb. The whole ensemble is a mixture of neoclassical and baroque revival motifs of splendour and wealth. This is further stressed by the centre of the tomb, as it is arranged into two levels. The first level, up two steps and occupying two-thirds of the depth and breadth, is the burial level dominated by the large heavy metal lid of the underlying vault. The vault lit itself is inscribed with eight names on round name plaques with space for a further eight more plaques (not used largely as the family emigrated initially to the United States). A further two steps up is the second level. Between two benches carved from stone stands a low plinth-like altar.

Inscribed on the right is the name of the family Franz Schlobach in its paternal nomenclature, and on the left that of the Leipzig borough of Böhlitz-Ehrenberg and the year A.D. 1907. This means there is a clear dominance of the wealth creator's name above all other family members, the locality of the sawmill clearly speaks of a certain local pride or even of *Heimat* (that particular German sense of belonging to a locality), and the rather unusual usage of the classical date convention further underscores the design and its reference to high culture.

However, most instructive is the main frieze of the four adult figures who, unlike the ancient Greek reference points, mostly are shrouded, following the convention of the late nineteenth century. On the left stands a female representation

Figure 3.1 The family tomb of Franz Schlobach.
Source: Reproduced courtesy of SLUB / Deutsche Fotothek / Straube, Stefan.

of commerce holding the model of a ship. The only male is a representation of industry signified by his holding a hoe and the hand of the second female figure, representing motherhood. That figure in turn is holding the hand of a naked boy who is pointing to the wine jug in the hand of the fourth female figure. This is a female representation of spirituality since the jug is called an *oinochoe* and often appears in scenes of libations to the gods. Even more interesting is her other gesture of *anakalypis,* that of plucking drapery away from the shoulder which has its roots in a nexus of ideas surrounding marriage, sexual surrender (unveiling) and modesty (veiling). All these classical references are juxtaposed by the last significant aspect, the clear backdrop of a large saw blade and a number of tree trunks, all clear references to the origins of Franz Schlobach's wealth.[17] The assembly offers us a clear late nineteenth-century public expression of wealth and cultural sophistication using the artistic and architectural language of the time. It was clearly commissioned on the understanding that a family tomb was an expression of sophistication and the cemetery a stage. This tomb is thus not only the site of mourning and commemoration of family and friends, it is also a site for the public display of wealth and learning as well as of civic pride.

Cities similarly invested considerable amounts in building communal buildings that demonstrated civic prowess and advanced thinking. Thus, large urban cemeteries were the key feature of the second stage of sepulchral change, driven by demographic and economic growth and accelerated by the desire for clear urban planning. This meant increased urgency for better public hygiene, and an affirmation of administrative power or commercial interests – for not all countries went with municipal cemeteries as we also see the emerging of cemetery co-operations especially in the United States and the United Kingdom. The churches continued to play a role, but one generally more removed; municipal chapels were often consecrated, but they were not churches as such. Slowly, contemporary public taste with regard to celebrating death changed, and more radical ideas such as freethinking and above all the cremation movements began to have an impact. It is no coincidence that the cremation movement had two distinct origins: one firmly rooted in the bourgeois desire to embrace romantic notions of this new technology or to challenge – 'overcome' – religious ideas; the second based firmly on the self-organisation of the working class that combined socialist dislike for religion with the fact that cremation could be a much more affordable alternative.[18] In addition, it is important to underline that there was very little difference between cemetery development driven by the public or the private sector. Large municipal or commercial cemeteries of the period saw parallel developments in terms of large cemeteries offering a multitude of burial options. Indeed, in a large number of countries, reactions against the perceived excesses of this sepulchral culture started at the beginning of the twentieth century. It was this mixture of concern for and tension between efficiencies, practicalities and popular tastes that led to the third stage of the emergence of the modern cemetery: the increasingly different approaches of reforming the cemetery and safeguarding it from the perceived ravages of modernity. This meant different things in different places, but all these movements have in common a shift away from the private or artificial and an establishment of the public or natural as well as the fact that individual specialists and administrators began to re-shape sepulchral culture. In Germany, this meant the emergence of the reform movement and its key idea, the woodland cemetery, and the radical break with the artificiality of the park and its perceived pomposity.

There are few places that better demonstrate this process than the case of the *Sennefriedhof* in Bielefeld. The Westphalian city, east of Dortmund and the Ruhr, had experienced rapid growth based on its linen and light engineering industry as well as its transport connection lying on the mainline linking Cologne to Berlin. In 1900, the city had expanded to about 63,000 inhabitants. This rising demographic pressure meant that the city's new cemeteries opened in 1874 and 1875 on the then periphery were deemed unable to cope with the demand for burial space in the medium term (then about 935 burials per year).[19] The town council therefore decided to look for a new location as the main burial ground for the city and this time the new cemetery was to be a longer-term solution. In 1902, the city began to buy the necessary parcels of relatively cheap heather and woodland for the nearly 62 hectare site that was to become the *Sennefriedhof*, today one of Germany's largest cemeteries at 102 hectares. The planning and design took a decade under the leadership of the city's architect Friedrich Schultz and the city's park planner Paul Meyerkamp. Together these two men executed a design that in its conception, execution and governing regulations was radical. Bielefeld's main cemetery, therefore, can only be compared with the three historically important cemeteries of Munich (1905), Hamburg-Ohlsdorf (1877), and Berlin-Stahnsdorf (1909). Ever since the first 32 hectare stage of the cemetery was opened on 15 August 1912, it has had a central position in the modern history of cemeteries in Germany. Especially since the relatively small size of the city allowed the cemetery to retain much of its original character, despite a number of staged expansions.

Central to the entire design, as in the cases of Munich and Berlin, was the very location of the cemetery and its marked abundance of trees. What made the location a little more difficult was that the planned terminus for the local tram-line had to be moved further into the direction of the cemetery, since only then did it allow for the linking of the central cemetery to the city a full seven kilometres away. This cemetery on the picturesque sandy foothills of the Teutoburg Forest, characterised by heather and woodland, had its very own charms, but it was quite remote for many of the mourners. However, it fitted neatly with the ideas of replacing the artificiality of the park with natural beauty as well as the concept of controlling the environment. From the beginning there was a clear plan to have a strict set of rules and regulations of what could and could not be done at this new cemetery. Therefore, the entire concept was centred upon the preservation of the character of the landscape and the purpose of the site was not to be as blatant as, for example, in Leipzig or Vienna. The different design concept in Bielefeld was one that got enormous intellectual support and applause:

> The manifold attempts over the last years to deliver our sepulchral culture from dismal barbarism and to lead it back into worthy forms is, here and there, beginning to bear fruits. A very pleasing achievement in this direction was accomplished by the city of Bielefeld: It created a new large cemetery as a woodland cemetery. . . . We might be temporarily drawn to the marble splendour and the spacious architectural fabric of the Southern cemetery; yet our love belongs to local places, places where Mother nature will take the dead corpse in her arms.[20]

Hence the antithesis to the marble splendour was nature's simplicity and the re-embracing of the understated and the local. This meant Meyerkamp designed both the first stage as well as the later executed second stage of the cemetery around the woodland and its terrain. So unlike in Ohlsdorf, where trees were planted, in Bielefeld they were preserved and thus they became the eponymous feature of this kind of cemetery. It is all too easy to disregard vegetation and the terrain of cemeteries in the light of the more obvious gravestones, but the often carefully curated flora too tell much about the history of a place. In this case, it tells of the German desire to ensure preservation of nature as well as the desire to mitigate the ravages of modernity and their enormous social impact at the end of the nineteenth century by providing green spaces to the urban masses. What is obvious when walking through the *Sennefriedhof* from observation, as well as historical documents, is that the basic design was based on avoiding artificial sameness in favour of variation and natural flow. While not a park, this was still very much a municipal green space.

Upon entering the cemetery through the main gate, with a two-storey house on either side that served as living quarters for the cemetery director and other staff, one could not see the main building looming on the horizon because of the vegetation as well as a deliberate slight bend in the main avenue after about 100 metres. This underlines the entire concept of the cemetery being integrated fully into the forest. Furthermore, the areas designated for burials were only a small percentage of the overall area. In addition, the burial locations were set at least 175 metres back from the wall running the circumference of the site, giving the whole cemetery a very spacious feel. The whole design was based around the spine of the meandering central avenue emanating from the main gate and a second internal rather wonky oval avenue connecting all the elements of the initial design and yet based on the existing paths through the woodland. Later the design was to be added by further ovals in the latter part of the acquired area. Yet, it is not symmetry that dominates this initial stage, the landscape with its dells and small hillsides, and thus the first oval is clearly offset from the centre to the east by a significant degree. In addition, the original four sections for graves were all on the western side of this avenue along an organically curved oval path centred around the main building. This design strongly emphasised the organic nature of the cemetery, a place at peace with nature, not imposing on it. Later, the efficiency of straight lines would begin to reassert itself in the second and third stage of the extension of the cemetery. Similarly, the natural was to dominate the actual burial sites; the arrangement of the burials was designed in sections each devised into four fields of 100 to 200 plots that were set with clearings in the trees. These fields would be adjacent to yet separated from each other in order not to overwhelm the landscape. Bielefeld at the time was known for its very low density of burials, further underlying that this was much more than a mere cemetery.

Cemeteries, and in particular German cemeteries, in the twentieth century were regularly designed for other purposes than to be used merely by the bereaved. The rules and regulations became more restrictive, as the professionals who were in charge were of the opinion that they knew best. In 1914, two years after the first 32 hectares had been opened, the garden architect Walter von Engelhard, then teaching at the prestigious *Kunstakademie* in Düsseldorf – and who later took over as the horticultural director for the city of Düsseldorf – summed up the revolutionary nature of the *Sennefriedhof*:

> The local implementation of the newly discovered creative possibilities has to be welcomed even more joyously, as on one hand it will encourage the timidly biding passivity of many local governments into deliberate emulation and on the other hand it will deliver the decisive argument against disparaging and demoralised shrugging, since the so-called utopian or starry-eyed

idealists can indeed achieve significant progress in the direction of ideal development.[21]

The keyword here is the word 'ideal', since it is this word that dominates a lot of twentieth-century thinking with regard to the cemetery. To ensure and preserve the ideal took active measures by those in charge of the cemeteries. In Bielefeld this is encapsulated by the inaugural regulations that governed the cemetery right from 1912. These are very clear on the usual rules such as dimension of graves, but swiftly the regulations go beyond what is strictly needed for the running of a cemetery. All commissions for gravestones and grave markers, for example, needed to be pre-approved; that is to say, a drawing had to be submitted to the cemetery committee made up of bureaucrats, art critics, and academics, and passed by them. The committee thus became the arbitrator of what was tasteful and suitable. In order to help the public the cemetery kept a book of approved patterns but excluded all industrially produced gravestones. Furthermore, specific sections of the cemetery necessitated certain designs, and no graves were to be framed by stones since this broke the natural design. Similarly the regulations were very strict as to who could look after a grave, what to plant on a grave plot, and when the city could intervene and take control.[22] Most significant is not the actual regulations, but that they were drawn up especially for the new cemetery and did not govern the other cemeteries of the city. Moreover, these regulations regularly drew praise, especially from those who held clear views on what was good for the public.[23]

Widespread professional approval for the *Sennefriedhof* did not stop with the design of the landscape; many contemporary professionals equally approved of the design of the buildings. These followed the design idea of fitting into the landscape. Since the cemetery was so far outside the city, what had to be built was the entire infrastructure necessary for a cemetery to function on a day-to-day basis. On the north side closest to the tram stop and furthest from the main entrance, the city built a tavern that utilised the design language of a local rural house with visible timber-framing. The main tavern bar and the kitchen was on the ground floor, the tenant's flat on the first floor, and to the side was a large hall. The interior was designed to be functional but in keeping with a rural tavern, the main function of which was to serve those using the cemetery and even more importantly to accommodate and provide for the wakes that are an integral part of German funerals. Underlining that the cemetery was also built as a destination for urbanites on an outing, the main entrance was flanked by three solid stone columns either side, forming a porch with space for a few benches and tables welcoming thirsty guests after a walk through the cemetery. Just behind the tavern was the cemetery nursery, with its glass houses and its horticultural areas as well as accommodation for the head gardener, again designed in order to fit in and be central to running a self-sufficient cemetery since the cemetery rules did not allow for anybody but the deceased family and the city's gardeners to maintain the graves. Therefore, the next, more challenging, addition was strictly necessary. Halfway between the tavern and the main entrance, the city erected a modest single-storey outlet for the nursery that also functioned as a point of sales for the local stone mason. The single most important design feature of this outlet was the arches forming five decent-sized arcades reminiscent of the arcades of medieval market squares. Hidden, well past the main gate in the direction from which few would approach the cemetery, those buildings that secured transportation were built, that is stables, the mews and the coachman's house – all again kept in the half-timber frame typical in Westphalia.

All these buildings, however, were secondary to Friedrich Schultz's chapel and mortuary building opened in June 1913, since it is this building that ensured the hygienic cold storage of the body prior to burial as well as providing a dignified backdrop to every funeral conducted. The solution the city's architect developed is one that married form and function into a quintessentially modern chimera [See Figure 3.2].

What one encounters is a building made up of three distinct parts: a chapel and a mortuary, both connected by an open cloister-like inner courtyard that was referred to as the hall of flowers. Breaking with the main design idea of fitting with nature, considerable space was created in order to ensure the rough east-west orientation of the building – so that the door of the chapel is facing in the traditional direction. It sits to the west of the main avenue with a sizeable mirror pond to the east, placed there to capture the reflection of the main design feature of this tripartite building: its dominating copper cupola of 24 metres height resting on 18 columns and marked with a cross on top. Clearly taking inspiration from the Pantheon in Rome, the whole chapel exudes what can only be described as a stout solidity. This impression is further underlined by the tuff stone cladding and the basalt stone foundations as well as the large portico, with its four rather chunky square columns of seven metres height. The gable of the portico is decorated with a figurative frieze of about three metres width. The work was created by Hans Perathoner, who was teaching at the local art academy, and depicts a winged depiction of death sitting with a serious expression on a throne holding in his left hand an inverted extinguished torch. To his left there is a kneeling nude female figure casting her sad closed eyes downwards. She is depicted against the backdrop of a starry night sky. As a contemporary article explains, it is the depiction of grief and loss, juxtaposed with a second female figure gestured towards by death on the right.[24] She represents the embodiment of hope and resurrection, with her gaze looking hopefully upwards and depicted against the background of a cross and the symbol of a palm leaf. Inside the chapel there is the lofty interior, 16 metres high, with space for up to 200 mourners, with walls decorated with classic symbols such as the cross, the *gladius*, and the scarab. While the main windows were undecorated in order to let light flood the chapel, the smaller row of windows above were commissions from a local artist who created a colourful set of windows of angels, crosses, and the four evangelists. The rest of the interior was dominated by the altar niche at the back with its large plain wooden cross and in front of it a catafalque. This can be Hydraulically lowered to allow for the transport of the coffin through the cellar. The middle section is made up of a low covered walkway made of seven arches on either side, thus framing an inner courtyard; the walkways lead to the mortuary in the back, a single story build with

Figure 3.2 Friedrich Schultz's Chapel and Mortuary Building.
Source: Photograph by Felix R. Schulz, 21 May 2019.

18 storage rooms for the deceased under a pyramid hip roof of simple design. Hence, this building links the desire to represent the municipality artistically with the technological desire to create an efficient funeral as well as the mundane need to store the dead in one edifice.

60 *Felix Robin Schulz*

After the funeral the coffin, or later the ashes (Bielefeld opened its crematorium in 1929), was transported to the graveside for burial. In Bielefeld, as was common for the time, there were two major forms of burial: (1) the burial in row graves, plots of 2.20 metres length and 1 metre breadth that were assigned by the cemetery administration, generally in chronological order and that were only available for 35 years; and (2) burial in chosen burial plots of 2.50 metres length and 1.30 metre breadth that were rented for renewable fixed terms up to 100 years by the cemetery administration. The major difference was not merely the price and the length of the period of usage; the key difference was the ability to personalise the grave within the strict rules as well as the ability to ensure burial with family members. These two major forms of burial still dominate the German sepulchral landscape, but it is important to understand that in this connection with the final resting place a whole multitude of options had emerged, ranging from columbaria to mass burials.

On the eve of the First World War, the *Sennefriedhof* was very close to the ideal of how German sepulchral culture should develop. What changed this, as well as the character of many European cemeteries, was the First World War, since the mass death of citizens necessitated different forms of commemoration. Besides public squares, workplaces, and public buildings, the cemetery became a site that saw the more widespread introduction of public memorials. The public death of hundreds of thousands meant that cemeteries became even more public spaces, with the addition of war graves and memorials. This hastened the already begun depersonalisation inherent in the new cemetery aesthetics, since the cemetery had become a staging area for public memory. Inherent in this is the tension between the public and private, the tension between the special sites and fields reserved for those deemed worthy of public attention and those buried in the increasingly regulated other areas. To a certain extent, the cemetery had become even less the site of private memory. The interwar period also brought more worries about excess and a desire to turn towards modernity. In Britain and beyond, this meant the emergence of the Lawn Cemetery with its easy to care for lawn in front of a gravestone and often the clear rule only to lay down flowers on the plinth of the gravestone.[25] After 1945, there was the continuation of the processes of the interwar period, with the more public memory being located in the confines of the urban cemetery, a revival of the desire to be efficient, and the desire to regulate. In Northern and Western Europe, cremation rates continued to rise as did the rate of those who do not want to be buried in a marked grave. While in the interwar period, anonymous burials by choice remained rare and even radical, this changed from the 1960s in areas with a high rate of cremation. One might thus argue that the cemeteries of the second half of the twentieth century are not as revealing as earlier ones, and that the design ideas were increasingly dominated by the attempt to enable the cheap upkeep of both cemeteries and graves. However, like most anonymous burial sites with their central memorials and other features, those with open eyes will still find a lot to be discovered in post-45 cemeteries.

The gravestone in Figure 3.3 demonstrates this vividly. The gravestone of the Borsch family can be found in a rural cemetery in Westphalia, evidently rural

Figure 3.3 The gravestone of the Borsch Family.
Source: Photograph by Felix R. Schulz, 5 November 2016.

since these remained less restrictive about what clearly is an industrially produced gravestone. The black granite gravestone sits on a plinth with a highly polished front and finely chiselled matte edges. In this execution, it is quintessentially a 1950s design often found in West Germany – similarly the font used for the inscription is reminiscent of the more traditional German lettering that was out of fashion by the 1960s. The stone, and please note the lack of anything but lawn, marks the burial site of five family members and tells the intimate story of a family. With the help of dates and the lay-out we can decode some of the family history. We know the maiden name of Frederike who went to on to marry Friedrich Borsch, as the names are set next to each other. We also know that Karl Borsch was in all likelihood Friedrich's father and that Karoline was Friedrich's older sister. Due to the inscription, we also know she chose to devote her life to the Protestant church and served as a deaconess. Religion thus played a role in the family, and this is further underlined by the large white cross. The gravestone also tells us that Frederike and Friedrich had a son who sadly died only a few months after being born. In addition, the gravestone also commemorates a lost homeland as this was clearly a family of expellees. The gravestone stresses that the family members' roots were in the Masurian village of Rohmanen in East Prussia. This gravestone is thus a public commemoration of the legacy of expulsion after 1945.

For thousands of families this was a common way to commemorate publicly villages and even family members lost and rendered inaccessible by the Cold War. Hence, this simple gravestone tells of small and large tragedies.

The burial of a society's dead clearly leaves a multitude of traces to be analysed, potentially nowhere more so than in the plethora of cemeteries with their graves, chapels, fields, sections and monuments, and crematoria. Being a close observer allows for the unlocking of some of the information even without access to the written archive, even, as we have seen, in the case of more anodyne modern gravestones. What might challenge this approach is a fundamental change in the sepulchral culture such as the rise of anonymous burials. Yet, this presupposes monolithic cultural change. As David Sloane underlines in his provocative yet insightful work, change in sepulchral culture is much more gradual and should not be seen as a zero-sum game. Sloane rightly points out that things do not change in exclusion of others.[26] Clearly, sepulchral culture is perpetually changing: funeral ceremonies are becoming more diversified; online memorials once rare are much more common place; various forms of anonymous burials are spreading; potentially most noticeable is the natural burial movement.[27] However, I am more sanguine about this, since sepulchral culture by definition is a complex decentralised system. Moreover, I once encountered an arch-critique of the late-twentieth century cemetery from an East German student advocating for the abolition of the cemetery as we know it. He favoured doing away with the highly organised and centralised site at the outer reaches of the city and replacing it with burial sites amidst the living, at the centre of social housing.[28] The burial site next to the playground for the children in his eyes was the ideal communal resting ground for the cremains of the former residents of the block of flats, since it would unite the memory of the dead with the living spaces of those who came after.

This might be too radical for some, but not too dissimilar is another trend worthy of further research. That trend is the rapid growth of memorial benches in the UK and beyond.[29] These dedicated benches, often adorned with plaques and flowers, can be found at beaches, beauty spots and even in cemeteries. Moreover, they can range from the Great War memorial benches beneath the Tyne Bridge in Newcastle to individual donations, but in every incarnation, even at the cemetery, they clearly represent the desire to locate the memory of the beloved one in a different and practical setting far removed from the sometimes impersonal central site of memory that the modern grave in a modern cemetery can be. As such they are a reminder to this historian that these benches can also be read like gravestones and cemeteries, and that like these sites they also need more scholarly attention on how they are used.

Notes

1 While Thomas Browne wrote about pre-historic urn burials as early as 1658, it was only in the early twentieth century that French anthropologists (predominantly) such as Robert Hertz and Arnold van Gennep wrote about the ritual side of sepulchral culture.
2 P. Ariès, *Western Attitudes Towards Death from the Middle Ages to the Present*, London: Marion Boyars, 1994, pp. 103–6.

3 For a detailed case study, see: F. Schulz, *Death in East Germany*, New York: Berghahn, 2013.
4 G. Gorer, *Death, Grief and Mourning in Contemporary Britain*, New York: Doubleday, 1965; T. Walter, *Revival of Death*, London: Routledge, 1994.
5 Indeed, one could make the argument that some cemeteries have taken on an additional aspect of having become tourist destinations. This challenges the argument of invisibility (too vague), see: A. Seaton, 'Thanatourism's final frontiers? Visits to cemeteries, churchyards and funerary sites as sacred and secular pilgrimage', *Tourism Recreation Research*, 27.2, 1996, 73–82.
6 Both in terms of cemetery and sepulchral culture, I could arguably include the prefix Western (as Ken Worpole does), but I deliberately decided against this for twofold reasons: (1) this is a deliberately condensed history and a practical guide and as such the elements to look out for analysis remain the same; and (2) fundamental demographic developments have led to technical convergence with regard to disposal that cannot be ignored and should not be painted in terms of hegemony itself. For a discursive treatment centred on the landscape and architectural dimension, see: K. Worpole, *Last Landscape: The Architecture of the Cemetery in the West*, London: Reaktion, 2003.
7 For an exemplary study, see: J. Rugg, *Churchyard and Cemetery: Tradition and Modernity in Rural North Yorkshire*, Manchester: Manchester University Press, 2013.
8 S. Schama, *Landscape and Memory*, New York: A. Knopf, 1995, p. 24.
9 For the contemporary use of London cemeteries see the pioneering work of D. Francis, G. Neophytou, and L. Kellaher, *The Secret Cemetery*, Oxford: Berg, 2005; additionally A. Mandrel and J. Sidaway (eds), *Deathscapes: Spaces for Death, Dying, Mourning and Remembrance*, Farnham: Ashgate, 2010.
10 The outlier to this is the Jewish cemetery, which, owing to continuation of traditions and a distinct identity, acts as a link between the early modern and the antique. For an overview, see: ICOMOS (eds), *Jewish Cemeteries and Burial Culture in Europe*. Berlin: Bäßler, 2011, www.icomos.de/admin/ckeditor/plugins/alphamanager/uploads/pdf/Bd_LIII_juedische_friedhoefe.pdf.
11 A. Ruschel, *Der Handwerkerfriedhof Sankt Rochus zu Nürnberg: Was Epitaphien erzählen können*, Norderstedt: BoD, 2016, pp. 6–7.
12 R. Sörries, *Ruhe sanft: Kulturgeschichte des Friedhofs*, Kevelaer: Butzon & Becker, 2009, pp. 101–16.
13 W. Biedermann, 'Friedhofskultur in Wien im 19. Jahrhundert – Das Bestattungswesen von Josefismus bis zur Gründerzeit', Unpublished dissertation, Universität Wien, 1978, p. 50.
14 C. Rädlinger, *Der Verwaltete Tod: Eine Entwicklungsgeschichte des Münchner Bestattungswesen*, München: Buchdorfer, 1996.
15 T. Laqueur, *The Work of the Dead: A Cultural History of Mortal Remains*, Princeton, NJ: Princeton University Press, 2015, p. 260. He contrasts Paris with the interesting case study of the Park Street Cemetery of Calcutta (1767).
16 For a mixture of history and travelogue on the cemetery, see: P. Standford, *How to Read a Graveyard: Journeys in the Company of the Dead*, London: Bloomsbury, 2013, pp. 93–115.
17 Finding the right reference to decode classic references can be tricky – a good starting point is a database like this: www.carc.ox.ac.uk/tools/pottery/shapes/oinochoe.htm.
18 For Europe, see: L. Mates and D. Davies, *Encyclopedia of Cremation*, London: Routledge, 2005, for the US and especially the working class element: S. Prothero, *Purified by Fire: A History of Cremation in America*, Berkeley, CA: University of California Press, 2001.
19 Stadtarchiv Bielefeld, 108,14, Friedhofsamt, No. 512, Gutachten über die von der Stadt Bielefeld in Aussicht genommene Friedhofsanlage, 23 May 1910.
20 G. Brandes, 'Der Sennefriedhof in Bielefeld', *Niedersachsen*, 18.12, 15 March 1913, 226.

21 W. von Engelhardt, 'Der Sennefriedhof in Bielefeld', *Architektonische Rundschau*, 1914, 9.
22 Stadtarchiv Bielefeld, 108,14, Friedhofsamt, No. 512, Friedhofs- und Bestattungsordnung für den Sennefriedhof der Stadt Bielefeld, 1 April 1912, pp 8–9.
23 Stadtarchiv Bielefeld, 108,14, Friedhofsamt, No. 512, Letter by Prof. Högg (Bremen), 21 October 1911.
24 'Die Kapelle auf dem Sennefriedhof', *Westfälische Zeitung*, 17 June 1913.
25 J. Rugg, 'Lawn cemeteries: The emergence of a new landscape of death', *Urban History*, 33.2, 2006, 213–33.
26 D. Sloane, *Is the Cemetery Dead?* Chicago, IL: University of Chicago Press, 2018, particularly pp. 235–44.
27 Those who regularly watch the football of the German second division, for example, will have spotted the regular large advertisements representing one of the two leading natural death companies in Germany. These companies are themselves a massive departure for Germany, since for the first time private cemeteries are being run in the country.
28 H. Keller, 'Möglichkeiten zur Ermittlung des Friedhofsflächenbedarf', Belegarbeit Humboldt Universität Berlin, quoted in B. Happe, 'Die sozialistische Reform', in R. Sörries (ed.), *Vom Reichsausschuß zur Arbeitsgemeinschaft Friedhof und Denkmal*, Darmstadt: Schnell+Steiner, 2009, p. 185.
29 E. Saner, 'Memorial benches: Inspirational reminders, or grave eyesores?', *The Guardian*, 14 March 2018.

Further reading

Colvin, Howard, *Architecture and the After-Life*, New Haven: Yale University Press, 1991.
Curl, James, *Death and Architecture*, Thrupp, Stroud: Sutton, 2002.
Laqueur, Thomas, *The Work of the Dead: A Cultural History of Mortal Remains*, Princeton, NJ: Princeton University Press, 2015.
Rugg, Julie, *Churchyard and Cemetery: Tradition and Modernity in Rural North Yorkshire*, Manchester: Manchester University Press, 2013.
Sloane, David Charles, *The Last Great Necessity: Cemeteries in American History*, Baltimore, MD: Johns Hopkins University Press, 1991.
Worpole, Ken, *Last Landscape: The Architecture of the Cemetery in the West*, London: Reaktion, 2003.

4 War memorials
Associative meanings

Corinna M. Peniston-Bird

I first encountered the memorial to the British Home Front in the Second World War in Coventry (2000) through an oral history interview in which the memorial was described as resembling a 'man-hole cover'.[1] In the context of the interview, the derogatory description served to underpin the speakers' experience of the inadequate public recognition of the contributions of the Home Front to the British war effort. That description stuck in my mind as a caption to the memorial until I visited it in situ and found that it had much less in common with a manhole cover than the bird's-eye images available over the internet would have one believe [Figure 4.1].[2] At around two metres in diameter, framed by a railing, and constructed out of slate on stone, its scale and materials provide the first points of differentiation.[3] The memorial's horizontality draws one in to read its central inscription: In gratitude to God and to commend to future generations the self-sacrifice of all those who served on the Home Front during the Second World War.

Then there is the matter of its location. [Figure 4.2] The memorial is set in the roofless ruins of the bomb-damaged St Michael's Cathedral in Coventry, the only city which competes with London in Britons' cultural memory of the Blitz. It shares the immediate delineated surroundings of the architectural shell of the wartime cathedral with other memorials, including a cross shaped from fallen roof timbers and a bronze cast of Reconciliation (originally named Reunion, Josefina de Vasconcellos, original 1977). The latter can also be found in the Hiroshima Peace Park in Japan in 1995, as well as in Berlin, and Belfast. The gold lettering on the sanctuary wall reads 'Father Forgive' (Luke 23: 34).[4] The juxtaposition of these different memorials in close proximity leaves the subject of forgiveness suitably ambiguous: 'forgive them' as in the biblical citation, or 'us' for the British role in the devastation? It is therefore this location which recasts the words on the slate: the deixis of 'those' – 'all those who served on the Home Front' – to invoke the British population on a front given increasing emphasis since the fiftieth anniversary of the end of the war in 1995. In that space, however, the memorial does not easily suggest nationalistic victimhood or a self-satisfied invocation of the so-called 'People's War'.[5]

The memorial is in dialogue with both material and intangible associations, specific but not unique to me. For example, the lack of acknowledged designer precluded creator contextualisation, but that anonymity, the subject matter, the

66 *Corinna M. Peniston-Bird*

Figure 4.1 The memorial to the Home Front in St Michael's Cathedral, Coventry
Source: Photograph by Corinna M. Peniston-Bird, 4 October 2013.

design and materials reminded me of the plaque on stone at the National Memorial Arboretum (Staffordshire, United Kingdom) which is 'a tribute to those who worked on the home front to support the war effort'.[6] The railing recalled unpoliced crowd-control in heritage spaces, at cultural events or in cultural and spiritual institutions. I had visited bombed-out churches serving as memorials in

Figure 4.2 St Michael's Cathedral, Coventry, the view of the exposed interior looking away from the memorial

Source: Photograph by Corinna M. Peniston-Bird, 4 October 2013.

Southampton and Liverpool, and I subsequently visited the Memorial Church in Berlin [Kaiser-Wilhelm-Gedächtniskirche] which was sent a cross of nails by the people of Coventry. Given my research interests, I was well-versed in the emphases and omissions in the narrative of the civilians' war, the growing impetus of diverse claims for recognition and the significance of the gender-neutral language of the inscription.

The layers of meaning of the Home Front memorial are created by its materiality, its physical location, its temporal context and the host of individual and collective associations it invokes. However, the research trip to Coventry underlined the importance of Simon Schama's 'archive[s] of the feet'.[7] It seems all the more pertinent to reflect on the spatial dimensions of these layers of association when much research on memorials begins (and, more significantly, ends) with online searches. In Britain, a sensible starting place for research on war memorials is online – The Imperial War Museum's Memorials Register – a national register of over 80,000 UK war memorials and growing.[8] It includes, where possible, both an image of the memorial and a map showing its location. The individual can choose to search by district, town, county or country; of relevance also is location on a smaller scale (interior to public building, such as a church, village hall or hospital, or private property such as an individual home or estate; exterior sites, such as the village square or a park), but these smaller-scale categories emerge only through inclusion in a keyword search. This is true also of War Memorials Online, created to document the condition of war memorials in Britain, which permits searching by keyword or location within a one-mile radius of a place name.[9] In print, physical locations (in the plural) are most likely to appear as an organising principle in guidebooks on sites or localities. Virtual memorials that exist only in cyberspace are designed for that space, but even those frequently draw on conventional vocabularies of representation.[10]

The argument here is that nothing can substitute for approaching, circling and gazing at a memorial in situ if the historian is to understand anything beyond its most rudimentary characteristics. An online image search spits out a wonderful array of reproductions on a screen dislocated from context, neither of original website nor physical locality. This is not to denigrate the potential of online searches, which create their own unexpected contexts, juxtapositions and associations, particularly if the researcher plays with reverse image searches. They allow individuals to be aware of a range of sources they might otherwise never have encountered. But they seldom permit engagement with all the key elements of physical memorials, summarised by Machin and Abousnnouga as elevation, angle, size, gaze/interaction, proximity and distance.[11] The authors recommend undertaking the 'commutation test' on these different elements of a war memorial: 'we can hypothetically change features or qualities, replacing them with others, or removing them completely and consider what kind of difference this makes.'[12] Such a test challenges Pierre Nora's claim that 'Statues or monuments to the dead . . . owe their meaning to their intrinsic existence; even though their location is far from arbitrary, one could justify relocating them without altering their meaning.'[13] As the guidelines of Westminster City Council stated (with regard to the siting of a statue to Sir Walter Raleigh),

> Any proposal for a statue or monument must have a clear and well defined historical or conceptual relationship with the proposed location. Proposals for new statues and monuments where there is no relationship between subject and location will not be acceptable.[14]

Raleigh's statue was removed from its site on Whitehall, where it had little connection either to its site, the surrounding architecture or to the other statues nearby. A new home was found for the statue at the former Royal Naval College at Greenwich, a site with suitable maritime associations.

The commutation test is equally telling applied to spatial and temporal contexts. Consider the difference it would make, for example, if the memorial to African and Caribbean service personnel (Nubian Jak Community Trust (NJCT), London, 2017) [Figure 4.3] stood not in Windrush Square, Brixton (London) but in Westminster Cathedral or at RAF Cranwell (Lincolnshire) or Traprain Law in East Lothian, Scotland, and had been unveiled in 1957, 1967 or 1987, not 2017.[15] As Nuala Johnson argues, 'new sites of memory are not simply arbitrary assignations of historical referents in space but are consciously situated to connect or compete with existing nodes of collective remembering'.[16]

Memorials can be categorised along a variety of thematic axes: public/private, sacred/secular, site-inspired or site-divorced, representational/abstract, utilitarian and non-utilitarian and intentional/coincidental, to name but a few. These are most usefully explored as spectra rather than binary opposites. For example, in his study of American military commemoration in Britain and France after 1943, Sam Edwards explored 'commercial commemoration' as the site where the sacred and profane meet and cross-fertilise.[17] Existing methodologies for research on war memorials are usually encountered in specific case studies, for example, of Maya Lin's Vietnam Veterans Memorial Wall (Lin, Washington D.C., 1982).[18] Investigations of memorials in the plural are usually grouped by specific events, in which the American Civil War, the First World War and the Holocaust dominate.[19] Combining archival research with the specifics of materiality, historians have explored the various functions of war memorials to promote selective national or militaristic ideals to political ends, the focus they provide to the emotional labour of grief, the competing agendas of the different agents behind every memorial and their significance to collective memory.[20] Christine Boyer defines monuments and memorials as mnemonic devices, which are erected 'to stir one's memory'.[21] Similarly exploring memorials as mnemonic devices, Ahenk Yilmaz has explored the relationship between form (the 'image') taken by the physical representation of the commemorated past and its 'locus', its place in physical reality. In some contexts, the image and locus are indistinguishable: battle fields and concentration camps, for example. Analysis of locus includes an identification of the parameters of the area and its overt or fuzzy boundaries, and the manner in which individuals are guided through it. The 'image-locus relation' refers to the physical interaction between the representation and its place, and Yilmaz's argument is that 'the image becomes memorable owing to the relevance with its place'.[22]

War memorials are defined here as, by the War Memorials Trust, 'any physical object created, erected or installed to commemorate those involved in or affected by a conflict or war'.[23] As Historic England points out, there is an 'astonishing diversity, including locomotives, trees, drinking fountains, chapels, windows, gardens and complete streets': this chapter focuses for the most part on sculptural war memorials as some of the most overt forms of memorialisation that reconfigure and are reconfigured by their spatial context.[24] This chapter explores the

Figure 4.3 The memorial to African and Caribbean Service Personnel, London
Source: Photograph by Corinna M. Peniston-Bird, 24 June 2019.

interplay of denotation and connotation, exploring the significance of physical and temporal contexts and associations in analyses of (war) memorials. Malcolm Barnard discusses 'denotation' as meaning involving a broad consensus: 'The denotational meaning of a sign would be broadly agreed upon by members of the same culture', whereas 'nobody is ever taken to task because their connotations are incorrect' – one could never list all possible connotations.[25] Nonetheless, as Kaja Silverman argues, connotations are also shared by members of a culture since they are 'aligned with a cluster of symbolic attributes'.[26] The case studies are drawn predominantly from Anglophone or European contexts, with a preponderance towards the British: the associative approach explored here requires the historian to be deeply immersed in both overt and more elusive networks of meaning, a requirement which mitigates against making broad transnational claims or drawing too readily international comparisons of connotation.

Positioned in space and time

As the opening description of the memorial to the Home Front in Coventry suggests, the associative dimension of setting is one of the most elusive but also one of the most fundamental elements in memorial analysis. At the level of the material design elements, the associative significance is easy to capture: the reiteration of the carved inscription 'Lest we forget', for example, or of lines from Laurence Binyon's 'For the Fallen' (the National Memorial Register lists 11742 hits for citations of Binyon). Assimilating materials from one location at another takes on symbolic meaning connecting spaces: The Flanders Fields Memorial Garden (Piet Blanckaert, Wellington Barracks, London, 2014) was planted with soil from 70 battlefield cemeteries in Flanders, gathered by over a thousand Belgian and British schoolchildren: visitors can sit on a bench made from Flemish Bluestone or meander under trees indigenous to the Belgian battlefields. On the other hand, practicality and pragmatism is also a factor: the popularity of Portland stone for English war memorials is in part a consequence of the size of blocks that can be sourced and because it is soft enough to be worked by hand.[27]

Just how wide the associative dimensions of the 'historical relationship between places' are is suggested by Historic England, in its description of the setting of heritage assets:

> The historic character of a place is the group of qualities derived from its past uses that make it distinctive. This may include: its associations with people, now and through time; its visual aspects; and the features, materials, and spaces associated with its history, including its original configuration and subsequent losses and changes.[28]

These are not simple to disentangle, as the battle over the form and location of the Scottish National War Memorial to the fallen of the First World War suggests. In 1917, in response to a proposal to erect a national war memorial in Hyde Park, the Duke of Atholl instigated the erection of a national war memorial in Scotland, 'put up by Scottish hands, with Scottish money, on Scottish soil'.[29] Scottish losses in the First World War were disproportionately large in relation to the size of population.[30] In January 1918, the Secretary for Scotland suggested in the House of Commons that

> no site could be found so appropriate to a Scottish National memorial associated with the present War and with other wars by land and sea in which

the Scottish nation, Scottish troops or regiments or men of Scottish birth or descent have played a part, as the castle of the ancient capital of Scotland.[31]

This choice of location and the proposed design caused some public controversy in the pages of *The Scotsman*. It was seen as too inaccessible, in need of preservation, and Sir Robert Lorimer's pre-Gothic architecture inappropriate for 'the rock, where hitherto nothing of the kind has existed.'[32] Of particular concern was the impact any erections or lights would have on the Edinburgh sky-line, which the Duke came to describe in frustration as both 'blasted' and a 'fetish'[33] The Executive Committee of the Glasgow and South Western Area Council of the British Legion were affronted by the slight suggested by Glasgow being rejected as the potential site, claiming higher casualties gave it a greater claim to site the Scottish National Memorial. Atholl was consistent in arguing that after his 'initial gravest doubts', Edinburgh Castle was the one and only place where a memorial, representative of the whole of Scotland, and worthy of being called National, could be placed, not least because 'it appears to be the only place in Scotland on which both Glasgow and Edinburgh can meet without quarrelling'.[34]

The siting of a memorial can thus be fundamental or peripheral to the conception of the design. At the fundamental end of the spectrum, the space is a memorial to itself, its meaning vested in authenticity of location: Graceland, or Gettysburg, for example, the footprints of the Twin Towers, marked by two one-acre pools (New York, USA, 2011), or the Gavrilo Princip footprints memorial that was embedded in the pavement where the assassin stood in Sarajevo, Bosnia in 1914 (Vojo Dimitrijević, 1951).[35] A striking memorial in the Lake District in both location and conception is the memorial to the men of the Lake District who fell in the Great War: it encompasses the rocks, buttresses and recesses of Lingmell, Great End, Allan Crags, Green Gable, Great Gable, Kirkfell and other peaks east and west of Sty Head Pass. It marks not death but the preceding lives and regional identities. Lord Leconfield gifted all land above 3000 feet – 'spaces of power and light' – to the National Trust. At the unveiling, the President of the Fell and Rock Climbing Club, Arthur Wakefield, 'described the great mountain park which lay in the mist and silence below and around, and which for memory had been presented to the nation, a possession for ever'.[36]

The connotations of a space may also be invoked by its representation in the memorial design especially in narrative friezes: the Battle of Britain memorial (Paul Day, London, 2005), for example, includes the local landmark of St Paul's, the building perhaps most associated with British resilience to the Blitz, while the memorial frieze to the Liverpool Pals at Liverpool Lime Street Station (Tom Murphy, Liverpool, 2014) depicts scenes on a platform. More frequently, however, the local dimensions of a memorial are more likely to be expressed by site rather than explicit depiction: William Goscombe John's Northumberland Fusiliers Memorial 'The Response' in Newcastle upon Tyne (1923), for example.

In both 'footprint' cases, authenticity of location is fundamental to the purpose and impact of the memorial. The controversy over Alexandra Hildebrandt's art installation of 2004 that rebuilt a section of the Berlin Wall in an inaccurate location is testament to the investment in accurate siting,[37] However 'x-marks-the-spot' can also change in its relationship to the message of a memorial when the characteristics of that location change over time. For example, when the premises of J & N Philips were demolished in Manchester in 1969, two plaques listing eighteen employees killed in the Second World War were rehung at the new erection on the site in Church Street, Manchester: a multi-storey carpark.[38] Conversely, a sacred space can also serve to elevate the mundane: the most stark example is perhaps the Tomb of the Unknown Warrior in Westminster Abbey, London, where an anonymous soldier is interred in a space otherwise occupied by British monarchs and national figures from Geoffrey Chaucer to, more recently, Stephen Hawking (2018). As these examples suggest, there is a complex interplay between memorial, location and status. The National Policy Planning Framework notes that, 'elements of a setting may make a positive or negative contribution to the significance of an asset, may affect the ability to appreciate that significance or may be neutral'.[39] In the Manchester example, the memorial is reframed by the mundane. The impact of relocation underlines the distinction that must be drawn between the survival of denotation and the disruption of connotation. Many of the company war memorials erected within factory or office premises after the First World War lost their homes over time, as buildings were demolished or repurposed, for example. Some were discarded, some were lost and some were preserved and rehoused, for example at the National Memorial Arboretum, discussed later. There, the memorial remains exactly as designed – often a scroll of names with an appropriate surround – but the shift in location and the temporal distance from the original loss transforms the memorial's dialogue with local memory and corporate identity into a flatter statement of abstract national loss.

Conversely, however, a mundane location can also be fundamental to the impact of the memorial, such as that at Smithfield market in London. In 2005, a memorial was added to the first one at that location which remembered the men 'who went forth from this place' in the First World War. The new memorial commemorated 'all men, women and children of Smithfield who lost their lives in conflict since the Great War'. As suggested in an online exposition, locals see this to be an allusion to the 110 men, women and children, 'queueing to buy meat, who died when a V2 rocket hit the market during the final days of WW2 in 1945', busy with their everyday lives in a way likely to parallel those reading the memorial today.[40] The mundane is particularly powerful where local, shared knowledge enhances the meaning of the memorial in situ and underpins community identities.

The significance of the contextual and associative relationships of heritage assets exemplifies the definition of 'context' given in the European Landscape Convention:

> The context of a heritage asset is a non-statutory term used to describe any relationship between it and other heritage assets, which is relevant to its significance, including cultural, intellectual, spatial or functional. Contextual relationships apply irrespective of distance, sometimes extending well beyond what might be considered an asset's setting, and can include the relationship of one heritage asset to another of the same period or function, or with the same designer or architect. . . . Setting may include associative relationships that are sometimes referred to as 'contextual'.[41]

A powerful example of the impact of contextual relationships on academic interpretation is provided by Sarah Crellin, who has written a convincing disruption of the traditional interpretations of two memorials juxtaposed in Hyde Park, London: Charles Sargeant Jagger's Royal Artillery Memorial and Francis Derwent Wood's Machine Gun Corps Memorial both unveiled in 1925.[42] Since the 1980s, a standard art-historical view has juxtaposed the two memorials as 'opposites illustrating a critical binary': 'the collision of a late Victorian/Edwardian aesthetic with the bitter, bone-splintering realities of modern war'. While Jagger's memorial has been seen as the appropriate and modern response to the horrors of war, Wood's Renaissance-inspired David 'exemplified the reactionary, irrelevant, even sickening attitude of an ignorant middle-aged non-combatant (and Royal Academician to boot.)'. However, such an interpretation ignores not only the associative significance of the figure of David in 1925, but also the significance of the sculptor's choice suggested by comparison with his other works. As Crellin points out, Wood had predated Jagger's horizontal representation of the dead in his sculpture of a recumbent officer in the parish church at Ditchingham, Norfolk (1919–20). Wood was also a pioneer of facial prostheses, spending much of war helping to disguise the wounds of disfigured soldiers: 'He was therefore better placed than most to understand the terrible impact of modern warfare on the human body'. The juxtaposed memorials suggested ready metaphors in the postwar interpretations of the First World War as a journey from naive innocence to brutal modernity, the coincidental spatial relationship between the two creating the unsympathetic, simplistic dismissal of Wood's interpretation.

Case studies: urban and rural spaces

Spatial location and juxtaposition became wholly intertwined with the status sought for the monument dedicated to 'The Women of World War II' [Figure 4.4]. 'The Memorial to Women in World War II Fund' was established in 1998 under the chairmanship of Major David Robertson, the President of a Royal Artillery Association Branch for the Auxiliary Training Service (ATS). The unveiling of the resultant memorial 'to honour over seven million service and civilian women who made such an important contribution to the war effort during World War II' took place in 2005.[43] The memorial was originally intended for the fourth plinth in Trafalgar Square, a site chosen for its central location and iconic visual status in VE day celebrations.[44] However, the memorial lost out to the Continuing Rotation of Art. The next contender, Raleigh Green, even after the statue of Walter Raleigh had been relocated, turned out to have a 20,000 gallon oil tank under it, which precluded any building on the site, and the Victoria Embankment was rejected by the Charity as meaningless, as it was a

> [d]elightful area, but in so far as the Memorial is concerned it would soon become marginalised in the general melee of the area and would hold no particular significance to the invaluable work done by our Women who helped to save our Country and have much to our shame, been ignored for so long. Sadly it does not meet the prime site criteria deserving of this Memorial. In

Figure 4.4 The memorial to The Women of World War II (John Mills, London, 2005)
Source: Photograph held by Corinna M. Peniston-Bird, 10 July 2005.

siting the Memorial we must also be very aware of inadvertently offending the sensitive and high profile issues of equality and gender.[45]

This allusion to the gender equality was a deft ploy to underline that the charity would be sensitive to status imbued by location and not be fobbed off with a site of insufficient import to articulate respect to the subject matter. As Ahenk has noted, 'the more the relation between the image and locus is established, the more effective remembering will become'.[46] The charity succeeded in finding one of the only possible locations of equal stature to Trafalgar Square: Whitehall. A road in Central London lined with listed buildings, and numerous departments and ministries, including the Ministry of Defence and the Cabinet Office, Whitehall has become as a metonym for the civil service and government of the United Kingdom. Most significantly, the final site for the memorial lay between the Cenotaph and the grade II listed statue of Field Marshall Earl Haig. The memorial stands directly outside the Ministry of Defence, and adjacent to three Field Marshals of the Second World War (Viscounts Slim, Alanbrooke and Montgomery). Robertson argued

> there is a compelling case for locating this monument of national significance at the heart of government in London. A position along one of the main

processional routes, close to memorials of considerable commemorative significance reflects the degree of acknowledgement sought by the proposers.[47]

As one petitioner for the site wrote, it was also deemed appropriate 'as convenient to visitors to other centrally placed memorials; as in the vicinity of many decision-making War Service headquarters; and where England endured some of the heaviest bombing'.[48] Westminster City Council gave support to this location when it came before the Major Planning Applications Committee on 25 July 2002 (despite the opposition to the design by their art panel).[49]

It was the siting of the memorial in such close proximity to the Cenotaph rather than its central location in London that was contentious, precisely because of the question of (appropriated) associative meaning. The Cenotaph has held a unique place in British commemorative practices ever since the original wood-and-plaster structure of 1919 designed by Sir Edwin Lutyens attracted such public outpourings of emotion that the War Cabinet decided that a permanent memorial should replace the wooden version and be designated Britain's official national war memorial. The Cenotaph became the site of multiple annual remembrance services, including the National Service of Remembrance, since 1945, held at 11:00 am on Remembrance Sunday in November. The Charity had to tread carefully: it sought to benefit through the proximity to the Cenotaph but avoid the accusation of thus detracting from it, an issue particularly significant in gender terms because of the lowering of status of roles once these become associated with women.[50] Thus according to Robertson, 'its placement in line with the Cenotaph is ideal because it is the only location that speaks a similar vocabulary, and is connected to it by an intimate historical link'. The application for planning consent claimed there would be a valuable dialogue between the two memorials and their immediate surrounds. This dialogue was underlined in sculptural form: although the monument to The Women of World War II could not be designed with its ultimate location in mind, when the plan for a top figure was dropped, the solution to refining the top of the plinth was found in what Mills' labelled 'a Lutyens'-style capping', creating a visual dialogue between the memorials.

Westminster City Council received support for the application from veteran organisations, members of parliament, and in particular a supportive letter from the Lutyens Trust, whose strap line is 'To protect the spirit and substance of the work of Sir Edwin Lutyens'. There were twenty letters of objection, including those from the Westminster Public Art Advisory Panel, The London Society, Thorney Island Society and Lutyen's grandson, Charles. There were multiple issues at stake here: the artistic merits of both of the sculptures were questioned as was the remit of the project – should it commemorate all contributions on the Home Front, both male or female; should it commemorate the efforts of women in both World Wars; should it fulfil its original remit and celebrate only the women of the auxiliary services? While some veterans welcomed the innovative design, others pointed to the memorial at Coventry to suggest that civilians on the Home Front had already had sufficient recognition. For those female veterans angered by the elision of their contributions with those of civilians, the location was fundamental to the argument: as one outspoken critic wrote to the *Daily Mail* '*If* approval *is* given for this particular memorial – the main purpose of which is to commemorate wartime civilians – it plainly should not be sited in Whitehall. Whitehall has long since been widely recognised as a strictly military zone', an argument dependent on the location of the Cenotaph rather than the buildings sited there.[51] The main thrust of objections focused on the memorial's proximity to the Cenotaph. The Thorney Island Society, a voluntary conservation and amenity group founded in 1985, complained:

> The Lutyens memorial is a universal memorial to all those who were lost or suffered in our national conflicts. The scale of the Lutyens memorial depends so much on the space in which it stands, and particularly when the National Service is held. This proposal would greatly detract from the setting of the Lutyens memorial, and destroy the ambiance of that particular setting.[52]

The Art Advisory Panel concurred, commenting also that 'the link to Haig is important and the purity of this symbolism would be irrevocably altered' by the erection of the memorial between the Cenotaph and Field Marshal Haig. Whether intended by Alfred Hardiman or not, their proximity had created a symbolic relationship: Haig is bare headed and appears to be paying homage to the fallen.[53] In response, the Charity drew on the defence of English Heritage who had spoken in favour of the site claiming that the relationship between Haig and the Cenotaph was ensured as the memorial was lower than Haig and off axis. Robertson again mobilised the issue of gender discrimination when he argued the memorial could not be seen as competition to the Cenotaph, 'it is intended to complement it, in the same way as men and women are not "in competition", but are complementary. In fact the Art Panel's view verges on discrimination against the equally important effort of women during the war'.[54] The Charity was ultimately successful in its defence and the monument was unveiled in 2005. The monument appears every year on television as part of the surroundings of the Remembrance Day Parade and its message continues to be underpinned by the efforts of the 'Raise your Hats' campaign.[55]

'The Women of World War II' was set apart on a traffic island: it invites the viewer to circle, and to view each uniform individually as well as in juxtaposition. Its height suggests it is not intended to encourage haptic interaction, although in 2015, the large, plain, flat surface at human height was spray painted with the graffiti 'Fuck Tory Scum' in street protests against austerity measures: it provided a canvas for protest not only because of its individual design features but precisely also because of its location in Whitehall.[56] In the defilement of memorials, frequently through urination, it is the site chosen not merely the public space that secures the act as a provocation.[57] The targeting of any memorial also draws upon the associative significance of all other memorials particularly in the context of war memorials which form the focal point of Remembrance Day rituals. In the contemporary cultural context in which the concept of 'sacred' is under attack, whether in relation to faith or truth, secular memorials still have the associative power to provoke discussion of the complex boundaries of propriety and respect, and to punctuate the geographies of protest.[58]

The significance of curtilage (the legal term for the area around the memorial defined by factors such as ownership, physical boundaries and functional association) can be explored by contrasting its impact on viewer behaviours.[59] Many memorials are set apart from the area in which they are placed by a pedestal, or by a railing or green space, for example. By suggesting a sacred space, or one distinct from everyday activities, these encourage modified behaviours, lowered tones, for example, or bowed heads. Such regulation can also be underlined by prohibitions: no smoking signs at Dachau, no ice creams permitted at the Terezin Memorial.[60] In the *New York Times* Kimmelman wrote of the 9/11 Memorial Plaza, 'The place doesn't feel like New York. It feels like a swath of the National Mall plunked in downtown Manhattan: formal, gigantic, impersonal, flat, built to awe, something for tourists'. Objecting to a design which is uninviting to the New Yorkers who will be using the site every day, he also took issue with the 'astonishing' lists of don't on the site: 'You can't sing, much less raise a protest or demonstration. I think that does raise some very profound questions about a site that is supposed to speak to our liberties' [Figure 4.5]. Such signs also remind us that the experience of a memorial is also a co-creation between viewers: the consequence of coincidental juxtapositions bringing together random individuals at a certain place at a certain time.

Memorials have increasingly taken the form of architectural spaces that people can freely enter, move around, and occupy, and that thus appeal to all the senses, not just sight. The National Memorial for Peace and Justice (Montgomery, Alabama, the Equal Justice Initiative, 2018) consists of 805 rusting steel columns dedicated to victims of lynching. Suspended from a ceiling, the columns are first at eye-level, but the wooden floor slopes downward, so that as the viewers walk, they come to gaze up as at bodies strung from trees inciting an emotive response, whether of empathy or complicity.[61] Memorials placed into urban spaces punctuated also by public sculpture can attract different styles of interaction. This issue has been explored by both academics and artists particularly in the context of the Memorial to the Murdered Jews of Europe (Peter Eisenman and Buro Happold, Berlin, 2005), a 4.7 acre space covered with 2711 concrete stelae of varying heights, on which *flaneurs* pose and lounge [Figure 4.6].[62]

Quentin Steven explored the significance of the absence of any clear delineation between urban space and the memorial:

> The stelae are lower towards the site perimeter, allowing views into the site. Some stelae at the perimeter are only flat shapes that extend out across the sidewalk paving, so that passing pedestrians are already stepping on some stelae without necessarily knowing it. In representational terms, the memorial is treated like a sidewalk.[63]

This was the deliberate intention of Eisenman, who sought to make the memorial part of 'the wider public realm, rather than a sacred space set apart from everyday life where all visitors would consciously focus their attention on the past and its meanings'.[64] He deliberately did not detach visitors from the actual flow of time and space, the condition which Ahenk argues creates 'a suitable milieu for concentrated contemplation but also creates a different reality for the individual whereby a spatial experience and therefore a specific mode of remembering can be manipulated'.[65]

Figure 4.5 Instructions at the 9/11 Memorial Plaza

Source: Photograph by Corinna M. Peniston-Bird, 27 August 2019.

The artist deliberately provoked a variety of ways of interacting with the memorial, where children run in the slopes between the stelae, teens jump them, and couples kiss in the claustrophobic spaces of hidden corners and sudden encounters. Nonetheless, such behaviours also provoke a sense of blasphemy by deliberate or inadvertent defilement. In 2017, the Jewish satirist Shahak Shapira captured public

Figure 4.6 Visitors around the Stelae, Berlin
Source: Photograph by Corinna M. Peniston-Bird, 14 July 2015.

attention in his project 'Yolocaust'. Shapira gathered twelve photos taken at the memorial and their associated captions such as 'Jumping on Dead Jews @ Holocaust Memorial' that were subsequently posted online. Shapira photoshopped the subjects into historic photographs of extermination camp victims.

Eisenman, however, responded by drawing a clear distinction between the Berlin memorial and sites such as Auschwitz, which he said was 'a different environment, absolutely':

> There are no dead people under my memorial. My idea was to allow as many people of different generations, in their own ways, to deal or not to deal with being in that place. And if they want to lark around I think that's fine.[66]

When I visited the memorial, I stayed a long time, not only wandering through it, but observing behaviours and staying with my discomfort: the memorial rendered all the more impact-laden by the varied responses it provokes and the associations of those behaviours.

A final case study: the National Memorial Arboretum

Thus far this chapter has considered the intertwining of location, status and meaning; of memorials located to mark a site; or in locations chosen for their associative implications. As we have seen, where memorials proliferate in a concentrated area, the area begins to bestow a gravitas on any further memorial permitted to be located there. This is true of the urban spaces explored earlier, also evident at the Mall in Washington, D.C.[67] It is particularly interesting to explore in the context of a rural space, the National Memorial Arboretum in Staffordshire, England. In 2001, the Arboretum was established on former gravel quarries. It constitutes a major shift in the British geography of war memorialisation because of the concentration there of memorials commemorating numerous wars in which Britain was involved.[68] It is also an example of the trend towards the large scale in memorialisation – such as the Berlin Memorial to the Murdered Jews of Europe, which occupies 19,000 square meters of urban real estate – but does not have the singular focus of those memorials. Located near Alrewas in Staffordshire in the heart of England, and opened to the public in 2001, the National Memorial Arboretum occupies over 150 acres of woodland landscape with 30,000 trees and over 350 memorials, the final figure constantly growing. Although the majority of the memorials are linked with the military, there are also memorials which feature emergency service, charity and civilian organisation tributes. The Armed Forces Memorial, dedicated in 2007, provides an alternate focus for Remembrance Day outside of the capital: indeed, one argument for locating the Memorial in Staffordshire was to counterbalance the dominance of London.

The Arboretum has also fostered a new way of consuming memorials in bulk, a day out complete with a land train and coffee shop. The juxtaposition of memorials in close proximity to each other and in a dedicated space offers a very different experience to coming across an isolated memorial set apart from everyday life, or passing by one sharing the space with countless other functions and objects and people, as, say, in Whitehall, which houses over 300 statues and memorials, 47 percent of all the memorials in London being concentrated there.[69] The Arboretum underlines the diversity of the experience of 'War' by amassing monuments dedicated to specific wars, specific groups, specific experiences and stakes the claim that each memorial there tells a story of national import. Such a concentration also encourages comparison between the design and messages of different memorials and suggests much about contemporary aesthetics. To pick an example from a tiny section of the Orange Zone, in the space of a minute's stroll, the visitor will pass the memorials to the Bevin Boys, the Y Group, Operation Market Garden, the 1st Airborne Reconnaissance Squadron, the General Post Office, the Fauld Explosion, the Royal Airforce Halton Apprentices Memorial Garden, the Inner Wheel Grove, the Trefoild Guild Willow Sculptures, British Limbless Ex-servicemen Association and the Ack Ack. As perusal of the Arboretum archives suggests, placement depends on availability of sites, some thematic groupings, such as that commemorating the UK police service and environmental factors in the former quarry.[70] Such deliberate accrual suggests a new type of experience in the act of consumption: a targeted visit or a meandering one will both involve coincidental spatial juxtapositions. It is nigh on impossible not to engage with multiple memorials on any visit, the latter rendered inescapably comparative by such random juxtaposition and concentration.

Conclusion

This chapter has asserted the significance of physical location in a period when virtual experience offers immense academic potential. We have explored a wide range of associate meanings derived from monuments located in space and time, suggesting the significance of material, scale, authorship; different dimensions of location – urban and rural, mundane and sacred, alone and in juxtaposition – and the ways in which those factors shape audience engagement. The temporal dimensions are layered similarly, as the meaning of the monument, its location and any related national narratives develop over time. Although the focus has been on war memorials, many of these layers of meaning are equally relevant for the analysis of any artefact considered in physical location.

Notes

1. Interview conducted by Emma Vickers with members of the Timber Corps, 2003, personal communication with the author.
2. See, for example, 'Coventry and Warwickshire', *BBC News*, 24 September 2004, www.bbc.co.uk/coventry/content/articles/2008/07/31/home_guard_feature.shtml, last accessed 22.08.19, or www.alamy.com/stock-photo-wwii-home-front-memorial-plaque-in-the-old-coventry-cathedral-west-77996437.html, and for a contextualised photograph, www.alamy.com/memorial-in-coventry-cathedral-to-the-self-sacrifice-of-those-who-image6475530.html, last accessed 23.08.19.
3. Description entered in database of the Public Monuments and Sculpture Association: www.pmsa.org.uk/pmsa-database/7142/, last accessed 22.08.19.
4. 'Then said Jesus, Father, forgive them; for they know not what they do'. See: War Memorials Register (WMR), 17718.
5. A. Calder, 'Britain's good war', *History Today*, 45.5, 1995, 55–61. See: also J. Watson, 'Total War and total anniversary: The Material Culture of Second World War commemoration in Britain', in L. Noakes and J. Pattinson (eds), *British Cultural Memory and the Second World War*, London: Bloomsbury Academic, 2014.

6 Stone of Remembrance (National Memorial Arboretum (NMA), 2006): NMR 68580.
7 S. Schama, *Landscape and Memory*, 1st edn., New York: A.A. Knopf: Distributed by Random House, 1995, p. 24.
8 War Memorials Register (WMR), www.iwm.org.uk/memorials, last accessed 22.08.19.
9 Other categories include such factors as conflict, maker, material or condition. See, also: War Memorials Online, at www.warmemorialsonline.org.uk/, last accessed 22.08.19.
10 See, for example, H. T. Nguyen, 'Wiring death: Remembering on the Internet. *Культура/Culture*, 5.11, 2015, 65–75.
11 G. Abousnnouga and D. Machin, *The Language of War Monuments*, 1st edn., Bloomsbury Advances in Semiotics, London: Bloomsbury Publishing, 2013.
12 Ibid., p. 326. This is exploited in counter-memorials, commemorations of negative, tragic, or shameful events, often sponsored by victims' groups. They frequently invert the formal conventions of earlier memorials: sunken rather than raised, void rather than solid, dark rather than light, dispersed rather than spatially concentrated. See: Q. Stevens, 'Visitor responses at Berlin's Holocaust Memorial: Contrary to conventions, expectations and rules', *Public Art Dialogue*, 2.1, 2012, 34–59.
13 P. Nora, 'Between memory and history: *Les lieux de mémoire*', *Representations*, Special Issue; Memory and Counter-Memory, 26, 1989, 7–24, p. 22.
14 Westminster City Council (WCC), *Statues and Monuments in Westminster: Guidance for the Erection of New Monuments Supplementary Planning Document*, www.westminster.gov.uk/sites/default/files/uploads/workspace/assets/publications/S-and-M-FINAL-VERSION-1243433604.pdf, last accessed 29.05.19.
15 These sites are not random selections: Ulric Cross, the Trinidadian RAF navigator, was initially trained at RAF Cranwell, and Traprain Law was one the first camps set up for the British Honduran Forestry Unit in 1941.
16 N. Johnson, 'Cast in stone: Monuments, geography, and nationalism', *Environment and Planning D: Society and Space*, 13.1, 1995, 51–65.
17 S. Edwards, 'War and Collective Memory: American Military Commemoration in Britain and France, 1943 to the present', Unpublished PhD thesis, Lancaster University, 2008, subsequently published as *Allies in Memory: World War II and the Politics of Transatlantic Commemoration in Europe, c. 1941–2001*. Studies in the Social and Cultural History of Modern Warfare 41, Cambridge: Cambridge University Press, 2015.
18 See, for example, J. Reston, *A Rift in the Earth: Art, Memory and the Fight for a Vietnam War Memorial*, New York: Arcade Publishing, 2017.
19 See, for example, J. Winter, *Sites of Memory, Sites of Mourning: The Great War in European Cultural History*, Cambridge: Cambridge University Press, 2014; J. E. Young, *The Texture of Memory: Holocaust Memorials and Meaning*, New Haven, CT: Yale University Press, 1993; J. E. Young, *The Art of Memory: Holocaust Memorials in History*, Munich and New York: Prestel, 1994.
20 For a good overview, see: T. G. Ashplant, G. Dawson, and M. Roper (eds), *The Politics of War Memory and Commemoration*, Routledge Studies in Memory and Narrative, London: Routledge, 2000.
21 M. Christine Boyer, *The City of Collective Memory: Its Historical Imagery and Architectural Entertainments*, Cambridge, MA: MIT Press, 1994.
22 A. Yilmaz, 'Memorialization as the art of memory: A method to analyse memorials', *METU Journal of Faculty of Architecture*, 27.1, 2010, 267–80.
23 Historic England, *Conservation and Management of War Memorial Landscapes*, January 2016 edn., p. 1
24 Historic England, *Conservation*, p. 1.
25 M. Barnard, *Fashion as Communication*, London: Routledge, 1996, p. 83.
26 K. Silverman, *The Subject of Semiotics*, New York: Oxford University Press, 1983, p. 36.
27 Portland stone was also the preferred choice of the Imperial War Graves Commission. See: 'Principal Material', in Historic England, *Conservation*; and Burslem Memorials,

'Natural Stone Memorials using local materials', www.burslem.co.uk/2017/04/29/natural-stone-memorials-uk/, last accessed 16.09.18.
28 Historic England, *The Setting of Heritage Assets: Historic Environment Good Practice Advice in Planning Note 3*, Liverpool: Liverpool University Press, 2017.
29 Supplement to *The Caledonian*, December 1922, Federated Caledonian Society of South Africa; National Library of Scotland (NLS): Papers of the duke and duchess of Atholl concerning the Scottish National War Memorial, Acc. 4714/2.
30 'We cannot forget that 26% of Scots in First World War didn't come home', *The Herald*, 27 February 2013.
31 NLS, Acc 4714//36: Miscellaneous correspondence, 28 June 1917–11 February 1920 (66 letters).
32 NLS, Acc 4714/43 i-vi: Miscellaneous.
33 NLS, Acc 4714/29: Correspondence and press-cuttings concerning the Cockburn Association, 1923–1953.
34 NLS, Acc 4714//36: Miscellaneous correspondence; see, also; J. Macleod, 'Memorial and location: Local versus national identity and the Scottish National War Memorial', *Scottish Historical Review*, 89.1, 2010, 73–95.
35 For the complicated history of this memorial, see, for example, the Carl Savich blog, 'Disputed Legacy: The Destruction of the 1953 Gavrilo Princip Plaque October 4, 2015', http://serbianna.com/blogs/savich/archives/2813, last accessed 24.08.18. For landscapes of memory in the context of memorialisation, see, for example, the special issue of *History & Memory*, 'Landscapes of Violence: Memory and Sacred Space'. 23.1, 2011.
36 W. T. Palmer, 'Unveiling the War Memorial Tablet', *The Journal of the Fell and Rock Climbing Club of the English Lake District*, 6.3, 1924, 365–8.
37 The controversy was extensively covered in the press, and is discussed in R. E. Klemke, 'Between disappearance and remembrance: Remembering the Berlin Wall today', in A. Kaminsky (ed.), *Where in the World is the Berlin Wall?* Berlin: Berlin Story Verlag, 2014. My thanks to Naomi Parker, research student at Lancaster University, for drawing this issue to my attention.
38 WMR, 13099, www.iwm.org.uk/memorials/item/memorial/13099, last accessed 29.09.19.
39 Ministry of Housing, Communities and Local Government, National Planning Policy Framework, 2012, Annex 2: Glossary.
40 Smithfield War Memorial on 'London Remembers', www.londonremembers.com/memorials/smithfield-war-memorial, last accessed 26.05.19.
41 Glossary, 'Guidelines for Landscape and Visual Impact Assessment', 3rd edition, published by the Landscape Institute and the Institute of Environmental Management and Assessment, p. 157, based on the definition in the European Landscape Convention, European Treaty Series – No. 176, Florence, 20.x.2000, p. 2.
42 [Sarah Crellin], 'The Machine Gun Corps Memorial', PMSA. Public Monuments and Statues Association, www.pmsa.org.uk/news/2019/3/22/the-machine-gun-corps-memorial, last accessed 29.09.19.
43 News Release, 'National Heritage Memorial Fund gives nearly £1 million to create UK's first national memorial Women of World War II', 29 April 2004, www.nhmf.org.uk/news/memorial-women-world-war-ii, last accessed 29.09.19. For the debates over the design, see: C. M. Peniston-Bird, 'The People's War in personal testimony and bronze: Sorority and the Memorial to the Women of World War II', in Noakes and Pattinson (eds), *Cultural Memory* and C. M. Peniston-Bid, 'War and peace in the cloakroom: The controversy over the Memorial to the Women of World War II', in Stephen Gibson and Simon Mollan (eds), *Representations of Peace and Conflict*, Basingstoke: Palgrave Macmillan, 2012. I would like to thank David Robertson and Bill Moralee for sharing the Charity files and photographs with me.
44 Charity Archive, 13 April 00 YG5506 Two. HQ York Garrison. Women's Memorial Planning and Erecting. See, for example, www.dailymail.co.uk/news/article-2623277/

The-day-young-Princess-Elizabeth-celebrated-jubilant-nation-Trafalgar-Square-awash-flags-recreation-VE-day-exactly-69-years-real-thing.html which includes both an image of VE Day in the Square, and its reimagining in the film 'A Royal Night Out' (Julian Jarrold, Atlas Distribution Company, 2015).
45 Charity Archive, 1 Jan 01 YG/4700; Planning. DMR comments to Ken Livingston on 5 July 2001 'You will notice the Cenotaph bears only the figures of men'. The Cenotaph bears no figures.
46 Yilmaz, 'Memorialization', p. 10.
47 Charity Archive, 1 Jan 03 YG/4700 HQ York Garrison: Memorial to Women of WW2 Planning.
48 Letter of support from F. L. Lewis, Charity Archive, 1 Jan 02 YG/4700 Women of WW2 Memorial Planning HQ York Garrison.
49 Giles Quarme, chartered architect, 11 July 2003, Charity Archive, 1 Jan 03 YG/4700 Memorial to Women of WW2 Planning.
50 See, for example, M. Randolph Higonnet and J. Jenson (eds), *Behind the Lines: Gender and the Two World Wars*, New Haven, CT and London: Yale University Press, 1987.
51 Joy Bone to the *Daily Mail*, 6 August 2003, Charity Archive, JB file.
52 Chairman to Planning Committee in Charity Archive, 1 Jan 02 YG/4700 HQ York Garrison Women of WW2 Memorial Planning.
53 S. Heathorn, '"A 'matter for artists, and not for soldiers"? The cultural politics of the Earl Haig National Memorial, 1928–1937', *Journal of British Studies*, 44.3, 2005, 536–61.
54 Letter from Robertson, 11 March 2002, Charity Archive, 1 Jan 02 YG/4700 HQ York Garrison Women of WW2 Memorial Planning.
55 'Raise your Hats: The Monument', www.raiseyourhats.co.uk/the-monument/, last accessed 29.09.19.
56 D. Bolton, 'War memorial vandalised: Anti-Tory protesters spray 'f**k Tory scum during anti-government protests', *Independent*, 10 May 2015.
57 'Gore Park war cenotaph urinated on, wreaths spit on', *Hamilton Spectator* (Ontario, Canada), 14 November 2009; 'Men fined for urinating on cenotaph', *Central Western Daily* (Orange, Australia), 22 September 2011; D. Wilcock, 'Man who urinated against cenotaph on Remembrance Sunday ordered to apologise to veterans', *Independent*, 12 November 2017; A. Hough, 'Student pictured urinating on city cenotaph subject to police investigation', *The Telegraph*, 5 October 2010; 'Blackpool war memorial urine woman avoids jail', *BBC News*, www.bbc.co.uk/news/uk-england-lancashire-11080456, last accessed 29.09.19: (this offence which took place in Blackpool, UK was the only one in this list with a female perpetrator); N. Parveen, 'Man who urinated on Manchester Cenotaph told to clean memorials', *The Guardian*, 20 April 2016; B. Farmer and C. Gordon, 'Rock star's son in Cenotaph case pleads ignorance', *Independent*, 6 October 2011.
58 B. Foreman and C. l'Anson, 'Is vandalising a war memorial ever OK?', *The Tab*, https://thetab.com/2015/05/11/is-vandalising-a-war-memorial-ever-ok-37821, last accessed 29.09.19.
59 Historic England, *Setting of Heritage Assets*, p. 14.
60 J. Sacks, 'A day trip to Dachau, Germany from Munich – Visiting the former concentration camp', *Everybody Hates a Tourist*, Blog: https://everybodyhatesatourist.net/trip-reports/travel-diaries-photos/dachau-germany-visiting-former-concentration-camp-day-9/#.W57B4-hKjIU, last accessed 29.09.19; *The Terezín Memorial – Visitor Code of Conduct*, www.pamatnik-terezin.cz/visitor-code, last accessed 29.09.19.
61 Shot at Dawn can be viewed from all angles, but the most logical positions the viewer from the perspective of the firing squad. For the growing emphasis on memorials as emotive experience, see: E. Doss, *Memorial Mania: Public Feeling in America*, Chicago, IL: University of Chicago Press, 2010.
62 See, for example, P. Oltermann, '"Yolocaust" artist provokes debate over commemorating Germany's past', *The Guardian*, 19 January 2017; see, also: G. Knischewski

and U. Spittler, 'Remembering in the Berlin Republic: The debate about the Central Holocaust Memorial in Berlin', *Journal of Contemporary Central and Eastern Europe*, 13.1, 2005, 25–42.
63 Stevens, 'Visitor responses', pp. 40–1.
64 Eisenmann cited in Stevens, 'Visitor responses', p. 40.
65 Yilmaz, 'Memorialization', p. 275.
66 J. Gunter, '"Yolocaust": How should you behave at a Holocaust Memorial?', *BBC News*, 20 January 2017, www.bbc.co.uk/news/world-europe-38675835, last accessed 29.09.19.
67 K. Savage, *Monument Wars: Washington, D.C., the National Mall, and the Transformation of the Memorial Landscape*, Berkeley, CA: University of California Press, 2011. The US Congress declared the mall to be a 'substantially completed work of art' (quoted in Savage p. 311). Savage argues that the memorials of the mall created an expectation that national memorials 'are to be spaces of experience, journeys of emotional discovery, rather than exemplary objects to be imitated' (p. 21). He calls it the 'spatial turn in monumental design' to create a highly charged space of collective introspection, political strike, and yearning for change (p. 20).
68 National Memorial Arboretum, 'A spiritually uplifting place which honours the fallen, recognises service and sacrifice, and fosters pride in our country', www.thenma.org.uk/about-us/, last accessed 29.09.19.
69 WCC, *'Statues and Monuments'*. They are diverse, including, for example: the Diana, Princess of Wales memorial; Lutyens' Cenotaph; and Jagger's Royal Artillery memorial; Australian and New Zealand War Memorials; Charles I, Lord Nelson and Albert; As WCC point out, 'Victoria Embankment Gardens is one of Westminster's most densely populated areas. Here, monument saturation has resulted in the surprising juxtaposition of Robert Burns and the Imperial Camel Corps memorial'.
70 National Memorial Arboretum Archive, email from the director, Jane Findlay, regarding the Bevin Boys Memorial, dated 6 July 2010, in which she discusses the importance of avoiding a woodland glade becoming a 'forest' of memorial stones, and the need to identify sites for memorials within the arboretum in advance, so to enable direction of applications to specific plots in the context of broader planning (for example, for tree planting and paths).

Further reading

Ashplant, T. G., Graham Dawson, and Michael Roper, *The Politics of War Memory and Commemoration*, Routledge Studies in Memory and Narrative; 7, London: Routledge, 2000.

Machin, David and Gill Abousnnouga, *The Language of War Monuments*, London and New York: Bloomsbury, 2013.

Nora, Pierre, 'Between memory and history: *Les lieux de mémoire*', *Representations*, Special Issue; Memory and Counter-Memory, 26, 1989, 7–24.

Tilley, Christopher, 'Introduction: Identity, place, landscape and heritage', *Journal of Material Culture*, 11.1–2, 2006, 7–32.

Yilmaz, Ahenk, 'Memorialization as the art of memory: A method to analyse memorials', *METU Journal of Faculty of Architecture*, 27.1, 2010, 267–80.

5 Masque and opera
Staging performance

Andrew Pinnock

This chapter will explore three multimedia stage productions designed to honour Britain's King Charles II (reigning 1660–85), while at the same time entertaining him.[1] All three relate very specifically to spaces and places that the king considered important and were easily recognized by his contemporaries. They animate political events vividly remembered by most of the people likely to attend early performances, giving the events a distinctive propagandistic spin through the use of powerful visual symbols. Their stage settings, characterization, and verbal (mostly poetic) content tell us how Charles and his advisers wanted history to be read. To modern historians this evidence of intention supplies valuable insight. It can only be retrieved through close study of the productions in question.

All three are generically ambiguous. When their texts were published, the first was labelled a 'masque', the second an 'opera', and the third a 'dramatick opera'. The first addressed a privileged court audience present by invitation only, as masques in in seventeenth-century England were understood to do. The second and third addressed paying public theatregoers but sent them masque-like messages, allowing them temporary access to courtly art-worlds and encouraging strong emotional commitment to the royalist cause.

Generic ambiguity is a pervasive feature of late seventeenth-century English drama. Neat distinctions between play/masque/opera/dramatic opera cannot really be made. When modern scholars insist on categorization by genre, forcing works into boxes of best fit, they inhibit comparisons which to authors and audiences of the period felt both natural and fruitful. These are the sorts of comparison attempted here.

All three productions served the ideals of the dynasty of the Stuarts, which held the British throne between 1603, when the patriarchal architect of united Great British islands, James VI of Scotland, became king of Great Britain; and 1714, when the dynasty foundered (in official terms at least) on the failure of his great-granddaughters Mary II and Anne to produce an heir.[2] Charles I and his clique of courtiers reached such heights of secluded elitism that social and political cohesion collapsed to the point of civil war. Charles I was executed outside James I's showcase Whitehall Banqueting House, in sight of Rubens' lavish ceiling celebrating the glories of early Stuart monarchy.[3] The anti-monarchists' greatest piece of theatre was to sever the corporeal head from the head of state to create a polity which continued to function. The third Stuart monarch of Great Britain, Charles II, son of Charles I, reclaimed his English throne in 1660, and the period was dubbed 'The Restoration'.[4]

Restoration politicians and their officials rebooted royalist institutions in priority order: the House of Lords, abolished in 1649, reopened for business; the military and an Anglican Established Church followed. Parish priests received copies of royal proclamations to read from their pulpits and ceremonial was reinstated, which included rebuilding cathedral organs smashed up by disapproving puritans, and choirs started to sing again, so that through this national ecclesiastical network a royalist infrastructure penetrated to local level. Charles I's art collection, one of the largest and finest in Europe until sold off by parliamentary agents, was reassembled as far as possible, willingness to sell or gift liquidated artwork back to the monarch serving as a test of loyalty that few thought it prudent to fail. Coins were minted with Charles II's portrait head on one side and the arms of Stuart Great Britain on the other. The task was first to secure the Restoration then to envelop Charles II and his royal relations in a hegemonic aura, putting the Restoration's permanence beyond doubt. The Restoration as a process – cementing the monarchy and ideals on which it relied: standing military, national church, the ideal of Great(er) Britain – was not accomplished fully until the 1690s. There was further rebellion in 1688 and the joint rule of the victors of the 'Glorious Revolution', Dutch William III of Orange-Nassau and his co-ruler, James I's great-granddaughter Mary II Stuart. Mary's sister, Anne (1702–1714) would be the last (recognized) Stuart ruler of Great Britain.

Charles II failed to produce a legitimate heir; though he was sexually voracious and had numerous illegitimate children. His likeliest successor was therefore his brother James, Duke of York, a confessed Roman Catholic. In fact, both Charles (closetly) and his queen, Catherine of Braganza (openly), were themselves Catholics which posed an obvious threat to the Anglican ecclesiology at the heart of the Restoration Settlement. There was little here to idealize: not a picture of domestic bliss, moral uprightness, and marital fecundity such as Charles I and Queen Henrietta Maria had presented in the 1630s. This was almost its opposite: a sleazy monarch running a sleazy court and running the country down.

The court masque – *Calisto*

Though reality could not be wished away, a grand artistic statement somehow rationalizing it looked to be both possible and worthwhile. The result was *Calisto*, the first full-scale court masque since 1640, in which Charles's nieces, Duchess Mary and Duchess Anne, starred as two unimpeachably virtuous woodland nymphs. Thus they signalled to older courtiers their readiness to succeed to the Stuart throne should events move further in that direction. John Crowne, who scripted *Calisto*, fitted the 1675 published version with a sheepish preface claiming that his choice of subject had been made 'in haste'.[5]

On re-reading Ovid he discovered too late that there Calisto is raped by Jupiter and then, to make approximate amends, turned by Jupiter into a star. It was nevertheless a story ideally suited to the masque's purpose, since alterations to it could turn Duchess Mary into a paragon of chastity invulnerable to rape even with Jove himself the would-be perpetrator. Jove, as chief of the gods, would inevitably be identified with Charles II, adding a threat of incest with which Crowne also had to deal. The manner of his escape from this seemingly impossible mythological bind evidently convinced contemporaries: according to Crowne *Calisto* was rehearsed on 'innumerable occasions', and when finally ready was performed at court four or five times.[6] Duchess Mary played the title role without dishonour.

Crowne made brilliant use of the multimedia masque art form to accommodate contradictions which, if left unresolved in a single-medium artwork such as a painting or a poem, would have destroyed its coherence. In a masque, conventionally flattering and strongly disapproving messages could be conveyed simultaneously, each reaching the audience via a different medium. Lavish presentation – splendid costumes and scenes, and the involvement of several dozen thoroughly rehearsed singers, dancers, and royal musicians – turned satire into a spectacle of state, honouring Charles as a peerless patron of the arts while, behind a veil of allegory which could be easily penetrated, asking awkward questions about Charles the man and Charles the lord of a thoroughly corrupt moral universe. Matthew Jenkinson puts it well:

> *Calisto* was . . . more than magnificent royal theatre. It was a piece of counsel to the court . . . demonstrat[ing] what happened to human relations, to conventional Christian morality and to (female) victims when the amorous ideas and justifications espoused by the Restoration court wits, and indulged by Charles II, were followed.[7]

Before counselling the court, Crowne paid it necessary compliments. *Calisto* opened with a thoroughly conventional prologue praising Charles as guarantor of the City of London's prosperity, and by extension that of the rest of the country. Cries of distress could be heard wafting over from mainland Europe. Augusta and Thamesis, allegorical representations of London and the River Thames, worried that 'complainings of some neighbouring shore' would cross the channel to embroil them, causing Peace and Plenty (nymphs personifying each) to abandon London for somewhere safer. Britain had only recently exited from the Third Anglo-Dutch War (1672–4), on terms not entirely favourable, leaving French former allies to carry on fighting without help from the British navy.[8] Plans for a world-dominating partnership between French and British monarchs were never realistic, and never came close to fruition. Peace with the Dutch, celebrated in the *Calisto* prologue and widely welcomed by Charles's war-weary subjects, marked, in John Miller's words, the death of 'The Grand Design [that] had been Charles's first and only major policy initiative . . . dreams of conquest had died with it'.[9]

Locating performance: Windsor Castle

Calisto marked the crucial turning point at which Charles stopped thinking of himself as a forceful player on the world political stage and retreated into a world of self-affirming make-believe. Later in *Calisto*'s prologue the Genius of England appeared along with British heroes wearing naval and mural [martial, or castle-wall-like?] crowns, to take credit for alleged victories over 'mighty monsters of the seas', rioting satyrs and giants 'chac'd . . . from their caves'. A Temple of Fame appeared. Europe, Asia, America, and Africa appeared to pay tribute to Charles and to his politely acknowledged though practically estranged queen. Rural gods and nymphs danced in celebration; then everyone important left the stage. 'Slaves' summoned to set scenes for the masque proper turned out to be dancing carpenters, amusing the audience while real carpenter employees borrowed from Charles's Office of Works got on with the real job.

The London-centred commercial structures enabling British merchant adventurers to build a global business empire were established in Charles's reign, to be sure; but Charles was not their architect. Tribute from the Four Parts of the World accrued mainly to investors backing the trading companies. Collectively, London merchants and financiers were vastly richer than the king himself. Charles owned little of his capital's prime real estate and was popularly blamed for causing the fire that had burned down much of London in 1666: court debauchery had attracted divine retribution. Charles liked London less and less. Neighbours, including too many parliamentarians, opposed his political will. After the collapse of the 'Grand Design', he spent as much time as possible in royal strongholds outside London, which, with Louis XIV's continuing subsidy support, he set about improving and beautifying. It was not coincidental that in 1674, the year that funds to keep war with the Dutch going ran out, and the year of *Calisto*, Charles embarked on his Windsor Castle 'Great Works'. This was the biggest crown-estate investment project of his entire reign, completed only months before he died in February 1685. Windsor

> was of particular significance to the restored monarch: alone among his palaces it was also a fortress that could be garrisoned effectively. The castle housed St. George's Chapel and St. George's Hall and was the headquarters of the Order of the Garter, England's prime order of chivalry, which the Stuart monarchs fostered with especial enthusiasm; and it had the personal significance of being the burial place of his martyred father, Charles I.[10]

The Great Works radically transformed royal living space at Windsor. Hugh May, the architect in charge, created 'a sequence of spaces which exploited variety of space and [natural] lighting in a way that had not been attempted before in England'. These state apartments – separate sets of rooms for the king and queen, each set with its own official entrance – occupied the first floor of a new three-storey accommodation block called the Star Building: a carved-and-gilded Garter Star on its outward-facing north wall, ten feet in diameter, was visible for miles around.[11] The Neapolitan artist Antonio Verrio and a large team of assistants painted every state apartment ceiling and several staircases.[12] As doors between the rooms opened and the ceilings were revealed one after another, visitors experienced a series of dramatic transformations, alluding to '[t]he circumstances of

Charles II's own early life, his restoration . . . the political upheavals of his reign' and the stable political future he had fought to bring about.[13] Verrio told a story teeming with heroic incident using visual-allegorical language strongly theatrical in flavour, readily transferable to the theatre.

All but three of Verrio's ceilings were destroyed when Windsor Castle underwent another round of modernization in the 1820s. However, Pierre Vandrebanc made prints of three of the ceilings in the 1680s, when they were new, allowing non-courtiers at least a glimpse of Windsor's interior splendour. W.H. Pyne commissioned a series of watercolour paintings around 1810, showing the state apartments as they then appeared, and in each painting a portion of Verrio ceiling is clearly visible. Pyne had engraved versions of the paintings made for reproduction in the first volume of his three-volume illustrated guide *The History of the Royal Residences* – today they are better known in that guise – and to complement the engravings he supplied an extensive prose commentary. Ceiling descriptions in this chapter follow Pyne's.[14]

The Windsor Great Works were about half complete in 1679, when a storm of exceptional ferocity broke over Charles's head, fixing the next historico-political date in our narrative: the so-called Exclusion Crisis. Two fortune-hunting informants (Drs Israel Tonge and Titus Oates) broke fake news of a Catholic plot to assassinate Charles and install James his brother as king in his place. An anti-Catholic witch-hunt followed, and bills to exclude James from the succession were debated in Parliament. Charles won the day, not by the debate, but by dissolving his fractious Parliament in March 1681. From then until his death in February 1685, Charles ruled without recalling Parliament. His court allies, including artists on the court payroll, thought it a 'Time proper for Triumph', a 'Second Restoration'. Revolution had been averted and the Exclusionists' design defeated just as Charles's 1660 restoration had defeated those revolutionaries whose execution of his father had forced him into exile. The artistic celebrations which ensued were by British standards unprecedentedly ambitious and unprecedentedly well coordinated, with artists in every genre supporting each other's efforts and thus reinvigorating the multimedia celebration of royal will.

Locating time: from masque to opera

In this final stage of Charles's reign – the return to non-parliamentary royalism – the means of cultural production in England were radically expanded.[15] Revived with triumphalist zeal and a serious propaganda purpose, the court masque tradition bifurcated. One branch morphed into all-sung English opera; the other used spoken words as well as music to address paying theatre audiences, rather than court insiders. Both were momentous developments. Both happened between 1683 and 1685, though the première production of the first outward-facing spoken and sung masque was delayed until 1691.

We know that two all-sung operas were presented at court before King Charles II between 1683 and 1685: *Venus and Adonis* (music by John Blow, words anonymous) and *Albion and Albanius* (music by Louis Grabu, words by John Dryden).[16]

One more, *Dido and Aeneas* (music by Henry Purcell, words by Nahum Tate), may well have been designed for performance before Charles II.[17] The 'Dramatick Opera' *King Arthur* (words by Dryden, music eventually supplied by Henry Purcell) was in Dryden's own words 'the last Piece of Service, which I had the Honour to do, for my Gracious Master, King Charles the Second'.[18] Act I of *Albion and Albanius* was originally meant to serve as *King Arthur*'s all-sung prologue; *King Arthur* being a five-act spoken drama with musical episodes interspersed, precisely following the structure of *Calisto*. But Charles's intensifying interest in all-sung opera forced a change of plan.

In August 1683 the London theatre supremo Thomas Betterton was dispatched to Paris at Charles's expense, to 'treat . . . with some persons capable of representing an opera in England'.[19] Betterton returned with only one, a French composer wearily familiar to English court musicians. As Charles II's Master of Music, Grabu had directed the court string orchestra from 1666 to 1673. After six years working as a freelance musician in London he left for France: Popish Plot revelations and the anti-Catholic climate had made that advisable. Now he was back to show English court musicians how to do all-sung opera properly.[20]

Sensing the direction in which operatic winds were blowing, Dryden (so he said) 'propos'd to the Actors, to turn the intended [*King Arthur*] Prologue into an Entertainment by it self . . . by adding two acts more to what I had already Written'. A full-length, all-sung English opera would result when Grabu had supplied the necessary extra music. How far *Albion* and *King Arthur* had progressed by autumn 1684 may be inferred from a letter that Dryden wrote in August or September that year to his publisher Jacob Tonson. Dryden mentioned 'the opera' on which he was working. Four of its five acts had already been written but the last would have to wait until he had time to focus on it. Dryden asked later in the same letter for news of his 'singing opera', hoping that Tonson would be able to tell him how Betterton was getting on with preparations for its public première (Dryden was out of town, Tonson still in London). By 'the opera', Dryden probably meant *King Arthur*, a five-act piece as planned and eventually realized. Three-act, all-sung *Albion and Albanius* was in production by this stage: 'singing opera' made a meaningful distinction setting it clearly apart from spoken-and-sung *King Arthur*.[21]

With the Exclusion Crisis. Charles's patience with London snapped. Though his victory over the Exclusionists looked definitive, in the capital they remained an angry and resentful presence. Taking inspiration from Louis XIV – who now lived much of the time in Versailles, pleasantly remote from central Paris, running his country with the help of ministers and civil servants quartered there – Charles ordered the construction of a brand new palace complex in Winchester.[22] Sir Christopher Wren designed it and oversaw the project personally.

Winchester Palace stood on high ground to the west of the city, on the site formerly occupied by Winchester Castle. The Castle was in ruins by this time: workmen cleared the rubble unceremoniously away. They spared and repaired the Castle's Great Hall however: Wren's plan assimilated it into the new Palace complex as an overt symbol of ancient hereditary right. 'King Arthur's Round Table' hung, and still hangs, on one wall of the Great Hall: Charles and his companions of the Order of the Garter could dine in Arthur's hall, in sight of the Round Table and in imagination seated at it. Acres of land in other parts of Winchester were bought by Charles's agents so the city could be redeveloped along architecturally harmonious Versailles-like lines.[23] Plans show that a wide avenue was to have led downhill from Winchester Palace to the great West Door of Winchester Cathedral, the burial place of a number of Saxon kings whose forebears the mythical Arthur was said to have subdued.

Inside the cathedral a feature no longer there emblematized the Stuart principle of orderly royal succession with startling clarity, no doubt reminding Charles II of the rightness of his decision to uphold it despite the political risk involved in doing so (compare Figure 5.1 with Figure 5.2). A stone choir screen designed by Inigo Jones, at right angles to the west-east line running from Winchester Palace to the High Altar of Winchester Cathedral, created an inner sanctum to which the only access was a round arch, flanked by life-size bronze statues of James I (to the left) and Charles I (to the right). Charles I had paid for these statues personally. They were made by Hubert Le Sueur, a French sculptor who achieved professional celebrity after moving to London and whose equestrian statue of Charles I became a famous London landmark after the Restoration (see what follows). In

Figure 5.1 The Banqueting House, Whitehall. Designed by Inigo Jones for James I (1619); the backdrop for Charles I's execution in 1649

Source: © The British Library Board, Thomason Tract Collection, 669.f.12 (87).

Figure 5.2 The Choir Screen, Winchester Cathedral (Inigo Jones, 1637–1638), with life-size bronze statues of James I (left) and Charles I (right). Engraving in Samuel Gale, *The History and Antiquities of the Cathedral Church of Winchester* (1715)

Source: Reproduced by courtesy of the Special Collections, Hartley Library, University of Southampton.

Winchester Cathedral, no one could come to Holy Communion without passing between Charles II's father and grandfather standing guard. Their role in life, as Defenders of the Faith, continued in effigy even after death.[24] It had been Arthur's role – repelling heathen Saxon invaders – and now descended to Charles II. Charles would have liked, like Arthur, to attend to Christian fundamentals and avoid invidious choice between Rome and Canterbury.

A number of court masques produced for James I and Charles I had made elaborate use of Arthurian imagery, unpacking meaning from the richly suggestive anagram 'Charles Iames Stuart Claimes Arthur's Seat': Charles James Stuart was James I's baptismal name.[25] At the end of his reign, Charles revived that claim with zeal and ingenuity. It is hard to imagine Charles driving the project forward personally. He was, for a king, ill-read and poorly educated. '[H]e could never overcome his distaste for reading or writing', and the research effort needed to connect mythical Arthur with the Carolean present would have been completely beyond him.[26]

Charles had inherited custodial responsibility for three close-to-sacred Stuart texts: the Authorized 'King James Bible', the complete works of James I (available in Latin and English versions), and the mainly apocryphal 'Works of King Charles the Martyr'. To these, by commissioning or endorsing work by the right people, certainly not by writing them himself, he was able to add three more: the 1662 *Book of Common Prayer*, Ashmole's account of the Order of the Garter, and Sandford's history of the kings of England.[27] Together the original very bulky folios provided an immense weight of evidence supporting Charles's political position. Stuart monarchs owned the conduit through which God spoke to believers in plain English. Historical continuity could be traced from Britain's earliest Christian rulers through to Charles II; and the chivalric code to which seventeenth-century Knights of the Garter supposedly subscribed had ancient origins. The building work at Windsor and Winchester gave concrete physical expression to the key religious, political, and historical ideas contained in these monumental literary works. Charles, his courtiers and – most importantly – the visitors he wished to impress, could in an almost literal sense, inhabit stories prefiguring their even more glorious present.

Opera as public spectacle – *Albion and Albanius* and *King Arthur*

The work of opera was to bring these stories to wider public notice, get them discussed and internalized by London audiences (perhaps), and show London audiences a series of powerful visual images otherwise only accessible to those who could afford travel or expensive books. A film-of-the-book analogy would not be too far-fetched. *Albion and Albanius* and *King Arthur* were designed for commercial production in London's best-equipped public theatre, not (as the prewar masques had been) for purposely exclusive performance at court. High production costs could only be recouped if audience interest in the shows justified regular revivals. Through *Albion* and *King Arthur*, therefore, Charles II's artist-advocates sought to make an unforgettable impression on contemporary theatre-goers and sought in addition to address posterity – the paying customers of the future.

Albion and Albanius opened in London:

> *The Curtain rises, and there appears on either side of the Stage . . . a Statue on Horse-back, of Gold, on Pedestal's of Marble, enrich'd with Gold, and bearing the Imperial Armes of* England: *one of these Statues is taken from that of the late King, at* Charing-Cross; *the other, from that Figure of his present Majesty (done by that noble Artist Mr.* Gibbons) *at* Windsor.
>
> *The Scene, is a Street of Palaces, which lead to the Front of the* Royal Exchange . . .

Two gold kings-on-horseback demonstrated Stuart continuity. The Hubert Le Sueur larger-than-life-size bronze of Charles I was finally erected on its present Charing Cross site in 1675.[28] Theatre technicians made a copy of it; or possibly a *tromp l'oeil* painting. The Grinling Gibbons Charles II had been installed at Windsor in 1679. It too is still there. London had its own equestrian statue of Charles II, installed in the Stock Market in 1672, but that was a gift to the city from the Royal Goldsmith and major royal creditor Sir Robert Vyner, far inferior in quality, and not so well suited to a role in royal opera.[29] Dryden and Betterton sacrificed geographical accuracy to encomiastic duty. The buildings represented had been carefully chosen: palaces (plural) to show London at its architecturally imposing best – a phoenix city rising from the ashes of the Great Fire – while the Royal Exchange signified commercial prosperity under royal patronage.

After the overture – several minutes of instrumental music giving the audience plenty of time to admire the scene just described – Augusta and Thamesis appear on couches '*in dejected postures*'. Paintings on the side of Augusta's couch show '*Towers falling*' and an odd collection of symbols representing the dereliction of civic duty. Broken reeds, weeds, and an upturned urn lie on the ground in front of Thamesis. The river is sick like the city it serves. Augusta and Thamesis explain their problem to Mercury, the messenger of the gods, who '*descends in a Chariot drawn by Ravens*'. Their rebellion against Charles I had resulted in punishment. Mercury is reassuring: all will be well if they repent, welcome Charles II's Restoration, ask his forgiveness, and have nothing further to do with the opera's principal villains Zelota [Zeal] or Democracy.

After some blatantly allegorical action summarizing political and military events paving the way to the Restoration – with scene changes to accompany the action – Albion (Charles II) appears with Albanius (James Duke of York) by his side. '[T]*he 4 Triumphal Arches erected at his Majesties Coronation*' are revealed. Augusta, Thamesis, and the chorus salute Royal Albion. They make no mention of Albanius. An elaborate danced entry follows, '*Representing the Four parts of the World, rejoycing at the Restauration of* Albion'. Then the chorus returns to end Act I with a slightly varied repeat of 'Hail, Royal Albion'. London's dejection has lifted, giving way to a loyal royalist frenzy.

The Four Parts of the World had appeared in the *Calisto* prologue and, after about 1678 (when Verrio finished painting it) were prominently visible on the ceiling of Charles II's Windsor Castle Presence Chamber, looking in awe at a bust-length portrait of the king unfurled by Mercury in front of them.[30] They appeared on the ceiling in the King's Bed Chamber, paying tribute to a painting of the King in Garter Robes seated on a throne, and on the ceiling in the Queen's Guard Chamber presenting their offerings to Queen Catherine, dressed as Britannia seated on a globe. Allegorical devices tested out on stage, in *Calisto*, migrated to the Windsor ceilings, and in *Albion and Albanius* were retrieved from the ceilings for a stage comeback. Mercury and the Four Parts of the World were stock characters, of course; Dryden could have deployed them without reference either to Crowne's published *Calisto* text or to Verrio; but as some of the imagery in Albion is explicitly derived from Windsor, and captioned accordingly, I think it likely that other, possible connections were real and were intended.

Act II covers the Exclusion Crisis. Its first scene is set in a 'Poetical Hell', the Exclusionists' rightful home; scene ii in Whitehall, viewed from the middle of the Thames so that buildings on both riverbanks seemed to stretch away into the distance. This route out to sea will shortly be taken by Albanius sailing to exile on the continent, hoping that the crisis will subside. Dancing watermen arrive to collect him; Tritons, sea-nymphs, and other watery deities gather to wish him a safe and pleasant voyage. Overhead the clouds part to reveal the sun-god Apollo in his fiery chariot, to assure Albion and Albanius that Providence is on their side: they are 'The Gods peculiar care'. Troubles borne with patience will soon pass. Charles himself was pictured as Phoebus-Apollo in the centre of Windsor Castle's Drawing Room ceiling, in a similar flying chariot.[31] It is not Dryden's intention, in the opera, to suggest that Charles-as-Apollo addressing Charles-as-Albion is literally the author of his own destiny, but the Windsor ceiling echo here practically eliminates the status gap between them.

The scene shifts to Dover at the start of Act III. From where Charles had landed in 1660, now Albion looks wistfully out to sea, wishing Albanius could be recalled. Nereids emerge from the waves to lament his sad and lonely situation. Democracy, Zelota, Tyranny, and Asebia ['Atheism or Ungodliness'], sensing they have the king in their power, present a mini-masque intended to celebrate impending victory. Teams of dancers representing different non-conformist Protestant factions, at first united in their hatred of Catholicism, soon start to squabble. Their coalition of Exclusionist interest falls apart. Once again, Albion emerges as the country's only credible leader; the only authority figure around whom most of its citizens are prepared more or less willingly to unite.

> *Albion.* See the Gods my cause defending,
> When all humane help was past!
> *Acacia* ['Innocence']. Factions mutually contending
> By each other fall at last.

Albion and Acacia visit the cave of the sea-god Proteus, hoping to learn from him how the Exclusion Crisis will be resolved. Proteus, who can change shape at will, demonstrates this repeatedly while Albion and Acacia attempt to pin him down. (Extreme changeability should give him an innate understanding of British religious sectarianism.) He hints at an answer but will not deliver it straight out.

98 *Andrew Pinnock*

Next, Democracy, Zelota, and their associates plot to assassinate Albion, solving the Catholic succession problem at one murderous stroke. Albion when dead will have no further power to impede the Exclusion Bill's passage through Parliament into law. But before their marksman can shoot '*A fire arises betwixt them and* Albion'. Albion is saved. The rebels 'sink together' to some imagined hell beneath the stage. Everyone in the audience would have recognised this reference to the 'Rye House Plot' of spring 1683. Charles and James returned to London earlier than expected when a fire at Newmarket races put pay to their sport. Plotters who had assembled at Rye House in Hoddesdon, Hertfordshire, on the London-Newmarket road, were not ready to strike when the royal party passed by. At the time, the fire was widely interpreted as direct heavenly intervention in the nation's affairs, and so it is presented in *Albion and Albanius*.

With the end of the opera in sight, Albanius returns from exile in '*A Machine ris*[*ing*] *out of the Sea: It opens and discovers* Venus *and* Albanius *sitting in a great Scallop-shell, richly adorn'd*'. Another of the paintings on Charles's Windsor Presence Chamber ceiling (at the end of the room farthest from his throne) showed 'Venus, in a majestic sea-car drawn and attended by Nereides, Tritons, and other aquatic divinities'.[32] This sea car or one very like it now brought Albanius home, rendering Albion's triumph and his happiness complete.

Neither lasted long. As Dryden put it in the preface to *King Arthur* (1691), 'when He [Charles II] had just Restor'd His People to their Senses, and made the latter End of His Government, of a Piece with the Happy Beginning of it, He was on the suddain snatch'd away'. *Albion and Albanius*, designed to celebrate Charles's 'Second Restoration', had now to accommodate the king's sudden and unexpected death. The opera had been extensively rehearsed (Charles himself watched it in rehearsal, according to Dryden, 'twice or thrice'), but some changes were now necessary before it could be performed in public. Dryden and Grabu worked on these during the two-month period of official mourning that followed Charles's death, throughout which Betterton's Dorset Garden Theatre had to stay shut.[33]

Between the opera's grand finale and the return-of-Albanius scene immediately preceding it, Dryden and Grabu added one short additional scene. Here Albion joins Apollo on a glorious golden machine lowered from heaven to collect him: not the chariot of the sun as in Act II but an oval cloud formation '*in the midst of* [*which*] *sits* Apollo *on a Throne of Gold*'. Angels and Cherubims can be seen '*flying about* [*the clouds*], *and playing in 'em*': this is a joyous occasion, not a tearful one, for Albion will be welcomed into heaven as a '*new Deity*'. Albanius will succeed him as Britain's earthly ruler and is amply qualified for the position: 'Ador'd and fear'd, and lov'd no less'.

A new, sumptuously gilded throne for Charles had recently been installed in St. George's Hall, Windsor Castle.[34] Apollo's may well have been modelled on it. Neptune, present along with Venus and Acacia to witness Charles's apotheosis, refers explicitly to the mythical family tree linking Charles with Venus:

Ven[*us*]. What Stars above shall we displace?
Where shall he [Charles] fill a Room Divine?

Nept[*une*]. Descended from the Sea Gods Race,
Let him by my *Orion* shine.

Apollo has other plans, but this brief Neptune-Venus exchange is another strategic pointer to Windsor Castle's visual-allegorical scheme. A painted Star of Venus hung above the throne and canopy in Charles's Windsor Presence Chamber, captioned '*Sidus Carolinum*': Charles's Star. A star widely though wrongly identified as Venus had been seen in the sky at noon on the day of Charles's birth, 29 May 1630 – a portent to which propagandists working for Charles could and did refer whenever they wanted shorthand proof of his divine right to rule.[35] Charles had inherited his sexual appetite from the love goddess Venus: behaviour hard for subjects to forgive in a monarch lacking that excuse could be indulged in Charles's case. He was powerless to control it. This is why the Windsor Castle Presence Chamber ceiling carried two painted representations of Venus: as a star guiding Charles the monarch, and as a temptress (mis)guiding Charles the man. From *Calisto* on, Venus makes prominent appearances in every court masque and court-originating opera devised for Charles II.

The final scene in *Albion and Albanius*, on a lavish set designed and largely built before Charles died, brings a literal re-creation of new-look Windsor Castle to the London stage:

> *The Scene changes to a walk of very high Trees: At the end of the Walk is a view of that part of* Windsor, *which faces* Eaton: *In the midst of it is a row of small Trees, which lead to the Castle-hill: In the first Scene, part of the Town and part of the Hill: In the next the Terrace Walk, the King's Lodgings, and the upper part of St.* George's *Chappel, then the Keep; and lastly, that part of the Castle, beyond the Keep.*
>
> *In the Air is a Vision of the Honors of the Garter, the Knights in Procession, and the King under a Canopy: Beyond this, the upper end of St.* George's *Hall.*
>
> *Fame rises out of the middle of the Stage, standing on a Globe; on which is the Arms of* England: *The Globe rests on a Pedestal: On the Front of the Pedestal is drawn a Man with a long, lean, pale Face, with Fiends Wings, and Snakes twisted round his Body: He is incompast by several Phanatical Rebellious Heads, who suck poyson from him, which runs out of a Tap in his Side.*

The man with a long, lean, pale face and fiends' wings is Anthony Ashley Cooper, First Earl of Shaftesbury, chief-Exclusionist (dead himself, by this time), personifying evil and setting a poisonous example to malcontents everywhere. Shaftesbury really did have a tap in his side, to drain a permanently suppurating abscess. Even Shaftesbury had a place on the Windsor ceilings, in the St. George's Hall centre panel: Verrio pictured him among a group of rebels being beaten into submission while Charles II looked imperturbably on. The vision of the Honours of the Garter, the Knights in procession, and the King under a Canopy is a painted realisation of two full-page engravings in Ashmole's *The Institution, Laws and*

100 *Andrew Pinnock*

Ceremonies of the Most Noble Order of the Garter (see Figures 5.3 and 5.4). This was a large and expensive book with which only a minority of theatregoers would have been familiar, but Garter symbols taken from Ashmole festooned Verrio's walls and ceiling of St. George's Hall. Tradition, far from scrupulously observed under Charles II and James II, required the Garter Knights to gather for an annual St George's Day chapel service and feast: Verrio prepared St. George's Hall for the latter.

At the end of *Albion and Albanius* everything came together: the chivalric heritage that Ashmole had reconstructed for Charles II, Windsor ceiling paintings celebrating that heritage and blending it with Venusian myth; and a '*full Chorus of all the Voices and Instruments*' echoing the words of trumpet-wielding Fame as she praised Great Albion's Name over and over. Fame did the same job at Windsor, blowing a mute fanfare while Mercury unfurled Charles's portrait on the Presence Chamber ceiling.[36]

Judith Hook, writing in 1976 about 'The function of the Work of Art' in late seventeenth-century England, noted perceptively that the 'literary counterpart

Figure 5.3 A display of garter regalia. Engraving by Wenceslaus Hollar, in Elias Ashmole, *The Institution, Laws and Ceremonies of the Most Noble Order of the Garter* (1672)

Source: Photograph by Christopher Guy, Worcester Cathedral Archaeologist. Reproduced by permission of the Chapter of Worcester Cathedral (UK), shelf mark OA11; bound in after p. 202.

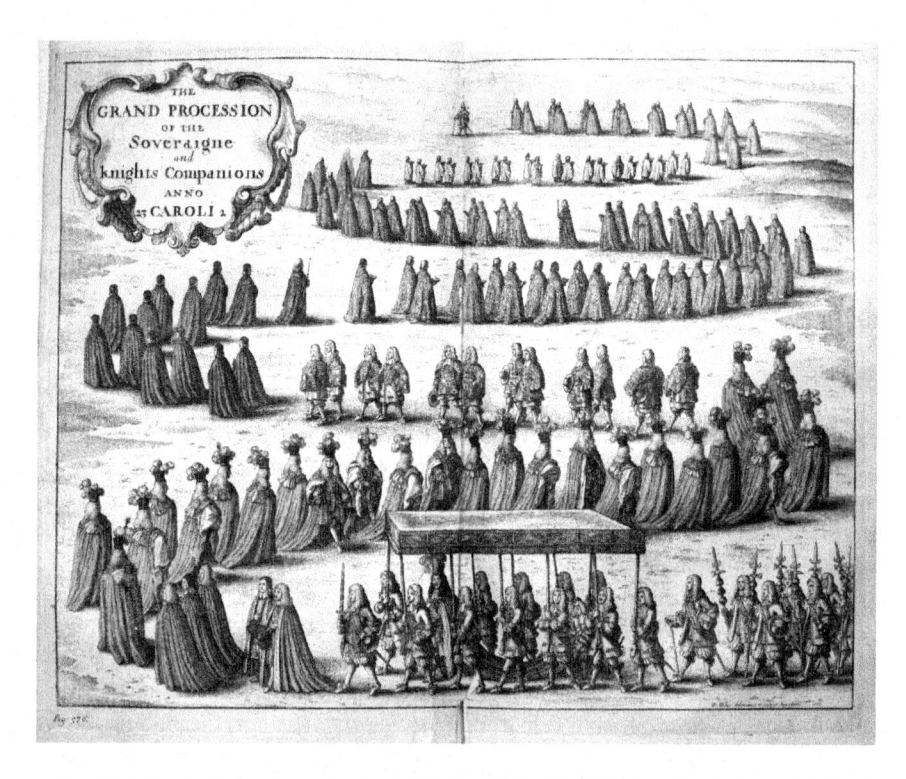

Figure 5.4 Garter Knights processing to St George's Hall, Windsor, for their annual feast. Charles II walks behind them under a canopy. Engraving by Hollar in Ashmole, *The Institution, Laws and Ceremonies*.

Source: Photograph by Andrew Stewart. Reproduced by courtesy of Sherborne School Archives (UK).

to Verrio's Windsor decorations was Dryden's libretto for the opera of *Albion and Albanius* which celebrated the apotheosis of Charles II, Dryden's "best of kings"'.[37] Albion's apotheosis was an afterthought: *Albion and Albanius* had been designed to celebrate the political triumphs of a king still very much alive. But Hook's main point holds. Since 1976, much more information about the detailed appearance of Verrio's Windsor ceilings has come to light.[38] Now we can see that *Albion and Albanius*, when performed in 1685, would have been recognized not as a literary counterpart to Verrio but as a brilliantly imaginative multimedia animation of Verrio.

Dryden's libretto was a means to that performative end: judged simply as literature it is baffling. The scene descriptions included in Dryden's published libretto, some of which I have quoted in this essay, were written not by Dryden but by Thomas Betterton the theatrical mastermind responsible for staging *Albion*. Dryden thanked him graciously: 'Mr. *Betterton* . . . has spar'd neither for industry, nor cost, to make this Entertainment perfect, nor for Invention of the Ornaments to beautify it'. Where Inigo Jones had designed for James I and Charles I self-contained, purposely transient masque-worlds which would live on only in the memory once curtains had fallen and sets had been dismantled, Dryden and Betterton, more ambitiously, used London, Dover, and above all Windsor Castle as dramatic and imaginative backdrops, making for Charles II masques that were permanently anchored to iconic landscapes and to buildings with a lengthy life expectancy.

To achieve a permanent place in the repertoire, *Albion and Albanius* would need to prove itself at the box office. But political tension following the accession of James II made this an impossible test to pass: distracted audiences stayed away. Grabu's detractors attributed this commercial failure to artistic weaknesses for which the composer could be blamed, and since English court musicians resented his royally patronized presence on the London scene, the 'Party . . . maliciously endeavour[ing] to decry him' recruited well. A small number of satirical poems, written after *Albion* had closed, mocked Grabu, Dryden for agreeing to collaborate with Grabu, and the whole *Albion* experiment. It would be a mistake to treat this highly partisan bad press as honest or accurate criticism; but Grabu's reputation had suffered irreparably. It was left to Dryden, Betterton and a different composer to rescue Charles II's outward-facing masque project from the edge of oblivion.

This would be *King Arthur*. Its concept must have been discussed with Charles in 1683: Dryden had written most of the script by September 1684. Act I of *Albion and Albanius* was to have served as prologue to *King Arthur*; Acts II and III were added later. Work to prepare full-length *Albion and Albanius* for public performance was still going on when Charles died and work on *King Arthur* had halted completely. It re-started around summer 1690, when political conditions looked reasonably favourable and when the theatre could once again afford to invest.[39] James II, Charles's brother, had been deposed in the revolution of 1688: Albanius was out of the picture. The victors, William and Mary, looked secure. Purcell and Betterton had scored a major hit with *Dioclesian* (premièred May 1690), leaving audiences hungry for more. Dryden was no longer Poet Laureate – a convert to Catholicism, he fell victim to William and Mary's re-imposed tests of conformity to Church of England doctrine – but he was still one of London's leading literary figures: a new Dryden-Purcell semi-opera would sell. And with care, Dryden and Betterton thought they could get moth-balled *King Arthur* past William and Mary's stage censors.

Care involved assuring the censors and assuring readers when the published version of Dryden's *King Arthur* text appeared in 1691, that the work had been comprehensively revised. Passages with capacity to 'offend the present Times' had been deleted; lyrics suited to Grabu's style of composition but not to Purcell's had been replaced: 'I have been oblig'd so much to alter the first Design, and take away so many Beauties from the Writing, that it is now no more what it was formerly, than the present ship of the *Royal Sovereign*, after so often taking down, and altering, is the Vessel it was at the first Building'. But Dryden was lying. His *King Arthur* preface is brazen in its disingenuousness, shot through with key words and phrases signalling the truth to readers curious to know what that might be.

King Arthur opens at a turning point in history: 'Then this is the deciding Day, to fix/ *Great Britain*'s Scepter in great *Arthur*'s Hand. / . . . Or put it in the bold Invaders gripe'. (Act I of *Albion and Albanius* ended with a re-enactment of Charles II's coronation procession. This would have dovetailed beautifully with a slightly earlier *King Arthur* opening moment had it survived as the prologue to *King Arthur*). Arthur's Britons have defeated Saxon invading forces in 'Ten set Battles' thus far.[40]

None of the scenes in *King Arthur* has a precise geographical location assigned to it – a *'place of Heathen worship'*, a *'Deep Wood'* (*etc.*) could be anywhere – though for the first and last that can be inferred from clues in the text. Arthur strikes out from his castle – in Winchester, as Charles II wanted to believe – to carry the fight to the Saxons wherever they may be. Winchester is nowhere mentioned; nor is the Round Table. Winchester Palace was not completed in Charles's lifetime and was never fitted out in proper palace fashion, serving in the eighteenth and nineteenth centuries as a prison, a barracks and a hospital. Ceiling paintings complementing Verrio's at Windsor surely would have been commissioned for Winchester Palace had Charles lived several years longer: no high-baroque palace was complete without them. But their moment never came.

When writing *King Arthur*, then, Dryden's task was not to find contemporary political meaning in extant palace artwork but to invent an archetypal politico-religious power struggle between long-ago Britons led by an exemplary Christian king against a misguided enemy threatening what Britons held most dear: national unity and their true religion. That power struggle would foreshadow Charles's and predict its outcome. Arthur and his knights set patterns of virtue and valour to which Charles and his supporters centuries later, much to their credit, can be seen to be conforming. Charles's enemies follow equally ancient bad precedent. Since history repeats itself, we can learn what will happen in the future. *King Arthur* puts Charles II squarely though ahistorically on the winning side.

In Act I, on St. George of Cappadocia's Day – a good omen – Arthur's troops engage the Saxons and notch up their eleventh victory. This should, like Charles II's Restoration and St. George's Day coronation, have been the end of the story. But Arthur will have to overcome enemies much more dangerous than a rival army: devils are ranged against him too, invisible and unbeatable without supernatural assistance. Merlin in *King Arthur* has a role analogous to Apollo's in *Albion and Albanius*, assuring Arthur that things will turn out well and occasionally intervening to make his prophecies come true.

Arthur's bride-to-be, Emmeline, had been blind from birth – blindness preventing her full appreciation of his kingly virtue. Her sight is restored in Act III, when the good spirit Philidel administers magic eye-drops supplied by Merlin. Arthur and Emmeline, rejoined by God (acting through Merlin) at the 'restoration', are now assailed by dark forces trying to put them asunder; whence the Saxon magician Osmond's attempt to rape Emmeline – foiled at the last moment – and spells with which Osmond enchants a wood through which Arthur must pass. Osmond's sidekick Grimbald is a winged fiend whose description roughly matches that of Shaftesbury in the *Albion and Albanius* stage direction quoted earlier (p. 99).

Arthur struggles to overcome fleshly temptation in Act IV: two naked sirens bathing in a stream urge him to join them. Osmond's hold over the enchanted wood can only be broken when Arthur gets a grip, asks advice from Merlin and follows it to the letter (also Act IV).

In Act V, Arthur and the Saxon leader Oswald fight a duel: single combat to avoid any further unnecessary bloodshed. After several passes 'they appear both Wounded'. Saxon magician Osmond knocks Arthur's sword out of his hand; Merlin gives it back. This a fight between good and evil. Arthur has a valiant part to play – slugging things out with Oswald for as long as necessary – but he can only win when Merlin the magician outwits Osmond. This is of course the outcome. With Arthur and Emmeline safe in each other's arms and Oswald though still alive no longer a threat (spared by Arthur, 'As Merciful and Kind, to vanquisht Foes, / As a Forgiving God' we learned at the outset), Merlin conjures up a prophetic masque showing cast members gathered on stage – and by extension the whole theatre audience:

> ... what Rouling Ages shall produce:
> The Wealth, the Loves, the Glories of our Isle,
> Which yet like Golden Oar, Unripe in Beds,
> Expect the Warm Indulgency of Heav'n
> To call 'em forth to Light –

King Arthur, set in the distant past, ends by looking forward to a Carolean present, around 1684. Britain under Charles II has become the country whose future Arthur and his knights fought to secure.

> Merlin *waves his Wand; the Scene changes, and discovers the* British *Ocean in a Storm.* Æolus *in a Cloud above: Four Winds hanging, &c.*
> Stern words from singing Aeolus calm the waves, whereupon
> *An Island arises, to a soft Tune;* Britannia *seated in the Island, with Fishermen at her Feet, &c.* . . .

Britannia – representing the whole island of Britain, not just England – appeared in two of Verrio's Windsor ceiling compositions, and there her face was clearly recognizable at that of Charles II's queen Catherine of Braganza. *King Arthur* thus starts to align with Windsor. The fishermen come ashore to dance; Pan and a Nereid sing a duet praising the abundance of British fish stocks.

Next, Pan, the Nereid, and an uncharacterized other eulogize the excellence of British wool in a 'Song of three Parts'. Comus and three peasants dance their way on stage to sing a curious song about harvest festival binge drinking, interminably long sermons preached by country parsons, the iniquity of tithe payments benefiting country parsons (justifying tithe evasion) and loyal toasts to Old England: tankards will be raised and drained repeatedly until the peasants fall over. This is a comedy number, inviting sophisticated Londoners to laugh at their country cousins, yet the loyalty seems real enough. The peasants worked hard both to grow the crops and to bring them in. They deserve a holiday.

Venus enters, to sing a solo (indecently beautiful as set by Purcell: 'Fairest Isle, all Isles Excelling') identifying Britain as her chosen home. Faith in the doctrine of free love will spread from Venus's formal Windsor headquarters through the whole nation. Where Charles impelled by Venus leads, those of his subjects young and fit enough to count as nymphs and swains will willingly follow.

The 'SONG by Mr HOWE' coming next – a rather formulaic he/she duet setting words by Queen Mary's Vice Chamberlain John Grobham Howe – disrupts the flow and logic of the rest of the masque. Elsewhere I have argued that Dryden and Betterton included this song to curry favour with Howe, hoping he would use his influence over court playscript scrutineers to get *King Arthur* the performance licence it needed.[41] A prominent writer's credit in the published version may have been his reward. The song in question also bought extra time, around five minutes, during which the stage crew could prepare their final scenic revelation.

'Fairest Isle' and the Howe duet lead in to '"A Warlike Consort", a vision of the Order of the Garter. a procession of heroes and a royalistic trumpet air evoking St George and the English monarchy', but Dryden's stage direction is very brief.[42] Unlike those in the published version of *Albion and Albanius* his *King Arthur* stage directions were not supplied by Betterton, and in Dryden's note-to-self form they made no attempt to describe *King Arthur*'s actual scenic splendour. Probably *King Arthur* recycled the whole of the set created for use at the same climactic moment in *Albion and Albanius* seven years before. In *King Arthur*, 'Honour [*enters*], *Attended by* Hero'*s*'. Merlin, speaking from the mythical past, invites present-day spectators to

> . . . look above, and in Heavn's High Abyss,
> Behold what Fame attends those future Hero's.
> Honour, who leads 'em to that Steepy Height,
> In her Immortal Song, shall tell the rest.

The description here requires an upward march, as in Figure 5.4. The utmost height of fame to which heroes could aspire in Carolean Britain was, according to Ashmole, a Garter Knighthood and a place at the table in St. George's Hall on Garter feast days.

Albion and Albanius ended with a three-stanza solo song for Fame, praising the King and praising the Garter. Two of these three stanzas had full choral repeats. According to its 1691 published text, *King Arthur* ended with a three-stanza solo song for Honour expressing almost the same sentiments, 'A full Chorus' repeating 'the whole Song'. No plausibly Purcellian setting of the song's first stanza survives. The extant choral setting of stanzas two and three may or may not be by Purcell. All three stanzas would have troubled stage censors in 1691.

1.

St. George, *the Patron of our Isle,*
   A Soldier, and a Saint,
On that Auspicious Order smile,
   Which Love and Arms will plant.

106 *Andrew Pinnock*

2.

Our Natives not alone appear
To Court this Martiall Prize;
But Foreign Kings, Adopted here,
Their Crowns at home despise.

3.

Our Soveraign High, in Aweful State,
His Honours shall bestow;
And see his Sceptr'd Subjects wait
On his Commands below.

The first invokes saintly aid, a Catholic practice which Anglicans swearing their oath of allegiance to Protestant monarchs had solemnly to renounce; the second implies criticism of foreign kings, for abandoning their subjects, and might have sounded to some like a swipe at King William; and the third ('*Our Soveraign High... His Honours*', etc.) assumes one all-powerful male monarch. William and Mary were joint heads of state, sharing equal honours on ceremonial occasions. None of these objections could have been anticipated in 1684–5: they surfaced subsequently. If the 'St. George' stanzas needed replacing in 1691 – to comply with stage licensing conditions perhaps, or to pre-empt the censor – then Purcell would have set words supplied in lieu.

Queen Mary died in 1695. By then, Dutch William was more at home and more popular in his adopted country. As a widower, he reigned alone. St. George could crack a smile without threatening the state. But Purcell also died in 1695. Others had to prepare the music for subsequent *King Arthur* revivals. To anyone checking the 1691 published text to see how words and music were supposed to fit together, it would look as though music for 'St. George' (presumably Purcell's) had gone missing. More would have to be composed to plug the gap in a style compatible with Purcell's but unlikely to match it exactly. This would explain the presence, in several music manuscripts copied in or after 1698, of a pseudo-Purcellian last chorus ('Our Natives not alone appear', *etc.*), with or without a pseudo-Purcellian 'St. George' solo preceding it.

Dryden's 1691 *King Arthur* preface hints that the published text preserves two kinds of lyric: words set by Purcell, and words not set by Purcell but nevertheless worth reading as part of the original design. I put 'St. George' in the latter category. I suspect that Honour and the Chorus sang something else to conclude *King Arthur* performances from 1691 through to 1695 or later.[43] To make sense in context, that something else, whatever it was, would have had to acknowledge the Order of the Garter hanging overhead and explain its role as master-symbol of the Stuart monarchy.

The Verrio paintings in St. George's Hall made that role explicit. There in the centre ceiling panel a portrait of Charles II in Garter habit held majestic sway over more than a dozen high-ranking allegorical figures gathered round him. The panel over Charles's throne – at the east or upper end of the Hall – contained 'St. George's cross, encircled with the garter, with a star of glory supported by infant genii' (Pyne). Garter regalia filled the panel at the lower end of the Hall, over the musicians' gallery. A huge mural on the north wall of the Hall showed Edward the Black Prince's triumphal procession into London after his unlikely victory in the Poitiers campaign, 1356–7 (beating far larger French forces). Edward III (King of England, father to the Black Prince and reputed founder of the Order of the Garter) welcomes him home. The Prince had been sent to France to protect English territorial interests to which Charles II laid vestigial claim. This is why one quarter of the Stuart coat of arms contained *fleurs-de-lys*, and why, on the King's Bed Chamber ceiling in Windsor, robed-and-enthroned Charles had 'a figure personifying France . . . placed at his feet in a suppliant posture' (Pyne). Dryden also recalled in a 1693 essay that 'Edward, the Black Prince, subduing Spain' was one of two English historical subjects he had once considered writing an epic poem about. The other was King Arthur, conquering the Saxons. Edward fought in Spain about a decade after his Poitiers victory: Dryden may have conflated the two campaigns.[44]

In two short speeches at the end of *King Arthur*, framing its last musical inset, Merlin and Arthur underline the opera's fundamental political message:

[*Merlin*] *To Osw*[*ald*]. Nor thou, brave Saxon Prince, disdain our Triumphs;
Britains and *Saxons* shall be once one People;
One Common Tongue, one Common Faith shall bind
Our Jarring Bands, in a perpetual Peace.

Arth[*ur*] to *Merl*[*in*]. Wisely you have, whate'er you please, reveal'd,
What would displease, as wisely have conceal'd:
Triumphs of War and Peace, at full ye show,
But swiftly turn the Pages of our Wo.
Rest we contented with our present State:
'Tis anxious to enquire of future Fate.
That Race of Hero's is enough alone
For all unseen Disasters to atone.
Let us make haste betimes to Reap our share,
And not Resign them all the Praise of War:
But set th' Example; and their Souls Inflame,
To Copy out their Great Forefathers Fame.

The nation will unite, in time. Getting there will require collective effort, willingness to set differences aside ('One Common Tongue, one Common Faith'), strong human leadership, and divine grace. 'Our Jarring Bands' – racial, religious, and linguistic sub-groups – can stop jarring if they decide to. The prize awaiting a united country, apart from 'perpetual Peace' welcome in itself, is perpetual prosperity.

Connections

This progressive programme for 'Great Britain', far from coincidentally, exactly matches the one unveiled by King James I in his very first speech to the House of Lords in London, delivered on 19 March 1603. The speech had been included in James's collected works and was reprinted separately in 1689. Dryden managed to summarize James's genuinely eloquent but highly ornate address:

> I [said James] am the Husband, and the whole Isle is my lawfull Wife [Arthur-Emmeline?]; I am the Head, and it is my Body; I am the Shepherd, and it is my flocke. [He went on:] 'For as my faith is the Trew, Ancient, Catholike and Apostolike faith, grounded upon the Scriptures and expresse word of God so will I ever yeeld all reverence to antiquitie in the points of Ecclesiasticall pollicy.

James had real respect for the Catholic laity; less for Catholic clergy taking the laity for fools. He proclaimed the benefits of peace. His personal motto was *Beati Pacifici*, blessed are the peacemakers, insisting too that a country at peace with itself, economically and militarily strong, would have little trouble co-existing peacefully with foreign neighbours.[45]

God had favoured James with

> healthful and hopeful Issue . . . for continuance and propagation of that undoubted right which is in my Person [as he put it], under whom I doubt not but it will please God to prosper and continue for many yeeres this Union, and all other blessings . . . which I have brought with me.

The execution of Charles I appeared to falsify James's confident prediction. This is why the principle of divine-right hereditary rule mattered so much to Charles II, and why he wanted to defend that principle against Exclusionist attack more or less whatever the cost.

By 1683, when they started discussing *King Arthur*, Charles and Dryden were both embracing Catholicism. Both converted soon after: Charles on his deathbed, Dryden sometime in 1685. Dryden was 'seen attending Mass in January 1686'.[46] Both had a big emotional stake in the Christian-ecumenical future to which Merlin looks forward at the end of *King Arthur*.

Paul Hammond, in a stimulating essay on *Albion and Albanius*, published more than thirty years ago (approaching the work from angles other than mine), describes it as 'a late scion' of the vanished court masque tradition; as of course it is.[47] Hammond mentioned *King Arthur* in passing but placed it outside the masque tradition. Dryden called it a 'Dramatick Opera' admittedly, not a masque, because in 1691, he and Betterton needed to obfuscate connections between *Albion* and *King Arthur*. Dryden at the same time drew coded attention to them in his *King Arthur* preface – a typically bravura move. My concern here has been to make these connections explicit. By tying together elements and linking the motifs and allegories from the visual arts, theatrical and musical traditions, we can show how *King Arthur* advanced on *Albion and Albanius* by generalizing the political messages that both were designed to convey.

Allusions to the Exclusion Crisis or the Rye House Plot are unlikely to be picked up by modern opera audiences. But *Albion and Albanius* is unintelligible without that knowledge, and basically pointless unless people reading or watching it performed identify with the protagonists. *King Arthur* is different: a typological enterprise, not an allegory. There were echoes of the Restoration narrative, but not a simple pre-run with names and locations changed. Dryden designed *King Arthur* to echo on through phases of real history that were still to come, to comment on the politics of his own age while sharing a generous vision of the future that neither he nor Charles II would live to see. Underpinned by Dryden's lyrics, Purcell's music for *King Arthur* has been performed continuously from 1691 through to the present.[48] Stage productions of *King Arthur* still happen from time to time, and whenever they do, seventeenth-century debates about the nature of Britishness are rekindled. Dryden deserves more credit than he is usually allowed for pulling durable threads from the time-bound fabric of the Stuart masque and weaving them (*pace* Hammond) 'into the eternity of true art'.

Albion and Albanius and *King Arthur* make good sense to readers who understand the context in which the works originated, but not much otherwise. The more we understand about that context, the more we will find to admire in writing intimately bound to it, and in modern performances that take the writing (even the stage directions) seriously. Through the study of court-originating culture at its most ambitious we can make a contribution to grand historical debate. Did Charles II and the Stuart dynasty want absolute rule?[49] Even if he did, was this a realistic ambition? In the last year of his life, Charles 'had been pleas'd twice or thrice to command, that [*Albion and Albanius*] shou'd be practic'd, before him, especially the first and third Acts of it' (Dryden: postscript to the *Albion and Albanius* preface). One of those practice runs happened at Windsor Castle on the king's birthday, 29 May 1684: Charles and his courtiers had gathered there to celebrate.[50] In Acts I and III, Charles-as-Albion triumphs gloriously. Because the lonely and dejected Albion of Act II pleased the king less, he commanded practice runs omitting it. This is what Dryden implies.

Merlin's Vision of Britain at the end of *King Arthur* centres on Charles II's Windsor Castle. The 'future Hero's' to whom Merlin entrusts the safety of the nation are Charles II and his Knight Companions. Charles saw himself as an absolute monarch, but in worlds of the imagination expensively created for him, not in the political day-to-day. Truths bravely acknowledged in *Calisto* – about his flawed character and morally corrosive leadership style – were not for telling in the public theatre. (*Calisto* of course had only been performed at court.) There was no longer humour to be found in that sort of satire. Charles was absorbed in absolutist role-play near the end of his career, but he must have known deep down that play was not the real thing.

Notes

1 J[ohn] Crowne, *Calisto: Or, the Chaste Nimph. The Late Masque at Court, as it Was Frequently Presented There, By Several Persons of Great Quality. With the Prologue, and the Songs Betwixt the Acts*, London: Tho[mas] Newcomb, 1675; 'Written by Mr. Dryden', *Albion and Albanius: An Opera. Perform'd at the Queens Theatre, in Dorset Garden*, London: Jacob Tonson, 1685, [compare with] *Albion and Albanius: An Opera. Or, Representation in Musick. Set by Lewis Grabu, Esquire Master of His Late Majesty's Musick*, London: Printed for the Author, 1687: 'Written by Mr. Dryden', *King Arthur: Or, The British Worthy. A Dramatick Opera. Perform'd at TGE Queens Theatre By Their Majesties Servants*, London: Jacob Tonson, 1691.

2 Much of the late seventeenth and early eighteenth century in Britain and Europe was concerned with monarchical dynasties compromised by their inability to produce stable, legitimate heirs. Charles II's illegitimate son claimed the throne in 1685. Charles II's brother, James II, was ousted for his Catholicism and that of his son, James, 'the Old Pretender', and his grandson, Charles Edward Stuart, 'Bonnie Prince Charlie', 'The Young Pretender', who launched a series of 'Jacobite' rebellions between 1689 and 1745 to reclaim the British Crown for the Stuarts and Catholicism.

3 S. Barber, 'Belshazzar's feast: Regicide, republicanism and the metaphor of balance', in J. Peacey (ed.), *The Regicides and the Execution of Charles I*, Basingstoke: Palgrave, 2001, pp. 71–116.

4 The best survey of the events and the period is T. Harris, *Restoration: Charles II and His Kingdoms, 1660–1685*, London: Allen Lane, 2005.

5 J. Crowne, 'Calisto, or, the Chaste Nymph (1675)', in J. Maidment and W. H. Logan (eds), *The Dramatic Works of John Crowne: Volume the First*, London: H. Sotheran, 1873.

6 E. Boswell, *The Restoration Court Stage (1660–1702), with a Particular Account of the Production of Calisto*, Cambridge, MA: Harvard University Press, 1936, pp. 180–2; A. Walkling, *Masque and Opera in England, 1656–1688*, Abingdon, NY: Routledge, 2017, pp. 96–101.

7 M. Jenkinson, *Culture and Politics at the Court of Charles II, 1660–1685*, Woodbridge: Boydell Press, 2010, p. 111.

8 Hardly anyone other than Charles knew why he had embarked on the Third Anglo-Dutch war in the first place. His 1670 secret treaty with France's Louis XIV (the pair were cousins) remained surprisingly secret till the early nineteenth century, and when the truth finally came out historians were scandalized. In return for subsidies supplied by Louis, Charles undertook to convert to Roman Catholicism himself, to lead his subjects back to Rome as soon as practicable, to soften or remove laws discriminating against Catholics in the meantime, and to join with Catholic France in a(nother) war against the Protestant Dutch Republic.

9 J. Miller, *Charles II*, London: Weidenfeld and Nicolson, 1991, p. 219.

10 See: H. M. Colvin and J. Newman, 'Windsor Castle', in H. M. Colvin (ed.), *The History of the King's Works*, London: HMSO, 1976, pp. 313–14, p. 318.

11 Colvin and Newman, 'Windsor Castle', p. 317.

12 C. Brett, 'Antonio Verrio (c1636–1707): His life and work', *British Art Journal*, 10.3 2009–10, 4–17.

13 J. Hook, *The Baroque Age in England*, London: Thames and Hudson, 1976, p. 138.

14 I have reproduced artwork from Pyne and Vandrebanc in a previously published article (Pinnock, 'Deus ex machina', see: n. 17) and do not intend to duplicate either the images or my full discussion of them here; W. H. Pyne, *The History of the Royal Residences, Vol. 1: The History of the Royal Palace of Windsor Castle; the History of the Queen's House, Frogmore*, London: A. Dry, 1819.

15 Charles I's suspension of parliamentary government in the 1630s was a major grievance that ushered in civil war to England.

Masque and opera 111

16 J. Dryden, *Albion and Albanius: An Opera*, London: Jacob Tonson, 1685.
17 Evidence pointing to this conclusion is open to interpretation and evidence showing that any planned performance(s) actually happened is entirely lacking: A. Pinnock, 'Deus Ex Machina: A royal witness to the court origin of Purcell's *Dido and Aeneas*', *Early Music*, 40.2, 2012, 265–78; A. Pinnock, 'Which genial day? More on the Court Origin of Purcell's *Dido and Aeneas*, with a shortlist of dates for its possible performance before King Charles II', *Early Music*, 43.2, 2015, 199–212; Walkling, *Masque and Opera*, 136–7. To avoid unproductive controversy, this chapter focuses on works about which more can be said with certainty.
18 J. Dryden, *King Arthur: Or, The British Worthy. A Dramatick Opera*, London: Jacob Tonson, 1691.
19 J. Milhous and R. D. Hume, *A Register of English Theatrical Documents 1660–1737*, Vol. 1, 1660–1714, Carbondale, IL: Southern Illinois University Press, 1991, p. 242.
20 B. White, *Louis Grabu: Albion and Albanius*, London: Stainer & Bell, 2007, Purcell Society Companion Series, 1, xi.
21 For the letter in full, see: C. E. Ward (ed.), *The Letters of John Dryden, With Letters Addressed to Him*, Durham, NC: Duke University Press, 1942, pp. 22–4.
22 S. Gale, *The History and Antiquities of the Cathedral Church of Winchester*, London: E. Curll, 1715.
23 Colvin and Newman, 'Windsor castle', pp. 311–12; B. Weiser, *Charles II and the Politics of Access*, Woodbridge: Boydell Press, 2003, pp. 46–53; S. Thurley, 'A country seat fit for a King: Charles II, Greenwich and Winchester', in E. Cruickshanks (ed.), *The Stuart Courts*, Stroud: Sutton Publishing, 2000, pp. 214–39.
24 G. Parry, *Glory, Laud and Honour: The Arts of the Anglican Counter-Reformation*, Woodbridge: Boydell Press, 2006, pp. 53–4.
25 See, for instance: Parry, *Glory*, p. 64.
26 R. Hutton, *Charles the Second: King of England, Scotland and Ireland*, Oxford: Clarendon Press, 1979, p. 453.
27 James I, King of England, *The Workes of the Most High and Mightie Prince, James [,] by the Grace of God, King of Great Britaine, France and Ireland, Defender of the Faith, &c.*, London: 'Printed by Robert Barker and John Bill, Printers to the Kings most Excellent Majestie', 1619 [Facsimile reprint 1971, Hildesheim: Georg Olms]; Elias Ashmole, *The Institution, Laws and Ceremonies of the Most Noble Order of the Garter*, London: N. Brooke, 1672 [facsimile reprint, London: Frederick Muller, 1971]; F. Sandford, *A Genealogical History of the Kings of England and Monarchs of Great Britain From the Conquest, Anno 1066, to the Year 1677*, London: Thomas Newcomb, printed for the author, 1677.
28 It was completed in 1633 but hidden away during the Commonwealth period (Parliament wanted it broken up): C. Stevenson, *The City and the King: Architecture and Politics in Restoration London*, New Haven, CT: Yale University Press, 2013, pp. 192–4.
29 Stevenson, *City and the King*, pp. 196–9.
30 Pinnock, 'Deus ex machina', p. 269 [Figure 4].
31 Ibid., p. 268 [Figure 3].
32 Pyne, *History of the Royal Residences*, Vol. 1, p. 170.
33 Hume and Milhous, *Register*, i, 253.
34 K. Gibson, 'The decoration of St George's Hall, Windsor, for Charles II: "Too resplendent bright for subjects' eyes"', *Apollo*, 147.435, 1996, 33–40, p. 36.
35 The brightest of seven stars comprising 'Charles's Wain', probably; Charles's Wain being the 'English cognomen for the hindquarters of the constellation Ursa Major ("The Big [or Greater] Bear")'. M. A. Brown, 'The Pleiadic Age of Stuart posie: Restoration uranography, Dryden's judicial astrology, and the fate of Anne Killigrew', Unpublished MA thesis, Georgia State University, 2010, pp. 48–9.
36 As n. 30.
37 Hook, *Baroque Age*, p. 136.

38 Gibson, 'Decoration of St George's Hall'; Brett, 'Verrio'; Pinnock, 'Deus ex machina'; Pinnock, 'Which genial day?'.
39 Years of cheap and cautious programming followed *Albion*'s commercial flop.
40 Dryden may have arrived at the number ten by subtracting two from the total number of Arthurian victories given in John Milton's *History of Britain*: there are two battles yet to come: J. Milton, *The History of Britain* (1670), 2nd edn., London: James Allestry, 1677. Despite claims in his *King Arthur* preface, Dryden may not have read much beyond Milton when researching the historical background.
41 A. Pinnock, 'A double vision of albion: Allegorical re-alignments in the dryden-purcell semi-opera *King Arthur*', *Restoration: Studies in English Literary Culture, 1660–1700*, 34, 2010–11, 55–81.
42 R. W. Bevis, *English Drama: Restoration and Eighteenth Century, 1660–1789*, London: Routledge, 2014, p. 180.
43 A. Pinnock, '*King Arthur* Expos'd: A Lesson in Anatomy', in C. A. Price (ed.), *Purcell Studies*, Cambridge: Cambridge University Press, 1995, pp. 243–56; Pinnock, 'Double vision'.
44 J. Dryden, 'A discourse concerning the Original and Progress of Satire (1693)', in G. Watson (ed.), *John Dryden: Of Dramatic Poesy and Other Critical Essays*, Vol. 2, London: J.M. Dent & Sons, 1962.
45 R. Strong, *Britannia Triumphans: Inigo Jones, Rubens and Whitehall Palace*, London: Thames and Hudson, 1980, pp. 19–20.
46 J. A. Winn, *John Dryden and His World*, New Haven, CT: Yale University Press, 1987, p. 420.
47 P. Hammond, 'Dryden's *Albion and Albanius* and the Apotheosis of Charles II', in D. Lindley (ed.), *The Court Masque*, Manchester: Manchester University Press, 1984, pp. 169–83.
48 Generally, modern performances of early operas are semi-staged. One recent staging was at the Royal Opera in Versailles, 7–9 December 2018 (Hervé Niquet for Le Concert Spirituel; Production: Opéra National de Montpellier Languedoc-Roussillon, co-production with the Festival de Radio-France et Montpellier Languedoc-Roussillon): with the gloss that 'The legend comes back to life conducted by Hervé Niquet, one of the masters of this repertoire, directing the Concert Spirituel, in a staging by Corinne and Gilles Benizio, aka Shirley and Dino, who combine poetry and fantasy, without affecting Purcell's powerful music: an original and fascinating evening which enchanted the public when it was created!'.
49 G. Tapsell, *The Personal Rule of Charles II, 1681–85*, Woodbridge: Boydell Press, 2010, p. 32.
50 Pinnock, 'Which genial day?', pp. 206–8 and Figure 4.

Further reading

Burden, Michael, 'To repeat (or not to repeat)? Dance cues in Restoration English opera', *Early Music*, 35.3, 2007, 397–418.

Cant, Sarah G. and Nina J. Morris, 'Geographies of art and the environment', *Social & Cultural Geography*, 7.6, 2006, 857–61.

Dent, Edward J., *Foundations of English Opera: A Study of Musical Drama in England During the Seventeenth Century*, Cambridge: Cambridge University Press, 1928.

Hume, Robert D., 'The politics of opera in late seventeenth-century London', *Cambridge Opera Journal*, 10.1, 1988, 15–43.

Remshardt, Ralf, '*Die Dreigroschenoper* (The Threepenny Opera), and: The Masque of the Red Death (Review)', *Theatre Journal*, 60.4, 2008, 639–43.

Viljoen, Martina, '"An aesthetic of redemption": Reading *Masque* as public culture', *MUZIKI*, 3.1, 2006, 114–33.

Walkling, Andrew R., *Masque and Opera in England, 1656–1688*, Abingdon: Routledge, 2017.

6 Radio

Listening to the airwaves

Tony Stoller

For nearly a century, sound broadcasting – 'radio' – has been ever-present in the Western world, and beyond. After it began to be used for wide-scale public purposes in the early 1920s, by the 1930s virtually everybody in Britain listened to the radio. Even now, in the post-television age of the internet and digital media, in the UK 90 percent of adults still listen to the radio each week.[1] Not only has it been ever-present, it is also ubiquitous, going into every aspect of public and private life. It can hold your attention in the foreground of your awareness, and/or you can listen to the radio while doing virtually anything else. This combination of being both a primary and secondary medium at the same time gives radio a unique salience.

It is therefore an unrivalled resource for the historian, both in its own right and for the light it throws on social, economic and political history in general over the past century. If the historian can become an effective time traveller, addressing radio in the context of its time, they can literally eavesdrop on the past. Sterne, Street and Hendy have all highlighted the power of sound as a point of entry into cultural history (and the cultural present).[2] From the moment (in the 1920s) when radio recordings became available, that potency is released for the historian as an increasingly wide-ranging and comprehensive resource.

This chapter will consider first the history and next the nature of sound broadcasting, including the debate about foreground or background listening, and how this affects the relevance of radio for the enquiring historian. It will then look at the opportunities and methodological challenges posed by the various sources of information, which include written archives, increasingly available online data and recordings of the radio programmes themselves, before considering in detail how to access and listen to the wide range of available sound recordings.

In conclusion, three case studies will demonstrate the importance of radio as a source both for the media historian, and to illustrate broader social and political events: the contrast between state-sponsored BBC radio and intrusive continental commercial radio in the 1930s; the rise of offshore pirate radio in the 1960s; and the arrival of Classic FM, to challenge the BBC's final monopoly – national radio – in the early 1990s. The chapter will then conclude with some observations about how radio can be used by the historian to understand more about the events and context of social political and economic history.

A very brief history of radio

The technology of sound broadcasting has been around for over a century. Although historians may dispute who was the actual 'founder' of radio, we usually date the beginning of wireless transmissions from 12 December 1901, with the Italian inventor Guglielmo Marconi's successful transmission of signals from Cornwall on the western tip of England to Newfoundland in Canada.[3] Probably the first example of 'radio', as we understand it, was the programme transmitted by R. A. Fessenden in Branch Rock, Massachusetts, on Christmas Eve 1906.[4] In Britain, the Marconi Company's experimental station MZX provided the first radio broadcast in January 1920, and after a brief attempt by the British government to reserve sound broadcasting for military and official purposes, the Marconi Company once again was first on air with 2MT from Writtle in February 1922, and then 2LO in London.[5] A slew of other companies rushed to join the enterprise, and in October of that year formed the British Broadcasting Company which was to translate into the intentional monopoly of the British Broadcasting Corporation, set up by Royal Charter in January 1927.

This sketch of radio's earliest years already illustrates how the development of the medium was interwoven with the social and political requirements and prejudices of its time and how understanding the way in which sound broadcasting came to Britain is a route into appreciating the broader context. The free market ruled in the US, which released its commercial vibrancy, but it also produced what the British Postmaster General regarded as 'a sort of chaos'.[6] In Britain, the new medium was to be carefully contained within a regulated structure to operate in what those who then dominated society regarded as the public interest.

For the BBC's founding Director General, John Reith, that meant for example not broadcasting popular music to any great extent and not at all on Sundays. The BBC's monopoly, and its anti-populist approach, opened the way for rival, commercial radio services to broadcast from the near continent into Britain.[7] Throughout the 1930s, stations such as Radio Luxembourg provided a well-received service of popular music and light entertainment, and might well have led to a similar approach on the British mainland had the Second World War not intervened – literally in the case of the transmitting stations, which were overrun by German Panzer divisions in May 1940.

After the war, thanks to the BBC's real achievements in radio, and the reputation that it had carefully cultivated, there could be no thought of a challenge to the Corporation's radio monopoly in the UK. Change came much sooner in television, where Independent Television (ITV), as part of a statutorily regulated duopoly, began broadcasting from 1956 onwards. The wartime radio pattern, however, had been very different from the more monolithic prewar BBC radio service. Alongside a more serious Home Service, there were extensive popular broadcasts in first of all a Forces Programme, and then the General Forces Programme, indicating the breadth of demand for radio.[8] The BBC responded in 1945 by establishing three national services: the Home Service, the Light Programme and the highly innovative Third Programme, described by Hennessy as 'the kind of cultural gem that could only have been produced in early postwar Britain under conditions of broadcasting monopoly'.[9]

This pattern of three quite broadly based radio services, national but with some regional opt outs, continued until the end of the Sixties. At that point, in the wake of a report commissioned from management consultants McKinsey and entitled *Broadcasting in the 70s*, the BBC shifted to four national radio stations, each aiming to be generic: Radio One for pop music; Radio Two for light music and light entertainment; Radio Three for classical music and some serious cultural output; and Radio Four for news, commentary on current affairs and drama.[10] From late 1967 onwards, some local radio stations in England and gradually developing national services in Scotland, Wales and Northern Ireland had been added to this mix.

The reason for the changes advocated by *Broadcasting in the 70s* was not hard to seek. On Easter Day 1964, Irish entrepreneur Ronan O'Reilly began broadcasting Radio Caroline from the ship *Mi Amigo*, moored outside UK territorial limits, which was swiftly followed by a fleet of pirate radio stations.[11] These offshore, non-legal radio services were hugely successful. Discussed in more detail as the second case study, they provide a striking example of how cultural and societal change hugely altered the pattern of radio, and how the new radio services themselves both played into and help to explain what was happening more generally within British society.

Although the offshore pirate stations were shut down (more or less) in 1967, one of their legacies was the breaking of the BBC's radio monopoly. From 1973 onwards, once again in the type of tightly regulated context which had applied to the arrival of ITV, Independent Local Radio (ILR) stations spread across the UK; haltingly at first – as the political considerations needed to be resolved – but then covering the whole of the country by the end of the 1980s.[12] That system moved steadily towards increasing deregulation, so that full-scale commercial radio had arrived at the turn of the century. ILR was joined in the early 1990s by Independent National Radio (INR), as first Classic FM and then Virgin and Talk Radio infiltrated the last remaining citadel of BBC exclusivity. The arrival of Classic FM comprises the third case study in this chapter.

As society evolves, so radio changes with it. The arrival of digital transmission technology from the 1990s onwards represents and will continue to represent the next great change for what used to be 'the wireless', just as digitisation is changing the nature of the UK economy and polity, and the position of the individual within it.[13] Once again, an understanding of what is happening more broadly will inform future media historians, while an appreciation of the development of radio will help the general historian identify the broader trends within society and provide extensive individual illustrations of their impact.

The nature of radio listening

The nature of the auditory experience changed irreversibly from the start of the twentieth century. With the 'invention' of the telephone by Alexander Graham

Bell in 1876 and the gramophone by Thomas Edison in 1877, sound could be reproduced mechanically. In that form, it became all-pervasive for people in the developed world. Nothing was more instrumental in this than radio. Walter Benjamin identified the availability of art and culture for 'simultaneous reception by large numbers of people' as a defining feature of the changed world of the twentieth century.[14] Yet radio made the change even greater, multiplying the dissemination of culture and of cultural artefacts through the mechanical reproduction of every available sound. More than that, it continued through virtually all other quotidian activity. David Hendy, in his *History of Noise*, reports a BBC observation of one family in South Wales in 1938: '[e]ven if they are not listening with their full attention, they are still listening. Even in the background, radio's burble is still more than a meaningless noise. And if it wasn't there they would miss it like hell'.[15]

The capacity of radio to function as both a primary and secondary medium is central to its significance for the historian. For those studying the medium itself, the key is radio's ability to be at the same time a background entertainer and a foreground informer and educator, which gives it its unique impact, and has allowed it to survive all the rival media and technological changes of the past hundred years. The same listener can and does switch between treating radio as part of their background auditory atmosphere to giving it the very closest attention. In that way, they remain entirely fixed in, and representative of, the times and circumstances in which they are living. Kate Lacey's exploration of the nature of listening publics stresses the primacy in this respect of sound over visual electronic media:

> radio probably survived (which means people actively continued to invest in it, promote, support and listen to it) because listening-without-looking meant music and the worlds conjured by the spoken word in the imagination could be woven into the patterns of everyday life, accompanying domestic and mobile routines and providing incidental companionship. But it might also have had something to do with the elective affinity between a listening and a pluralistic, public sensibility.[16]

This is not necessarily always benign. As societal and economic contexts change, so the role of radio shifts also. Susan Douglas has noted with alarm the way in which, in the United States, the disappearance of traditional locality and community-based radio has diminished the broadcast output and the listening experience:

> This same device that worked so powerfully, through comedy and drama, sports and news, to forge a powerful sense of national identity in the Thirties is now working ... to cultivate and encourage cultural segregation. ... Changing corporate imperatives – first for national markets, now for niche markets – have influenced our sensory relationships to the outside world. And at the end of the century our modes of listening, once so varied and rich, are truncated. Story listening and news listening on the radio, with their

requirements for dimensional listening and detailed imaginings are virtually gone from the dial, except on NPR.[17]

Although commercial radio in the UK has followed the American model of consolidated ownership and networking, the very existence of the BBC has made its impact less significant, which is a further example of how radio as a medium affects and is affected by the wider context in which it operates and is a valuable signifier of that context.

The experience of listening to the radio has been differentiated from other auditory participation through the twentieth century by its typical 'liveness'. As James Cridland has observed,

> there is a difference between 'radio' and 'audio' in terms of consumption. . . . The difference between them is one of liveness and connection. If you are listening to a live radio signal there is a (subconscious) knowledge that you are listening along with other people.[18]

Yet that poses a particular challenge to the historian. Recorded sound in the form of, for example, gramophone records has a good long 'shelf life'. Radio, in its essence, is broadcast and gone (or was so, until the arrival of 'listen again' technology in the new century). To access this ephemeral resource requires an approach to archives different from any other primary source.

Methodological opportunities and challenges

Radio as an historical source can be approached in three ways: (1) through written archive material; (2) increasingly through the availability of online records and analysis; and (3) through the radio programmes themselves. This chapter draws upon the author's experience of research in the UK, and the examples are drawn from British experience. In other Anglophone countries, reflecting their geography, archive sources are more dispersed, but comparisons will be offered where they are appropriate.

The primary documentary source is the BBC's own paper archive. The Written Archive Centre (WAC) in Caversham, Reading.[19] It provides access to an immense range of files from the start of the Corporation up until 1979. The catalogue and the files themselves can be consulted by appointment, and this is very much the first port of call for any historical analysis of BBC radio. There are some obvious limitations. More recent material is not available unless it is specially cleared by the BBC's archivists, which is a demanding and time-consuming process. Some material is restricted or redacted in order to protect the privacy of individuals. Nevertheless, this is a key primary source. For the US, the Records of the Federal Communications Commission and the Office of Education offer equivalent materials, as do a number of collections within the Library of Congress. The National Public Broadcasting Archive, housed at the University of Maryland, and the Library of American Broadcasting is the central source, although material is widely dispersed in individual collections held in universities across the country.[20] For Australia, the Australian Broadcasting Corporation archives provide a service analogous to that of the BBC in the UK and the National Film and Sound Archive (NFSA) holds some broadcast content of key national events.[21] In Canada, the CBC Digital Archive offers radio clips from over 75 years of broadcasting by CBC/Radio Canada, while in New Zealand 70,000 sound recordings from Radio New Zealand have been preserved by transfer to the New Zealand Film Archive in 2013.[22]

For non-BBC radio in the UK, the files of the Independent Television Authority and the Independent Broadcasting Authority are now held in a specific archive within Bournemouth University, and can be consulted by bone fide researchers.[23] The Bournemouth archive is much less exploited so far, and can yield much original and unexpected material. More recent archive material for the commercial sector is still held by the successor regulatory body, Ofcom, both its own materials and the archive of the Radio Authority. At present, this can only be accessed through Freedom of Information requests, but there are moves to bring it together with the ITA/IBA archive so that it can become more easily available. In both the UK and the US, there is much less archive material available from the commercial sector. The National Association of Broadcasters archive in Washington is a members-only resource.

A further central written primary source is programme listings, in *Radio Times* for BBC (and to a very small extent national commercial radio) and in *Radio Pictorial* for the pre-war European commercial radio stations broadcasting into Britain. Although programmes listed were not invariably broadcast as such, those listings can be checked against the actual production logs which are available at the WAC. Of great recent significance is the BBC Genome Project, that makes available in an online archive all of *Radio Times* listings and can be searched by a whole range of parameters.[24] This is a developing facility. At the time of writing this chapter, it is reported that the BBC intends to make available online all of the scripts from its news broadcasts on radio, possibly across the entire period of the Corporation's existence. Once again, that will provide a major research source for the historian, which can be searched by keyword terms for any period required.

Professor Hugh Chignell regards the act of listening to programmes to be fundamental, and that failing to do so 'is a mistake because it assumes that sound content of different types can be reduced to a written or other visual record. What old programmes and other content sound like should I think be given priority wherever possible'. He urges a similar approach for the both the media historian and the general historian:

> As more archive material becomes available I think general and especially cultural historians will turn to sound archives for particular subject areas. This is a complicated area but I would argue with reference to my current research that attitudes towards gender and class in particular are revealed in some detail by listening to post-war radio drama. A more straightforward example is the Falklands War which the general historian can now study

using the daily IRN news reports sent by Kim Sabido who was with the task force. I have done similar work on the Suez crisis and radio news does provide a particular type of unfolding record of events.[25]

There are three main sound broadcasting archives in Britain: (1) the British Library; (2) the BBC; and (3) the British Universities Film and Video Council (BUFVC).

The British Library Sound collection is outstanding, although it requires the researcher to get used to the particular ways in which it can be accessed. In essence, there are two separate services: the first provides access to a quarter of a million hours of radio recording, which can be listened to at the Library itself; the second is on-request access to around one million additional hours within the collections of the BBC sound archive. The range of material is astonishing, from the oldest surviving British radio recording of George V opening the British Empire exhibition in 1924 through to the present day. Paul Wilson, the radio curator at the British Library (who has provided much of the material for this section), reports that since 1963 radio broadcasts have been recorded off-air to create a core collection of around 60,000 hours. This has been augmented by around 200 individual named collections acquired from industry sources, such as Capital Radio, LBC/IRN and Resonance FM, and from producers, engineers, musicians, academics, journalists and home record recording enthusiasts and collectors. In addition, the Library holds thousands of BBC archive discs and BBC transcription discs.

Owing to rights issues, currently only a small proportion of the radio collections can be accessed offsite from the Library's online collection of British Library sounds but a significant increase in the amount available is anticipated as the Library's *Unlocking Our Sound Heritage* project (the core element of the *Save Our Sounds* programme) progresses.[26] The *Save Our Sounds* programme is currently in the process of digitising much of the Library's unique sound content, including many of its hitherto unavailable radio collections. A new *Sounds* website is also being designed to present these expanded collections of historical content online. A second strand of the *Save Our Sounds* programme, the National Radio Archive, is a pilot project aimed at building a more representative archive of UK radio today, captured from the output of around 50 stations around the country and representing all broadcast sectors: BBC network, nations and local, commercial radio sector, community radio and independent producers. A third strand of the programme will additionally collect podcast content and other radio-type media now being published online.[27]

In addition to the material available through the British Library, the BBC is gradually making available more sound archive material. It is, however, conditioned by what was for many years a restrictive attitude towards a recording of programmes of broadcasting, let alone for archive purposes. All early programmes were live, to the extent that there was hardly any recording machinery available. In his introduction to the online archive, BBC Sound Archivist Simon Rooks notes also that there was 'some kind of prejudice against recordings being broadcast, as not being quite real'.[28]

The continental commercial stations which were broadcasting radio into Britain needed to have better recording and play-out facilities. As Street notes, 'the mass audience stations required fare of a more elaborate kind to maintain their audience figures and such artists as George Robey, Geraldo and his orchestra and Debroy Somers could only be captured by recorded means, mostly in London'.[29] Gradually, recordings on location became more common, and it became credible to develop an archive of actual programmes. Rooks again notes that, while this included 'the great and the good – the Churchills, the Chamberlains, Nancy Astor, the first woman MP to take her seat – so all kind of eminent people that you might expect' there was an increasing understanding of the importance of keeping the experiences of ordinary people.[30]

In recent years, the BBC has begun to make more sound recordings available. In the main, it has so far chosen to release sound archives of 'prestige' programme series. *Desert Island Discs* is available online in fragmentary form between its launch in 1942 and 1959, and fully thereafter, as are Alistair Cooke's *Letters from America* from 1946 to 2004. The historian will find these of value but may also fret at the unavailability of more routine and less polished output, which is in itself also very revealing of events and times. For the years between 1973 and 1990, that omission can be partly rectified through the British Universities Film and Video Council (BUFVC) archive of output from the ILR station LBC, and the Independent Radio News (IRN) service which supplied national and international news across all ILR stations. Chignell recounts his own experience of accessing the LBC/IRN archive:

> One of the most accessible sound archives is the LBC/IRN archive hosted on the BUFVC website. If we take a subject like football fans, or HIV/AIDS, it is possible to find a number of short clips from the mid Seventies to the Nineties where reporters using vox pops or discussions in studios reveal attitudes to something from several decades ago.[31]

A potential major development in the availability of sound material is the BBC's Connected History project, based at the University of Sussex.[32] Begun in 2017, this is intended to bring into the public realm the BBC's 'oral history' archive, which comprises over 600 interviews with former BBC staff and is a valuable tool chiefly for the media historian. The availability of the transcripts had been quite constrained hitherto, with the BBC only releasing these to the researcher when the subject is no longer alive, and the material has been checked (and often partly redacted). As Professor David Hendy explains, the new project 'aims not just to make these individual records available to researchers and the general public; it aims to make them available as a unified, fully searchable, and robustly accurate collection'. This involves preparing an online catalogue, creating new digital transcripts and managing the relevant metadata. At this stage, it is unlikely that the bulk of the material will be available until the end of 2021. However, in parallel with this, Hendy notes that 'the BBC Connected Histories project will be "releasing" extracts and sample downloadable typescripts from the collection through a series of BBC-hosted websites: "100 Voices that Made the BBC".'[33] At the time of writing, there have been three such websites launched covering the history of election broadcasting (2015), the birth of television (2016) and the re-emergence of radio in the 1960s (2017). Five more are currently planned, in line with the BBC's usual enthusiasm for anniversaries with an eye to their topicality. The recorded sound collection in the Library of Congress in the US is an outstanding and multifaceted archival resource. Its website also offers wide-ranging listings of sound archival collections.[34]

Case studies

The case studies presented here are three examples of specific historical events examined through the medium of sound broadcasting. Many iconic incidents in the history of radio might have been chosen, such as the BBC's response to the 1926 General Strike, wartime radio or the introduction of the Third Programme in 1946. These case studies cover less well-trodden ground and look at the sound broadcasting medium as a whole rather than just the institutional arrangements within the BBC. Each throws new light on a separate decade in British history, illuminating a pivotal time in both media and general history.

Case study one: British commercial radio in the 1930s

The accomplished student of history quickly learns to be suspicious of the pervasive historical myths, especially where those have entered uncritically into casual discourse. One of those, affecting both the general historian and the media historian, is of an all-powerful, benign and paternalistic BBC through the 1930s, which by winning the hearts and minds of the British people prepared them for the existential struggle of the Second World War in which it played such a major and uniquely positive role.

The last of these observations is probably true, up to a point. However, the standard version of the role of BBC radio in the 1930s suggests a society that was deferential and formal to an improbable degree, with that radio monolith playing the only broadcasting part. That was not the case, as Street has demonstrated in *Crossing the Ether*.[35] The story of those 'other' radio services says a great deal about the nature of society at that time, and the seeds which were stirring within it and which would find fruit in the social and political radicalism of 1945 to 1951.

This first case study therefore looks at Britain in the Thirties through the little-used lens of the huge popularity of commercial radio stations broadcasting into the UK from the near continent: Radio Luxembourg, foremost among them. In most contemporary memory, Radio Luxembourg is its postwar incarnation. A popular music broadcaster, what has stuck in public consciousness is the novelty of its advertisements for Ovaltine, Horace Batchelor's football pools advice and Bulova watches. It was listened to through the 1950s on an increasingly unsatisfactory medium wave channel of 208, in the evenings and overnight often under the bedclothes to avoid parental disapproval. There were equivalent developments in the

US in this period. Goodman writes of the role of American commercial radio in supporting the democratic paradigm of American society. In a reversal of modern expectations, for example, the commercial giants of US broadcasting were extensive providers of classical music, seeing that as both a civic and a business imperative.[36]

The prewar pattern was much grander and of much greater importance. Radio Luxembourg, Radio Paris, Radio Normandy, Radio Toulouse and the other continental English-language stations attracted audience levels in their millions and challenged not only the BBC but the wider prevailing social image of a dour and deferential society. They were also avowedly commercial, taking advantage of the opportunities left by a strait-laced BBC, especially in the provision of popular music and overwhelmingly on Sundays, when Presbyterian John Reith would not permit dance music to sully the Sabbath.[37]

Although there had been some English language broadcasts by continental stations in the late 1920s, it was the newly formed International Broadcasting Company (IBC), which was the key operator throughout the 1930s of what was initially Radio Fecamp and then Radio Normandy, and from the middle of 1933, a new Radio Luxembourg English language service on longwave from a powerful transmitter.[38] The aptly named Captain Leonard Plugge was the driving force behind the IBC. Street speaks of him as 'one of the most remarkable personalities in British broadcasting, a man who went on to become a millionaire through radio and about whom legends grew up'.[39] He was MP for Chatham from 1935 until the outbreak of war in 1939, had driven trains during the General Strike and owned a yacht in Cannes and a villa overlooking Hyde Park. He could scarcely have been more unlike John Reith – except perhaps in the force of his personality and his eccentricity – and between them they represented not just the twin poles of radio broadcasting but the divided character of British society between the wars.

The competition between state-sanctioned and intrusive commercial radio in the UK in the 1930s was paradigmatic of British society in these years. The BBC was a creature of the British state, self-consciously worthy, serious, high-minded, culturally aspirational and – for all its supposed popularity – rather 'above' the ordinary people, even when they were committed listeners. The commercial alternative lived outside British jurisdiction, and was commercial, populist and brash. Both attracted very substantial audiences. Commercial radio's audience research in 1938 claimed an improbably high level of listening, but even the BBC's own research suggested that perhaps 10 percent of radio listening was to these commercial stations on weekdays, rising to as much as 27 percent on Sundays.[40] There is little doubt that the BBC was rattled by competition, which felt – and at times was presented as being – *lese majesté*.

It is customary to view the great divide in Britain in the 1930s as being between Mosley's fascist Black Shirts and their communist opponents. That is valid at the extremes, but closer to the centre an equally telling juxtaposition would be between those who defended the BBC at all costs and those who promoted an alternative commercial radio approach. For the majority of listeners, it was unlikely to have been one or the other, but patronage of both according to mood and circumstances. It may be credibly argued that this division persists to the present day, and that disputes about over-elitism on the one hand and dumbing-down on the other represent a continuation of the argument and its historical significance.

Primary audio sources are quite limited for this period. As discussed earlier, there was a presumption within the BBC against making recordings. The commercial stations on the other hand owed much of their success to the ability to record material in the UK that could then be shipped across to Luxembourg for broadcasting.[41] Even so, relatively little remains for the historian today. The key primary sources are listings magazines: *Radio Times* for the BBC, and – less thoroughly mined by scholars – *Radio Pictorial* for the commercial sector.

Case study two: offshore pirate radio 1964–1967

For the general social and political historian (and for that matter for the media historian as well), the offshore pirate radio phenomenon between 1964 and 1967 provides a telling case study for understanding how the varied influences of the 1960s played out in a practical way both in Parliament and in people's everyday lives.

Rock 'n' roll arguably began in earnest when Elvis Presley recorded *Heartbreak Hotel* for RCA in Nashville on 10 January 1956. The explosion of pop music that followed it linked perfectly with the growing social empowerment of young people in the Western world. The devising of the transistor in 1948 by Bardeen, Brattain and Shockley meant that the old symbol of prewar and wartime patriarchal authority – the wireless set – was replaced by affordable, plastic, portable receivers that would be produced in the tens of millions. The relevance of artefacts to historical study has become more significant in recent years, and the transistor radio holds a significant place in this lineage, representing in physical form the significant postwar opportunity for radio to reinvent itself as a medium and to escape from the dominance of television.

Britain however adjusted uneasily to the social revolution of the 1960s, and nowhere was that better demonstrated than in the response of the providers of sound broadcasting.[42] The BBC decided it would promote the more wholesome British equivalent, skiffle, and would try to keep the 'pollution' of rock 'n' roll 'at arms length'.[43] As a consequence, while the market for record 'singles' exploded, radio offered barely more than a couple of hours of pop music a week. There were political moves to introduce some form of alternative, popular radio services in the early 1960s, but these were dashed by successive centrist Conservative and Labour governments.[44]

Seizing the opportunity, an armada of offshore pirate radio stations sprang up around the coasts of Britain. As noted earlier, their flagship was Ronan O'Reilly's Radio Caroline, which began broadcasting on Easter Day 1964. It was followed by Radio Atlanta on 27 April 1964, and before long, Radio London, Radio Invicta, Radio City, Radio Northsea, Radio Scotland, Radio England, Radio Britain, Invicta Radio and others. The young (invariably male) disc jockeys followed what they understood to be the American pattern of pop music radio: 'Atlanta had about 150 long playing records and about 500 singles. Their music was for a family type of programme consisting of pop ballads'.[45] The most popular of stations, Radio Caroline and Radio London, were soon each claiming 8 million listeners each week.[46]

'Pirate radio' as it was universally known, was the lodestone of young people's experience in the later 1960s. It is possible to argue an equivalence between these illegal stations and the illegal listening to radio in the communist bloc, then and later, although UK pirate radio had a peculiarly British flavour. It was not even necessarily illegal, and it took a new Act of Parliament – the Marine &c Broadcasting Offences Act of 1967 – to shut the stations down.[47] By then, however, there was no going back to the pre-lapsarian days when the thirst for popular music could be slaked by middle-of-the-road broadcasts such as *Family Favourites* and *Housewives Choice*. The BBC launched its own pop music channel, Radio One, and the grand institution of the Corporation was never to be quite the same again. Even that was not enough, and an incoming Conservative government in 1970 initiated the introduction of a competitive radio service, funded by advertising, although still not freed of all the constraints of public service.

General broadcasting historians devote little attention to this phenomenon. Volume V of Asa Briggs' monumental *History of Broadcasting* (better thought of as the history of the BBC) allots it only some 15 pages from a total of over 1,000.[48] A fictional feature film, *The Boat that Rocked*, offers a pastiche of life on board these elderly and uncomfortable ships; Radio Caroline for example had launched on a converted Baltic ferryboat, the *Frederica*. But to understand it properly 'you had to be there', and no one reports on that better than pirate DJ – and later BBC stalwart, then legitimate radio manager – Keith Skues, in his two books entitled *Pop Went the Pirates*. To read these is to get a genuine flavour of aspirational life in the 1960s, where young people were trying to throw off the shackles of postwar conventionality but were substantially conditioned and limited by those conventions. The sound of the stations is chiefly available on CDs produced by and for Radio Caroline and Radio London, providing an audio entry into the impactful yet essentially bourgeois nature of this peculiarly British revolution.[49]

The heroes of Paris in May 1968, such as Tariq Ali and Danny Cohn-Bendit, went on to become public intellectuals or politicians. The UK heroes of the pirate radio stations between 1964 and 1967 went on to become household names in the bourgeois institution of the BBC: Tony Blackburn, Tommy Vance, Ed Stuart, Johnny Walker, Emperor Roscoe, John Peel, Kenny Everett and Roger Day. Revolutionary social upheaval and change was averted in a manner illustrated by the way in which offshore pirate radio was first anathematised, then legislated against, then replaced by a sanitised state-based alternative, then moved into the commercial sector and eventually absorbed into the body politic and mainstream popular culture.[50]

Case study three: the arrival of Classic FM

Of all the developments in terrestrial broadcasting in the 1990s, the arrival of Classic FM was one of the most significant and dramatic. As first analogue satellite and then digital technologies began to challenge the hegemony of 'old style' broadcasting, Classic FM broke the last remaining BBC monopoly – on national radio – and both encapsulated and spoke to the culture of what was described as 'Mondeo man', foreshadowing Tony Blair's New Labour Britain.[51] That it came within a whisker of not happening illustrates precisely the mixture of ambition and muddle which characterised the shift from social liberalism to market liberalism in these years.

These events are still relatively recent, and many of the sources are journalistic rather than documentary. This writer's own book, *Classical Music Radio in the United Kingdom 1945 to 1995* is the only major work examining the phenomenon of Classic FM in detail, although the context is set out well in Humphrey Carpenter's *The Envy of the World* that is centred upon the BBC's Radio Three and its predecessor, the Third Programme.[52] Nevertheless, for the media historian or the general historian there is a wealth of sound material available which enables one to listen to the output. Through the British Library's sound collections, the BBC's Genome information about programme listings and the websites of both Classic FM and Radio Three, the researcher is well placed to inhabit and understand the sound world of the Nineties.

Politics and broadcasting intertwined in the 1980s and 1990s. The government of Margaret Thatcher, which had shown scant faith in the existing public service-obligated ITV system, was completely shattered when Thames Television broadcast the documentary *Death on the Rock* on 28 April 1988. It reported on the killing by SAS soldiers in Gibraltar of three unarmed (at that moment) IRA terrorists who had planned to bomb a military parade in Gibraltar. Memories of the attempt by the IRA on 12 October 1984 to assassinate Prime Minister Thatcher, with a bomb in her Party Conference hotel in Brighton, were still fresh, and the fury unleashed by the Thames TV programme was the catalyst for a complete reshaping of commercial television and radio in 1990.

For radio, this involved three new commercial national radio services, from 1992 onwards. Imitating the new approach to licensing ITV, these radio licences were to be awarded by a new regulator, the Radio Authority, to the highest cash bid, but beyond that there were no initial stipulations. However, typical of evolution rather than revolution in UK governance, the new services were still to be overseen by a regulator that retained some of the powers and much of the attitude of its predecessors.[53] It had among other things to decide which of the three possible services would operate on FM, with the other two consigned to the increasingly outdated platform of AM. That allowed it to bring into play at least some of the value judgements from the pre-1990 social liberal approach to the regulation of broadcasting in the public interest.

The Authority therefore sought from government powers that were not in the original legislation, to be able to require that the national FM service not be a popular music service.[54] Confirming this in a House of Lords debate, the Conservative minister, Earl Ferrers, seemed to hope that not all of the qualities of the old were being sacrificed in the pursuit of the new: 'I am pleased to reassure your Lordships that it will not be all thump, thump, thump.'[55]

Nevertheless, although they were aware of the possibility of an application from the group describing itself as Classic FM, the Radio Authority was not permitted to specify a classical music service, and the highest cash bid was received from a group calling itself Showtime, which offered light music from the shows.[56] In a less nuanced and serendipitous world than Britain in the early Nineties, that would have been that. However, Showtime was unable to raise its promised capital funding by the deadline. The Radio Authority, therefore, turned to the second highest bidder, Classic FM, to invite it to try to provide the necessary wherewithal for a classical music station. It managed to do that with just 20 minutes to spare, delivering the documents to the Radio Authority at 11:40 am on 30 September 1991.

Thus, Classic FM came about through a combination of the aspiration of the regulatory establishment, legislative imprecision, and good luck. This was an accidental revolution in British radio, but one with huge impact nevertheless. The story of its arrival is for media historians perhaps the last flourish of the old terrestrial, analogue broadcasting. For historians of the UK generally, it demonstrates how an archetypal change came about partly through a shifting governing philosophy, and partly through sheer accident. For most of the benign consequences of the last two decades of the twentieth century, that may be seen as archetypal.

Classic FM was immediately successful. The first audience research into the station demonstrated that it had attracted over four million listeners – roughly double that of Radio Three – and it retained and increased that level of patronage thereafter.[57] Classic FM spoke to the newly socially enfranchised and property-owning middle-class; those who had benefited from the reforms of the Thatcher government and who now looked for their own place in the cultural sun. While Alan Bennett might deride them as 'Saga louts', these were ordinary people enjoying the tunes and more provided by classical music from which they had previously been excluded.[58] After the Third Programme had launched on 26 September 1946 and attracted an audience almost one in three of whom were working class, the BBC had lamented that these listeners would be 'unable to engage in with it on equal terms'. When Classic FM launched on 7 September 1992, its multimillion audience was celebrated in *The Times*:

> For those who believe that exposure to high art – of which great music is one of the most approachable forms – can benefit everyone, the popularity of Classic FM must be immensely cheery. Even in small, easily digested doses, the enjoyment of fine music is a civilising pastime. If the presentation of it can be divested of the intimidating, class-bound order with which it has tended to be surrounded in Britain, then a great many lives will be enriched.[59]

Conclusion

Radio is a prime and underutilised source for the general historian, as well as the media historian. Throughout the last 100 years in the United Kingdom, it has provided a unique insight into social, political and commercial developments during that period. To take full advantage of it, the researcher will need a basic understanding of how the medium developed and to master the methodological challenges involved in seeking to eavesdrop on the auditory experience of the past. The fact that radio can be both a primary and secondary medium for the same listener at almost the same time means that it is a rich and a wide resource.

The potential is immediately obvious in radio's coverage of news and current affairs and in its speech programmes. These need not only be the self-consciously 'serious' output; demotic and the everyday broadcasts are at least as revealing as the set-piece features. These are the broadcasts in which close analysis of the 'spoken-text' can yield benefits but demands a different form of reading from the historian who has to detect authenticity or disguises from voice alone. Can a 'music station' yield information about its times? Its choice of recorded and concert music, the style of its presentation and the accessibility (or otherwise) of the programmes to the generality of listeners can be highly revealing of the social attitudes of the times. In this case, the sound of the broadcast is less important while the contexts of listening come to the fore.

The three case studies examined in this chapter demonstrate how the developments in the radio medium itself are paradigmatic for wider society. They can correct prevailing myths, such a sense that Britain in the 1930s was overwhelmingly a BBC-style, restricted society (case study one); they can bring to life times of intense social firmament, illustrated by the role of the offshore pirate stations in the fabled decade of the 1960s (study two); or they can provide an approachable understanding of the social and cultural aspirations of an emerging meritocracy during the 1990s, when market liberalism was delivering benefits but had not yet revealed its downside (number three).

Still unclear is the extent to which the digitisation of radio, and its increasing move off-line onto podcast and other platforms, will put at risk what archived, linear radio had made available up to the end of the twentieth century.[60] It is unlikely that comprehensive audio archives will exist into the future, and probable that some of the audio material that would have been most valuable will appear elsewhere than in the current institutional framework. The British Library's *Save Our Sounds* initiative, referred to earlier, may be one way of tackling this, but it remains a crucial unknown.

Throughout the past hundred years, radio has been always with us. It has survived the challenge of television, and the early years of digital transformation. The historian of the twentieth century can turn to it with confidence when looking for a guide to past events and the trends which underlie them. It will not disappoint. It offers the historian a resource and an aural vantage-point wholly unknown until the 1920s and the arrival of broadcasting. To give three very different parallels from more conventional written examples, Pliny the Younger delivered a written account to Tacitus describing the eruption of Vesuvius which was sent perhaps a quarter of a century after the event; St. Bede's account of the Anglo-Saxon raids into Britain in the seventh century drew on contemporary written sources but was probably not composed until 50 years after the crucial Battle of Hatfield Chase in 633; while Tolstoy's magnificent fictional reconstruction of Napoleon's occupation of Moscow in 1812, in *War and Peace*, was published in complete form only in 1869. These come as close to living accounts of history as were previously available. With sound broadcasting archives, the historian can become his or her own Pliny, Bede or Tolstoy. Better still, an historian can become immersed in minute-by-minute actuality, enhanced by a range of contemporary, contrasting and sometimes conflicting reports. This chapter is about the potency of sound that becomes almost overwhelming for the middle and late twentieth century, where the main limitations are the skill to select and the time to absorb all the radio material that is available.

Notes

1. Radio Joint Audience Research (RAJAR) data for quarter ending March 2018, www.rajar.co.uk/listening/quarterly_listening.php, last accessed 10.09.19.
2. J. Sterne, *The Audible Past*, Durham, NC and London: Duke University Press, 2003; S. Street, *The Memory of Sound: Preserving the Sonic Past*, London: Routledge, 2014; D. Hendy, *Noise: A Human History of Sound and Listening*, London: Profile Books, 2013.
3. A. Briggs, *The History of Broadcasting in the United Kingdom*, Vol. I, Oxford: Oxford University Press, 1995, p. 23.
4. R. A. Fessenden (1866–1932) was Canadian-born: J. S. Belrose, 'Fessenden and Marconi: Their differing technologies and transatlantic experiments during the first decade of this century', International Conference on 100 Years of Radio, 5–7 September 1995, www.ieee.ca/millennium/radio/radio_differences.html, last accessed 30.08.19; J. S. Belrose, 'Reginald Aubrey Fessenden and the birth of wireless telephony', *IEEE Antenna's and Propagation Magazine*, 44.2, 2002, 37–47.
5. S. Street, *A Concise History of British Radio*, 2nd edn., Tiverton: Kelly Publications, 2005, pp. 11–18.
6. *Hansard*, House of Commons, 3 April 1922, vol. 152, col. 1869w.
7. S. Street, *Crossing the Ether*, Eastleigh: John Libbey Publications, 2006, pp. 137–86.
8. A. Briggs, *The History of Broadcasting in the United Kingdom*, Oxford: Oxford University Press, 1970, iii, pp. 125–59.
9. P. Hennessy, *Never Again: Britain 1945–51*, London: Cape, 1992, p. 312.
10. T. Burns, *The BBC: Public Institution and Private World*, London and Basingstoke: Macmillan Press, 1977, p. 255.
11. K. Skues, *Pop Went the Pirates*, Sheffield: Lams Meadow, 1994; R. Chapman, *Selling the Sixties: The Pirates and Pop Music Radio*, London: Routledge, 2012; R. Chapman, 'The 1960s pirates: A comparative analysis of Radio London and Radio Caroline', *Popular Music*, 9.2, 1990, 165–78.
12. T. Stoller, *Sounds of Your Life: The History of Independent Radio in the UK*, Barnet: John Libbey Publications, 2010, pp. 96–111.
13. T. Stoller, 'Foresight, fudge or facilitation? The making of United Kingdom digital radio policy 1987–2008', in M. Mollgaard (ed.), *Radio and Society: New Thinking for an Old Medium*, Newcastle upon Tyne: Cambridge Scholars, 2012, pp. 149–64.
14. W. Benjamin, *The Work of Art in the Age of Mechanical Reproduction*, London: Penguin, 1934/2008, p. 27.
15. D. Hendy, *Noise, a Human History of Sound and Listening*, London: Profile Books, 2014, p. 293; quoted in P. Scannell and D. Cardiff, *A Social History of British Broadcasting*, Oxford: Basil Blackwell, 1991, i, 375.
16. K. Lacey, *Listening Publics: The Politics and Experience of listening in the Media Age*, Cambridge: Polity Press, 2013, p. 38.
17. S. J. Douglas, *Listening: Radio and the American Experience*, Minneapolis, MN: University of Minnesota Press, 2004, p. 354.

18 James Cridland quoted in Street *Memory of Sound*, pp. 35–6.
19 BBC Written Archives Centre, www.bbc.co.uk/informationandarchives/access_archives/bbc_written_archives_centre, last accessed 30.08.19.
20 Library of American Broadcasting, University of Maryland, www.lib.umd.edu/libraryofamericanbroadcasting, last accessed 30.08.19.
21 National Film and Sound Archive, www.nfsa.gov.au/, last accessed 30.08.19.
22 Canadian Broadcasting Corporation, www.cbc.ca/archives, last accessed 30.08.19; T. Pedwell, 'CBC is destroying its broadcast archives after they're digitzed', *The Star*, 19 April 2018; Ngā Taonga Sound & Vision, www.soundarchives.co.nz, last accessed 30.08.19.
23 www.bournemouth.ac.uk/students/library/using-library/archives-special-collections/broadcasting-history-collections, last accessed 30.08.19.
24 BBC Genome Project, https://genome.ch.bbc.co.uk/, last accessed 30.08.19.
25 Hugh Chignell, private communication, 17 April 2018.
26 British Library (BL), Unlocking Our Sound Heritage, www.bl.uk/projects/unlocking-our-sound-heritage, last accessed 30.08.19.
27 BL, National Radio Archive, www.bl.uk/projects/national-radio-archive, last accessed 30.08.19.
28 S. Rooks, *The BBC Sound Archive*, BBC Written Archive Centre, undated, last accessed 12.05.2018.
29 Street, *Crossing the Ether*, p. 116.
30 Rooks, *BBC WAC*.
31 Chignell, Private communication.
32 University of Sussex, Connected Histories, www.sussex.ac.uk/broadcast/read/39459, last accessed 30.08.19.
33 David Hendy private communication 1 May 2018; '100 voices that made the BBC: The story of the BBC, as told by the people who made it', www.bbc.com/historyofthebbc/100-voices, last accessed 30.08.19.
34 Library of Congress, Washington DC., National Recording Preservation Board, www.loc.gov/programs/national-recording-preservation-board/resources/organizations/, last accessed 30.08.19.
35 Street, *Crossing the Ether*.
36 D. Goodman, *Radio's Civic Ambition: American Broadcasting and Democracy in the 1930s*, Oxford: Oxford University Press, 2011, pp. 139–43.
37 Briggs, *History of Broadcasting*, ii, p. 54.
38 Street, *Concise History*, p. 40.
39 Street, *Crossing the Ether*, p. 54.
40 R. Silvey, Memorandum to Maurice Farquharson, 4 February 1938, 'Audience for foreign programmes in the mornings on weekdays and Sundays', The BBC Written Archives Centre (BBC WAC), R 34/960 quoted in Street, *Crossing the Ether*, p. 177.
41 Street, *Crossing the Ether*, pp. 115–33.
42 A. Marwick, *The Sixties: Cultural Revolution in Britain, France, Italy and the United States*, Oxford: Oxford University Press, 1998, pp. 16–20.
43 S. Barnard, *On the Radio: Music Radio in Britain*, Milton Keynes: Open University Press, 1989, p. 38.
44 Stoller, *Sounds of Your Life*, p. 18.
45 Skues, *Pop Went the Pirates*, p. 16.
46 M. Baron, *Independent Radio, the Story of Independent Radio in the United Kingdom*, Lavenham: Dalton, 1975, pp. 36–7
47 Marine, &c. Broadcasting (Offences) Act 1967: UK Public General Acts, 1967, c.41: www.legislation.gov.uk/ukpga/1967/41/enacted, last accessed 30.08.19.
48 Briggs, *History*, pp. 502–15.
49 *The Boat that Rocked* (2009) Working Title Films, written and directed by Richard Curtis; *The Wonderful Radio London* story (1997) East Anglian Productions, written by Chris Elliot, narrated by Keith Skues.

50 Stoller, *Sounds of your Life*, pp. 201–2.
51 A term supposedly coined by Tony Blair: O. Stone, 'Who's the new Mondeo Man?', *BBC News Channel*, 2 January 2005, http://news.bbc.co.uk/1/hi/4119695.stm, last accessed 30.08.19.
52 H. Carpenter, *The Envy of the World: Fifty Years of the Third Programme and Radio Three*, London: Weidenfeld & Nicolson, 1996.
53 Stoller, *Sounds of Your Life*, pp. 201–2
54 T. Stoller, *Classical Music Radio in the United Kingdom, 1945–1995*, London: Palgrave, 2017, p. 197.
55 *Hansard*, House of Lords, 23 May 1991, vol. 529, col.423.
56 Stoller, *Classical Music*, p. 198.
57 Ibid., p. 216.
58 A. Bennett, 'What I did in 1996', *London Review of Books*, 2 January 1997. The phrase is a pun based on the name of the insurance and holiday company, Saga, specialising in providing services for the over-50s, and the 'lager-louts' slur of the same decade. The reviewer attributes the phrase 'Saga louts' to Hugh Stalker, but it has attached itself firmly to Bennett.
59 'High culture for the people', *The Times*, London, 30 January 1993, p. 15.
60 A. Leemann, 'Documenting sound change with smartphone apps', *The Journal of the Acoustical Society of America*, 137.4, 2015, https://asa.scitation.org/doi/10.1121/1.4920412, last accessed 30.08.19; M. Droumeva, 'Curating everyday life: Approaches to documenting everyday soundscapes', *M/C Journal*, 18.4, 2015, www.journal.media-culture.org.au/index.php/mcjournal/article/view/1009, last accessed 30.08.19.

Further reading

Adena, Maja, et al., 'Radio and the rise of the Nazis in prewar Germany', *The Quarterly Journal of Economics*, 130.4, 2015, 1885–939.

Avery, Todd, *Radio Modernism: Literature, Ethics, and the BBC, 1922–1938*, London: Routledge, 2006.

Douglas, Susan J., *Listening In: Radio and the American Imagination*, Minneapolis, MN: University of Minnesota Press, 2004.

Feldman, Matthew, Erik Tonning and Henry Mead (eds), *Broadcasting in the Modernist Era*, Historicizing Modernism, London: Bloomsbury Publishing, 2014.

Hangen, Tona J., *Redeeming the Dial: Radio, Religion, & Popular Culture in America*, Chapel Hill, NC and London: University of North Carolina Press, 2002.

Hilmes, Michele, *Hollywood and Broadcasting: From Radio to Cable*, Urbana and Chicago, IL: University of Illinois Press, 1990.

Price, Monroe and Marc Raboy (eds), *Public Service Broadcasting in Transition: A Documentary Reader*, European Institute for the Media, 2001, Scholarly Commons, http://repository.upenn.edu/cgcs_publications/1.

7 Television
Capturing performance

Philip Kiszely

In this chapter I offer contextual and textual analyses of an appearance of Mick Jagger on Granada Television's current affairs series *World in Action*.[1] The programme in question, broadcast on 31 July 1967 – the day Jagger and his Rolling Stones band-mate Keith Richards had their drug-related criminal convictions quashed – addressed some difficult social questions. It tried to understand why Jagger and Richards, along with fellow Rolling Stone Brian Jones, had in their travails come to represent a schism in society that seemed to pit young against old, progressive against conservative, and a burgeoning pop culture against the somewhat beleaguered British Establishment. My purpose here is much the same in that I am concerned with charting processes of social and cultural change in Britain. But as the focus on the *World in Action* broadcast itself would indicate, it is the nature of the encounter between Jagger and the 'great and the good' – William Rees-Mogg, Rev. Thomas Corbishley, Dr John Robinson and Frank Soskice (Lord Stow Hill) – that lies at the heart of this enquiry.[2] How is the televised *World in Action* debate useful as an historical document? What does it reveal about the nature of pop culture's challenge to the British class/social hierarchy?

Gimme . . . historiography: ways of seeing

My approach to the historical work can be broadly described as constructionist in that it follows in the tradition of scholars such as R.G. Collingwood and Leon Goldstein.[3] I deal in testimony and evidence, the latter triangulating examples of the former. I call upon theory, too, in order to offer a conceptual framework within which to address the research questions.

But what does 'theory' mean in this context? And what is its organizational function? My starting point in writing this chapter was of course the document itself. The 'Mick Jagger' *World in Action* programme offers an on-the-spot Establishment response to a pop culture *cause célèbre*, and as such it is something of a trailblazer in British broadcasting history. That status alone makes it interesting. What makes the programme important, however, is the particular combination of its participants. These men constitute the central meaning-bearing element around which my analysis works. I will come back to that point in a moment. In the meantime – and as a means of properly highlighting the importance of a focused approach – it is helpful to reflect on the enormous scale of social change associated with that historical moment of July 1967, the legendary Summer of Love. In this chapter, I claim that an analysis of social class is an effective means to measure aspects of that change. I should add something by way of qualification. Equally effective might be a consideration of gender, or of ethnicity, or sex and sexuality, or any number of other potential alternatives. The problem is clear enough. While television broadcasts like the *World in Action* programme can offer a wealth of information to the historian, they only go so far. Happily though, the answer to the conundrum lies in the restriction itself – it solves the problem of choice.

The all-male Establishment-versus-pop-star dynamic conveys nothing of, say, the female experience, but it does reveal a lot about contemporaneous (male) attitudes towards class. Public debates in which class played a part tended to be masculine affairs in those days (a situation remedied only with the deepening influence of second-wave feminism, on the one hand, and newer incarnations of the New Left on the other). And on those terms, the *World in Action* participants offer an insight into the workings of a creaking but still functioning social hierarchy. The subject of the programme's debate was freedom – its expression and its limitations – but the terms on which the participants engaged were, ironically enough, wholly bound up in the constraints of the English class system. Thus, the document provides an organizing principle for the chapter. With class as a touchstone, then, other discourses intersect in meaningful ways.

Tell me . . .: television, pop culture, and communication

In order to understand the impact of pop culture during the 1960s, it is important to appreciate the role of the broadcast media in its dissemination – and in particular the growing influence of television. As the decade progressed, television consolidated its position as the primary means of entertainment for most people; it provided a focal point of interest in practically every sitting room in the nation. *World in Action*, first broadcast in January 1963, was one of several additions to the schedules which demonstrated that the medium had come of age. The series appeared in the wake of *The Pilkington Committee Report on Broadcasting* (1962). The committee's findings, along with the provision of the subsequent Television Act (1964), proved instrumental in setting a more serious tone, especially for the commercial stations.[4] If, by 1967, current affairs series like *World in Action* were keen to cast light into the murkier corners of youth culture (see what follows), then their enquiries were in part a response to the youth-oriented entertainment boom that had become a staple of both channels.

Ready Steady Go (ITV 1963) and *Top of the Pops* (BBC 1964) offered a glimpse into a brave new world hitherto only dreamt of by music and fashion-obsessed teenagers. These weekly music shows complemented the new magazines and pirate radio stations to form the basis of the rock/pop-based youth subculture. Television and the other media proved indispensable to the hordes of young people who were unable to go out and find pop culture for themselves, either because they were removed geographically from the blues, beat and pop clubs of the larger cities and towns, or because they were simply too young to participate properly. Moreover, while bands like the Rolling Stones and the Beatles toured incessantly throughout the early and middle years of the 1960s, Britain's live music infrastructure at that time was that of the old variety circuit – and thus inadequate. Television played an important part in making accessible Jagger, Jones, other comparable icons such as John Lennon and Paul McCartney, and more run-of-the-mill pop stars. The medium had begun to bring popular music to a wider audience, with the shows such as *Six-Five Special*, which ran from 1957 to 1958. This programme tried to replicate the ambience and atmosphere of the famous 2i's Coffee Bar, in Compton Street, Soho, where Teddy Boys and Girls gathered to listen to rock 'n' roll. The newer series beamed pop stars straight into the home, their extreme close-up camera work offering a heady proximity. The relationship between pop star and viewer depended for its intimacy on the former occupying the personal space of the latter – and it is on these terms that Jagger addresses his audiences on *World in Action*.

The far-flung reaches of pop culture had become complex territories of self-expression for young people, easily transcending anything that had gone before. These new identities drew on a variety of exotic influences, ranging from 1950s bohemianism to international iterations of the counterculture.[5] British television kept pace, documenting pop culture evolution with ever more sophisticated levels of coverage. But it took a US show to first catch something of the real spirit of this change. On 20 May 1965, the Rolling Stones made a remarkable appearance on *Shindig!* At one point in the show Jagger and Jones joined presenter Jack Goode in introducing blues legend Howlin' Wolf. They enthused about his influence on the band, and that of black blues and rhythm 'n' blues performers in general. Jones then told Goode to 'Shut up!' – he wanted to hear Howlin' Wolf perform 'How Many More Years?' – and Jagger drawled sarcastically, 'Howlin' Jack Goode . . . Howlin' Jack Goode'. Such behaviour, tongue-in-cheek though it was, would have been unthinkable twelve months previously.

A steady but definite decline in deference to authority manifested itself as the 1960s gained pace. By 1963–1964, such behaviour had become pronounced enough to be noticed.[6] Arthur Marwick offers a balanced view on developments, noting changes in behaviour in large sections of society, not just the young. Of the youth subculture itself, however, he described '"healthy scepticism" [taking] the form of greater openness, frankness and contempt for adult hypocrisy; even among the more restrained and conformist there tended to be an admiration for the more daring'.[7] Nowhere is the power of this kind of posturing illustrated with more eloquence than by Keith Richards. Famously bullish at his drugs trial, his conduct in the dock captured the spirit of the time. 'We are not old men,' he told Mr Morris (Prosecuting) in answer to a question concerning Marianne Faithfull, the infamous girl in the rug: 'We are not worried by petty morals.'[8]

The rate of cultural change had become staggering – alarming, even – as the summer stretched out across the middle months of 1967. And it was fuelled by the mercilessly sensationalized drug debate. The press busied itself in communicating the involvement of celebrities, its reportage by turns responsible or libellous. Along with all other forms of media, television ran with the story. The Rolling Stones and the Beatles would occasionally cooperate, as a matter of expediency as much as anything else: they could set the record straight or express a desire for privacy. In a television interview, for example, McCartney admitted to taking LSD four times. But he added:

> If I had my way, I wouldn't have told anyone, y'know. I'm not trying to spread the word about this, but the man from the newspaper is the man from the mass medium. I'll keep it a personal thing if he does too, y'know – if he keeps it quiet. But he wanted to spread it. So it's his responsibility to spread it, not mine.[9]

The binary of personal freedom versus public responsibility, bound up with the communicating role of the media, was an issue that Jagger would himself take up a month later in the *World in Action* broadcast. It was for him, as it was for anyone with a vested interest, the essence of the pop culture question as posed in 1967. In the light of what was to follow, McCartney's estimation of his own influence – 'I don't think my fans will take drugs just because I did' – would seem somewhat naïve. It soon became apparent that the kind of freedom the pop stars wished to enjoy, secure in the privacy and comfort of their own homes, took on a different inflection when expressed on the streets. Television responded accordingly, with the experiences of ordinary young people now providing the raw material for sociological scrutiny. Most hard-hitting in this respect was a BAFTA-nominated *Man Alive* documentary, 'Gail is Dead' (1970), the story of a 19-year-old heroin addict whose body had been found in a derelict Chelsea house. Television traced the arc of social and cultural change as it happened. And one thing was for certain: that change was understood to be profound, irrespective of its pros and cons.

Something happened to me yesterday . . .: changes and new ideas

It has become something of a commonplace to suggest that the spirit of a particular decade takes time to manifest itself properly. Its cosy familiarity notwithstanding, this idea is sound enough for application at any time and place, and certainly it is true of Britain and the 1960s. Rock writer Nik Cohn (1970) made much the same point when he described pre-1962 musical output as remarkable only for its blandness, a far cry from the richness that was to follow.[10] The 1960s came to gain a recognizable identity, in broader pop culture as well as in musical terms, in the October of 1962. It was during this remarkable month that Britain saw the release of the Beatles' debut single, 'Love Me Do', the cinematic premier of *Dr No*, and the first airing on television of *The Saint*. And it might be argued (in that same spirit of cataloguing) that while the era was up and running at the end 1962, it was only in the late spring of 1963, with the appearance of the Rolling Stones and their debut single, 'Come On', that the 1960s properly started 'swinging'. Yet, useful though these high-profile pop culture markers are, the contexts within which they made their impact were set long before. The processes of history, as E.H. Carr observed, concern themselves with particular combinations of micro and macro narratives, the interplay between long and short term influences, and the dovetailing of related sequences of events.[11]

The Labour Government of 1945 ushered in a sweep of social change that would echo down the years, with subsequent developments building towards a culmination that was the cultural revolution of the 1960s. The founding of the National Health Service, the dismantling of Empire, changing attitudes towards sex and gender, multiple waves of immigration, and the steady erosion of the class system were all factors that made for a healthier and fairer environment. However, the greatest beneficiaries of this longitudinal national reconstruction were too busy building the Britain of today to concern themselves overly with a history in which they had had no hand. It was the self-styled 'modernists' among the Baby Boomer generation who tended to set the pop culture pace in the early and middle 1960s, and their impatience with the past is understandable. Their collective memory was, after all, that of an aftermath of conflict followed by years of austerity. This seeming indifference to the past was an expression of freedom. Most in the new generation simply ignored the constraints imposed by pre-war notions of decency and excellence. These were the standards by which the class-bound national identity had hitherto been measured – and that identity was changing.

The beginnings of social mobility can be traced to a recognizable figure of the early Welfare State years, the grant-aided student. Fictionalized versions of the archetype soon found their way into the mainstream of popular culture. Characters like John Osborne's Jimmy Porter were celebrated for their fashionable rebellion and lauded at length in the key literature and theatre surveys of the day, such as *The Angry Decade* and *Anger and After*.[12] Anti-hero of the seminal *Look Back in Anger* (1956), the Porter character would re-surface in the Woodfall Films' big screen version of the play (1958) before going on to serve as a working template for a seemingly endless stream of characters across various media. The defining characteristic of all these similarly alienated young men was class displacement. Real-life anti-heroes of comparable backgrounds traded on this attribute, which became a kind of shorthand for authenticity. Along with actors such as Kenneth Haigh (the original Jimmy Porter), Tom Courtney, and Albert Finney, were cutting-edge writers, filmmakers, political activists, and thinkers – 'angry young men' – who set out their store in high-profile collections of essays, such as *Declaration* (1957) and *Out of Apathy* (1960). It all suggested the dynamism of a movement.

Young(ish) men were breaching the class barriers, certainly, but other groups were driving change too, and on the same terms. It was a woman – notably – who was most eloquent in her appraisal of this first 'New Left'. In her far-seeing 'A House of Theory', Iris Murdoch closed the *Conviction* collection of essays with a call for conceptualization.[13] Her demand for structural rigor anticipated the influence of divisive figures like Perry Anderson and the embrace of continental philosophy. Moreover, full employment meant that women, often working in a part-time capacity, enjoyed unprecedented spending power – and, as a consequence, a measure of autonomy. And the same can be said of 'youth', whether male or female, as Mark Abrams observed in his 1959 book, *The Teenage Consumer*. In 1958, 13 percent of the population was single and aged between 15 and 24, a demographic that represented somewhere in the region of £900-million in spending power. These young people made up over 40 percent of the market for records and record players. Abrams discovered an important sub-division in this youth market. 'Not far short of all teenage spending is conditioned by working class tastes and values,' he noted: '[t]he aesthetic of the teenage market is essentially a working class aesthetic and probably only entrepreneurs of working class origin will have a natural understanding of the needs of this market.'[14] From consumer to producer, working class youth were not only purchasing pop culture in their droves, but they were also manufacturing it and dictating the terms on which it was produced.

The 1960s saw these new identities crystalize, with uninterrupted years of affluence resulting in broader processes of what J.P. Goldthorpe described as *embourgeoisement*.[15] Relative wealth served to bolster newly acquired forms of social and cultural capital. This winning combination fostered an unprecedented sense of confidence. The model of consumer-driven mobility could be seen most strikingly in the slender figure of Twiggy. But change was also evident in men. Suddenly, or so it seemed, attractive male role models were to be found in abundance. Stylish figures like the Beatles, Sean Connery, and Michael Caine forged effortlessly new, or 'modern', working class identities. And David Bailey's photographic *Box of Pin-ups* (1964) served to showcase the new masculinity.[16] His collection caught the spirit of the moment, and in its wake working class figures 'come good', so to speak, began to be treated with a new respect. A *Man Alive* episode, 'Top Class People', broadcast at peak time on 10 May 1967, celebrated some key figures in a rapidly developing new social order. Twiggy – again – took centre stage, but her manager/boyfriend Justin de Villeneuve shared the spotlight, as did graphic designer Alan Aldridge and screenwriter Johnny Speight.

Nowhere did the loosening of class bonds offer more potential for a challenge to convention than on the elite pop culture scene, which had by this time become inextricably linked with the smarter homes and haunts of the nation's capital. 'Swinging London', as it had been christened by *Time* magazine, consisted of an exotic mix of glamorous people whose talent, flamboyance and beauty were their defining features. That is not to deny, however, the intensely hierarchical nature of this high-achieving and competitive community. Indeed, the male contingent in its vanguard – the Rolling Stones, the Beatles, Christopher Gibbs, Michael Cooper, and Stanislaus 'Stash' Kowassala de Rola, along with a roll call of others – were decadently aristocratic in their tastes, attitudes, and demeanour. But the social constraints bequeathed by the great Victorian middle class were banished and the same can be said for the prejudices still straightjacketing the broader sweep of 'Little England'. As Christopher Booker (1969) noted at the end of the decade, these people personified a change that amounted to something of a revolution.[17]

Rebellion found exquisite expression through style, often in places like Chelsea and Knightsbridge. It could also be seen on (and off) Savile Row, Mount Street, and Jermyn Street. Tailors like Edward Sexton, Tommy Nutter, Rupert Lycett-Green, and Doug Hayward were vital to the scene. Boutique owners and designers were similarly important: Michael Fish, Barry Sainsbury and Christopher Lynch at Mr Fish; Michael Rainey at Hung On You; and John Crittle, Tara Browne, and Neil Winterbotham at Dandie Fashions. All of these men were style arbiters, facilitators of what would become known as the Peacock Revolution.[18] In their sartorial choices, the peacocks and dandies of Swinging London threw down the gauntlet. They at once challenged and appropriated the privilege of luxury and style hitherto the province of the Establishment. Individualism, like the aforementioned social mobility, was nothing new of course, a point detailed at length by Robinson et al.[19] But in the shape of the seductively libertarian Rolling Stones, it represented a particular affront to some elements of the British Establishment. Moreover, it set in motion the remarkable events that were to play out in the summer of 1967.

I can't get no . . .: the trials and tribulations of . . .

While on holiday in Marrakesh during the early spring of that year, the Rolling Stones encountered society photographer Sir Cecil Beaton. He was a fellow guest at the Mamounia Hotel. Beaton dined with Jagger, Jones, Richards, and their entourage on the evening of 14 March. 'I was intent not to give the impression that I was only interested in Mick', he recorded in his diary, '[b]ut it happened that we sat next to one another, as he drank a vodka Collins, and smoked with pointed fingers held high'.[20] The chance meeting is trivial enough in the overall scheme of things, but it is nonetheless instructive in that it offers an unsolicited opinion of Jagger from what might be termed an Establishment figure. 'His skin is chicken breast white, and of a fine quality,' the diary continued. 'He has an enormous inborn elegance'. Taken with Jagger, clearly, Beaton photographed the singer in the grounds of the hotel, capturing in those images something of a powerful and androgynous sexual quality. Jagger, for his part, was open and communicative, much more so, according to Beaton, than on the only other occasion their paths had crossed. Indeed, the singer expounded the virtues of LSD. He also talked of his legal wrangles with *The News of the World*.

The previous month, on 5 February, the tabloid newspaper had published the second of a five-part series about the drug habits of pop stars. The article in question alleged that Jagger had taken LSD. He promptly issued a denial and threatened legal action against what he considered defamatory comments. Seven days later he was arrested, along with Keith Richards and gallery owner Robert Fraser. The police had raided Richards's house, Redlands, on a tip-off from the newspaper. Jagger was accused of being in unauthorized possession of four amphetamine tablets, and Richards for permitting Redlands to be used for the purpose of smoking cannabis resin. Fraser faced the most serious charge: the possession of heroin.

138 *Philip Kiszely*

From here events moved swiftly. The two Rolling Stones appeared for a court hearing at Chichester, West Sussex, on 10 May. That same day, remarkably enough, Brian Jones and Stash Klossowski de Rola were arrested for possession at Brian's Courtfield Road flat, amid a flurry of press activity and on the most dubious grounds. On 22 June, Jagger, Richards, and Fraser were sent for trial at West Sussex quarter sessions. After electing for trial by jury, they were released on £100 bail. The trial was heard on 27 June, and two days later all three were convicted. Richards was sentenced to twelve months in prison and ordered to pay £500 costs, while Jagger received three months with £100 costs. They were subsequently granted bail, pending appeal, in their own recognizance of £5,000 each, plus sureties of £1,000.

In the midst of this chaos, on 13 and 14 June, the band repaired to Olympic Studios to record the Andrew Loog Oldham-produced 'We Love You', on which Lennon and McCartney over-dubbed backing vocals as a gesture of support. Then, on the day before Jagger's and Richards' appeal, the ever-resourceful Oldham commissioned director Peter Whitehead to make a film with which to promote the 'We Love You' single. Drawing parallels between the Rolling Stones and Oscar Wilde, its trial scenes featured Jagger as Wilde, Marianne Faithfull as Lord Alfred Douglas, and Richards as a court judge – the latter resplendent in a wig made from rolled tabloid newspapers. It is as powerful a piece of pop promotional footage as any produced throughout the decade. *Top of the Pops* declined an invitation to run it, however, and as a consequence Whitehead called the programme irresponsible, not to say cowardly. The major pop acts of the day were brave by comparison. Jagger, Richards, and Jones featured prominently in the international *Our World* ('All You Need is Love') broadcast, alongside the Beatles. Others were similarly demonstrative in their support. The Who, for example, placed large adverts in the *Evening News* and *Evening Standard*, announcing their decision to cover a series of Rolling Stones songs. The gesture was a sincere attempt to keep the band in the public eye should the worst happen.

Throughout July a body of public opinion was growing in support of the band, a point explored in-depth by Tony Sanchez.[21] Many were either nonplussed or angry at the convictions and the severity of the sentences. But it was *The Times* and William Rees Mogg's brave leader, 'Who Breaks a butterfly on a Wheel?', that struck at the heart of the matter.[22] 'There must remain a suspicion in this case', wrote Rees-Mogg, 'that Mr Jagger received a more severe sentence than would have been thought proper of any purely anonymous young man'. Much of Jagger's public image had been expertly manufactured by the precocious Oldham, who at 19 years of age had set about promoting Jagger and the band as the anti-Beatles. The backlash that followed, however, amounted to a twin assault by the law enforcement agencies and elements of the tabloid press. Bill Wyman accurately described the nature of the Rolling Stones' position at the time: 'To bust a Beatle would be to squash the dreams of millions of adults as well as their children. To bust a Rolling Stone was ok – most parents hated us anyway'.[23]

'It was a low-level Establishment conspiracy', reflects Stash Klossowki de Rola, whose own high-profile and close friendship with Jones and the other

Rolling Stones had placed him firmly in the firing line.[24] He continued: 'Andrew Oldham's development of the band's image had triggered a conflict with the Establishment – and they were frowned upon. The Stones were an insult to the overall sense of propriety. Their success went very much against the grain'. The tragic irony of the business was the decline of Brian Jones: the adverse publicity prompted his retreat into sense-numbing Mandrax use, a soft barrier against an increasingly hostile world. Jones' death, on 3 July 1969, profoundly affected De Rola: 'It is an unspeakable tragedy. Brian was killed by the attitudes of the Establishment'. Other members of the same circle, notably Marianne Faithfull, only just escaped a similarly tragic fate.

Vindication for Jagger and Richards, when it finally arrived on 31 July in the form of acquittal, prompted a renewed round of worrying at questions concerning the accountability of pop stars. But the world was now a slightly different place. If Rees-Mogg's leader had chipped away at the Establishment's moral authority on the subject, then Lord Parker's criticisms of Judge Block's conduct at the trials served to raise further questions. Dwelling on the power of the pop star in his summing up at the appeal, Lord Parker described Jagger as having 'grave responsibilities' as 'an idol of a large number of young people in this country'. Yet acknowledging those responsibilities, let alone bowing to pressure to act on them, was something Jagger was still loath to do. He was, however, amenable to discussing the subject – on a suitably high-profile media platform.

I'm alright . . .: Jagger in action

'Publicity since the case has shown up a split between the society which resents the anarchy of people like the Stones and that which favours greater individual freedom': so ran the voiceover introducing the 'Mick Jagger' *World in Action* programme. Beneath it and presented in the form of a dramatic long take, footage depicted a helicopter landing and a figure disembarking. Then – still the same shot – the camera followed the figure on his way. Now clearly recognisable as he strode across the expansive lawns of Spain's Hall near Ongar, in Essex, the kaftan-clad Mick Jagger perfectly embodied Cecil Beaton's description. For many of the viewing public this translated into something that spoke directly of danger, rather than exotic romance. It conjured an image of druggy decadence, pernicious in its influence on the young and impressionable. But nothing was quite as it seemed, even when at first glance the rights and wrongs of a situation appeared incontestable: the legal circus surrounding the acquittals had shown that all too clearly. Questions suddenly presented themselves. Attitudes towards drug-use were drawn cleanly along generational lines, weren't they? That was the conventional wisdom, wasn't it? As if to disabuse viewers of such assumptions, *World in Action* set out its stall by citing a survey which claimed 85 percent of young people agreed with the soundness of Jagger's conviction.

For all its provocative myth-busting, the broadcast did place the much-vaunted 'Generation Gap' at the heart of the matter. The idea was to mark difference from the outset, as indicated by the framing of Jagger's arrival. Future Director General of the BBC John Birt – then a young production assistant making his mark at Granada Television – said as much years later when he recalled the making of the show: 'On the day Jagger's appeal succeeded I persuaded him to meet the editor of *The Times* and other establishment luminaries in a coming together of the generations'.[25] Before he could attend Birt's summit conference, however, the 24-year-old singer had another appointment to keep.

Earlier in the day Jagger had made his way from the Court of Appeal to Battersea heliport. From here, and now accompanied by Birt and Marianne Faithfull, he flew to Granada TV's West End headquarters in Golden Square where he addressed a cramped, somewhat chaotic, press conference. Flanked by his lawyer and manager Allen Klein, he clarified the conditions of his acquittal and fielded questions about the increasingly serious business of pop stardom. He reiterated the substance of what had come to be a stock response for the Stones and Beatles alike, confident now that the day's events would add weight to its sentiment. 'One doesn't ask for responsibilities', he told the gathering:

> Perhaps one is given responsibilities when one is pushed into the limelight in this particular sphere, rather than asking to be. I didn't ask to be. . . . I merely ask for my private life to be left alone. . . . My responsibilities as far as that goes are only to do with myself. In the public sector – such as to do with my work, my records, etc – I have responsibility, but the amount of baths I take or my personal habits are of no consequence to anyone else, I don't think. I don't propagate religious views, such as some pop stars do. I don't propagate drug views, such as some pop stars do. This whole sort of thing was pushed upon me.[26]

When, finally, Jagger settled into his seat at Spain's Hall, Rees-Mogg set things in motion without further fanfare. 'Mick, you've had a difficult day', he said, 'and a difficult three months'.[27] This was putting it mildly, as the editor himself acknowledged with a grin. The true extent of the frustration bred by these difficulties, especially in relation to the police, was something that Jagger and his fellow Stones had kept to themselves. But the hidden irony of the first exchanges, in which Father Corbishley talked of corruption and the need to check it, cannot have been lost on the singer. In the wake of the Redlands bust, the band had tried to bribe West End division personnel who, according to Richards' friend and 'assistant', 'Spanish' Tony Sanchez, had made it known that they were amenable to a pay-off. Bill Wyman has detailed the circumstances in which Sanchez made a £7,000 payment to a man in a pub, all to no effect on the outcome of the case.[28] Jagger's response to Corbishley, therefore – 'it's always been in need of checking' – was no doubt heartfelt. The blackly comic nature of the subtext notwithstanding, these opening remarks set the serious tone for what was to follow.

In Corbishley, Rees-Mogg, and the other panellists, Jagger found a challenging but far from unsympathetic audience. *The Times* editor had, after all, taken something of a risk in passing comment on a case while an appeal was in progress. Progressive credentials of a kind were on display, too, in the softly spoken Frank

Soskice. Predecessor at the Home Office to Roy Jenkins, he could claim involvement in the abolition of the death penalty and direct responsibility for The Race Relations Act of 1965. But the level of his personal commitment to social justice was questionable, to say the least.[29] Rounding off the quartet was Dr John Robinson, a formidable intellect whose 1963 monograph, *Honest to God*, had caused a stir on its publication.[30] And it was Robinson, in fact, who would stimulate the most fruitful exchanges, his comments at once kindly and probing.

The nature of the interaction between Jagger and these men points to difference, certainly, but it also indicates a surprising amount of common ground. Jagger went out of his way to demonstrate thoughtfulness – diffidence, even – and to communicate on equal intellectual terms. It was a strategy that would both ingratiate and impress. 'I haven't until very recently been into this discussion at all because I haven't really felt it's been my place', he said; '[a]nd I don't think my knowledge is enough to start pontificating on these kinds of subjects'. This was a self-consciously refined kind of utterance from a voice similar to that of the suitor in 'Lady Jane', or to the wistful romantic in 'Ruby Tuesday'. It was a world away from that other Jagger of recent invention, the sneering mock-cockney commentator of 'Mother's Little Helper'. And, by the same token, the persona on display here was unrecognizable as the same Jagger of caricature in the popular press; that leader of the 'Great Unwashed' who, on 18 March 1965, had been fined £5 for urinating in the forecourt of an east London petrol station.

Years later, journalist Nick Kent reminisced about the disconcerting ease with which Jagger could slip between personas. He noted among other things an ability to mimic class traits.[31] It would be easy to make much of what might be described as Jagger's mixed-class background (as a means of explaining away the extraordinary chameleon-like nature of his personality as much as anything else). But to do so would be to overstate the case. Yet it is worth noting here, if only in passing, because on occasion he himself was given to comment on it: 'My Mum is very working class, my Father bourgeois, because he had a reasonably good education, so I came from somewhere in between that', – he told one interviewer – 'Neither one nor the other'.[32] Taken on its own, this remark about the transformative nature of the education system is interesting enough – it suggests a set of values that might have a deeper than expected root in tradition. But coupled with a similar observation, made on the programme itself, the sentiment is rather more revealing. The Jagger on display in *World in Action* was of a thorough-going middle class sensibility. He is the grown-up version of his grammar schoolboy former self – the cerebral ex-LSE student.

Jagger's ability to talk 'the same language', as it were, held some sway for Rees-Mogg, especially when it came to the central theme of the debate – freedom: 'I remember being struck by the fact that Jagger used the classic John Stuart Mill *On Liberty* argument: that you are entitled to do anything that does not affect somebody else adversely'.

> He argued that that is the test of permissibility of human action. The State has no right to interfere in anything merely because it may damage the person who chooses to do it. I did not believe, as some did, that Jagger's remarks were mere

142 *Philip Kiszely*

sloganeering. They represented, rather, a thought-out system of beliefs. When Jagger made these remarks in 1967, the British still made paternalistic assumptions about government; the young were beginning to revolt against the limits put on liberty by Victorian tradition and wartime necessities, and, to a considerable extent, socialist paternalism.[33]

The parameters of the freedom discussion were set by Corbishley, who broached the subject via the connected issue of mass communication. This was an area where Jagger and his ilk should take responsibility, he said, as they were the 'dominant generation' in waiting. 'It's the old [who should take responsibility], I think', Jagger countered, 'Because they're the ones in charge of the mass communication media. Politicians are really the ones that are putting over the messages more than anyone else'. It was a reasonable enough response; a reminder that the power structure still privileged the elite. It received nods of approval from all present.

Robinson then entered the fray, picking up on the mass communication idea and taking it in a different direction. He pondered what might be the ultimate impact on society of the mass communication media, in terms of encroachment and harm, suggesting that the real consequences might stem from the speed in which it worked. Freedoms touched on those of others far more quickly than in previous eras, he reflected, and they in turn affected other people's lives with breath-taking haste. 'We are immediately and very quickly up against this question of the limits of freedom'. Here was the nub of the problem, at least as far as Robinson was concerned. The ensuing exchange chased the philosophical idea of freedom. For Jagger, this meant the libertarian vision of unfettered individual expression, aforementioned by Rees-Mogg, with the only proviso being the harm principle. Robinson, for his part, queried boundaries and sought definition. Jagger historicized with remarkable insight but was vague in his response to Robinson's assertions.

The conversation took a turn towards a more classical liberal-versus-communitarian debate with an interjection by Soskice, who maintained that the law intervened to protect people and their individual sphere of freedom. It was in response to this statement that Jagger was at his most impressive, his recent experiences no doubt utmost in his mind: 'Quite often the law works to protect a minority of interests, or to protect interests which one would think were rather empty'. Drawing on the situational ethics that were Robinson's province, he built an argument centred on relativism and change. There were several examples: the recent US 'race riots' and the Civil Rights Movement; young people, their particular interests and spheres of experience; the disenfranchisement of various groups and communities. 'For instance', he went on to say, 'there was a time when attempting to commit suicide was a criminal offence – which was changed. But it's not so very long ago it was changed. The law on homosexuality – it was a crime. It's been changed'. He continued along similar lines, speaking eloquently of victimless crimes. In so doing, he functioned effectively as a mouthpiece for the Permissive Society: 'Taking drugs – heroin – it's a crime against themselves, not a crime against society'. When, finally, asked – again by Soskice – where he predicted freedom would end and prohibition begin, Jagger replied, 'A real *crime* against society should be punished by society – but it should be punished in a way to suit the case. And they must really *be* crimes against society, not just fears of society which could be groundless'.

The debate concluded with Jagger's grateful acknowledgement of Rees-Mogg's intervention in 'Who breaks a butterfly on a wheel?'. He declared himself happy at the overall outcome of his case, and there were nods of approval from the panel. In foregrounding the genteel aspect of his identity, the singer succeeded in positioning himself favourably. As much any other single individual, Mick Jagger represented a new breed. He was the archetypal Englishman of the Permissive Society, the personification of the new individualism. Yet, through his understanding of the English Class system, he managed to broker, if not a gentleman's agreement as such, then at least a gentleman's disagreement. As the closing credits roll, the ease with which the participants occupy their shared space offers a final impression of clubbable companionship.

Conclusion

This chapter has considered some aspects of social and cultural change in Britain, 1967, by analyzing a television text closely associated with a set of era-defining events. In orchestrating an encounter between a pop star and a set of influential Establishment figures, the 'Mick Jagger' *World in Action* programme sought to understand the new ideas, new values – new freedoms. The Rolling Stones in general, and Mick Jagger in particular, were potent symbols of a threat, either real or imagined, to any status quo as it stood at that time – more so, certainly, than the women and minorities still in the relatively early stages of a journey towards equality. Jagger and his ilk were wealthy and ubiquitous, thanks in part to television, the wider media, and a thriving music industry. The Rolling Stones were the idols of millions; they had inspired a devotion that almost rivalled Beatlemania in its scope, before going on to become the public face of the Permissive Society. Their drug trials, convictions, and acquittals, therefore, offer a lens through which to view the bigger issues. Their exploits not only set the context for the *World in Action* programme itself, but they also map on to broader discourses which deal with the same overarching theme – freedom. The chapter has illustrated this point.

On the surface, the *World in Action* programme sketched its generational conflict in bold strokes: young buck versus old order, the upstart against the Establishment – all the delicious sensation of an Andrew Oldham publicity headline. Yet, as the nuances of the screen debate indicate, the interactions between the participants were anything but simplistic. Spicing the instant concoction of Generation Gap politicking was the added ingredient of social convention. Stash Klossowski de Rola illustrated the nature of its influence when he recalled talking with his solicitor, Sir David Napley, about his association with the Rolling Stones. 'Now you, sir, *are* a gentleman', Napley told him: 'What on earth are you doing associating with *these* chaps?'[34] While the subject of class was never broached directly at Spain's House – nothing quite so vulgar in so grand a space – it did nonetheless dictate the terms on which the subject of freedom was discussed. As

144   *Philip Kiszely*

this chapter has shown, Jagger acquitted himself well. His demeanour, accent, articulation, and display of taste and education were effective in offsetting the initial shock of his outlandish appearance. Years later, Rees-Mogg reflected on his 'incisive' argument, concluding that he had 'got the better' of the panel – besting Robinson in particular.[35] Jagger held his own in the debate, a point this chapter acknowledges, but it would be stretching that point to say that he vanquished his opponents. Then again, Jagger did prove himself to be a gentleman – and Rees-Mogg liked him.

The Baby Boomers were, according to Jagger, different than the previous generations. 'One's parents have been through two wars and a Depression, and we've been through none of this – it's all in history to us', he told the panel: 'We haven't been influenced by it – only in as much are parents could influence us'. This chapter has charted that difference, linking it to notions of freedom by narrating bottom-up processes of social mobility. It remains something of an irony, then, that Jagger should actively mobilize class convention in order to represent that freedom.

Notes

1   The show is available on vol. 1 of the *World in Action* DVD set, Network, 2005.
2   William Rees-Mogg was the editor of *The Times* newspaper from 1967–81. Father Thomas Corbishley was Master at Campion Hall and later Superior at Farm Street. He had published *The Contemporary Christian* the previous year. Lord Stow Hill was previously Sir Frank Soskice, Home Secretary from 1964–5, in Harold Wilson's Labour Government. Dr John Robinson was the Bishop of Woolwich and lecturer at Trinity College, Cambridge. He was author of the controversial *Honest to God*, which introduced situationalist ethics to an anglophone audience: J. Robinson, *Honest to God*, London: SCM Press, 1963.
3   R.G. Collingwood, *The Idea of History*, Oxford: Oxford University Press, 1946; L. J. Goldstein, *Historical Knowing*, Austin, TX: University of Austin at Texas, 1976.
4   For a debate on the Pilkington Report, see: Hansard, House of Lords (HL) Debate, 18 July 1962, vol. 242, cc605–765.
5   A. Marwick, *The Sixties: Cultural Revolution in Britain, France, Italy, and the United States, c.1958–c.1974*, Oxford: Oxford University Press, 1998.
6   F. Sutcliffe-Braithwaite, 'Class, community and individualism in English politics society', Unpublished thesis, University of Cambridge, 1994.
7   Marwick, *The Sixties*, p. 74.
8   Transcript materials from the trials are reproduced in Bill Wyman with R. Coleman, *Stone Alone: The Story of a Rock 'n' Roll Band*, London: Viking, 1990, pp. 422–77. For Richards' own account, see: Keith Richards, *Life*, London: Weidenfeld & Nicolson, 2010, pp. 225–30. Marianne Faithfull was found at the drugs' raid wearing only a rabbit-fur rug. She subsequently said of the incident: 'It destroyed me. To be a male drug addict and to act like that is always enhancing and glamorising. A woman in that situation becomes a slut and a bad mother'.
9   McCartney made these comments in an ITN interview that was broadcast on 19 June 1967. Two minutes of this interview are available widely online, www.youtube.com/user/beatlesbible/videos, last accessed 22.09.19.
10 N. Cohn, *Awopbopaloobop Alopbambooom: Pop From the Beginning*, London: Paladin, 1970.
11 E.H. Carr, *What Is History?* Reprint, Basingstoke: Palgrave, 2001, p. 45.

12 J. Osborne, *Look Back in Anger: A Play in Three Acts*, London: Faber & Faber, 1958; K. Allsop, *The Angry Decade: A Survey of the cultural Revolt of the 1950s*, London: Peter Owen, 1958; J. R. Taylor, *Anger and After: A Guide to the New Drama*, London: Pelican/Penguin Books, 1961.
13 I. Murdoch, 'A house of theory', in N. MacKenzie (ed.), *Conviction*, London: MacGibbon & Kee, 1958, reprinted in P. J. Conradi (ed.), *Existentialists and Mystics: Writings on Philosophy and Literature*, London: Penguin, 1997, pp. 171–87.
14 M. Abrams, *The Teenage Consumer*, London: Press Exchange, 1959, p. 3.
15 J.H. Goldthorpe, et al., *The Affluent Worker: Industrial Attitudes and Behaviour*, Cambridge: Cambridge University Press, 1968.
16 This collection contained containing individual portraits of the new icons – Jagger, Lennon, McCartney, Caine, Terence Stamp, Rudolf Nureyev, David Hockney, and even the Kray Twins.
17 C. Booker, *The Neophiliacs: The Revolution in English Life in the Fifties and Sixties*, London: Harper Collins, 1969.
18 G. Aquilina Ross, *The Day of the Peacock: Style for Men, 1963–73*, London: V & A Publishing, 2011.
19 E. Robinson, C. Schofield, F. Sutcliffe-Braithwaite, and N. Thomlinson, 'Telling Stories about Post-war Britain: Popular individualism and the "crisis" of the 1970s', *Twentieth Century British History*, 28.2, 2017, 268–304.
20 H. Vickers (Ed,), *Beaton in the Sixties: More Unexpurgated Diaries*, London: Weidenfeld & Nicolson, 1993, p. 160.
21 T. Sanchez, *Up and Down with the Rolling Stones: My Rollercoaster Ride with Keith Richards* (1979), Reprint, London: John Blake, 2010, pp. 59–79.
22 The quotation is from the Augustan poet, Alexander Pope, who in 1735 wrote 'Epistle to Dr Arbuthnot'. The latter had cautioned against satirising the Establishment of the day, and Pope in response alluded to the torture of the Catherine wheel: A. Pope, 'Epistle to Dr Arbuthnot', l. 308. The original was *'upon* a wheel'. [William Rees Mogg], 'Who breaks a Butterfly on a Wheel?', *The Times*, Saturday 1 July 1967, issue 56982, p. 11.
23 B. Wyman with R. Coleman, *Stone Alone: The Story of a Rock 'n' Roll Band*, London: Viking, 1990, p. 425.
24 Telephone interview: Philip Kiszely with Stash Klossowki de Rola, 6 January 2019.
25 John Birt's comments taken from his MacTaggart Lecture delivered to the Edinburgh International Television Festival in 2005.
26 The words of the press conference in Soho on 31 July 1967 are reported in M. Paytress, *Rolling Stones: Off the Record*, London: Omnibus Press, 2009, n.p.
27 On 31 July 2017, the conservative tabloid, *The Daily Express*, published a review of the event after fifty years: D. Robson, 'Sympathy for the devil: 50 years ago today Mick Jagger faced the Establishment on TV', *Express*, www.express.co.uk/life-style/life/834968/rolling-stones-mick-jagger-faced-establishment-on-tv, last accessed 22.09.19.
28 Wyman, *Stone Alone*, pp. 408–9.
29 A commentary on his attitude to the immigration question can be found in G. K. Fry, *The Politics of Decline: An Interpretation of British Politics From the 1940s to the 1970s*, Basingstoke: Palgrave MacMillan, 2005, pp. 206–7.
30 Robinson, *Honest to God*, see: n. 2.
31 N. Kent, *The Dark Stuff: The Best of Nick Kent*, London: Penguin Books, 1994, p. 128.
32 Miles (ed.), *Mick Jagger in His Own Words*, London: Omnibus Press, 1982, p. 9.
33 W. Rees-Mogg, *William Rees-Mogg: Memoirs*, London: Harper Press, 2011, p. 159.
34 Blog, *A Dandy in Aspic*, 'Prince Stash Klossowski De Rola – 1960's Peacock Style Icon', posted 27 March 2012, http://dandyinaspic.blogspot.com/2012/03/prince-stash-klossowski-de-rola-1960s.html, last accessed 22.09.19.
35 Rees-Mogg, *Memoirs*, p. 158.

Further reading

Das, Saudamini, 'Television is more effective in bringing behavioral change: Evidence from heat-wave awareness campaign in India', *World Development*, 88, 2016, 107–21.

Durham, Kim, 'Methodology and praxis of the actor within the television production process: Facing the camera in *Eastenders* and *Morse*', *Studies in Theatre and Performance*, 22.2, 2002, 82–94.

Leichter, Hope Jensen, Durre Ahmed, Leoncio Barrios, Jennifer Bryce, Eric Larsen and Laura Moe, 'Family contexts of television', *Educational Technology Research and Development* (*ETRD*), 33.3, 1985, 26–40.

Messaris, Paul, *Visual 'Literacy': Image, Mind, and Reality*, Boulder, CO: Westview Pressm, 1994.

Paytress, Mark, *Rolling Stones: Off the Record*, London: Omnibus Press, 2009.

Rumsey, Francis, *Spatial Audio*, Oxford: Focal Press, 2001.

Sutcliffe-Braithwaite, Florence, *Class Politics, and the Decline of Deference in England, 1968–2000*, Oxford: Oxford University Press, 2018.

Wells, Simon, *Butterfly on a Wheel: The Great Rolling Stones Drugs Bust*, London: Omnibus Press, 2012.

8 Digital surrogates
Archaeological materialities

Adam Rabinowitz

In 2013, historian Robin Fleming was awarded a MacArthur 'genius' grant. The work for which Fleming was recognized centered on the incorporation of archaeological evidence into historical investigation. Several years earlier, she had argued that historians failed to pay attention to the material evidence for the periods in which they were interested, and thus missed the chance to write the stories of people who were invisible in the documentary evidence. Illustrating her point with the 'biography' of an anonymous seventh-century woman sketched from her skeletal remains, she concluded that 'the work of archaeologists can help us recuperate a world of intimate details about long-dead beings whose lives were never captured in words.'[1]

Fleming's observation reflects a broader 'material turn' in historical scholarship over the last half-century that has paralleled the development of social, cultural, and economic histories – that is, historical investigations that focus not on prominent men and literate elites but on the faceless masses and unrecorded daily interactions that shape any historical period. The convergence of the material and textual records was driven in part by new approaches to historiography: material culture allowed scholars reconstructing daily life to get at the physical reality behind household inventories and wills, fostered the investigation of long-term changes in land use through the combination of archaeological field survey and historical maps, and provided the raw materials to write the economic histories of periods for which documentary sources are scarce. And, as questions of identity, ethnicity, gender, and self-presentation captured the attention of historians, the archaeological record offered an opportunity to look behind or around the carefully fashioned images presented by the texts. Fleming's own work on Britain in the centuries following the ebb of the Roman Empire takes full advantage of these opportunities, and this and similar studies show how powerful this approach can be when done well.[2]

The effectiveness of material culture in bringing history to life has been reinforced by a series of public-facing works that explained long-term historical phenomena through the lens of individual objects. The highest profile of these may have been the 'History of the World in 100 Objects,' a BBC radio program presented by Neil MacGregor, then director of the British Museum, which became a web exhibit and eventually a book.[3] Like Fleming's biography of a skeleton, this approach centers on the close reading of a single object that acts as an example representative of larger historical trends. But in a new way it also draws on the possibilities offered by digital databases: the interactive website that accompanied the program made it possible to jump visually from one object to others connected to it, creating links from shared attributes in the descriptive information in the object records. For historians interested in the incorporation of archaeological material in their research, online databases have opened new doors. No longer is it necessary to find physical objects in museum storerooms or in the pages of obscure grey-literature reports stored in county archives. It is now possible to find online a digital surrogate of almost any object one might desire as an illustration of a particular point, often through simple keyword or image searches.

The proliferation of digital information about material culture has also made it possible to perform distant reading almost as easily as close reading. As individual databases absorb more information, and as it becomes easier to integrate records across multiple databases, historians are given access to something like the 'big data' that has transformed information science. The sheer volume of digital surrogates available facilitates quantitative argumentation and the identification of long-term social and historical processes, as two competing interpretations of the fluctuations of the Roman economy based on coin-hoard distribution and archaeological evidence for lead pollution have recently demonstrated.[4] Similarly, access to data about the material record of the past makes it easier to connect disparate historical sources to build a global narrative, as historian Monica Green currently seeks to do with the history of *Yersinia pestis*, the bacterium responsible for the Black Death.[5] Online archaeological information thus not only facilitates the 'material turn' by presenting a vast number of individual objects for close reading but also feeds a more 'quantitative turn' inspired by the availability of large historical datasets covering long timespans.

The potential of these digital archaeological surrogates for historical research should be immensely exciting to historians working today. But there are also risks. This is particularly true when scholars from one field fail to apply a rigorous critical perspective to evidence from the other. Both archaeologists and historians are trained to recognize the importance of context in their engagement with their primary sources, and to take a sober view of the limitations of those sources. It can be tempting, however, to borrow knowledge from another domain uncritically – either by blindly trusting a claim made in secondary scholarship, or by selecting only that piece of primary evidence that reinforces one's argument. Such borrowing can be especially dangerous at the intersection of history and archaeology, since it tends to create a feedback loop in which an unsupported assumption in one discipline engenders a second in the other. This is true on the level of the individual object: where literary references to the Viking invasion of northern England might lead an archaeologist in the area to assume that the burials of Scandinavian individuals must be recognizable, and therefore to treat an object in a burial as conclusive evidence of an individual's ethnicity, an historian might point to the archaeologist's identification of 'Scandinavian' burials as evidence that confirms the historical accounts.[6]

Both historians and archaeologists, therefore, must be careful to apply the same critical perspective they bring to their own sources to sources from other fields of knowledge – not only each other's evidence but also to evidence from a widening range of scientific disciplines, from genetics to geosciences. The increasing online availability of digital surrogates for primary sources, from manuscript scans to excavation records, makes this point even more important. It is now both easier to find primary evidence in digital form and harder to sort, filter, and understand the contexts of specific items within that flood of material.[7] Furthermore, search algorithms tend to favor popular information, creating bubbles in which 'celebrity' items are overrepresented and lower-profile material is invisible. It becomes increasingly difficult to know what we do not know, which makes it more difficult to treat evidence critically. Meanwhile, we are presented with an abundance of decontextualized objects from museum databases, encouraging object-centric approaches that engage with the formal properties of an artifact rather than its associations.

For the historian who wishes to work with digital archaeological evidence, therefore, it is critical to remember that context is central to interpretation. Fortunately, there is an expanding set of online platforms that provide rich context for individual artifacts while still offering the analytical advantages of large datasets. Most of these platforms feature visualizations that help place records in space and time, and many of them also use semantic-web principles to connect their contents to external reference points and additional data sources. They operate at various scales: some of them aggregate data from multiple sources, while others focus on a single research project. All of them, however, give the historical researcher a chance to understand both the archaeological context of objects of interest and the social and methodological processes that shaped their current digital context. They are therefore an extremely valuable resource for holistic historical inquiries that seek to integrate textual and material sources.

An historian who wishes to incorporate material evidence into historical analysis is usually driven by some of the research questions mentioned earlier, questions related to long-term change, non-elite experience, large-scale social or economic phenomena, cultural interaction, and identity. An historian who plans to use online resources to help answer these questions, however, must begin with a more practical set of queries. First is the question of where to find a particular artifact or object type, and of how many examples are necessary for the research – that is, what is a valid sample size on which to base an argument? Archaeological knowledge is based on the repetition of forms and patterns, and in many ways unique objects are the least informative. One of the greatest advantages of digital archaeology is the possibility to bring together large quantities of data that might otherwise be scattered across numerous storerooms or publications, but this still takes work, and the historian should begin with a sense of how much data will be required.

Once one has found information about the relevant materials, one must interrogate the digital platform in which records of the object(s) are housed: for what audience and purpose was it built? What collection and selection processes dictated its content and the ways in which that content is described? What is missing, and what stated or unstated biases or agendas are responsible for that absence? Finally, the historian must turn to more traditional questions of context. On the most general level, at the macro-scale, such questions tend to be quantitative, concerned with identifying comparable spatial and temporal coordinates for objects from disparate datasets, a prerequisite for reliable data visualization. At the most granular micro-scale, on the other hand, the historian must seek to understand the qualitative archaeological context and documentation of individual objects within a single digital platform, in order to reconstruct the way an object was used, deposited, and recovered – and thus how it can be used to reconstruct aspects of past life not included in textual sources.

In the sections that follow, three specific case studies exemplify the promise and problems of historical research using digital archaeological surrogates in context. Each case study focuses on a particular archaeological database, a particular analytical scale (macro, meso, and micro), and a particular set of challenges and opportunities for historical interpretation. All three are connected, however, by a shared focus on a specific category of archaeological material: coins. They have long played a role in the fields of ancient and medieval history and are simultaneously intensely contextual and easily decontextualized. On the archaeological side, coins are almost always documented because they provide crucial chronological information; on the historical side, they are frequently used as evidence for economic trends, political developments, and cultural interaction. They also have both quantitative and qualitative facets: one can count them or map their distribution, or one can assess the ideological value of the images they bear. Coins are thus an ideal lens through which to explore the use of digital archaeology in historical research.

The macro-scale: data discovery and aggregation

Finding old coins online is easy: simple search-engine trawls for 'Late Roman coins' return 11.4 million hits, many of them with high-quality photographs. But it quickly becomes apparent that the most popular results are from commercial coin dealers, whose items tend to lack context. An isolated coin can provide information about iconography but not about social or economic history. A large-scale analysis of the frequency of certain types might be more useful for those questions, but it would be very difficult to carry out with dealer information: although coin descriptions are highly standardized, the underlying databases maintained by dealers are not publicly available, and thus any data aggregation would involve matching text strings across websites. Even if such an analysis could be carried out, the frequency of specific types could not necessarily be understood as a reflection of historical developments. Those statistics could be just as easily interpreted as the result of modern market preferences: do coins of a certain mint appear more often because more coins were being minted there in the past, or because they are simply more desirable for collectors in the present?

Fortunately, commercial search engines are not the only route to discovery. The historical disciplines have been helped in this regard by two relatively recent developments: the so-called 'spatial turn' in the humanities and the rise of the Semantic Web and Linked Open Data. Together, these developments have made it easier to place objects in space and to bring together records from different databases that refer to the same entities, whether ancient cities or object types. Historians working on topics like long-distance trade have made good use of digital mapping technologies and better access to object records across databases.[8] And Linked Open Data standards, which make the contextual associations of objects searchable, have allowed third-party platforms to bring together information from heterogeneous datasets for unified complex searches. The Pelagios project, for example, has built a Linked Open Data ecosystem for the ancient world centered on shared gazetteers of ancient places, like Pleiades (https://pleiades.stoa.org).[9] Standards for spatial references shared by a number of data contributors underlie the Peripleo map browser (http://peripleo.pelagios.org/), which displays ancient places and the records associated with them in an interactive map [Figure 8.1].

A similar aggregation portal is provided by the EU-based ARIADNE project (www.ariadne-infrastructure.eu/), which maps a variety of archaeological datasets from European partners to a single formal ontology.[10] In contrast to the Pelagios project, categories rather than space are the primary tools for integration and search. Whereas the net cast by Pelagios pulls in everything that might be related to an ancient place, leaving the user to sort out what is useful, ARIADNE allows very precise filtering through numerous facets, but relies on the user to have a very clear idea of the object of the search. It also aggregates metadata for whole datasets, not just individual records, which increases the chances that a user will

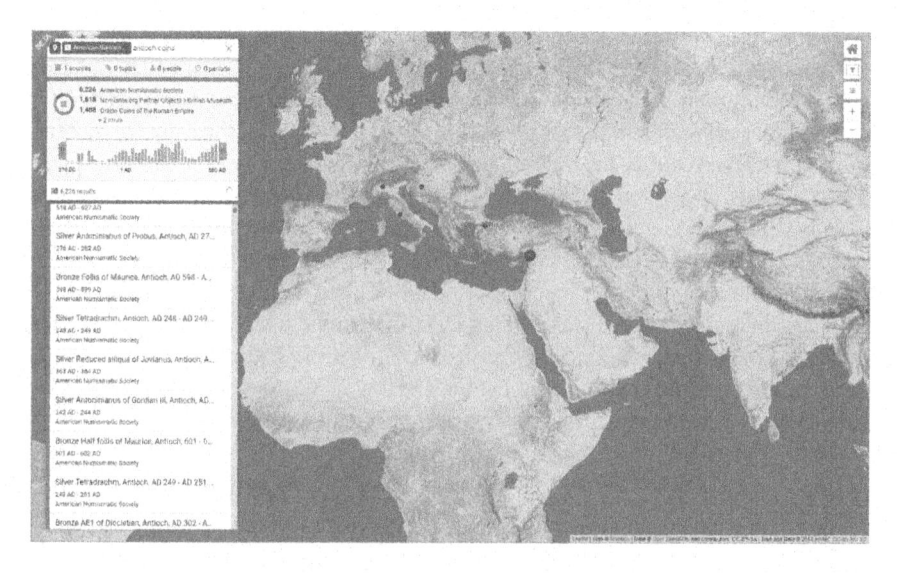

Figure 8.1 Screen capture of a search in the Peripleo browser for coins from Antioch

Source: Peripleo, an initiative of Pelagious Commons, http://peripleo.pelagios.org/; map data courtesy of Ancient World Mapping Center (accessed 29 August 2019).

discover relevant sources of information but decreases the likelihood of finding individual objects.

Both of these platforms offer a view from 30,000 feet. Under the right circumstances, the temporal and spatial visualization and dynamic filtering of data in massive aggregation platforms can allow a user to see very large-scale patterns that would not be visible in an individual dataset. On the other hand, neither platform offers enough information about the datasets being visualized to allow the user to understand the context of a set of search results. For that, it is necessary to explore records in the individual databases in which they are located. Both platforms are primarily reconnaissance tools – starting points for further research, not resources for historical argumentation. While they will probably direct a researcher toward material of interest, they may not even provide a useful answer to the question of how much information is globally available (a search of records related to the place-concept 'Antioch' returns more than 4,000 records in Pelagios, most of them related to coins; a search of records with the string 'Antioch' and the formal subject 'coins' in ARIADNE returns just one). To identify and understand a body of digital archaeological data in better context, we need to zoom in a bit for our first case study. Here, as in the following case studies, the examination of objects in context will be framed by a hypothetical research agenda focused on the role of the mint at Antioch in Late Roman economic history.

Case study one: Open Context

For an historian using a search engine to explore the distribution of coins minted in the Antioch mint in the fourth century CE, a very broad set of criteria returns too many false positives, while a very narrow set of criteria omits too much. These problems can be alleviated by a platform that hosts full datasets mapped to a shared data structure and some common vocabularies. This combines the potential for detailed faceted search, like that provided by ARIADNE, with the capacity of Pelagios to retrieve records for individual objects. In the best case, it can also place those records in context within the research project that produced them. This is exactly what Open Context (https://opencontext.org) seeks to do. Defined by its developers as an online data publication platform, Open Context maps datasets from individual archaeological projects to a common data structure and publishes the resulting integrated datasets as Linked Data in a single interactive interface. This makes it much easier to find all the instances of a particular object type across those datasets, while ensuring that the underlying data is documented properly for future reuse.[11] At the same time, the platform's attention to preserving the original context of the data – and thus the form and structure of the original database or dataset – means that the user has access to all the information provided by the contributing project. Where the data supplied are both dense and consistent, the platform has supported important integrative research, such as a study showing how the domestication of the pig spread across the Near East and Anatolia.[12]

The strengths and weaknesses of this contextual, integrative, single-platform approach to sharing archaeological data become visible when our hypothetical ancient historian seeks to use Open Context to identify the frequency and distribution of Late Roman coins minted at Antioch. As a result of the shared mapping and vocabularies, the search can unfold through filters as well as free-text queries: one moves from general to specific, selecting first the data category 'object' and then, within that, the category 'coin,' and then further narrowing those results by selecting 'origin place' from another filter menu. The locations on the accompanying map diminish as this process unfolds, indicating to the researcher that each further refinement limits the results to a smaller number of datasets containing those values. Only two – the Anatolian Neolithic site of Domuztepe and the Great Temple excavations at Petra – recorded the 'origin place' of the coins recovered. Nonetheless, there are still more than 350 coins that can be matched to a mint, and of those more than 150 are associated with Antioch. The project markers on the map view are sized according to the number of records, which shows that Domuztepe has the most coins, while the temporal histogram indicates that the vast majority of the results fall within the fourth century CE [Figure 8.2].

Selecting 'Antioch' as a further filter confirms this visual impression. Of the coins from that mint, most are from Domuztepe, and only a few are from Petra. Because each dataset provides different information about context, it is most useful at this point to filter the results further by project – and here the differences in documentation become obvious. The coins from Petra, most of which date from the same range between 200 CE and 350 or 360 CE, can be placed in the stratigraphic unit from which they were excavated, and this well-described stratigraphic unit can in turn be located within a broadening spatial frame (the trench where the unit was found, the part of the site at Petra where the trench was found, and so on). This helps the researcher to understand the nature of the deposition event that left a coin in a particular place, which is critical for historical interpretation. The coin minted at Antioch between 351 and 361 and designated '97-C-21,' for example, was found in a deposit of fill related to the abandonment of the theater area of the Great Temple, and therefore it is probably a residual item that had moved around the site between the time it was dropped and the time it came to rest in this layer.[13] The usefulness of this and other coins of the Antioch mint at Petra is to show that such coinage was circulating there during the fourth century, but it makes up a relatively small percentage of the coins from that period (the project as a whole records 760 coins, more than half of which are from the same time range).

When the Domuztepe data is isolated, on the other hand, a very different picture emerges. The temporal visualization indicates that all 140 coins from Antioch are from the same very narrow fourth-century CE date-range, and when those are put in the context of all the other coins at the site, it becomes clear that this phenomenon applies to the entire set of 296. By contrast with the small proportion of coins minted at Antioch in the Petra data, coins from the Antioch mint make up almost half of the total number of coins. On a simple distribution map, these quantitative results suggest that the site was more economically engaged with the eastern Roman economy in the fourth century CE than was the major trading center of Petra. But because the contextual information in the database is limited to whatever the project has provided, the explanation for the pattern is not

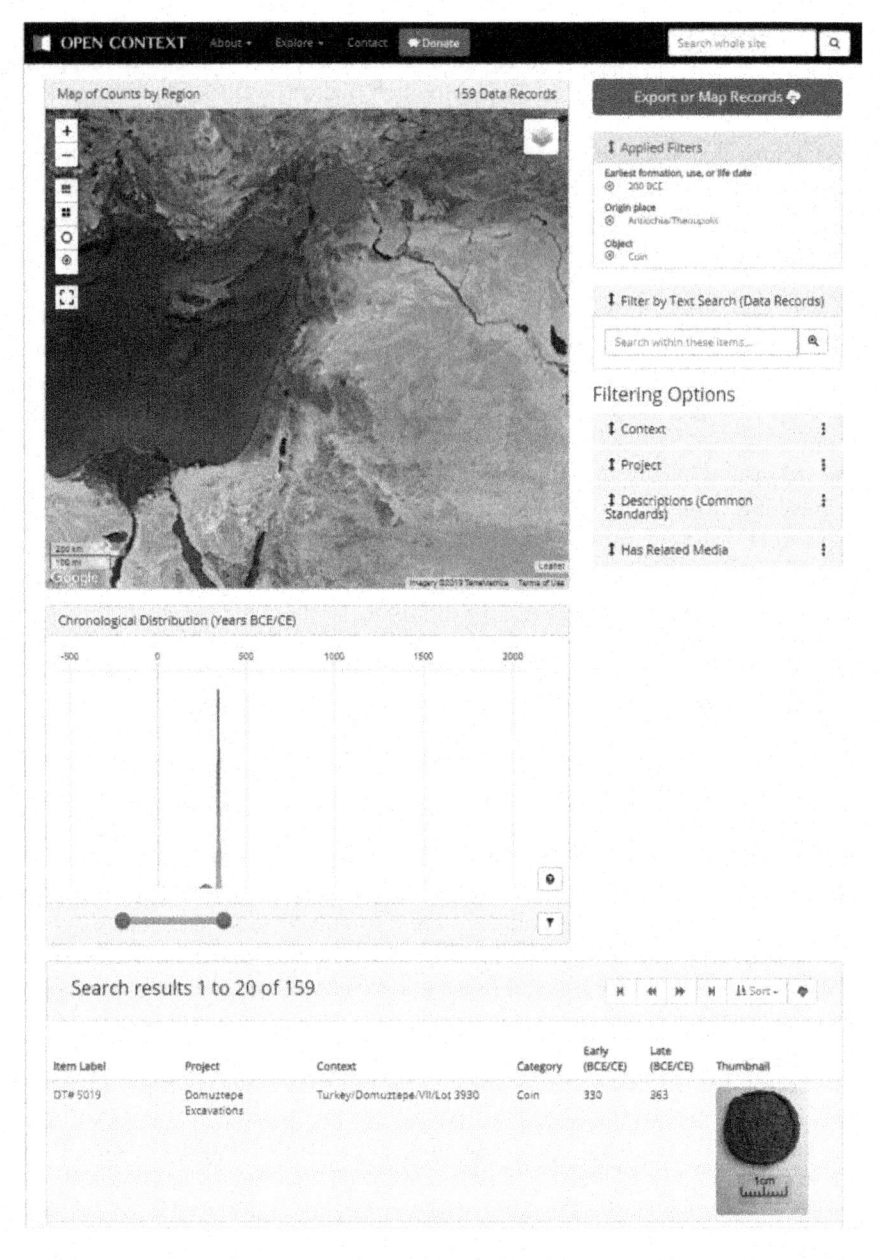

Figure 8.2 Screen capture of search results in Open Context for records marked 'coin' including a value for 'origin place.'

Source: Open Context, https://opencontext.org (accessed 29 August 2019).

immediately obvious. Selecting DT# 5019, one of the coins in this series, shows that it belongs to 'Lot 3930,' which includes 95 other coins and nothing else, and is not clearly identified as a stratigraphic unit or some other documentation unit.[14] The lot is in turn part of 'VII (Operation),' which groups together a series of other lots, all of which consist exclusively of coins. While it is not clear at this point what Operation VII is, the large number of coins grouped together suggests the presence of a hoard, rather than a representative sample of currency across the site, as does the inconsistency between the coin dates and the site's primarily Neolithic occupation.

Our historian, having gathered this information, must now consider how best to use it. On the one hand, the ease of extracting these data, and the spatial coordinates provided, make it easy to visualize the results of the research as an online map or in a GIS platform. On the other hand, for the historian's research question about the role of the Antioch mint in the Late Roman economy, the data aggregated are not sufficiently comparable, since individual coins and hoards provide very different sorts of information. In the future, better aggregation may make it possible to address a question this specific with a quantitative argument, but for the moment, the visualization of these search results does not actually reveal a macro-level economic pattern. At this point, it would make more sense for the historian to look instead at a meso-scale case, where a geographically limited database might contain a sample of coins or hoards large enough to be representative of an entire region, but consistent enough in description to make it easy to find Late Roman coins minted at Antioch.

The meso-scale: spatial and social context

When we move from an international dataset to a national or regional one, detail, consistency, and spatial resolution often increase. It is easier to manage data from a smaller area, especially if there are governmental bodies that oversee archaeological fieldwork and mandate certain standards. Databases organized on a national level are a good starting point for research into the spatial distribution of particular object types or classes, but there are often restrictions on the use of governmental databases, and even there, data structures can be inconsistent or opaque to the non-initiated. They can also be biased toward the type of archaeology that national or regional governments are tasked to manage, generally in connection with development – so a distribution map in such a dataset may be a better reflection of where modern roads or pipelines have been built than where objects were used and deposited in the past. There are, however, a few exceptions that manage to balance openness, standardization, and information provided by a wider range of contributors. One of those, the Portable Antiquities Scheme, serves as our second case study. Here we will see the power of a high-resolution view of spatial distribution, but we will also grapple with the social context of the dataset and the effect of that context on quality and coverage.

Case study two: the Portable Antiquities Scheme (PAS)

The Portable Antiquities Scheme (https://finds.org.uk/) was an initiative of what is now the Department for Culture, Media & Sport in the government of the United Kingdom. It was established to encourage the voluntary reporting of chance archaeological finds by members of the public, many of whom participate in a robust culture of metal-detecting on private land. Its timing coincided with the passage of the Treasure Act, which was intended to update laws stretching back to the Middle Ages on the discovery of 'treasure troves' and to clarify the state's claims over objects of precious metal found in the ground. The heritage community was concerned, however, that objects not covered by the Act would simply disappear from sight, and so PAS was established as a place where members of the public could report these less spectacular finds. The British Museum became increasingly involved in its administration in the early 2000s. Since then, PAS has adopted Linked Data principles that permit the description of PAS records with external identifiers that can connect them to other resources.[15]

It is thus a platform that takes advantage of citizen science carried out by a large and enthusiastic amateur community while standardizing its contents in such a way that descriptions are internally consistent and externally linked. There are a very large number of records, with fairly broad and regular coverage across the country, and one can search not only for 'coin' as an object type but also for the specific mint as defined by the Pleiades spatial gazetteer and the Nomisma numismatic metadata standard (http://nomisma.org/). This search produces more than 200 results, of which more than 80 have attached spatial data: these are found from Newcastle in the north to the very southwest tip of Cornwall [Figure 8.3]. Furthermore, PAS also records hoards as separate records, so that the scatter of lost coins can be compared with deliberately deposed collections that also contain coins from the mint at Antioch: only three appear in a search, but one of them (London hoard LON-B81CC8, https://finds.org.uk/database/artefacts/record/id/488876) reflects the very end of the Roman period in Britain and includes a single gold coin from the Antioch mint among 133 others, almost all from mints at sites in France and Germany. This is useful information about the shape of economic currents at a moment of major political and historical transition.

The context provided for this hoard, however, highlights some of the drawbacks of PAS's crowdsourced approach. Although this deposit was in fact scientifically excavated, the only contextual information within that record indicates that it was found 'in an ill-defined cut through the backfill of a ditch that served as the northern boundary of a late Roman cemetery.'[16] The nature of the database, which was designed to collect information about sporadic finds, precludes extensive information on context, which means that it works best for research that is concerned with general spatial and statistical patterns. Because of the quantity of information in PAS, and because of both policies and information architecture designed to facilitate the sharing and reuse of data, it has generated a substantial amount of quantitative historical research, including several recent studies that have based their analyses primarily on the PAS dataset.[17] Interestingly, a subgroup

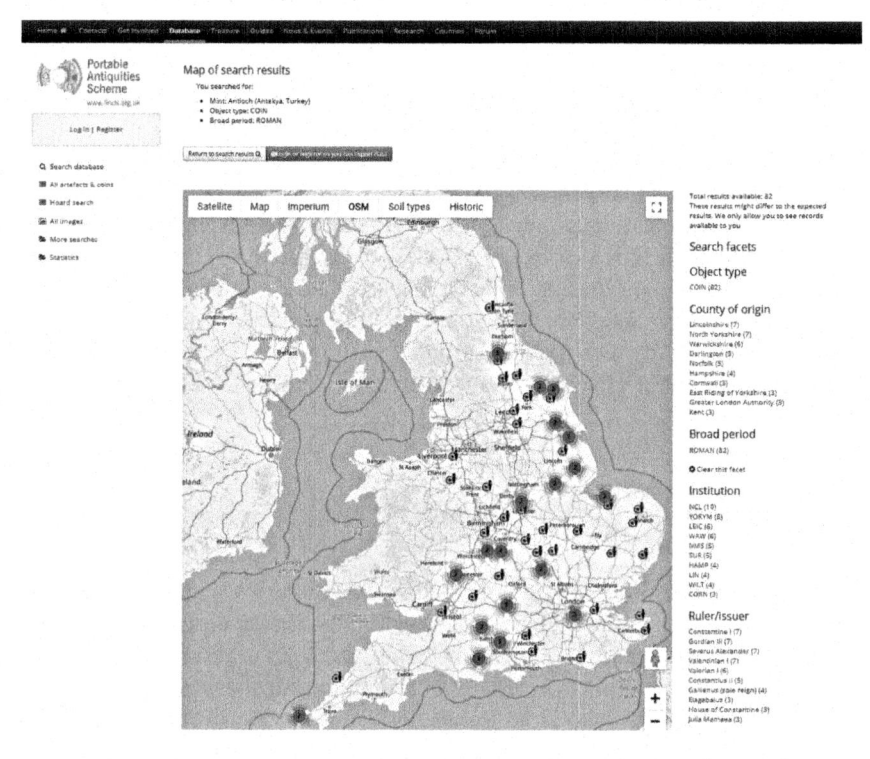

Figure 8.3 Screen capture of the spatial distribution of results of a PAS search for coins minted at Antioch

Source: The Portable Antiques Scheme/The Trustees of the British Museum, https://finds.org.uk (accessed 29 August 2019).

of these studies have focused on both the biases in the dataset itself and the degree to which it reflects (or even encourages) illegal excavation and the destruction of archaeological heritage.[18]

Such studies bring to the fore the trade-offs required by the social context of PAS. One of the original intents of the platform was to transform metal-detectorists into collaborators in archaeological science, rather than simply treasure-hunters, and to inspire the English public at large to contribute to the documentation of their own heritage. Critics of PAS have argued, however, that it has done little to diminish illicit metal-detecting activity, and, moreover, that its database represents a substantial underreporting of the finds recovered by detectorists.[19] This should inspire caution in the historian who seeks to treat the PAS dataset as a surrogate for the archaeological landscape of the UK: if only some finds are reported, and if there is no clear pattern in what is chosen for reporting, interpretations based on quantitative analysis of the dataset can only be preliminary. Furthermore, on a qualitative level, the platform's managers note that the quality of information can be variable from record to record, both because the database has changed over time and because the information is collected from public contributors with varying degrees of expertise.

Open Context incorporates multiple datasets from both excavation and survey archaeology across the world and facilitates research into very large-scale historical trends. PAS is limited in its spatial coverage, and the data in its single dataset is mainly equivalent to the sort of data produced by survey archaeology, fostering higher-resolution quantitative analyses of regional contexts. At the micro-scale of digital archaeological data, where individual objects and their contexts are extensively documented, lies the excavation database. Just as digital data aggregators provide new opportunities for distant reading of long-term spatio-temporal patterns that can only be seen through surrogate materialities, excavation databases offer richer potential for contextual interpretation and object biography than a single physical object in a museum display case.

The micro-scale: archaeological method and stratigraphic context

At the macro- and meso-scales of the Open Context and PAS, an object's digital surrogates are connected to other surrogates through shared descriptive information (place, period, type). As a result, the maps and tables of results that appear in response to a query in both platforms eclipse the practical aspects of the activities that produced the data. In an excavation database, however, the contextual associations of a single object are more visibly entangled with the methods and history of the excavation itself. Changes in excavation method or documentation strategies over the life of a project can leave some objects with less context than others, or with context that has to be reconstructed in a different way. Thus the database of a long-term project becomes a surrogate both for the physical objects and deposited documents, and for the changing social, historical, and scientific contexts in which that documentation was produced.

Strangely, historians have not yet begun to take much advantage of the opportunities offered by such databases, despite their ability to fulfil Fleming's calls for histories that capture the biographies of the voiceless, and despite their potential relevance for historians of science. The digital database of the Corinth excavations, which have been carried out by the American School of Classical Studies at Athens for more than a century, is a particularly good example. Not only does the database include a range of digitized and born-digital records stretching back decades, but the most recent excavation team has published a guide that explains how collection and documentation were carried out in the field in the more recent campaigns.[20] Yet to date there has been no systematic use of its rich information by historians of ancient Greece or those who study the history of archaeology. In contrast to the previous case studies, this last case study focuses on the untapped potential for close historical reading offered by ancient Corinth's digital surrogates.

Case study three: the Corinth archaeological database

The American School project at Corinth began in 1896 and has run continuously with only a few interruptions since then. As a result, archaeological practice at the site has tracked larger disciplinary developments across the twentieth and twenty-first centuries. The basic principles of this practice had already been established by the nineteenth century: the history of a site could be reconstructed by excavating it by layers in reverse order, from top to bottom, and the objects recovered could be associated with other objects by virtue of similar depth or co-presence in a particular deposit or feature. These associations in turn could be connected to historical events or cultures. But the level of attention to detail in Classical excavations – and, for that matter, the details considered worth recording – changed dramatically over the twentieth century, from a focus on the monumental architecture and sculpture of the Classical period at the beginning, to attention to historical questions of daily life, political and economic development, and diachronic change in society and beliefs across *all* periods by the end.

The recording system at Corinth developed in tandem with this disciplinary arc. Early excavations employed large numbers of workmen and had a particular focus on exposing the buildings of the Greek and Roman era. Record-keeping involved the trench notebooks of the supervisory staff and the running inventory of noteworthy finds.[21] By the 1960s, a more consistent recording system was in place. The central recording unit in this system was the 'basket,' named after the physical baskets in which associated finds were placed during excavation but referring essentially to a stratigraphic unit: if ceramic fragments or other evidence matched across baskets, those baskets would be joined after the fact as a 'lot.' In the 2000s, there was a gradual terminological shift from 'basket' to 'context,' as the project methodology shifted toward the system of open-area, single-context excavation developed in the UK in the 1970s and 1980s. During the same period, as digital technologies were increasingly employed for excavation recording in the field, the American School embarked on an ambitious program of digitization and data integration that brought together scans of the notebooks from the twentieth century, digitized object records from the paper inventory cards of the same period, and new information being generated in the course of ongoing excavations.

The result is an extensive, unified archaeological database that contains records from more than a hundred years of excavation at the same site. Unlike the material in Open Context and PAS, which was generated largely in the context of new work, this archival material facilitates the historian's digital access to objects found and published (or not published) as much as a century ago. Because the platform was built for legacy as well as new data, and because it reflects a single project with standards that changed across time, rather than different projects with different standards that must be unified, it does not attempt to align various categories of information to a single schema, as both Open Context and PAS do. Even when a researcher understands diachronic changes in methods, standards, and terms at the Corinth excavations, therefore, it can still be difficult to find specific

160 *Adam Rabinowitz*

objects or types of object in the database. Coins once again represent the lowest hanging fruit in this ecosystem. A search for coins from the mint of Antioch represents one of the most straightforward inquiries one can make of the Corinth database. Exploring the record of a single coin in its full archaeological context can be a revelatory experience for an historian interested in reconstructing a vivid picture of life in the past. But it also raises issues related to the consideration of objects in digital contexts and should alert the historian to the more complicated situations that will inevitably be presented by less-standardized material.

Searching for 'coins' as a class and 'Antioch' as a term leads quickly to coins from the Roman-period mint, and with some attention to cross-references to the notebook pages on which they appear, it is relatively easy to reconstruct a detailed context. Coin 1928–134, for example, a coin of Constantine I minted at Antioch in the early fourth century, is associated with p. 60, line 18 of Notebook 101.[22] The scanned image of that notebook page shows, at that line, the note that a group of 24 coins was found 'on the floor of vault passage south of [the] cavea' of the Odeion [Figure 8.4]. Because the coins were found in a group, this almost certainly

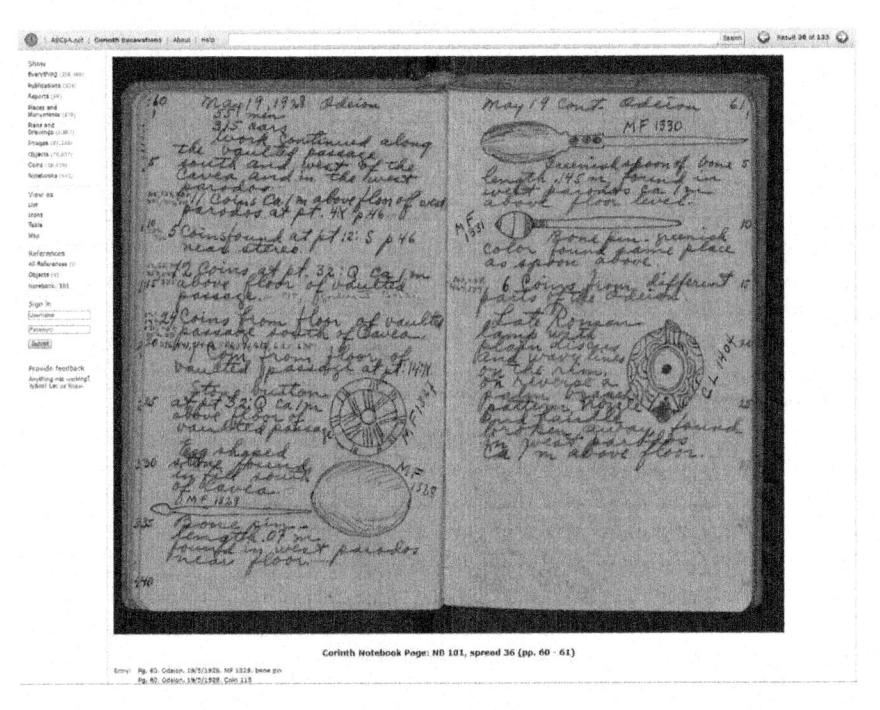

Figure 8.4 Scanned image of page 60 of notebook 101, from the 1928 excavations in Corinth

Source: (http://ascsa.net/id/corinth/notebookpage/nb%20101%2c%20spread%2036%20%28pp.%2060%20-%2061%29?q=corinth%20notebook%20101%2C%20spread%2036&t=&v=list&sort=&s=2). ASCSA Digital Collections, Corinth Excavations, http://corinth.ascsa.net (accessed 29 August 2019). Courtesy of the American School of Classical Studies at Athens, Corinth Excavations.

represents a primary deposition, which means that the coin was still circulating just before that deposit was formed. Consulting the other records for the Odeion reveals that the building was destroyed around the end of the fourth century, around the time that historical sources mention a sack by Visigoths; furthermore, the notebook entry for the previous day indicates that human bones belonging to at least one adult and one child were found in the same area (pp. 58–59). This contextual information raises the possibility that these phenomena were associated, bringing that particular coin to life in a way that its consideration in isolation cannot.

On the other hand, a coin numbered 134 does not appear on the list of coins appended to the record for page 60, making this association uncertain; and the other coins in this list cannot be located in the database from the information provided, making it impossible to understand the chronological and spatial patterns present in the assemblage as a whole. It is not unusual in archaeological workflows for items to be re-inventoried or re-numbered after their initial discovery, especially in long-running projects, and it is also possible that the original records for these coins have not yet been added to the database. But we also learn from page 57 that 53 men were working in that area that day, and that they moved 295 'cars' (narrow-gauge railway cars full of earth). The speed and volume of the excavations in this period should thus also be taken into account when considering the accuracy of the information.

Like Open Context, the Corinth database at its best allows the user to zoom in to the details of a particular object, and then to zoom out again to see that object in its digital and stratigraphic context. The researcher must remember, however, that the larger the archive and the longer the period over which it was created, the more potential there is for error and omission. Digital frameworks make it easier to find information, but this does not mean that all that information is reliable, even in an authoritative source. Before incorporating digital archaeological data into an argument, the historian must understand not only the possible sources of error or confusion in the data but also the scale and implications of the problems. In Open Context, the potential for confusion arises from the differences in data description between projects; in PAS, errors or biases may be introduced by the crowdsourcing processes that generate the data. In the Corinth database, inconsistencies are the natural product of many different people working on a very complex project over many decades, and of the transformation of paper records to digital surrogates.

Future directions for digital context

Contextualized digital surrogates for material objects have the potential to enrich the way history is written. They offer easier direct access to archaeological data for historians who may be unfamiliar with the esoteric world of archaeological reports and paper archives, and they can be connected more readily with related material within a single project and across multiple projects. They can be aggregated to identify macroscopic patterns that unfold across regions and centuries in ways that cannot be recognized from the perspective of an individual project or publication; or they can help the historian to explore in microscopic detail the single moment of fear and anxiety when a long-dead human being dropped a handful of coins in desperate flight. But these digital records cannot be approached uncritically: the social context of their production, the history of both the discipline and any given archive, and the uncertainties of archaeological research and documentation must all be taken into account before they can be used to reconstruct the past.

This critical perspective will be all the more important in the coming decades, as digital technologies open new horizons. In the near future, we should expect increasing semantic interconnection of data: as Linked Data principles are more widely adopted, it will be easier to find information we did not know we were looking for by following a trail of connections from one digital object to another, or by grouping widely separated records together by shared attributes. Ideally, the connection of data through semantic description will also make it easier for us to filter through the rising flood of information to find what we *are* looking for. This aggregation, however, will only be as good as the data that go into it, and the potential of Linked Data will only be realized in the historical disciplines if more researchers embrace shared vocabularies or gazetteers and publish their data openly online in structured formats.

As this happens, the historian can expect even greater payoffs. Semantic frameworks will make it possible to connect archaeological materials to datasets maintained by other scientific communities, with the result that it will be easier for historians to integrate information about past climate or human genetics with text-based accounts of political or social developments. Paradigms are emerging that integrate narrative and interpretation with primary data, providing object context that currently can only be reconstructed through the exhaustive examination of scattered records. These new publications will incorporate both an account of the excavation process and the results of analysis, so that the reader can understand how and when a hoard was excavated, then move seamlessly to the descriptions of individual coins and the statistics of the deposit, and then move back out to a discussion of the spatial and temporal distribution of hoards across the site. The first wave of these publications is already here: the recent digital publication of a Roman Late Republican house at Gabii, for example, puts object records in the context of both an interpretive narrative and three-dimensional reconstructions.[23]

In the longer term, if current trends continue, there is likely to be a shift from human-driven aggregation and analysis to machine mediation of information. As projects provide more classified data, it becomes easier for computers to make sense of that data through machine-learning protocols and artificial intelligence. A search process based on natural language processing and a sophisticated recommendation algorithm might use a database search to extract relevant information from the scan of a notebook in the archive of an apparently unrelated project. More intuitive and compelling data visualizations could then be used to contextualize large sets of search results in time and space, making apparent subtle patterns that would otherwise escape our notice.

These developments would be a boon to archaeologists and historians alike, vastly increasing our ability to write history from an interdisciplinary perspective.

Digital surrogates 163

At the same time, they would exacerbate problems related to decontextualized data and uncritical analysis. Visualizations create the impression of certainty precisely by selecting and filtering the underlying data in ways that are intended to be opaque to the viewer. And algorithms are not neutral; they encode the biases of the people who develop them and of the datasets used to train and refine them.[24] The user, meanwhile, is led to assume that both search results and visualizations are objective reflections of external realities. Historians who use digital surrogates to incorporate material perspectives into their research have more opportunities to give a voice to the voiceless and articulate vast patterns than ever before; but they must also examine relentlessly the contextual information associated with an object, the processes that led to the creation of the digital records that now describe it, and the mechanisms by which those records have been selected to appear on their computer screens. Only then can they use this online information to rise responsibly to Fleming's challenge to write material remains into history.

Notes

1 R. Fleming, 'Writing biography at the edge of history', *The American Historical Review*, 114.3, 2009, 610.
2 R. Fleming, *Britain after Rome: The Fall and Rise, 400–1070*, London and New York: Penguin, 2011.
3 N. MacGregor, *A History of the World in 100 Objects*, New York: Penguin, 2013. Object records and the podcast can be accessed at www.britishmuseum.org/explore/a_history_of_the_world.aspx.
4 P. Turchin and W. Scheidel, 'Coin hoards speak of population declines in Ancient Rome', *Proceedings of the National Academy of Sciences*, 106.41, 2009, 17276–9, https://doi.org/10.1073/pnas.0904576106; J. R. McConnell, et al., 'Lead pollution recorded in Greenland ice indicates European emissions tracked plagues, wars, and imperial expansion during Antiquity', *Proceedings of the National Academy of Sciences*, 115.22, 2018, 5726–31, https://doi.org/10.1073/pnas.1721818115.
5 M. Green, 'Taking "pandemic" seriously: Making the Black Death global', *The Medieval Globe*, 1.1, 2014, https://scholarworks.wmich.edu/tmg/vol1/iss1/4.
6 See the discussion of some of these difficulties in: J. Buckberry, et al., 'Finding Vikings in the Danelaw', *Oxford Journal of Archaeology*, 33.4, 2014, 413–34.
7 A. Bevan, 'The data deluge', *Antiquity*, 89.348, 2015, 1473–84.
8 See, for example, A. Wilson, 'Saharan trade in the Roman period: Short-, medium- and long-distance trade networks', *Azania: Archaeological Research in Africa*, 47.4, 2012, 409–49; or the series of clear and accessible posts on long-distance contacts provided by Caitlin Green on her blog (www.caitlingreen.org).
9 L. Isaksen, et al., 'Pelagios and the emerging graph of ancient world data', in *Web Sci '14. Proceedings of the 2014 ACM Conference on Web Science* (ACM, 2014), 197–201, http://dl.acm.org/citation.cfm?id=2615569.2615693.
10 F. Niccolucci and J. Richards, 'ARIADNE: Advanced Research Infrastructures for Archaeological Dataset Networking in Europe', *International Journal of Humanities and Arts Computing*, 7.1–2, 2013, 70–88, https://doi.org/doi:10.3366/ijhac.2013.0082.
11 E. C. Kansa and S. Whitcher Kansa, 'Open archaeology: We all know that a 14 is a sheep: Data publication and professionalism in archaeological communication', *Journal of Eastern Mediterranean Archaeology & Heritage Studies*, 1.1, 2013, 88–97.
12 B. S. Arbuckle, et al., 'Data sharing reveals complexity in the Westward spread of domestic animals across Neolithic Turkey', *PLoS One*, 9.6, 2014, e99845, https://doi.org/10.1371/journal.pone.0099845.

13 B. H. Kleine, L.-A. Bedal, and D. Barrett, 'Coin 97-C-21 from Jordan/Petra Great Temple/Temple/Trench 47/Locus 4/Seq. 47074', in M. Sharp Joukowsky (ed.), *Petra Great Temple Excavations*, 2009, Released: 2009-10-26, Open Context, http://opencontext.org/subjects/86511BD0-3E07-402B-BC00-5E43DBC90050. ARK (Archive): https://n2t.net/ark:/28722/k2cv4j380. One of the strengths of the Open Context platform is its ability to provide a persistent, resolvable URI for every individual record, making it possible for single records in a database to be cited with confidence in scholarly publications.

14 E. Carlson, 'DT# 5019 from Turkey/Domuztepe/VII/Lot 3930', in S. Campbell and E. Carter (eds), *Domuztepe Excavations*, Released: 2010-07-31, Open Context, http://opencontext.org/subjects/766ED8AA-3147-4CA2-6ECA-BD96BE0433BE. ARK (Archive): https://n2t.net/ark:/28722/k2p55kt83.

15 D. Pett, 'Linking portable antiquities to a wider web', *ISAW Papers*, 7.20, 2014, http://dlib.nyu.edu/awdl/isaw/isaw-papers/7/pett/.; A. H. Bevan, et al., 'Citizen archaeologists: Online collaborative research about the human past', *Human Computation*, 1.2, 2014, 183–97; T. Brindle, *The Portable Antiquities Scheme and Roman Britain*, London: The British Museum, 2014.

16 K. Creed, *LON-B81CC8: A ROMAN HOARD, PAS 2012*. https://finds.org.uk/database/artefacts/record/id/488876, last accessed 29.08.2019.

17 For example, P. J. Walton, 'Rethinking Roman Britain: An applied numismatic analysis of the Roman coin data recorded by the Portable Antiquities Scheme', Unpublished PhD dissertation, University College London, 2011; or S. Moorhead, 'Early Byzantine copper coins found in Britain: A review in light of new finds recorded with the Portable Antiquities Scheme', in O. Tekin (ed.), *Ancient History, Numismatics and Epigraphy in the Mediterranean World*, Istanbul: Ege Publications, 2009, pp. 263–74.

18 K. J. Robbins, 'Balancing the scales: Exploring the variable effects of collection bias on data collected by the Portable Antiquities Scheme', *Landscapes*, 14.1, 2013, 54–72, https://doi.org/10.1179/1466203513Z.0000000006; D. Gill, 'The Portable Antiquities Scheme and the Treasure Act: Protecting the archaeology of England and Wales?', *Papers From the Institute of Archaeology*, 20, 2010, https://doi.org/10.5334/pia.333.

19 S. A. Hardy, 'Quantitative analysis of open-source data on metal detecting for cultural property: Estimation of the scale and intensity of metal detecting and the quantity of metal-detected cultural goods', *Cogent Social Sciences*, 3.1, 2017, 1298397, https://doi.org/10.1080/23311886.2017.1298397.

20 G. D. R. Sanders, S. James, and A. Carter Johnston, *Corinth Excavations Archaeological Manual*, Grand Forks, ND: The Digital Press at the University of North Dakota, 2017.

21 'Corinth Excavations – ASCSA.Net', http://corinth.ascsa.net/research?v=default, last accessed 24.06.2018.

22 http://corinth.ascsa.net/id/corinth/coin/1928%20134.

23 R. Opitz, M. Mogetta, and N. Terrenato (eds), *A Mid-Republican House From Gabii*, Ann Arbor, MI: University of Michigan Press, 2018, http://dx.doi.org/10.3998/mpub.9231782.

24 See, for example: S. Umoja Noble, *Algorithms of Oppression: How Search Engines Reinforce Racism*, New York: NYU Press, 2018.

Further reading

Barker, Elton, Stefan Bouzarovski, Christopher B. R. Pelling, and Leif Isaksen (eds), *New Worlds Out of Old Texts: Approaches to the Spatial Analysis of Ancient Greek Literature*, Oxford: Oxford University Press, 2014.

Bodenhamer, David J., John Corrigan, and Trevor M. Harris (eds), *The Spatial Humanities: GIS and the Future of Humanities Scholarship*, Bloomington, IN: Indiana University Press, 2010.

Bowman, Alan K., *Quantifying the Roman Economy: Methods and Problems*, Oxford and New York: Oxford University Press, 2013.

Callataÿ, François de (ed.), *Quantifying the Greco-Roman Economy and Beyond*, Bari: Edipuglia, 2014.

Elliott, Thomas, Sebastian Heath, and John Muccigrosso, *Current Practice in Linked Open Data for the Ancient World*, ISAW Papers 7, New York: Institute for the Study of the Ancient World, New York University; Princeton, NJ: Princeton University Press, 2014. http://dlib.nyu.edu/awdl/isaw/isaw-papers/7/.

Gregory, Ian, *Historical GIS: Technologies, Methodologies, and Scholarship*, Cambridge and New York: Cambridge University Press, 2007.

Heath, Tom and Christian Bizer, *Linked Data: Evolving the Web Into a Global Data Space*, San Rafael, CA: Morgan & Claypool, 2011.

Lucas, Gavin, *Critical Approaches to Fieldwork: Contemporary and Historical Archaeological Practice*, London and New York: Routledge, 2001.

McCormick, Michael, Ulf Büntgen, Mark A. Cane, Edward R. Cook, Kyle Harper, Peter Huybers, and Thomas Litt, 'Climate change during and after the Roman Empire: Reconstructing the past from scientific and historical evidence', *The Journal of Interdisciplinary History*, 43.2, 2012, 169–220.

The Programming Historian, https://programminghistorian.org/.

Turchin, Peter, Thomas E. Currie, Harvey Whitehouse, Pieter François, Kevin Feeney, Daniel Mullins, and Daniel Hoyer, 'Quantitative historical analysis uncovers a single dimension of complexity that structures global variation in human social organization', *Proceedings of the National Academy of Sciences*, 115.2, 2018, E144–51, https://doi.org/10.1073/pnas.1708800115.

9 Objects
Dynamics of display

Sarah Ann Robin

This chapter provides guidance for students and academics beginning their journeys with the object. It may also be of use to object carers including those working for museums, trusts or with objects in private ownership, particularly if they are looking to collaborate with university researchers. I begin with an analysis of material culture itself, as well as an explanation of the array of terminologies that scholars will encounter when they begin to study objects. These terminologies impact upon the volume and type of objects we might research, and therefore upon those spaces we will investigate – as well as the types of histories we find ourselves alongside. I then offer a commentary on spatial influences and challenges that affect the ways we study and use objects situated within differing areas of display. Working with and managing both public and private dimensions of space will be of central importance to the analysis. My research has focused on objects in the early modern period, and while many of the reflections here can be applied to historical inquiry from any period, it should be noted that some (such as my analysis on colonisation and trade) have particular relevance to the period 1450–1750. However, the majority of observations, especially on influence and dynamics of display, are applicable to any period of study. Indeed, they may be even more pertinent for modern objects with stronger provenance and closer connection to well-known events and people.

During my Masters, I was fortunate to be inspired by two historians who wanted to unlock the value of none traditional sources and the potential histories therein: it was their influence that started me on my path with material culture. However, this was by no means a uniform consensus among many historians. When I began my research with the object, over a decade ago, the field of material culture seemed a very different landscape. While many scholars, including archaeologists, anthropologists and sociologists, had long used material culture to inform their work, as a discipline history was more hesitant to engage. Some believed objects were exclusively the tools of archaeologists and museum workers, while written documents were the preserve of the historian. At worst, I encountered a perceived hierarchy of sources, where written documents had greater credibility and value than material culture; where material culture revealed a simpler, illiterate way of living.[1] This reluctance to see material culture as a valid and informative source led one historian, Adrienne Hood, to summarise material culture as an 'academic orphan'.[2] The current situation is much improved with new publications on the methods and approaches to using material culture year-on-year, as well as events and workshops, and a greater appreciation for the multidisciplinary collaboration which working with objects facilitates.[3] However, many collections of material culture are stored away in an array of locations and have yet to be given the scholarly attention which will allow them to speak fully, and as such, material culture provides an excellent opportunity for scholars looking to use an untapped body of sources.

What is material culture?

When I began studying the object, one of the first things I had to grasp was an understanding of what material culture meant, as well as understanding an array of terminology in the existing literature. Researchers may use all or any of 'material culture', 'object', 'artefact', 'stuff' or 'things' as terms for the study of the same source. However, scholars also seek differentiation by using specific languages. I was left wondering if Tara Hamling and Catherine Richardson implied something different when they wrote of 'Everyday Objects' to Daniel Miller, who wrote of 'Stuff', and was he implying something different yet again to Arjun Appadurai when he spoke of 'things'?[4] These terminologies can be confusing enough, especially given the scholar's penchant for playing with the key terms, particularly 'material' and 'matter', such as Robert Friedel's 'Some Matters of Substance'.[5] For a budding researcher, grappling with these terms is often one of the first challenges of working, along with coming to terms with degrees of interchangeability and difference.

Different terminologies may imply a distinct approach to objects and have consequences for the spaces that the researcher investigates. These approaches relate to whether objects are studied as individual sources or as a collective. For example, 'stuff' typically relates to a collective body of material culture, while 'object'-centred works tend to focus on a particular source, or on a small number. These could be within a group of objects defined by landscape or space: for example, in a gathering or collection of objects in a domestic or religious sphere. Deciding whether a study will examine material culture as an individual object or collectively will dictate how many objects a scholar will use, and it will also inform how that scholar engages with the source. Studies which analyse objects on an individual basis will typically benefit from close examination and contact, whereas a more general analysis may be better suited to studies of collections. My research incorporated both: I examined around 100 objects in depth (handling, using and so on) from approximately 60 housing institutions and used this analysis to dictate my wider analysis of similar object types.[6] This was especially useful for collections that have been digitised. Scholars of material culture may feel a reluctance to engage with objects in a broader sense, particularly if this compromises an authentic and pure connection with individual objects. This is a valid argument; however, I found that for material culture to stand alongside other histories (especially of the early modern period), a larger number of sources was required in order to give the study greater credibility.

'Material culture' straddles both approaches, referring to large and small-scale investigations. Material culture is a notably complex term, as scholars employ it as the name of a field of study, as a description of a source base (the objects or stuff), and as a way of studying the past: material culture is therefore used as noun, adjective and verb.[7] Catherine Richardson, Tara Hamling and David Gaimster's *Handbook of Material Culture Studies* exemplifies this, with narratives on specific objects, wider contextual studies, accounts of methods and approaches, as well as histories measuring the impact of objects in the past.[8] 'Material culture' can be used in all of these scenarios. This wide range of usage can make material culture seem boundless, and therefore in order to feel less overwhelmed or intimidated, a researcher should set some boundaries early on to combat this issue. Boundaries might be a defined time-period, geographical location, institution affiliation, material type, or a parameter particularly relevant to the scholar's own work. These boundaries need a degree of flexibility. Objects are often placed together in a serendipitous manner, and this means that when one object is uncovered by a researcher, this may naturally lead to another relevant but unexpected source. A connection between the two (provenance, time period, *etc.*) may make the second object a useful discovery, but it may not fit within the set boundaries of say, object type or material.

Choosing a usage of terminologies has consequences for the argument that is made and to the areas of historical enquiry. The three under discussion here are histories of commerce, emotions and faith. For example, collective studies of material culture in early modern European histories may enhance and complement existing narratives on the growth and importation of goods and therefore correlate with histories of commerce, trade and colonisation. A growth in the production of goods led to an increase in the volume of available material culture, while exploration and trade routes produced a wider variety of materials.[9] These increases influenced patterns of social and cultural change. Anne Gerritsen and Giorgio Riello noted how global trade created a 'vast diversity of goods' for European consumers.[10] Likewise, Beverly Lemire identified a growth in material goods throughout the early modern period, and how these forms of material culture were essential in the creation and maintenance of connections between the Old and New Worlds.[11] Therefore, histories of trade and their vocabulary, including terms such as commerce, production and consumption, feature heavily in and alongside the language of material culture. As these histories comment upon the impact of a large volume of goods, scholars of this period and topic have often considered objects as a collective and their consequent impact upon wider social and cultural trends. Evelyn Welch's works on shopping and clothing in Renaissance Italy are key examples of histories merging object studies with commerce and cultures.[12] These approaches encompass large numbers of material culture and reflect upon material culture as a collective and active force. The extent to which we consider objects as 'active' in our approach has been a recent point of debate among scholars. As approaches have evolved, scholars have considered whether history comes 'from' or 'through' objects, whether we should consider material culture 'and' its histories, or more simply 'write material culture history'.[13] These approaches apply nuanced degrees of agency to objects. In my research, material culture was an active force in dictating and facilitating emotional communication, which stemmed from my interactions and analysis of the object.

Students of material culture will come across combinations of terminologies from the history of emotions and objects. Material culture is an enabler of emotional expression, and a growth in material culture and variety of objects enabled a greater degree and type of emotional expression. As a consequence, objects and emotion have an affinity, and objects have a strong presence in the history of emotions: for example, Stephanie Downes's, Sally Holloway's and Sarah Randles's recent *Feeling Things: Objects and Emotions through History* is just such an example of bringing together the two fields and their terminologies. Victoria Avery, Melissa Calaresu and Mary Laven's, *Treasured Possessions: The Renaissance to the Enlightenment* is a similar fusion of object analysis revealing emotive perspectives. A growth in material goods has also been strongly allied with religious belief, expression and defiance in the early modern period. As with the history of emotions, histories of the European Reformation have a natural affiliation with material culture because of the status of religious art and icons within Reformation debate. The Reformation has been seen by many as a radical and destructive overhaul of a material landscape. Eamon Duffy's *The Stripping of the Altars: Traditional Religion in England 1400–1580* is a key example. Material culture has formed the crux of many Reformation debates, particularly concerning the degree of impact and change.[14] The destruction, construction and use of religious artefacts, and the spaces they occupied, can help us to understand the success, limitations and nature of the European Reformation. Within these debates, one will likely see terminologies referring to material culture as 'art', particularly in studies of the life cycle and faith due to the high standing of Christian iconography and images.[15] Therefore, different areas of history – in these instances commerce, emotions and faith – influence and impact upon the terminologies of material culture and the stories which objects tell.

The history of art and material culture remain largely distinct fields, although as with most divisions in historical sources, the increased study of material culture has helped to erode past partitioning.[16] There does remain, however, a line between what is considered fine, high art, and what is usually considered everyday pieces made by everyday people. These distinctions have many implications and they often encourage the scholar to consider an object as either visual or material: something to be admired or something to be used. For example, Ludmilla Jordanova emphasised the importance of the interplay between how we look at objects and how we interact with their material nature:

> [t]he material world is a visual world, which impacts upon human beings through their eyes, and is intimately bound up with touch. Historians can only benefit from approaching the past with a vivid appreciation of these points, with a willingness to consider what people looked at, how they looked and the roles of objects designed to be looked at.[17]

Jordanova rightly puts such a focus on the 'visual' aspects of object study. How objects appear, their designs and their colours, are highly influential in what messages they were and are intended to convey. An awareness of the interplay between the visual and material, and that dual approaches are feasible, and rewarding is essential in capturing a fuller understanding.[18]

Visual aesthetics

The emphasis on the visual aesthetics of material culture is likely a legacy of fine art history, wherein objects were designed primarily to be looked at and appreciated in spaces where the viewer's gaze was distant rather than objects intended to be held or used as things in three dimensions. I believe this emphasis on the visual aesthetics of an object has been informed by the economic value and perceived preciousness of surviving objects, especially those that are believed to also possess significant historical value.[19] Handling, moving and using an object for any other purpose than looking at it can prove difficult and pose a risk to a fragile object. As the majority of objects that I have studied are between 300 and 400 years old, they have been considered valuable and precious, even if they were relatively crudely made and once common. This aspect of material culture study alters how we approach objects, how we interact and can impact how we write about them. Carving is 'fine'; metalwork 'intricate'; decoration is 'hand-finished'. Such words are descriptions of technique, but they also imply a contemporary value judgement that may not have attached to the object at the time of its creation. Furthermore, many objects, especially those with provenance, have been collected and cared for precisely because of a perceived value: this may compound the emphasis on the visual aesthetics of an object and reluctance to engage with it in a material sense. The space in which the object is kept could further emphasise these constructed feelings and associations, which will be discussed later in this chapter

Divisions and attitudes toward objects can be subtle and inflicted subconsciously, influencing the scholar through the way objects are positioned, photographed, previously written about and preserved. Continuing the emphasis on visual aesthetics, this approach can lead us to focus on the sides of the object or to see it flat. If one side is more visually appealing than another, this is likely to be the side on display or that which has received the most attention in terms of research, recording and photography. This would almost certainly be true of a painting or embroidery but potentially also of objects which have been fixed in cases, or those that have been on display for many years in the same position (such as in an entrusted house, for example). Objects have multiple sides and can have interiors as well as exteriors. If this is a chest or casket, the interior may not be accessible, or if it is, it may not be opened very often, to preserve the inside from sunlight damage or a delicate hinge from strain. In addition to an agenda of conservation, lost keys or seized locks have played a role in preventing access to caskets and chests on more than one occasion. Conversely, if the inside of an object is particularly interesting or attractive, then a conscious decision may be taken to put the interior on display, garnering greater attention than the exterior. Examples of this sort could be a cabinet with a richly decorated interior, or a piece of jewelry, with an internal space such as a locket or a ring with an inscription. These types of object are considered to have important sides or spaces within, and, as a consequence, much attention may be paid to that internal space, perhaps by a curator who ensures this is seen by a scholar or determines how it is displayed to the viewing public. However, this method of interaction may differ from the original maker's or owner's intention. For example, the inscription on the inside of a ring was typically a personal and intimate message, intended to sit against the skin. In this type of scenario, when the interior is exposed, we are interacting with an object in an artificially constructed way. Photographing a ring inscription is also problematic and forces us to represent a single inscription as two, potentially disjointed, segments; or to use technology to put two halves together. Either way, such a visualisation does not represent the experience of the object wearer. Disentangling our own interests and agendas from an object can be even more problematic if an object has undergone significant change, through alteration, damage and repair or modernising. The key is to ensure approaches encompass an awareness of multiple dimensions of the object, examining both its aesthetic and utilitarian functions.[20]

All of these aspects of display and ways objects are kept can influence our idiom and approaches. Scholars should note these distinctions, especially between the visual and material, as assumptions may have been imposed after the object's original creation and use. Most historical objects will have experienced multiple owners, and each episode can leave its mark on the object, whether this be sunlight damage, the removal of a religious icon, repairing frayed needlework or simply by accidentally being dropped. As each episode passed, an object's spatial surroundings and usage are also likely to have changed significantly, which may too have had a physical impact on the object. Awareness of this kind of change can help form a better understanding of the purpose and meaning of an object. Therefore, scholars should try to gain an understanding of the full lifecycle of an object where possible. I found myself leafing through issues of *Country Life* to try to determine if a lock was a twentieth-century addition or how long an object had been in the same position. Written documents, including inventories, wills and testaments, diaries and letters, can all help in creating this individual object history. Even when an object has no provenance, research of the object type, function or material might help to build a picture of the object's past.

Distinctions between how an object is named and how it is approached may require an 'either or' method. For example, the division between visual and material approaches, spatially and psychologically, may encourage a scholar to think of an object (perhaps a painting or brooch) as something to be admired from a distance, when in the past, that object may have been used and appreciated as *both* a visual and a material thing in multiple ways with many owners. Even objects that seem purely visual, such as a portrait miniature, may have been created to be a portable, wearable thing, small enough to be held or worn close to the body.[21] Disentangling these uses can be problematic when objects are typically displayed and distinguished according to their status as either art or material culture, as one type of object from another, as visual or physical, as valuable or inexpensive.

However, they were unlikely to have been so distinguished or displayed by their original creators and owners. This is why approaches to material culture which embrace multiple lines of space and time, making different subject approaches both rewarding and necessary.[22] Previously existing categorisation can also impose bounds around the researcher's work and as we have noted that material culture can seem boundless, a defined gathering of objects can be an appealing body of sources to use but often does not reflect the authentic experience of a person in the past.

Approaching the object

My research took me to many types of object locations: from the storerooms of the Victoria and Albert Museum to an independent antique dealer in Oxfordshire; from a rundown sixteenth-century pile to searching through digital auction files of lost paintings. Prior to my work with the object, I was accustomed to viewing documents in archives and increasingly researching documents online. The number of locations which I encountered research the object was much greater. This required a set of tools that I accumulated along the way (pencils, soft measuring tape, photography equipment, tracing paper and chalk, sketching paper and torch). Objects locations allow for and demand greater flexibility in approach than an archive, especially if an object is under the ownership of an individual in, for example, an antique shop. Museums and trustees have regulations to abide by, and due to a significant degree of interaction with the public, a greater conservation agenda. The variety of settings required innovative and unusual methods in approaching object owners. There is not space enough in this chapter to discuss locating objects, but object owners are likely to have their own agendas and priorities that can affect and possibly hinder their response to an academic query. For example, antique dealers would likely put a buyer's request above my questions, and some object carers may be cautious about providing object access to someone without a curatorial background. But in my experience, the most were passionate about their objects and in telling their stories, and saw the value in allowing an historian access, albeit in differing degrees. Furthermore, in the last decade, the field of museum studies has become increasingly professionalised, and a greater emphasis has been placed on how museums educate and inform people about the past.[23] This is of significant benefit to the researcher, though degrees of professionalization and staffing vary greatly depending on the size and funding of the housing institution.

The literature on material culture has increased over the last decade; however, guidance on approaching objects, the spaces around them, and how to use them as research sources, in order to write compelling histories, remains underrepresented.[24] Publications by Karen Harvey, Sarah Barber and Corinna M. Peniston-Bird, as part of the Routledge's *Guides to Using Historical Sources*, remain two staple examples for budding scholars of material culture.[25] Leonie Hannan's and Sarah Longhair's recent work is perhaps the most thorough and comprehensive attempt to establish robust methodologies for locating, approaching and using objects, and importantly how to successfully write up work using material culture.[26] These publications remain, however, small in number, and as objects come in great swathes of sizes and types, methodologies cannot always be easily applied across objects. Coupled with the variety of locations and spaces in which we find objects, more literature is needed. This is partly why there remains so many objects undiscovered and unexplored. As Hannan and Longhair stressed, even long established museums still have a wealth of objects that remain understudied.[27]

Guidance on methodologies for working with object display and storage has received notably less attention than object theory and meaning, especially for a scholar who does not have direct access to a museum collection and who does not have a curatorial background. This deficit is worse still for objects in storage, which have received even less consideration than objects on display, despite objects in storage accounting for 98 percent of some museums' collections. When objects in storage have been written about it has often been because it has been a point of controversy, especially in the public eye. Museums have had to defend their right to house and to 'hide' publically owned artefacts. This was noted by Mirjam Brusius and Kavita Singh recently in their book, *Museum Storage and Meaning: Tales from the Crypt*, when they touched upon the sensitive and often affecting colonial nature of museum collections, and whether museums have the right to own and to store 'other' people's artefacts. Objects that were taken under colonial rule typically carry emotive narratives and associations with specific, identifiable people and places.

Smaller institutes may have similar problems but on a different scale. For example, I have worked at and collaborated with several heritage homes where access to a site, spaces within the site, or artefacts was contested. Conflicts had grown up around access for the public, museum workers and researchers. To give an example, this could have occurred in an entrusted home where a long-established family, or a family member, was still in residence. Ownership and living arrangements can be complex and specific to the heritage site and family, wherein trusts have to juggle sensitive personal demands with their duties as conservationists and as a public attraction. A researcher may walk into an ongoing dispute when they request to examine an object or see a space. One heritage site may have particular rooms or sections that remain a private family home, while other spaces are 'public'. These agreements can be chaotic. For example, one site I have worked in had its content divvied up in the 1950s on the back of a napkin over coffee. The trust's subsequent access to the family collections was sporadic and uneasy, despite the trust owning the house in which the objects were located. The family also fought to prevent anyone from having access continuously to certain rooms and the objects therein. Given that this family viewed the house as their family home, their views were not unfathomable. However, it produced significant conflict between the trust's mission to conserve and protect the site and its contents, most notably when an overflowing bath destroyed a ceiling, and a lit cigarette started a substantial fire. Any scholar considering approaching charities, trusts or stately home collections should be aware that these complex arrangements and underlying tensions are, in my experience, not uncommon.

I found these conflicts to be even more pointed for objects with emotional narratives. Many of the pieces I have worked with are small, private pieces with great sentimental value, never intended to be on public display. For example, dozens of the objects which I researched contained body parts, most frequently hair, or on occasion, reputed fragments or stains of blood.[28] This is not uncommon in the world of early modern objects. I was searching for tokens of amorous love, but this also in this period meant objects containing body parts that conveyed monarchical or political allegiance.[29] There is also a wealth of medieval and early modern holy relics composed of body parts or similarly sacred materials.[30] These artefacts, which seem to offer the most direct of physical links to a person in the past with heightened political or religious significance, thereby accrete emotive cultural capital. An object which retains a connection to a family similarly gains emotional resonance and the family may well then be invested in granting access to such an object or in the way in which a researcher might present and photograph it. It is usually a family that has preserved the object over what may be hundreds of years. Custodians of objects such as this may also have considerable anxiety over damage or theft. There is no necessary connection between historical and monetary value, but in the case of objects with familial, religious or secular emotional charge, the link between the two can be strengthened or perceived to have increased. Objects become the target of thieves: such as the theft of the heart of Saint Laurence O'Toole's from Christ Church Cathedral in Dublin in 2012, or the instance of convicted burglar, Graham Geoffrey Harkin, who in the 2000s joined the National Trust (England and Wales) for the purposes of scoping its sites for thefts.[31] Emotions are heightened or compounded further by potential conflict over ownership.

Conflicted spaces

As a researcher in an environment such as this, I could be fed differing accounts, descriptions and narratives of an object. A particular example was a family member who attributed a painting to one artist, while a curator – possibly based on more recent scholarship – was sceptical of the painting's provenance. Lifting the lid, to maybe imply that someone's great, great aunt was either a liar or was conned, and that a signature or record was fraudulent, places the researcher in a supremely delicate situation at the heart of conflict when their *raison d'être* is objectivity. There could be consequences such as considerable financial loss, further emotional conflict as well as resentment, and greater potential for misinformation. Alongside this, I came up against barriers that had arisen when previous scholars had requested access to an object, and the trust or resident had been left unhappy with some aspect of the process; perhaps how the object was subsequently represented or photographed, or in how it had been handled and put away. Prior knowledge of a previous dispute or contention can make access and research easier, and therefore it is advisable, to research not only the object before visiting but also the space in which it is kept. Has the institution or object custodian experienced a theft or controversy in recent years? If the site remains a home, are a family still in residence? How often is the space open to the public? Answers to these questions can help a scholar judge how amenable object owners are to access.

However, a relationship, or even conflict, between a resident and trust was not always a negative experience and could be fruitful. On one particular visit to a site which still housed the last descendent of the family, this descendent was particularly keen to show me his house in great and full detail. This included deliberately removing barriers, which the owning charity had put in place, as the said descendent believed was his right, in his home. In this instance, the preexisting tension between the two object custodians worked to my advantage. This included the two of us moving a heavy 500-year-old chest out into the courtyard, while navigating the precious object around a rather excited terrier. This could have compromised the structural integrity of the object, but he wanted the object and its mysterious engraving to be viewed and photographed in full light. This I did and was able to later uncover the meaning of the inscription, in part due to the quality of those photos. Alongside this, I experienced a conflict between who owned the object and to whom I should reference the object as belonging, and whether I should publically thank him for his generosity in enabling access and photography without causing a backlash from the charity.

In this example, the tension between the charity and the family was resolved by the former's insistence that I photograph a mounted ivory disc that the charity had used to identify and catalogue the object decades before. I was then thrown unwillingly into the contentious curation of ivory as a material.[32] In 2017, *The Guardian* newspaper described how some of the greatest art in history, made from ivory, was being 'criminalised' and that the destruction of ivory antiques was a step toward cultural destruction.[33] The family descendent was very much aware of this controversy and keen for it to be highlighted and photographed. In relation to the object's story it was an important marker, informing the researcher of a stage in the object's life, as well as the wider cultural acceptance which ivory was once held in the UK. Fixing the ivory marker required puncturing a hole in the centuries' old cedar-wood: this was a deliberate and violent act, notwithstanding the violence we now associate with the material. Regardless of modern notions of heritage and curatorship, the history of an object, just as any history, is rife with mistakes, controversies and individual agendas. These actions did not always represent or benefit an object, the object's home or, arguably, the object's previous custodians. The example of the cedar chest reveals the shifting social and cultural sensitivities around objects and that what was once considered good practice may no longer be viewed in a positive light.

I likened these controversies and conflicts to a web around an object, a web which may influence and obscure the scholar's experience and that the scholar needs to know and understand, especially by the time they come to reflect and write up the research. The object may stay static within this web: for example, the ivory disc remains ivory while our perceptions of ivory shift dramatically. For the historian, this is frequently where we identify what for us is value in a source because it can reveal change over time. However, objects can be altered physically in an effort to make them less contentious or functional in a modern setting, particularly as cultural and social attitudes shift and change. Sometimes objects can be moved or 'returned' to a heritage site or community in order to appease conflict. The movement of an object from space to space can be a labour-intensive and difficult task, and yet this effort reveals exactly the importance and meaning of object location in understanding the object itself.[34] Therefore, the object's immediate surroundings and ownership can shift to respond to conflict. Take for example a sixteenth-century inlaid chamber (so called because of the intricate inlaid patterns in the wood panelling), which was removed from Sizergh Castle in Cumbria in the early twentieth century and sold to the Victoria and Albert Museum in London. There, it was put on display to the public. It was returned to Sizergh Castle in 1999 following pressure to send back the panelling, bed and windows to its original home.[35] While the panelling did not undergo significant change or damage in the process, the change in its surroundings was colossal, and there was significant tension over where the panelling 'should' reside. More famously, there have been several recent instances in which museums have offered to return objects to indigenous communities around the world. Over the past twenty years, hundreds of *Toi Moko* (preserved Māori heads) 'Western' museums have been returned to New Zealand.[36] Similarly, for several decades the Museum of Egyptian Antiquities in Cairo has been campaigning for the return of artefacts considered by many Egyptian historians and archaeologists to have been stolen from Egypt over several centuries. The narratives with an English focus that have been outlined here have been analysed from the perspective of localised, domestic and familial conflicts. But as the example of the label made from ivory reveals, there are likely to be wider, deeper and more intractable conflicting perspectives not far beneath the surface in disentangling the ethics of possessive individualism.[37]

Personal responses

Now that I have painted a somewhat messy and chaotic picture of object display and research, it should be noted that these intricacies add layers of substance and enjoyment to object research. The entrusted home in particular is filled with oral narratives of people, families and connections between objects and people. Stepping into a seemingly unchanged domestic interior unavoidably transports a scholar into a highly emotive and stimulating environment. Take for example, the apparently untouched sixteenth-century 'Hellens Manor' in Herefordshire, England. When I came across this property, I discovered that it was run by a private, family trust and that those responsible for the site claimed many of the rooms were in a state of undisturbed preservation. I was unable to find out much detail about the house or what lay within, but unperturbed, I decided to visit. This was an unusual tactic in my doctoral research but if there was a site relatively near to another with a confirmed object of interest, I did visit several sites and their collections haphazardly. Upon entering this particular site, I was subject to tales about its haunting atmosphere and ghostly stories. I had experienced this sort of imposed sentiment before and observed how surviving early modern interiors seem to, or are engineered, to instil a sort of gloomy atmosphere, which many attractions use to their benefit. While aware of this, I viewed these sorts of preserved interiors as useful spaces for my work. For example, there is a significant difference between examining embroidered stumpwork under lights, perhaps in a glass case or between sheets of paper, and in a domestic home where a researcher can observe the twinkle of metallic threads from small rays of sunlight passing through 400-year-old glass panes, while sitting in a 300-year-old chair.[38]

There were several moments during my impromptu tour of the house that I found stimulating, but one which particularly stood out happened when I entered the space called 'Hetty Walwyn's Room'. The guide began to tell us the story of Mehitabel (Hetty) Walwyn. Hetty was the daughter of John Walwyn (1622–1686) who had owned the house, Hellens Manor. At some point toward the end of seventeenth century she was purported to have eloped with a poor labourer named John Pierce. Later, Hetty reputedly returned to her parents 'in disgrace', though the reasons why the relationship ended are not known. Hetty was shut away in the room until her death. The guide pointed to her portrait, believed to have been painted during her 'imprisonment'. Judging by the portrait and its style, I wondered whether it was, in fact, painted in the century after her death, her narrative serving as inspiration to an artist. I was then informed by the guide that Hetty committed suicide, probably in the room, at the age of 50 (c.1728). This was indeed a sad story; the type of ill-fated love narrative which has come to be attached to many entrusted houses. The authenticity of this tale did not give me cause to wonder; it was merely a story that may or may not have been true and of a type I came across quite frequently when working with objects, usually in the space of an entrusted home.

However, the materiality of the tale did not end there. The guide then pointed directly to me, as it transpired that I was standing beside a piece of graffiti on a windowpane. This was believed to have been scratched into the glass by Hetty using a diamond ring. It read, 'It is a part of virtue to abstain from what we love if it should prove our bane'. As I studied the inscription, the scrawlings and markings seemed to match the period of the story (late seventeenth to early eighteenth century). I had encountered early modern graffiti elsewhere, on prison walls and wooden furniture, but nothing with quite the same setting and narrative.[39] Following the revelation of so close and authentic a segment of early modern philosophy on love, the guide pointed to a long bell pull, which was more-or-less in the centre of the room. It is not unusual for a home of this time to have a bell system, though this particular cord looked older than most I had seen. The guide explained that the bell pull was believed to date to the time Hetty spent in the room. However rather than leading to a discrete system of bells in the servants' quarters, this pull was connected to a large bell on the roof. The guide pulled the cord and a few moments later, a toll sounded from above. The accompanying narrative imbued the toll with a doleful, lingering tone.

With the assistance of a narrative, Hetty's room, bed, portrait, bell and window conjured a strong emotional response. I was left with an impression of the melancholy that her character (was deemed to have) experienced after the breakdown of love. The sound represented the unforgiving mind-set of her parents and the shame that the relationship between Hetty and John brought to her family. However, as with most material culture, it was impossible to prove that it was Hetty who scribed the window, or that the inscription referred to amorous love – hers or any others'. The significance of the experience is that this type of emotional narrative, woven by oral history and the presence of certain objects, was by no means an uncommon experience when visiting domestic houses. Typically, historians do not engage with such affecting spatial dynamics, but I found them impossible to ignore when using objects in entrusted spaces. Such narratives have not always been connected to the objects which I was examining, but still caught my attention. For example, when I went to Aston Hall in Birmingham, I could not help but see preserved damage from the English civil war in the oak staircase. As I ran my fingers round the silhouette of a cannon ball, I wondered where the ball could have come through the walls or windows of the house. The home became a mental scene of warfare and fear: an impression that was hard to shake off when interacting with something else. When I went to Woolsthorpe Manor in Lincolnshire, I was beset by the presence of one of its former occupants, Isaac Newton. From the preserved apple tree in the garden to the demonstrations of a prism and the refraction of sunlight in the rooms upstairs, the curators of the site ensured that his influence was stained into every object. This sort of inflicted presence can act as a distraction when trying to uncover relevant objects, as object carers are more likely to think of their collections in relationship to specific narratives and people, and not to a different research approach or question. A response may be that 'everything we have here relates to so and so, not to what you are looking for'.

The field of material culture studies is now established and widely respected. In conjunction, the increased professionalisation of museum studies means objects are more accessible and often better researched. However, the numbers that remain underappreciated in a research sense, especially in smaller trusts and private ownership, are still significant, and given the growth of credible methodological approaches and greater access, these objects are themselves calling out for their own research narratives. The spaces in which objects exist influence them in numerous ways, leaving physical changes, altering cataloguing and referencing, affecting interaction and most importantly, prompting a researcher's brain toward a particular type of analysis. One means to combat these influences is to try to create as full a timeline of an object's spatial history as possible. This is not always feasible, either because an object has little known provenance, or because, as with my research, using a large number of objects makes tracing all sources impossible. There is still value in researching an object's past if only for a handful of objects, as it allows a scholar to peel back years and layers of external influences and reach something of an original intent. Engaging with objects in a variety of settings is valuable in itself. It was only through interacting with objects in different heritage settings, from glass displays and storage drawers to bedrooms and shop floors, that I gained a fuller insight into how powerful spatial influences can be. Interacting with objects in different settings and with different people can be the key to understanding an object's past as well as its present.

Notes

1 J. Deetz, *In Small Things Forgotten: An Archaeology of Early American Life*, New York: Anchor Books, 1996, p. 11.
2 A. D. Hood, 'Material culture: The object' in Sarah Barber and Corinna M. Peniston-Bird (eds), *Beyond the Text*: *A Student's Guide to Approaching Alternative Sources*, London: Routledge, 2009, p. 187.
3 For example, The Australian Research Council Centre of Excellence for the History of Emotions now has a research cluster dedicated to Objects and Emotion in collaboration with the University of Manchester. Publications include: S. Downes, S. Holloway and S. Randles, *Feeling Things*: *Objects and Emotions through History*, Oxford: Oxford University Press, 2018; A. Gerritsen and G. Riello, *Writing Material Culture History*, London: Bloomsbury, 2014; L. Hannan and S. Longair, *History Through Material Culture*, Manchester: Manchester University Press, 2017.
4 T. Hamling and C. Richardson, *Everyday Objects: Medieval and Early Modern Material Culture and Its Meanings*, Farnham: Ashgate, 2010; D. Miller, *Stuff*, Cambridge: Polity Press, 2010; A. Appadurai, *The Social Life of Things: Commodities of Cultural Perspective*, Cambridge: Cambridge University Press, 1988.
5 R. Friedel, 'Some Matters of Substance' in W. D. Kingery and S. Lubar (eds), *History From Things*: *Essays on Material Culture*, London: Smithsonian Institution Press, 1993, pp. 41–50.
6 S. A. Robin, 'Pictures, posies and promises: Love, the object and the English in the seventeenth century', Unpublished doctoral thesis, PhD in History, Lancaster University, UK, 2016.
7 I. Woodward, *Understanding Material Culture*, London: Sage, 2007, pp. 3–4.
8 C. Richardson, T. Hamling, and D. Gaimster (eds), *Routledge Handbook of Material Culture Studies in Early Modern Europe*, Abingdon, NY: Routledge, 2016.
9 S. A. Robin, 'Male choice and desire: Material offerings in seventeenth-century England', *Cultural and Social History*, 2019 [Printed issue forthcoming Autumn 2019], 1–16, https://doi.org/10.1080/14780038.2019.16400.
10 A. Gerritsen and G. Riello (eds), *The Global Lives of Things*: *The Material Culture of Connections in the Early Modern World*, Abingdon, NY: Routledge, 2015, p. 6.
11 B. Lemire, *Global Trade and the Transformation of Consumer Cultures: The Material World Remade, c.1500–1820*, Cambridge: Cambridge University Press, 2018, chapter 6.
12 E. Welch, *Shopping in the Renaissance*: *Consumer Cultures in Italy, 1400–1600*, New Haven, CT: Yale University Press, 2009; M. O'Malley and E. Welch (eds), *The Material Renaissance*, Manchester: Manchester University Press, 2010.
13 S. D. Lubar and W. D. Kingery (eds), *History From Things: Essays on Material Culture*, Washington DC: Smithsonian Press, 1993; L. Hannan and S. Longair, *History through Material Culture,* Manchester: Manchester University Press, 2017; P. Findlen (ed.), *Early Modern Things*: *Objects and Their Histories, 1500–1800*, Abingdon, NY: Routledge, 2012; A. Gerritsen and G. Riello, *Writing Material Culture History*, (Bloomsbury Academic: London, 2015).
14 For example, T. Hamling, *Decorating the Godly Household: Religious Art in Post Reformation Britain*, London: Yale University Press, 2010; M. Miller, 'Introduction: Material culture and catholic history', *The Catholic Historical Review*, 101.1, 2015, 1–17.
15 For example, A. Gordon and T. Rist (eds), *The Arts of Remembrance in Early Modern England: Memorial Cultures of the Post Reformation*, London: Routledge, 2016; N. Llewellyn, *The Art of Death: Visual Culture in the English Death Ritual c.1500–c.1800*, London: Reaktion Books Ltd., 1991.
16 M. Yonan, 'Toward a fusion of art history and material culture studies', *West 86th: A Journal of Decorative Arts, Design History, and Material Culture*, 18.2, 2011, 232–48.
17 L. Jordanova, *The Look of the Past*: *Visual and Material Evidence in Historical Practice*, Cambridge: Cambridge University Press, 2012, p. 1.

18 J. Skelly (ed.), *The Uses of Excess in Visual and Material Culture 1600–2010*, Abingdon, NY: Routledge, 2014.
19 S. Berns, 'Considering the glass case: Material encounters between museums, visitors and religious objects', *Journal of Material Culture*, 21.2, 2016, 153–68.
20 K. Smith and L. Hannan, 'Return and repetition: Methods for material culture studies', *Journal of Interdisciplinary History*, 48.1, 2017, 43–59, p. 48.
21 K. Coombs, *The Portrait Miniature in England*, London: V&A Publications, 1998; G. C. Boettcher, *The Look of Love: Eye Miniatures From the Skier Collection*, London: D. Giles, 2012.
22 S. Woodward, 'Object interviews, material imaginings and "unsettling" methods: Interdisciplinary approaches to understanding materials and material culture', *Qualitative Research*, 16.4, 2015, 359–74.
23 J. Fritsch, *Museum Gallery Interpretation and Material Culture*, New York: Routledge, 2011, introduction.
24 Smith and Hannan, 'Return and Repetition'.
25 K. Harvey (ed.), *History and Material Culture: A Student's Guide to Approaching Alternative Sources*, London: Routledge, 2017; S. Barber and C. M. Peniston-Bird (eds), *History beyond the Text: A Student's Guide to Approaching Alternative Sources*, London: Routledge, 2008.
26 Hannan and Longhair, *History Through Material Culture*.
27 Ibid., 7.
28 Examples include Joseph Coney (maker), Penelope Winslow's Mourning Ring, Massachusetts, 1680. Diameter: 1.8 cm. Memento Mori Pendant, double-sided, 1699. Dimensions: 1.9 x 1.9 cm (excluding hoop). This pendant was on sale at Rowan and Rowan, London in 2013: Ref HM3. Hair Band, 1640–1680. The Victoria and Albert Museum: T.150-1963.
29 At the execution of Charles I Stuart of England in 1649, there was a huge market in mementos, royalist symbols and icons.
30 C. Freeman, *Holy Bones, Holy Dust: How Relics Shaped the History of Medieval Europe*, New Haven, CT: Yale University Press, 2011; A. Walsham, 'Skeletons in the cupboard: Relics after the English reformation', *Past and Present*, Supplement 5, 2010, 121–43; D. Lutz, 'The dead still among us: Victorian secular relics, hair jewelry, and death culture', *Victorian Literature and Culture*, 39, 2011, 127–42.
31 National Trust, Heelis, Kemble Drive, Swindon, Wiltshire, UK: Registered Charity 205846; K. Lithgow, S. Staniforth, and P. Etheridge, 'Prioritizing access in the conservation of national trust collections', *Studies in Conservation*, 53.sup.1, 2008, 178–85; M. A. Vargas, 'Pondering dysfunctions in heritage protection: Lessons from the theft of the *codex calixtinus*', *International Journal of Cultural Property*, 21.1, 2014, 1–21.
32 An entire issue of *Curator: The Museum Journal*, 61.1, January 2018, has recently been dedicated to the topic of housing and displaying ivory within museums.
33 J. Jones, 'Ivory tells the history of the world: It must never be banned', *The Guardian*, 16 February 2017.
34 H. P. Hahn and H. Weis (eds), *Mobility, Meaning and Transformations of Things: Shifting Contexts of Material Culture through Time and Space*, Oxford: Oxbow Books, 2013, preface.
35 See The National Trust online for further information on the inlaid chamber, www.nationaltrust.org.uk/features/the-return-of-the-inlaid-panelling-to-sizergh-castle, accessed 29.08.19; J. Musson, *How to Read a Country House*, London: Ebury, 2005, pp. 103–4; J. Musson, 'Sizergh castle, cumbria celebrates the reinstallation of the Castle's famous room of Elizabethan Inlaid panelling', *Country Life*, London, 2000; I. Goodall, 'Privacy, display and over extension: Walter strickland's rebuilding of sizergh', *The Antiquaries Journal*, 82, September 2002, 197–245.
36 Further reading: T. Jenkins, *Contesting Human Remains in Museum Collections*, New York: Routledge, 2011.

37 S. Ndlovu-Gatsheni, 'Decolonising research methodology must include undoing its dirty history', *Journal of Public Administration*, 52.1, March 2017, 186–8; C. Wintle, 'Decolonising the museum: The case of the Imperial and Commonwealth Institutes', *Museum and Society*, 11.2, July 2013, 185–201.
38 Stumpwork is the name given to a type of seventeenth-century raised or stuffed embroidery. It can be found on panels and small tapestries, as well as on domestic objects such as boxes, cabinets, baskets, purses and book covers. For further reading see: A. Morall and M. Watt (eds), *English Embroidery From the Metropolitan Museum of Art, 1580–1700*: "*Twixt Art and Nature*", New York: Metropolitan Museum of Art, 2009.
39 A significant narrative attached to heritage locations in England also includes the use of diamond rings to scratch into glass windowpanes.

Further reading

Downes, Stephanie, Sally Holloway, and Sarah Randles, *Feeling Things: Objects and Emotions Through History*, Oxford: Oxford University Press, 2018.

Findlen, Paula (ed.), *Early Modern Things: Objects and Their Histories, 1500–1800*, London: Routledge, 2012.

Fritsch, Juliette, *Museum Gallery Interpretation and Material Culture*, New York: Routledge, 2011.

Hamling, Tara and Catherine Richardson, *Everyday Objects: Medieval and Early Modern Material Culture and Its Meanings*, Farnham: Ashgate, 2010.

Hannan, Leonie and Sarah Longair, *History through Material Culture*, Manchester: Manchester University Press, 2017.

Harvey, Karen (ed.), *History and Material Culture: A Student's Guide to Approaching Alternative Sources*, London: Routledge, 2017.

Richardson, Catherine, Tara Hamling, and David Gaimster (eds), *Routledge Handbook of Material Culture Studies in Early Modern Europe*, Abingdon: Routledge, 2016.

Vergo, Peter (ed.), *The New Museology*, London: Reaktion Books, 1989.

10 Clothing

Reading what was worn

Laura R. Prieto

Clothing is a part of everyday human life, a necessity that is also a form of expressing identity and sometimes an exercise in frivolity. The things people wear are the product of often unsung labor, evidence of economic relationships and negotiations that are rarely recorded directly. Clothing styles reflect both tradition and innovation. Uniforms announce one's occupation, while the wearing of pants or of velvet trim broke laws in particular times and places. Clothing can thus mark class, gender, race, and other social boundaries. Specific items of apparel can consciously mark one's status and sense of belonging to a particular group. Wearing a chef's starched, white *torque blanche* or a baseball cap with a team's logo conveys information without need for words. The place where one wears something contributes to its message as well – a baseball cap at a black-tie dinner makes a different impression than a baseball cap at a stadium.

The meanings of clothing are thus always relative and performative, inseparable from their historical moment and the spaces in which the clothes are being worn. Tight stays – body shaping garments, precursors to the corset – were regarded as radical statements of women's sexual freedom in the late fourteenth century; in 1969, the refusal to wear a bra signaled feminist values. Each choice makes sense only in light of the 'look' that preceded it.[1] The same clothes may be seen as entirely different, depending on who is wearing them and ideas about appropriateness. For a woman to wear pants in mid-nineteenth-century San Francisco, for instance, marked her as either a prostitute, a women's rights militant, or a miner disguising herself as a man. For a man, wearing pants was an unremarkable choice.[2]

In consequence individuals can use clothing deliberately, not only to communicate personal identity but to challenge norms. They may choose to wear something out of playfulness, in conscious protest, or because of practical concerns. The language of clothes may signal conformity or self-expression. As Kathy Peiss argues, 'Style offers the powerless a potent means to communicate resistance.'[3] But it may communicate a point clearly or be misread.

This makes clothing a rich and complex primary source. As scholar Anne Hollander writes, 'Clothes can suggest, persuade, connote, insinuate, or indeed lie, and apply subtle pressure while their wearer is speaking frankly and straightforwardly of other matters.'[4] The object itself and its spatial context create meaning together; thus the meaning of an item of clothing changes across time, location, and situation. So how do we learn to understand, across time, what it means for a person to wear a particular article or combination of clothes? Many different disciplines and approaches, used singly or in concert, help make clothing 'readable' as a primary source. The more techniques one applies to analyze an item or type of clothing, the more clearly one will understand it. Close observation, reflection, contextual research, and analysis are all important parts of the process.[5] Visual and verbal sources add complexity to what clothes document in themselves, as material artefacts. It takes many types of sources and strategies to grasp fully what clothing can show about its makers and its wearers, about what it meant to signify and how viewers interpreted that message.

In an immediate sense, garments are intensely personal, for they have an intimate association with the body. Like other artifacts, their creation and subsequent history leaves material traces upon them: slipped stiches and stains, strained buttonholes and frayed cuffs, patches and raised hems. These too are clues that we can learn to decode, to reconstruct aspects of the wearer's life. Before the twentieth century, clothing had great monetary as well as functional and emotional value. It even served as a sort of currency until industrialization made new, mass-produced clothing available to the poor.[6]

But despite all their day-to-day significance, when their usefulness has run its course, clothes are discarded or altered. Very rarely is an article of clothing preserved through generations in its original form. One must usually rely on visual images or verbal descriptions to research clothing that no longer exists in material form. With or without the object itself, one must consult other kinds of sources for evidence of how a piece of clothing was actually made, worn, and regarded. As a result, clothing possesses rich potential rewards but also poses significant challenges as an historical source.

This chapter considers how various kinds of contextual research can help make clothing legible as a historical source. Taking its main examples from the history of women in the United States, it focuses in particular on how historians trace the experiences of under-documented people by studying the making and wearing of clothing, as well as clothing's depiction and regulation. It suggests ways that the history of clothing is interrelated to other histories. For example, the rise of ready-to-wear clothing is part of the narrative of industrialization and the factory production of textiles, as well as the history of technologies like the sewing machine. How did the mechanization of clothing production change labor conditions and opportunities? How did the availability of less expensive, mass-produced clothing alter the material lives of the poor and working classes? What did the 'democratization' of fashion do in turn to ideas about class status and rank?[7] The emergence of 'fashion' is connected to demographic changes, such as the rise in the average age of first marriage. Technologies in domestic heating led to lighter textiles and clothes.[8] Debates over the appropriateness of athletics for women included controversy over whether women had to wear skirts that made physical activity, from swimming to basketball, less safe than if women wore 'masculine' pants. Twentieth-century protest movements skillfully deployed the symbolism of clothing, from the white dresses representing women's purity and respectability in 1910s suffrage parades, to the African dashikis through which Black nationalist men and women voiced their racial pride in the 1960s. Considering clothing as a source can thus deepen the study of many topics, from economics to politics, from technology to sports.

The beginnings of a field

Many historians look to clothing as a valuable source for understanding human beings, but other scholars in the social sciences and humanities began using clothes as sources long before academic historians did. Antiquarians and popular writers in the eighteenth century were the first to chronicle what people wore in the past; they usually called their subject 'costume' or 'dress.'[9] By the turn of the twentieth century, social scientists and theorists regarded clothing as an important subject. In 1899, for example, the prominent Norwegian-American sociologist and economist Thorstein Veblen pioneered the concept of 'conspicuous consumption.' He perceived how women within the upper class had ornamental value; by adorning themselves, especially through intricate and expensive dress, they signified family wealth and elite status.[10]

Through the twentieth century, researchers increasingly asserted the legitimacy and importance of asking what people wore. Starting in the 1940s, collectors like Doris Langley Moore and curators like Anne Buck made the compelling case that clothing could function as evidence; Moore, for instance, studied thousands of examples of women's clothing to prove that women's average height had not increased since the eighteenth century, and that most women did not corset their waists to eighteen inches.[11] Working from a number of different disciplinary perspectives – prominently including art history – scholars founded what they called the history of dress or costume history. The purpose of their research is to understand clothing itself: its development and construction, its aesthetics, and its social meanings and functions. In the 1990s, 'fashion' arose as the subject of inquiry, in contrast to 'dress.' The new term looked beyond the material form of dress. 'Fashion' emphasizes a broader context, integrating the history of clothing's production and consumption, and most of all the cultural meanings ascribed to clothes temporally and spatially. By articulating the spectrum of meanings that clothing can convey, these multidisciplinary scholars reveal ideologies and practices. They recognize how, across time and place, clothing serves as a means of 'fashioning' one's self – that is, as a way of making and projecting a public persona. Sociologist Diana Crane uses clothing to 'trace changes in the nature of the relationship between social classes and lifestyle and between men and women' as well as 'to expand our understanding of material culture and its codes.'[12] Focusing on artists' depiction of clothes, Anne Hollander theorizes the necessity of 'visual desire' as an even stronger factor than utility or practicality in dress.[13] Anthropologist Emma Tarlo stresses the importance of 'controversial moments when individuals and groups choose to change their clothes or combine one type of clothing with another'; such moments 'reveal the active role that clothing has played in the identity construction of individuals, families, castes, regions, and nations.'[14]

Academic historians first added clothing to their arsenal of potential sources as part of the rise of social history. For instance, economic historians in the early twentieth century started to examine textile production but did not interrogate clothing itself as a relevant source until the 1960s.[15] This body of work thus still overlooked the potential of artifacts to provide evidence for human actions and ideas that were never articulated in written documents. In 1979, *Annales* historian Fernand Braudel wrote in defense of clothing as a 'serious' primary source: 'The history of costume is less anecdotal than would appear . . . it touches on every issue – raw materials, production processes, manufacturing costs, cultural stability, fashion and social hierarchy.'[16] Women's history as a field was notably receptive to fashion studies, as it was to feminist scholarship across disciplines. Researchers found clothing to be an especially rich means of illuminating both women's lived experience and ideologies of gender, which so often expressed themselves through differentiated norms of dress for women and men. The 'cultural turn' among academic historians in the 1990s, and the subsequent 'material turn' championing the evidentiary value of objects from the past, helped make fashion and dress more prominent in historical study. Fashion proved particularly attractive in transnational histories, as a means of tracing the global circulation of commodities (and related ideas).[17] A closer collegiality and fluidity between academic scholars and museum professionals has further encouraged research using artifacts, including clothing. Dress has always offered great potential insight upon the past. It now has also achieved a recognized place within the historian's repertoire.

Material contexts

Other sources have great value for understanding and interpreting clothing as historical evidence, yet they do not substitute for the artifact of the clothing itself, when it is available. As Leora Auslander writes, 'people's relationship to language is not the same as their relation to things; all that they express through their creation and use of material objects is . . . not reducible to words.'[18] Although historians do not always have access to actual clothing when conducting research, one can find clothes in the holdings of museums, historical societies, archives, and other repositories. An institution may have just a few articles or an expansive costume collection. While the larger collections will have digitized, searchable finding aids, and even photographs of their holdings, it often takes special effort to inquire (and discover) what historic clothing a site may possess.

Knowing exactly what a person wore can shed a singular light on her or him as an individual. For instance, the dresses that belonged to nineteenth-century missionary Mary Richardson Walker reveal her 'small stature' and 'slight build.' They also show abstract traits, especially how her expectations differed from the realities of a missionary wife in Oregon country. Her self-confident letters and diaries do not comment on the adaptations she clearly had to make to the climate and her new life, but her wardrobe does: her clothing conformed to convention, covering her 'neck to ankle,' but would have made her hot and uncomfortable as she labored at her domestic tasks,[19] Another young wife, Lee Ng Shee, came to America around 1906; she brought with her a pair of embroidered, silk trousers made in Hong Kong, a pleated two-panel skirt, and a *wei chu'u* apron. Like Walker's clothes, these too represented conventions and expectations – ideas about the proper dress of a merchant's wife. Mrs. Lee continued to wear traditional Chinese clothing throughout most of her life, though her husband and children adopted Western styles for everyday attire. Her clothing marked her as the bearer of their ancestral culture, while her family's choices in dress asserted their American identity and citizenship during a time of xenophobia and exclusion.[20] For both women, the clothing they chose to keep wearing came to mean different things in a new environment; their dress asserted a separate identity, all the more insistent because it seemed 'wrong' for their new circumstances.

Modern examples abound of wearers who purchased particular items to make a political point, from silk purses and ribbons with abolitionist emblems in the nineteenth century to the profusion of t-shirts with ideological messages in the twentieth. For instance, a white tank top in the collection of the GLBT Historical Society bears the image of a line of automobiles ablaze, and the words, 'Fight Back! Stonewall Inn '69, S.F. City Hall '79.' It references, and connects, two violent demonstrations. Patrons' sudden resistance against a police raid of the Stonewall Inn in New York City, 1969, became memorialized as a founding event in the gay liberation movement. The 'White Night Riots' in San Francisco ten years later protested the assassinations of the city's Mayor George Moscone and openly gay Supervisor Harvey Milk. A similar blue cotton T-shirt reads 'No Apologies! May 21st 1979 San Francisco' around the drawing of a burning police car. Sales of the shirts raised funds for the legal defense of protesters who were arrested during the riot.[21]

The path that an article of clothing takes to end up in a museum or archive is part of its context as a source. The provenance of clothing – from museum notes and object files to oral traditions – can provide such information, not only about who made and who wore the clothing, but who preserved and donated it. This context deepens the scholar's analysis of the clothing, in turn. Descendants of slaveholders donated much of the enslaved people's clothing in museums, for example. Slaveholding families tended to keep items that they believed showed their benevolence: gifts they had given or even made for their slaves, like a wedding dress in North Carolina's Alamance County Historical Museum that demonstrates its white maker's skill with the needle.[22] These were not everyday work clothes, nor were they garments that enslaved people took with them into freedom; they are part of a romanticized past, obscuring the workings of power and racism within slavery as an institution. Researchers have the ethical obligation to question this implicit narrative when they use slave clothing as a source. It is also worthwhile to take collection policies and the state of preservation of the item into account.

Any article of clothing represents a negotiation among a designer, maker, purchaser and wearer. The materiality of an actual article of clothing testifies not only to how it 'really' looked but to how it was made and even how it was worn. Its shape, fabric, stitching, signs of wear, alterations, and repair, all provide tangible evidence of a garment's social history.

Analyzing the *design* of a single article or group of clothing calls for a comparative context. That is, it takes cross-referencing with other pieces to identify a type and style of dress. Clothing has variations over time that reflect changing fashions, as well as variations due to individual preferences or utility. That is because dress does not simply meet practical needs for warmth and protection but also aesthetic sensibilities and cultural expectations. As fashion historian Anne Hollander explains, 'the shapes, lines, and textures of clothing . . . fluctuate according to their own formal laws.'[23] Scholars often refer to those 'laws' – the formal elements of dress – as a metaphorical 'vocabulary' or 'language.'[24] This visual language inscribes meaning into clothes. Each component – like the cut of a sleeve, the width of the lapels, the colors – may communicate something about the wearer's identity, preferences, or mood, but the ability to communicate those things depends upon what the clothing looks like. The ability to express ideas and aesthetic vision through dress also makes fashion an art form.

The creator of a garment is the foremost author of the language that the garment speaks, in this sense. Some of the 'words' (and their connotations) derive from rules and customs, like the association of ermine fur and purple dye with royalty. Others are the product of artistic vision and training. Beginning in nineteenth-century France, fashion designers came to win renown as artists. Consequently, certain designers richly documented their intentions and have been important biographical subjects: Charles Worth, Paul Poiret, and Coco Chanel, for example. Less prominent designers are also significant, however, as are tailors and dressmakers. Poiret and Chanel revolutionized *fashion* by creating new silhouettes and 'looks.' But whether or not a *modiste* seeks to change 'the laws of beauty,' the clothes she designs have an intention behind them. Clothing is the material expression of those ideas.

Designing sartorial styles for specific occupations made strategic use of the language of clothes. For example, uniforms were key to making the nursing profession respectable for middle-class women to pursue in the late nineteenth century. Dress historian Christina Bates writes that, 'The uniform is not just a symbol, but also an active participant in the formation of institutional and personal *mentalities*. Each day student nurses were physically reminded of the expectations of neatness, cleanliness and personal control when they donned their prescribed dress, pressed their caps, and tied their aprons.'[25] Contemporary fashions gave nursing uniforms a 'vocabulary' through which to suggest that nursing was appropriate for middle-class women, yet that it involved physical labor. Early uniforms for nurses used the basic form of the princess dress, a style that elongated the female body, making the torso appear more slender and thus 'elegant.'[26] Yet it added elements associated with both women's work and men's. The nursing cap and apron acknowledged the gendered and working-class associations of nursing by mirroring what female domestic servants wore. Yet other elements borrowed from masculine white-collar work to underscore nurses' professionalism. By the

1890s, nursing uniforms included detachable cuffs and collars such as men wore, and sometimes elastic sleeve holders to help keep the sleeves clean by pulling them up above the wrist [Figure 10.1].

The development of women's athletic attire illustrates how clothing design has to account for cultural expectations along with strictly pragmatic concerns. Neither culture nor pragmatism alone determined what women's swimming costumes should look like. Women bathers at the turn of the nineteenth century wore 'long, loose, and flowing dresses' of heavy material that 'ballooned out from the body' when wet.[27] The early bathing suit strove to cover and conceal the female body, to meet the standards of female 'respectability' in public. Over time, women were not content to limit themselves to the passive leisure of seaside 'bathing,' though. Arguments promoting the health benefits of physical exercise for women, and concerns over high rates of women's deaths from drowning, encouraged them to learn to swim.[28] This called for new attire. The Australian competitive swimmer Annette Kellerman designed her own line of swimsuits in response [Figure 10.2]. The one-piece 'Kellerman' had a scooped neckline and ended in shorts above the knee. Yet feminine modesty remained a consideration. American women typically wore not only pantaloons to swim, but a skirt over them.[29] This helped disguise the way any wet fabric clings to the body, showing the contours of one's 'figure.'

Similarly, the field hockey uniform that Radcliffe College student Elizabeth Wright Plimpton wore in the 1920s differed greatly from the gym suit her mother had worn. The first athletic clothing for women adapted the bloomer, or divided skirt – a compromise solution to the constricting nature of women's dress, in that it retained the billowy look of full skirts but allowed the legs freer movement without becoming entangled. In the 1920s, the baggy bloomers of the previous generation gave way to a short, loose pleated skirt. Long, full sleeves were replaced by a sleeveless bodice and a short-sleeved shirt. Paired with long knee socks or stockings, the 1920s outfit gave the wearer greater mobility while maintaining modesty. Moreover, a badge with a bold letter 'R' (for Radcliffe) and a more demure 'H' (for hockey) underneath proclaimed the wearer's identity as an athlete and a representative of her college.[30] From bicycling outfits to gym suits, the design of women's sportswear in the 1920s repeatedly balanced greater freedom of movement with culturally defined modesty, fashion with individualism.

Alongside silhouette, cut, and other aspects of design, the stuff of which it is made is intrinsic to the properties of clothing as material evidence. Is the fabric soft and comfortable, or stiff? Homespun or woven by machine? How costly was it? The significance of the fabric is not only tactile in a universal sense, but contextual. The plain white muslin of Sarah Tate's wedding dress, for instance, was relatively inexpensive; but compared to the much cheaper, coarser, homespun 'Negro cloth' that enslaved people like Tate typically wore, the fabric marked the dress as something special.[31] The very cloth of a garment connects it to economic and labor histories that raise new questions about the production and circulation of goods. For instance, the popularity of the color blue for eighteenth-century American clothing, from 'ball gowns' to 'military uniforms' to 'slave garments,' derived largely from the easy cultivation and use of indigo dye.[32]

Figure 10.1 Nurse in uniform, Liverpool, England, *c.*1870–1890
Source: Wellcome Collection, London, England. CC BY.

Figure 10.2 Swimsuit (*c.*1920). Asbury Mills, New York (manufacturer), Annette Kellerman (designer)

Source: National Gallery of Victoria, Melbourne. Purchased 2002. This digital record has been made available on NGV Collection Online through the generous support of Professor A. G. L. Shaw, AO Bequest.

Changes in preferred fabrics relate to other social, cultural, and economic developments. Women's swimsuits continued to have many layers into the 1920s in deference to modesty. But the fabrics employed helped make swimsuits easier for women to swim in. Technology addressed the deficiencies of wool, which was 'stretchy, saggy, itchy,' heavy and smelly when wet, and a sand magnet. Cotton, though lighter weight, 'didn't give at all in the water.' Enter Lastex, a new thread that incorporated rubber and was later combined with nylon.[33] Gym suits and nursing uniforms likewise turned away from heavy wool to lightweight cotton to afford greater mobility and easier washing. But all cottons were not the same. Unlike the princess style dresses in 'delicate cotton' that fashionable women wore, the nurse's princess cut uniform was made of 'serviceable' denim, the cotton twill 'first introduced for men's working overalls in the 1850s.' Its patterns and colors were also distinctive; out of practical considerations, especially the need to 'resist fading from frequent washing,' nursing uniforms came in stripes or patterns of white with 'blue from indigo' or 'pink from a synthetic version of madder dye,' 'the two most colorfast dyestuffs available.'[34]

The fabric of an article of clothing can demonstrate great personal, emotional value beyond pragmatic concerns or fashion trends. A piece of the fabric can become a synecdoche not only of the garment but of the person. Take, for example, a nineteenth-century pincushion belonging to Charlotte Thompson Richardson. Her two brothers had fought on opposite sides of the Revolutionary War. She made a pincushion out of scraps from each of their military uniforms. By combining the two contrasting fabrics into one object, she may have meant 'to 'mend' the family together after the conflict.'[35] The pincushion in turn came into service to sew and mend other clothing in the family, and was passed on to the next generation. In another instance of re-purposed fabric, in 1898, Eliza Philbrick took 'rough brown wool spun and woven on her grandparents' New Hampshire farm almost a century before and saved uncut in her mother's trunk.' Out of it, she made a gown after the colonial style, to wear to a gala for the Daughters of the American Revolution, a hereditary society. She purchased other colonial textiles 'from an antiques dealer' to add details to the skirt, and later to the neck and sleeves. Though Philbrick did not know it, the panel she added to the skirt was probably a bed valance originally, and the linen 'kerchief' had likely been a tea cloth.[36] As Laurel Thatcher Ulrich writes, Philbrick's dress 'falsified her family's past only in its details'; her choice of fabric 'revised her family's history' and attested to 'the impulse toward betterment that often lay beneath rural industry.'[37] Such interest in antique textiles also helped create the sentimental nineteenth-century myth of the Revolutionary era as the pre-industrial 'age of homespun,' an era in which women's domestic productivity proved their virtue, contributing to the nation through their labor for their families, snug and content within the female sphere.

At times, other sources can indicate what clothing was made from when the clothes themselves no longer exist. These may be artifacts like swatches or fabric samples. Home economist Mary Schenck Woolman not only collected textiles but included swatches in her published instruction manual, *A Sewing Course* (1901);

192 *Laura R. Prieto*

these can help identify contemporary fabrics [Figure 10.3].[38] Sometimes strictly verbal references must suffice. For example, the archival records and scrapbooks of the North Carolina Homemaker's Association, 4-H Club, and individuals reveal how rural women and girls in the 1920s and 1930s approximated the fashionable dress of urban women: they learned to repurpose materials like cotton fertilizer sacks for their dresses. A lace dress made from old curtains won a competition in North Carolina in 1933.[39]

As with other artefacts, determining 'authorship' poses special challenges with regard to dress. Clothes are almost always 'unsigned' work. If a garment is attributed to a creator, it is almost universally its designer who receives credit rather than acknowledgment of those who literally made it. The labor of factory operatives, piece workers, and home stitchers alike was undervalued and thus difficult to trace. One remarkable exception from the era of the American Revolution involves Esther de Berdt Reed and the other women of the Philadelphia Ladies Association. Each woman sewed her name on the sleeves of the shirts she made and donated to the Continental Army. In doing so, the sewer asserted her patriotism and her individual contribution to the War of Independence.[40]

Figure 10.3 Mary Schenck Woolman, *A Sewing Course*, 1901. Gift of Barbara White Haddad 1992.076.12

Source: Courtesy of the RISD Museum, Providence, Rhode Island, USA.

But a lack of recognition does not mean that the sewer is entirely invisible. The labor itself leaves physical traces. The stitching on quilted petticoats in museum collections, for example, reveals that each petticoat was the work of multiple people with varying levels of skill.[41] Indeed, any article of clothing attests not only to the method (hand or machine) but to the level of skill of its maker, the physical tasks of cutting, sewing, and fitting. The invention of sewing machines and the development of patterns and drafting systems 'democratized' the ability to make more elaborate clothes for oneself.[42]

For the majority of clothing through most of the past, the maker and wearer were likely to be closely related, even the same person. Thus a twentieth-century nursing student's uniform, like one in the Collection of the Alumnae Association, Montreal General Hospital School of Nursing, reveals much about the many forms of work that its wearer engaged in. Christina Bates models how much an attentive researcher can derive from close analysis of an individual garment:

> It is quite roughly machine sewn, with crude handmade buttonholes. The fabric is very soft and thin from repeated washing, still retaining its pink color, although much faded. There are many tears, especially around the collar, which are roughly darned. This bodice – wash-worn, threadbare, unlined, ripped, and worn until it almost fell apart – is material evidence of the other side of nurses in 'pretty pink dresses,' It alludes to the need for extreme economy on the part of some of the young students whose families could barely afford to send their daughters to school rather than straight into paying jobs. But even more evocatively, the garment bears witness to the nurse's hard labor of bending, lifting, washing, restraining, and scrubbing.[43]

A piece of apparel thus not only illuminates the creative vision of its designers; clothing attests to the physical labor of its makers and provides evidence of the experiences of the person who wore it. Clothing's physical properties aids in dating the origins of a piece and in filling in its history of use. For example, Courtney Crawford's raccoon coat, now in the Cornell Costume and Textile Collection, dates to the 1920s, when such coats became the rage among affluent male college students. But Crawford bought the coat second-hand in 1947, when a subsequent craze for raccoon coats infected a later generation of collegians. Crawford had a tailor replace the coat's lining with a plaid fabric, 'as similar to the Crawford tartan as he could find.' The exterior and lining thus date to different owners and different periods of wear. The material trace left by changing the lining demonstrates how individuals adapted clothing that was 'on trend'; not simply conforming to a style but adapting its details for personal expression.[44]

Alterations and repairs leave their marks on an article of clothing and signify its use. Among Mary Richardson Walker's belongings, her fan was repaired multiple times and its wood replaced, but a cotton capelet, decorative ribbons, and 'delicate "mitts"' survive in such condition that it seems she never had occasion to use them [Figure 10.4].[45] A tiny pair of moccasins, also unworn, may be her own handiwork, using skills learned from indigenous women at the Tshimakain

194 *Laura R. Prieto*

Figure 10.4 Mary Richardson Walker's lace mitts and fan. Manuscripts, Archives, and Special Collections, Washington State University Libraries, Pullman, WA

Source: Photograph by James Seckington.

mission where she was stationed.[46] Or it may have been meant for a *collection*, to be looked at rather than worn, to exemplify a 'foreign' culture or society, like other pieces acquired by missionaries or anthropologists. In contrast, enslaved women on a Georgia plantation wore and passed down a flowered cotton skirt decorated with dark brown bands near the bottom. Though it would have been 'saved . . . for special occasions,' historian Katie Knowles writes, 'an insert and a repair at the waist, along with the faded and soft quality of the fabric, indicate this skirt was worn frequently.' It serves as vivid evidence of how 'enslaved people created their own fashions through manipulating the clothing allowance given to then.'[47] The skirt's multiple repairs and resized waist also attest to how, in the slave quarters, items of beauty were precious, shared resources.

Beyond the material

Although the material object provides crucial evidence, using clothing as a source benefits from consideration of multiple contexts that extend beyond its physical properties. Without accounting for these other contexts, the analysis of clothing is incomplete. There are limits to the historical evidence that clothing as an artefact can provide, and the majority of what was worn no longer exists in material form anyhow. And the existence of an object in a collection, or a closet, does not definitively attest to its use. Careful examination of a cage-like corset, made of metal, will reveal how it fit the body; it may even show signs of wear. One might assume it functioned as a particularly tortuous form of body shaping for fashionable women. But medical texts and autobiographical writings identify iron corsets as orthopedic devices, employed 'to amend the crookednesse of the Bodie' in the manner of stays. In addition, 'accounts and illustrations of iron corsets seem to have resulted in the production of modern replicas or forgeries, just as we see with accounts of medieval chastity belts.'[48] These objects are evidence of twentieth-century fetish rather than of seventeenth-century fashion. Other visual and verbal sources help to document what was worn, how it was worn, and who wore it. They may record the same elements observable in clothing itself: silhouette, fabric, construction.

Non-material sources especially help to reveal the meanings ascribed to clothing: how clothing was *understood*. Returning to the example of slave clothing: one can turn to other texts, from daguerreotypes to runaway slave advertisements, logbooks to fugitive slave narratives, to help determine what antebellum enslaved people wore in bondage and in freedom.[49] By using these contextual sources as a lens, one can perceive the multiple meanings of clothing for enslaved individuals and slave communities. It is mainly verbal descriptions that reveal the distinctive aesthetic created by African-American slaves: not only altering the standardized clothing issued by slaveholders, 'of uniform cut and color and sewn of coarse, drab materials,' but combining these with 'old waistcoats, dresses, stockings, hats and petticoats from their owners, part of the rewards and punishments system on plantations . . . changing any details that they did not like.'[50]

Visual images of course help to compensate for the vast majority of clothing from the past that simply does not exist in material form. A plethora of sources – genre paintings and advertisements, cartoons and Hollywood musicals – all depict people wearing clothing. Still, as Leora Auslander reminds us, all such depictions are mediated; that mediation limits their value in one sense and accords them a new value as well. Although no representation is a perfectly complete and transparent view of its subject, the human decision to depict particular things in a particular manner provides insight into their context. Thus 'the mediation of the painter, photographer, or filmmaker, like that of the writer, both enriches and complicates the historian's work.'[51]

Researchers must be mindful of the selectivity and exclusivity of visual culture. Its exclusions can be subtle. Artists more often portray subjects who fit contemporary ideals of beauty, or who can afford to commission or buy images of themselves. As Zara Anishanslin notes, 'Who chose clothing shown in portraits – whether it was painter, sitter, sitter's family, commissioner of the job, or some combination – is often difficult to determine' and often resulted from multifaceted negotiations.[52] Fashion illustration employs its own iconography from one period to another.[53] And images can be didactic. The fashion plate, introduced in the late eighteenth century, demonstrated how clothing *ought* to appear; magazines like *Godey's Lady's Book* not only taught readers about the latest styles but about the 'correct' posture, demeanor, and body type that befitted ideal femininity in the mid-nineteenth century US.

Even images that seem to be straightforward can be misleading. Figures in art may be dressed in unusual, or at least more studied and formal ways, than a typical person. Ordinary people rarely commissioned images of themselves – and when they did, they did not necessarily want to appear ordinary. One might reasonably presume that individuals chose carefully from their best clothing when they sat for their portraits. But verisimilitude was not always the ultimate purpose of portraiture.[54] Artist John Singleton Copley sometimes painted his sitters in a dress that he copied from a print rather than one they owned; this is why Katherine Greene Amory, Mary Greene Hubbard, and Lucretia Chandler Murray are wearing identical dresses in their portraits from 1763 and 1764. Copley's strategy probably meant to associate his elite American sitters with the latest London fashions. Other patrons modified their images to conform to later fashions, like Jemima Wilkinson who had a simpler, solid-colored gown painted over the original flowered silk dress in her portrait by John Singleton Copley.[55] As print culture expanded, and the hunger for illustrations grew, magazines too 'borrowed' from one another, recycling the same fashion plates and other images over many years. They even interchanged English and American images, though in actuality the styles differed substantially in the two countries.[56]

Just as the clothing that tends to be kept and preserved is not the everyday dress of enslaved people or poorer folk, so are visual representations skewed towards the elite. Servants and slaves appear in paintings and photographs less often than the master class. Even genre paintings of the poor – John George Brown's *The Card Trick* (1880–1889), for instance – might sentimentalize their ordinary subjects.[57] Illustrators viciously satirized African American visitors to Chicago's World's Columbian Exhibition in 1893.[58] They not only exaggerated racialized facial features, but lampooned African Americans' place in society through depictions of their dress. Frederick Burr Opper's lithograph, 'Darkies' Day at the Fair' in *Puck* magazine portrayed African-American men in supposedly African loincloths, flashy band uniforms, and vividly colored, patterned trousers. These types of dress all marked the men as cultural outsiders. This visual strategy paralleled the mocking of the urban working class, like 'Bowery b'hoys' and g'hals,' for their brightly colored clothes and flamboyant sense of style. Middle-class observers regarded Bowery dress as an exaggerated imitation of elite fashions, gaudier and more revealing versions of what their 'betters' wore and thus manifestations of their defiant egalitarianism.[59]

Photographs sometimes served more explicitly ideological purposes as well. Such images show how clothing could serve as a measure of 'civilization.' The captions and guide to the Keystone View Company's educational stereographs make this clear: they explicitly label the traditional costumes of those in Africa as 'savage' and 'primitive.'[60] For Native Americans in the late nineteenth century, photographs purported to document their successful assimilation through capturing their changed appearance. A pair of photographs of the young Sioux woman Zie-Wie, for example, emphasizes her transformation before and after entering Hampton Institute in 1878. In the earlier image, Zie-Wie wears moccasins and covers herself with a plaid blanket. A year later, she poses stiffly in a Mother Hubbard dress, also plaid, rendered relatively formal by a belt.[61] The sewing implements in her lap suggest that Zie Wie might have made the simple dress herself. The high-necked, long-sleeved Mother Hubbard was ubiquitous as indoor daywear among Anglo-American women in the west; wearing it associated Zie-Wie with domestic, feminine, modest womanhood. It also evoked a history of religious conversion; American missionaries had urged Pacific Islander women to adopt the Mother Hubbard in place of traditional clothing that covered much less of their bodies.[62] Some Native American women, such as writer Sarah Winnemucca Hopkins (Paiute), publicly wore native dress to signal their support for Indian sovereignty.[63] Other elite women of color, including Hawai'ian Queen Liliuokalani and Filipina anti-imperial activist Clemencia López, strategically employed Western clothing at times, using it to refute their 'savagery' and to assert their equality with white American audiences.[64]

When used with care, visual sources afford a great advantage, however: they depict how garments look when worn. As art historian Anne Hollander points out, dressing is itself a form of 'picture making, with reference to actual pictures that indicate how the clothes are to be perceived.'[65] Photographs help answer whether and how ordinary people 'handled the often conflicting dictates of fashion, hard work, and economy in their clothing choices,' as scholar Joan Severa puts it.[66] They reveal what Diana Crane has termed 'alternative dress' for middle-class and elite women on both sides of the Atlantic in the late nineteenth century. Not all women, even in the upper classes, conformed to the 'exceptionally restrictive and ornamental' styles of fashionable dress in the period. Photographs show how some women co-opted elements of masculine dress, always in combination 'with items of fashionable female clothing.' Rather than fully replacing dresses or skirts with trousers, many women adopted neckties and cravats, suit jackets, waistcoats, and men's hats, as accompaniments to fashionable, feminine skirts and hairstyles.[67] An item might combine masculine and feminine elements; ties might be made of ribbon, flowers might ornament a straw boater, and a tailored shirtwaist might have feminine mutton sleeves. Or a woman would create an 'alternative' look by pairing differently gendered articles. Wearing cufflinks, for instance, changed the context of a bustle when a woman wore both together.

The effect was subtle but significant. Individual combinations of masculine and feminine fashions appealed most strongly to women who were moving beyond the separate 'female sphere,' for example, to attend college, practice the professions, or engage in public reform movements – anyone who found expectations of domesticity too restrictive. Through this syncretic style, women could lay claim to masculine independence without completely flouting convention. In fact, by the 1920s, aspects of 'alternative dress' had become dominant in fashion.[68]

Images made clothing more public than the material object could ever be; circulating images spread the visual influence of clothes and amplified the message of the wearers. That is, exporting a certain 'look' did not occur solely in material form through sending clothing itself from one place to another. Beyond depicting and promoting dress, visual technologies shaped fashion in turn. Hollander notes that, 'with the development of photography and film, 'black-and-white vision required a certain crispness of shape, texture, and grooming, while fashion in gesture and posture became freer and more expressive.'[69] The advent of abstract art made the fashion ideal more geometric.[70] Print culture – especially magazines, film, and other media with visual components – played a major role in the history of fashion. Clothing and images of clothing are often companion commodities.[71] For instance, the 'zoot suit' arrived in Trinidad through the film *Stormy Weather* (1943), in conjunction with US military occupation.[72] The visual representation of clothes increased public consciousness of its possibilities; as the types of images and their reach have expanded, 'the connotative power of dress' has proliferated.[73]

Seeing clothing through words

Written sources, even more than visual ones, help researchers reconstruct the intent of a style of dress and its cultural associations more fully. Discourse about clothing, along with images, suffused print culture. Yet like the visual images, the verbal texts range from idealized prescriptions to realistic descriptions. Fashion magazines, published starting in the nineteenth century, of course provide the most direct verbal commentary on the preferred styles, yet even they ranged beyond just illustrations. Early examples, like *Metropolitan, Delineator,* and *Demorest's Monthly Magazine,* included paper dress patterns in every issue; others integrated short fiction and advice, putting the fashion coverage into a refined yet domestic context.[74] Just about any periodical, from newspapers to fan magazines, chronicled dress even if it did not discuss fashion, merely by virtue of depicting people wearing clothes.

American writers imbued clothing with specific associations. Through words, they narrowed the multiple, ambiguous meanings that a style of clothing could have. For example, in 1943, hundreds of white soldiers, sailors, and civilians clashed violently with Mexican Americans in the streets of Los Angeles. Reporters tagged the riots to the 'Zoot Suit' that young Mexican American men often wore. Controversies in print connected the style to youth, defiance, and criminality. These attributes were not inherent in pegged pants and broad-shouldered jackets but rather in how people voiced their interpretation of the style and who wore it. Thus, newspaper accounts not only recognized the zoot suit as a popular style within the Mexican American community. They also further instilled this style of dress with a defiant identity and made it part of the public debate about race, ethnicity, citizenship, and patriotism.[75]

The wider the range of verbal sources that a researcher consults, the better situated one is to test their claims. Critics have singled out women, in particular, as the 'victims' or 'slaves' of fashion, misled by their feminine vanity or ignorance to look ridiculous, or to endanger their bodies – tight-lacing corsets to achieve an abnormally small waist, for instance. Yet careful research shows that few women actually practiced such extremes. The broader lesson, as Valerie Steele cautions, is that 'The discourse on fashion has tended to stress its negative connotations.'[76] Indeed 'dress reform,' as a movement in the US, began in conjunction with calls for women's rights. The movement objected to the constricting and increasingly ornamental dress expected of women, which impeded women's mobility and even their health.[77] As activist Sarah Grimké wrote in 1837, 'as long as we submit to be dressed like dolls, we never can rise to the stations of duty and usefulness from which [men] desire to exclude us.'[78] In response, Amelia Bloomer and other activists promoted 'Turkish dress' or the 'bloomer' costume, comprising a shortened full skirt over pantaloons. The bloomer received much press but also such widespread public ridicule that very few mid-nineteenth-century women ever wore it outside the home or water-cure resorts. Written sources document that the bloomer proved counterproductive to winning support for women's rights, so that even radicals and leaders like Susan B. Anthony returned to skirts after about a year.[79]

Correspondence, diaries, and other personal papers further enrich the context that publications provide for clothing. They do what periodicals mostly cannot: record the quotidian, personal, even private choices that individuals made regarding their attire. William Dillwyn wrote letters to his daughter Susanna in the 1770s, accompanied by dress patterns from London.[80] The correspondence of Samuel and Rebecca Shoemaker – Quakers and Revolutionary War refugees in London like Dillwyn – attests to their struggles to find fabrics and accessories to their taste instead of the different items that were fashionable there then. The Dillwyn and Shoemaker papers show how even Quakers, whose religion discouraged worldliness in favor of plain dress, could be concerned with fashion. Written sources illuminate not only the context of clothing's consumption, but also its production. The autobiography and financial records of African-American dressmaker Elizabeth Keckly, for instance, reveal much about the business of making and selling clothes in mid-nineteenth-century America. Keckly was able to use her skills in sewing and design as a path from slavery to freedom yet remained highly dependent on personal recommendations. Her shop in Baltimore failed before she re-established herself in Washington, D.C. and gained her most famous client, First Lady Mary Todd Lincoln. Keckly became not only a businesswoman but a tastemaker – until public criticism following her publication entitled *Behind the Scenes* damaged her reputation. She trained and employed dozens of other women throughout her life yet ended up as a lowly worker in someone else's dry goods shop.[81] Her career shows both the potential and the volatility of her occupation.

Published works and manuscript records also include enumerative and even quantitative information – inventories and account books, wills and probate – that help put clothing in its social and economic context. Census and tax records add many layers to rare memoirs, like Elizabeth Keckly's, for understanding the dressmaking trade. The growth of social science, social work, and home economics in the late nineteenth century meant researchers, government employees, and reformers began collecting data, on the working class in particular. In the 1870s and 1880s, Carroll Wright oversaw quantitative studies of family budgets. Other studies conducted by Progressive era reformers surveyed working-class women about what they wore and how much they spent on clothing.[82] These sources help document the rise of the shirtwaist among urban working-class women. Not only were young women drawn into industrial wage work by the advent of ready-to-wear clothing in the 1870s, they became its principal consumers, and their buying habits inspired anxieties among middle- and upper-class social reformers. The mass media exhibited a new fascination with working-class women that usually depicted them at leisure. At the same time, early sociological surveys collected information on what working-class women wore and how much they spent on clothing. This was meant to pressure employers to pay higher wages, as well as to urge women workers to enact more sober self-discipline. For researchers, these studies serve a different purpose: filling in the everyday aspects of how working women chose to dress, beyond the moments in which they caught a photographer's eye.

Lastly, context from verbal documents is essential to realize how deciding what to wear was not an entirely individual or private matter. Laws govern the importation and exportation, manufacture, and labeling of clothes and textiles. Laws and institutional policies also attempted to consciously control, contain, and direct who wore what clothing. The manner in which government concerned itself about dress indicates how much clothing mattered to identity. They thus help expose whether dressing a particular way was subversive. In sixteenth-century Mexico, Spanish colonial officials decreed that mestiza, mulata, and black women must wear Spanish rather than indigenous clothing. That is, they deemed indigenous clothing appropriate only for 'full-blooded' indigenous people.[83] In the British colonies, sumptuary laws restricted people's choice of wearing apparel to what seemed appropriate for their 'rank' and economic means. Lavish dress was grouped initially with other forms of immoral 'excess' like drunkenness. Thus most people could be prosecuted for wearing silk, gold buttons, or silver lace. In North America, Plymouth colony had no such laws, while Massachusetts Bay had various.[84]

Yet laws themselves do not indicate how they were enforced. Only actual court records reveal how laws were applied. In some instances, communities did not prosecute illegal attire. Sumptuary laws in Massachusetts Bay Colony grew so unpopular that by the 1660s, courts stopped prosecuting them.[85] The opposite also occurred: communities policed behaviors without there being specific laws in place. For example, relatively few statutes explicitly prohibited cross dressing in the nineteenth-century United States. Nevertheless, law enforcement utilized other, vaguer legislation to prosecute individuals, for instance anti-vagrancy or public nuisance statutes. Emma Snodgrass and Harriet French came to the attention of the Boston Police Department for wearing pants as they walked down the street in 1852; newspaper headlines like 'Arrest of Females in Male Attire' indicate the community regarded their dress as the transgression, but the official charge against them was vagrancy.[86]

Conclusion

The very everydayness of clothing makes its cultural meanings ubiquitous and submerged at the same time. Dress is so intrinsic to common experience that it does not seem to merit commentary unless it represents a new, outré style or a transgression. What could be more quotidian than waking up and getting dressed for the day? Styles and means of production may change, but the practice of wearing clothes unites human beings across culture, place, and time. In the modern era, clothes have become particularly cheap and plentiful; in the United States, cast-off clothing increasingly chokes landfills and overwhelms donation centers, straining global trade in recycled goods.[87] Clothing's very dispensability is what makes it a vehicle for self-expression and personal identity, in the moment.

Yet this omnipresence makes clothing all the more possible to discover as a piece of evidence, if one simply looks and asks the right questions. Close observation of a garment's material properties – fabric, color, silhouette, stitching, signs of wear and repair, and so on – can reveal much about how it was made and used. These are essential aspects of the article's individual history; they also help connect it to broader communities and economies. Visual images help place clothing in a geospatial and social contexts, as do verbal descriptions and commentaries. Clothing can thus illuminate specific and individual aspects of human experience, as well as broad patterns and abstract ideas.

Take, for instance, a pair of pants. How can they serve as historical evidence? Their material properties matter, to begin with, as we have considered with regard to a variety of other garments. The distinction between denim pants or silk trousers, for example, not only affects the individual experience of wearing them – the feel of the garment, its weight and warmth and sturdiness; the fabric also relates to the activities they are most appropriate for: heavy labor or leisure. This in turn connotes where one can expect to see them worn, what it means to wear them there, and what it means to see or wear them in other settings. A political candidate wearing jeans or silk pants at a fundraising event would create different impressions. And wearing blue cotton canvas pants for heavy labor, as Gold Rush miners did, would leave physical traces on the garment itself – besides which these traces differ from the ones on designer jeans worn to the mall by a teenager in the 1970s.

Manufacture and design are vital to interrogate as well. Mass production and standardized sizing revolutionized the garment industry starting in the mid-nineteenth century. The ready-to-wear 'sack suit,' with jacket and pants made from the same fabric, approximated a custom-made garment, making it affordable for the masses. Such clothing marks the historical effects of industrialization. Likewise, the cut of a pair of pants can convey a historically specific meaning. Nineteenth-century dress reformers broke a significant taboo in advocating pants for women; they thus tried to make the idea more palatable by proposing bloomers, with very full legs gathered at the ankle. The silhouette of the bloomer meant to resemble a skirt, thus seeming more feminine than the types of pants men wore; and women wore them under dresses, to emphasize the impression further.

Lastly, one needs to consider who wears an article or type of clothing, where and when. The baggy 'drape pants' and tight ankles of the men's Zoot suit in the 1940s, bore certain similarity to bloomers but connoted entirely different meanings: ethnic pride, masculine swagger, and even unpatriotic defiance in the eyes of some observers. Dr Mary Walker, the young, working-class Emma Snodgrass, and Chinese immigrant Lee Ng Shee all wore trousers when it seemed scandalous for women to do so – but the perceptions (and self-perceptions) of transgression were different in each woman's case. For Walker, her status in the almost exclusively masculine field of medicine rendered her use of male attire culturally acceptable. Snodgrass was regarded suspiciously as a cross-dresser and arrested in Boston in 1852 for vagrancy. Meanwhile, Lee Ng Shee wore trousers as a continuation of Chinese tradition, not a flouting of convention.

These meanings are thus not inherent in the garments themselves, but in how people have associated them with categories and characteristics, made rules about them, used them to do or communicate something in a specific setting. To understand clothing as evidence, then, we need to know how people have both worn clothes and thought about them – combining the material and the performative, the visual and the verbal. Indeed, interweaving different types of sources helps compensate for the shortcomings of each type so that the sum becomes stronger than its parts.[88] Though Henry David Thoreau wrote in *Walden*, 'Beware of all enterprises that require new clothes,' we need not shy away from making clothing part of our historical research. A careful consideration of clothing in context will add layers to our knowledge of human experience, in the past as in our own times.

Notes

1 A. Hollander, *Seeing through Clothes*, New York: Viking Press, 1975, p. 313.
2 C. Sears, *Arresting Dress: Cross-Dressing, Law, and Fascination in Nineteenth-Century San Francisco*, Durham, NC: Duke University Press, 2015, pp. 23–4.
3 K. Peiss, *Zoot Suit: The Enigmatic Career of an Extreme Style*, Philadelphia, PA: University of Pennsylvania Press, 2011, pp. 3–4.
4 Hollander, *Seeing through Clothes*, p. 355.
5 See; I. Mida and A. Kim, *The Dress Detective: A Practical Guide to Object-Based Research in Fashion*, London: Bloomsbury, 2015, for a clothing-specific adaptation of Jules David Prown's classic object-based methodology in Prown, 'Mind in matter: An introduction to material culture theory and method', *Winterthur Portfolio*, 17.1, 1–19.
6 D. Crane, *Fashion and Its Social Agendas: Class, Gender, and Identity in Clothing*, Chicago, IL: The University of Chicago, 2000, p. 3.
7 K. Honeyman, 'Snapshot: Fashion, the factory, and exploitation', in G. Riello and P. McNeil (eds), *Fashion History Reader*, New York, NY: Routledge, 2010, pp. 308–10.
8 N. Harte, 'The study of fashion and dress', in Riello and McNeil (eds), *Fashion History Reader*, 15–18, p. 16; Sarah Jones Weicksel, 'The dress of the enemy: Clothing and disease in the Civil War Era', *Civil War History*, 63.2, 2017, 133–50.
9 A. Ribeiro, 'Antiquarian attitudes: Some early studies in the history of dress', *Costume*, 28.1, 1994, 60–70.
10 T. Veblen, *The Theory of the Leisure Class* (1899, reprinted), London: George Allen & Unwin, 1924.
11 Mida and Kim, *Dress Detective*, pp. 18–20.
12 Crane, *Fashion and Its Social Agendas*, p. 24.
13 Hollander, *Seeing through Clothes*, p. 312.
14 E. Tarlo, *Clothing Matters, Dress and Identity in India*, London: Hurst, 1996, p. 1.
15 Harte, 'The study of fashion and dress', p. 15.
16 F. Braudel, *Civilization and Capitalism, 15th-18th Century: Vol. 1. The Structures of Everyday Life*, London: Collins, 1979, p. 311.

17 Peiss, *Zoot Suit*, p. 3; Modern Girl around the World Research Group, *The Modern Girl around the World: Consumption, Modernity, and Globalization*, Durham, NC: Duke University Press, 2008.
18 L. Auslander, 'Beyond Words', *The American Historical Review*, 110.4, 2005, 1015–45, p. 1017.
19 J. Thigpen, 'Desperately Seeking Mary: Materializing Mary Richardson Walker, Missionary', *The Public Historian*, 34.3, 2012, 74.
20 The youngest daughter, Virginia Lee Mead, donated several items of the Lee family's clothing to the National Museum of American History. See: "Clothes and Heritage," www.si.edu/spotlight/clothes-and-heritage-chinese-american-clothes-from-the-virginia-lee-mead-collection, last accessed 10.09.19.
21 The GLBT Historical Society Museum still sells replicas of the 'No Apologies!' T-shirt. 'Fight Back!' and 'No Apologies!' T-shirt collection box 42, GLBT Historical Society, San Francisco, California; digital images at http://wearinggayhistory.com/items/show/2865 and http://wearinggayhistory.com/items/show/2859; www.glbthistory.org/shop/no-apologies-t-shirt?rq=no%20apologies%20t-shirt, all last accessed 10.09.19. On the place of clothing in politics, also, see: Katrina Navikas, '"That Sash Will Hang You": Political Clothing and Adornment in England, 1780–1840', *Journal of British Studies* 49, 2010, 540–65.
22 K. Knowles, 'Expressions of self and belonging: Enslaved people and race-based fashion in the antebellum U.S. South', in C. Parfait, H. Le Dantex Lowry, and C. Bourhis-Mariotti (eds), *Writing History from the Margins: African Americans and the Quest for Freedom*, New York: Routledge, 2017, pp. 95–7; 100:79.08.02: Slave Dress, *c.*1850, linsey-woolsey homespun material. Provenance: Murray Plantation, Cross Roads Community, northern Alamance County. Alamance Museum, Burlington NC.
23 Hollander, *Seeing through Clothes*, p. 312.
24 See: R. Barthes, *The Fashion System*, New York: Hill and Wang, 1983, originally written and published in French in 1967, and *The Language of Fashion*, London: Bloomsbury, 2013; A. Lurie, *The Language of Clothes*, New York: Random House, 1981.
25 C. Bates, '"Their Uniforms All Esthetic and Antiseptic": Fashioning Modern Nursing Identity, 1870–1900', in I. Parkins and E. M. S Sheehan (eds), *Cultures of Femininity in Modern Fashion*, Durham, NC: University of New Hampshire Press, 2011, p. 153; Quoting J. Craik, *Uniforms Exposed: From Conformity to Transgression*, London: Berg, 2005, p. 106.
26 Bates, 'Their Uniforms All Esthetic and Antiseptic', p. 170.
27 P. Campbell Warner, *When the Girls Came Out to Play*, Amherst, MA: University of Massachusetts Press, 2006, p. 62.
28 M. Morgan, 'When Culture Kills: A History of Drowning in America', *Consuming Cultures*, 24 August 2012: www.consumingcultures.net/2012/08/24/when-culture-kills-a-history-of-drowning-in-america/, last accessed 10.09.19.
29 Warner, *When the Girls*, p. 68.
30 L. T. Ulrich, I. Gaskell, S. J. Schechner, and S. A. Carter, *Tangible Things: Making History through Objects*, New York: Oxford University Press, 2015, pp. 64–7.
31 Knowles, 'Expressions of self', p. 96.
32 A. Feeser, *Red, White, and Black Make Blue: Indigo in the Fabric of the Colonial South*, Athens, GA: University of Georgia Press, 2013.
33 Warner, *When the Girls*, pp. 80, 81. Spandex fiber, a breathable alternative to rubber, was developed in 1958.
34 Bates, 'Their Uniforms All Esthetic and Antiseptic', p. 170; A. Miller Stamper and J. Condra, *Clothing through American History: The Civil War through the Gilded Age, 1861–1899*, Santa Barbara, CA.: ABC-CLIO, 2011, is a good resource on fabric and other materials for that period.
35 Thigpen, 'Desperately seeking Mary', 77.

36 L. T. Ulrich, *Age of Homespun: Objects and Stories in the Creation of an American Myth*, New York: Vintage Books, a Division of Random House, 2001, p. 30.
37 Ulrich, *Age of Homespun*, p. 415.
38 A copy of Woolman's book is in the collections of the Rhode Island School of Design Museum, Providence, Rhode Island, https://risdmuseum.org/art-design/collection/sewing-course-199207612, last accessed 10.09.19.
39 B. Roberts, *Pageants, Parlors, and Pretty Women: Race and Beauty in the Twentieth-Century South*, Chapel Hill, NC: University of North Carolina Press, 2014, p. 125.
40 M. B. Norton, *Liberty's Daughters: The Revolutionary Experience of American Women, 1750–1800*, Boston, MA: Little, Brown, 1980, pp. 178–88.
41 B. Lemire, 'Draping the body and dressing the home', in K. Harvey (ed.), *History and Material Culture* 2nd edn., New York: Routledge, 2018, p. 100.
42 J. Spanabel Emery, *A History of the Paper Pattern Industry: The Home Dressmaking Fashion Revolution*, New York: Bloomsbury Publishing, 2014. Emery, a theater historian and curator, was instrumental in developing the Commercial Pattern Archive at the University of Rhode Island; the CoPA, https://copa.apps.uri.edu/index.php, is the largest collection of paper clothing patterns in the world. Also, see: B. Burman, *The Culture of Sewing: Gender, Consumption and Home Dressmaking*, New York: Bloomsbury Academic, 1999, and S. A. Gordon, *'Make It Yourself': Home Sewing, Gender, and Culture, 1890–1930*, New York: Columbia University Press, 2009.
43 Bates, 'Their Uniforms All Esthetic and Antiseptic', p. 174.
44 A. Dubin, 'The Power of a Winter Coat', 8 March 2018, Cornell Costume and Textile Coillection, https://blogs.cornell.edu/cornellcostume/2018/03/08/the-power-of-a-winter-coat/, last accessed 10.09.19.
45 Thigpen, 'Desperately seeking Mary', p. 75.
46 Ibid., pp. 78–9.
47 Knowles, 'Expressions of self', pp. 93–4.
48 V. Steele, *The Corset: A Cultural History*, New Haven, CT: Yale University Press, 2001, p. 5.
49 K. Haulman, *The Politics of Fashion in Eighteenth-Century America*, Chapel Hill, NC: University of North Carolina Press, 2011, pp. 27–9.
50 Roberts, *Pageants*, p. 158; Shane White and Graham White, *Stylin': African American Expressive Culture from its Beginnings to the Zoot Suit*, Ithaca, NY: Cornell University Press, 1996.
51 Auslander, 'Beyond words', p. 1024.
52 Z. Anishanslin, *Portrait of a Woman in Silk: Hidden Histories of the British Atlantic World*, New Haven CT: Yale University Press, 2016, p. 180.
53 Hollander, *Seeing through Clothes*, pp. 17–18.
54 M. M. Lovell, *Art in a Season of Revolution: Painters, Artisans, and Patrons in Early America*, Philadelphia, PA: University of Pennsylvania Press, 2005, pp. 75–6.
55 Anishanslin, *Portrait*, p. 180.
56 Warner, *When the Girls*, p. 68.
57 Hollander, *Seeing through Clothes*, p. 318 ('dressed people in ordinary life'), p. 322; www.joslyn.org/collections-and-exhibitions/permanent-collections/american/john-george-brown-the-card-trick/, last accessed 10.09.19.
58 B. R. Cooks, 'Fixing race: visual representations of African Americans at the World's Columbian Exposition, Chicago, 1893', *Patterns of Prejudice*, 41.5, 2007, 435–65.
59 T. Anbinder, *Five Points: The Nineteenth-Century New York City Neighborhood*, New York: Simon and Schuster, 2012, chapter 6.
60 Stereoview #572, for example, taught that 'The semicivilized and savage tribes [of Africa] wear very few clothes. A loin cloth wrapped about their bodies suffices,' while #573 adds that contact with European traders has led Africans on the west coast to be 'more clothed than their less civilized brothers of the interior.' Keystone View Company,

Visual Education: Teachers' Guide to Keystone 600 Set, Keystone View Company Educational Department, 1920, p. 540.
61 '(7) Dakota Zie-Wie, Yellow Moon, daughter of Indian Chief, Crow Creek Agency, Dakota, as she appeared on arrival at Hampton, Virginia. Age 15 years Date: November, 1878, BAE Copy Negative Number 55,518; (8) Dakota Zie-Wie, 14 months after her arrival at Hampton, Virginia February, 1880', BAE Copy Negative Number 55,519: James Owen Dorsey Photograph Collection, National Museum of Natural History, Washington DC.
62 E. Wood, R. Tisdale, and T. Jones, *Active Collections*, New York: Routledge, 2018, pp. 38–41; P. Marks, 'Belva Lockwood and the Mother Hubbard Dress: Social, moral, and political overtones in the popular press' *Journal of American Culture*, 39.3, 2016, 298–312; S. Helvenston Gray, 'Searching for Mother Hubbard: Function and fashion in nineteenth-century dress' *Winterthur Portfolio*, 48.1, 2014, 29–74.
63 J. Cohan Scherer, 'The Public Faces of Sarah Winnemucca', *Cultural Anthropology*, 3.2, 1988, 178–204.
64 L. R. Prieto, 'A delicate subject: Clemencia López, civilized womanhood, and the politics of anti-imperialism', *Journal of the Gilded Age and Progressive Era*, 12, 2013, 199–233; M. Roces, 'Gender, nation, and the politics of dress in twentieth-century Philippines', *Gender & History*, 17.2, 2005, 354–77.
65 Hollander, *Seeing through Clothes*, p. 326, p. 311.
66 Severa, *Dressed for the Photographer*, p. xvi.
67 A rare exception was Dr Mary Edwards Walker, who gained permission from Congress to wear pants as a commissioned physician in the Union Army during the Civil War.
68 D. Crane, 'Women's clothing behavior as nonverbal resistance', in *Fashion and its Social Agendas*, pp. 99–107.
69 Hollander, *Seeing through Clothes*, p. 344.
70 'Western dress requires the body to give clothes meaning, and Western art had always accommodated itself to this need until the possibilities of abstract vision made themselves visible to Western eyes. After that, clothes could aim at an ideal shape of their own.': Hollander, *Seeing through Clothes*, p. 337.
71 Peiss, *Zoot Suit*, p. 167.
72 Peiss *Zoot Suit*, p. 162; see, also: H. Neptune, *Caliban and the Yankees: Trinidad and the United States Occupation*, Chapel Hill, NC: University of North Carolina Press, 2007.
73 Hollander, *Seeing through Clothes*, p. 345.
74 F. L. Mott, *A History of American Magazines, 1865–1885*, Cambridge, MA: Harvard University Press, 1938, p. 97.
75 Peiss, *Zoot Suit*, p. 159.
76 Steele, *Corset*, p. 2.
77 M. Doak and M. Karetny, *How Did Diverse Activists Shape the Dress Reform Movement, 1838–1881?*, Binghamton, NY: State University of New York at Binghamton, 1999; P. A. Cunningham, *Reforming Women's Fashion, 1850–1920: Politics, Health, and Art*, Kent, OH: Kent State University Press, 2003, and G. Fisher, *Pantaloons and Power: A Nineteenth-Century Dress Reform in the United States*, Kent, OH: Kent State University Press, 2001.
78 S. Moore Grimké, *Letters on the Equality of the Sexes, and the Condition of Woman*, Boston, MA: I. Knapp, 1838, Letter XI 'Dress of Women', p. 66.
79 C. Mattingly, *Appropriate[ing] Dress: Women's Rhetorical Style in Nineteenth-Century America*, Carbondale, IL: Southern Illinois University Press, 2002. On the connection between the water cure movement and dress reform, see: S. Cayleff, *Wash and Be Healed: The Water-Cure Movement and Women's Health*, Philadelphia, PA: Temple University Press, 2010.
80 Haulman, *Politics of Fashion*, p. 198.

81 V. Reynolds, 'Slaves to Fashion, Not Society: Elizabeth Keckly and Washington, D.C.'s African American Dressmakers, 1860–1870,' *Washington History*, 26.2, 2014, 4–17.
82 See: C. Wright, *The Working Girls of Boston*, 1889, reprint New York: Arno Press, 1969; L. Marion Bosworth, *The Living Wage of Women Workers: A Study of Incomes and Expenditures of 450 Women in the City of Boston*, New York: Longmans, Green and Co., 1911; M. Brew, 'American Clothing Consumption, 1879–1909', Unpublished PhD dissertation, Home Economics, University of Chicago, 1945.
83 R. Earle, 'Clothing and Ethnicity in Colonial Spanish America', in Riello and McNeil, *Fashion History Reader*, p. 383.
84 A. Hunt, 'A Short History of Sumptuary Laws', in Riello and McNeil, *Fashion History Reader*, pp. 54–5.
85 L. M. Scott, *Fresh Lipstick: Redressing Fashion and Feminism*, Basingstoke: Palgrave Macmillan, 2005, pp. 23–4.
86 'Affairs in and about the City: Arrest of Females in Male Attire', *The Boston Daily Atlas*, Boston, MA, 1 January 1853. See: Clare Sears, *Arresting Dress: Cross-Dressing, Law, and Fascination in Nineteenth-Century San Francisco*, Durham, NC: Duke University Press, 2014.
87 See: E. L. Cline, *Over-Dressed: The Shockingly High Cost of Cheap Fashion*, New York: Penguin/Portfolio, 2012.
88 'Blending sources may minimize their inherent problems, and can help highlight interpenetration, similarities, and interplay between and amongst authors and works of art': K. Olson, *Dress and the Roman Woman: Self-Presentation and Society*, London and New York: Routledge, 2008, p. 4.

Further reading

Allman, Jean (ed.), *Fashioning Africa: Power and the Politics of Dress*, Bloomington, IN: Indiana University Press, 2004.
Boag, Peter, *Re-Dressing America's Frontier Past*, Oakland, CA: University of California Press, 2011.
Burman, Barbara and Carole Turbin (eds), *Material Strategies: Dress and Gender in Historical Perspective*, Oxford: Blackwell Publishing, 2003.
Dwyer-McNulty, Sally, *Common Threads: A Cultural History of Clothing in American Catholicism*, Chapel Hill, NC: University of North Carolina Press, 2014.
Ford, Tanisha, *Liberated Threads: Black Women, Style, and the Global Politics of Soul*, Chapel Hill, NC: University of North Carolina Press, 2015.
Gamber, Wendy, *The Female Economy: The Millinery and Dressmaking Trades, 1860–1930*, Urbana, IL: University of Illinois Press, 1990.
McMurry, Elsie Frost, *American Dresses, 1780–1900: Identification and Significance of 148 Extant Dresses*, Ithaca, NY: Cornell University, Digital Resource, 2001.
Schorman, Rob, *Selling Style: Clothing and Social Change at the Turn of the Century*, Philadelphia, PA: University of Pennsylvania, 2003.

11 Photo albums

Autobiographical narrations

Cord Pagenstecher

'Laugh at everything and forget it'. The former Dutch forced laborer Aart M. put this motto at the beginning of a photo album with pictorial memories of his years in a labor camp in Berlin during the Second World War. This motto highlights some contradictions inherent to private photo albums: Does such a seemingly 'cheerful' album help the owner to laugh about his experiences of forced labor? Are the pictures kept to remember or to forget? Who is addressed by this motto and by Aart's whole photographic narration? As sources for historical, anthropological or sociological research, private photo albums pose a theoretical and methodological challenge, constituting an 'interpretive problem'.[1]

Private photography is probably the most widespread source of the visual history of the nineteenth and twentieth centuries: In the year 1970 alone, around 15 billion private photos were taken worldwide.[2] For decades, many of these private snapshots were glued into albums, which their owners kept their whole life, until someday the albums ended up either at flea markets (many), were preserved by the owners' children (some) or given to archives and museums (few). To their creators, however, photo albums are very important; as irreplaceable souvenirs, prior to digital albums and cloud storage, they featured high on every list of the top ten things to save if your house was on fire. Albums are not only a widespread but also a meaningful source.

For many researchers, however, they are just 'boring pictures, predictable, conservative, and repetitive in both form and content'. In their aesthetic and fine-artistic approach, most histories of photography do 'not find family albums interesting enough to deal with extensively'.[3] So far, private photo albums have received little scholarly attention, especially not in German historiography, where my research is focused. Pioneering studies in France and the US have hardly been taken up.[4] In fact, the so-called iconic turn since the 1980s has inspired an increased interest in images and the gradual establishment of a 'visual history' as a research field. Timm Starl and other authors of the *Fotogeschichte* journal have presented inspiring interpretations. Gerhard Paul's work has advanced the analysis of photographs considerably.[5] Nevertheless, historians are still skeptical toward images as sources, especially toward non-professional and unpublished amateur snapshots.

They cared even less about the specific 'genre' of the photo album, which has hardly been studied even by photo historians – with the exception of literary and artistic productions.[6] In public archives, most albums remain in a non-inventoried shadow existence.[7] For their analysis, anthropological research and thematic exhibition catalogues have made important contributions to specific topics like company albums,[8] soldiers' albums,[9] holiday albums[10] or other topics.[11] These studies often are limited to individual albums or small collections and need a much wider and comparative follow-up.[12] With a more systematic research being absent, this paper can only give some initial suggestions for analysis and interpretation. After some theoretical and methodological considerations and a historical overview, I will present two case studies on albums from the National Socialist camps and from postwar German tourism.

Interpretative approaches and methods

Theoretical and methodological reflections about private photo albums should start with the specific quality of private photography – an inspiring but difficult historical source in many respects. Compared with professional pictures, their private contexts and goals render their scholarly interpretation more difficult. Professional photographs created and used in medical institutions, by the police or by architects have well-defined goals of identification, control, diagnostics or documentation. Images used in political propaganda or consumer advertising address their target groups with clearly defined objectives, which can be analyzed accordingly. With private snapshots, however, the creators' aims and ideas are less clear. We must consider their production as well as their storage context and ask about their specific functions in the private realm.[13]

What are the goals and functions of private photography? Private snapshots are taken to serve individual memory, biographical self-assurance and self-portrayal. They help to remember positive experiences like family celebrations and happy moments with friends. A large proportion of private photography is dedicated to holidays and travelling whereas work and daily life are often missing. When travelling, taking pictures structures the wide array of new impressions and enables a self-determined appropriation and processing of these impressions from the unknown world. Back home, the tourists' experiences can be communicated through the album presentation, acquiring prestige in relevant peer groups. Watching pictures together with the family also renews and strengthens family cohesion.[14] Over all, albums contain visual material of an extraordinary personal importance but also constitute a number of cultural practices with additional meanings: they are 'about social and emotional communication, they can be interpreted as ways of understanding and coming to terms with life'.[15]

To emphasize the private functions of these photo albums, however, does not mean ignoring their linkage to public imagery which always had a strong influence on private snapshots, as can be seen with tourist advertising,[16] racial stereotypes[17] or Nazi propaganda.[18] Most albums reflect common stereotypes and represent 'a reaffirmation of culturally structured values'.[19]

What is shown on the pictures? Compared with unsorted photo collections, albums usually have captions which can be helpful for the researcher. Yet a private photo album is an open narrative form meant to be complemented by verbal explanations.[20] Analyzing private photos with anonymous albums found in archives is therefore difficult. It can be a laborious detective's work to identify the portrayed persons and their relationships as well as the times and places of the pictures. Without the personal narration, sometimes it remains unclear why the owner stuck even blurred pictures with hardly recognizable motifs in their album.

When was the album created? The analysis of a photo album must take into account the photographs' and the album's twofold originating context; the creation of photos and albums must be dated separately. Has the album been successively filled with new photos, for example after each holiday? Or have existing pictures been compiled for a special occasion like marriage or retirement, maybe decades after the creation of the pictures?

Who was the author? The photographer does not have to be the same person as the one who selects, glues and labels the pictures into the album. In many families, a gender-specific division of labor exists: men shoot the pictures, women design the albums. This might correspond to the conventional gendering of technical activities as male and creative activities as female. Organizing the common visual narrative of the family by creating a photo album is part of the integrative emotional work, a traditionally female domain: 'Women guard the fireplace and the photo album'.[21]

The layers of creation become more manifold once commercial picture postcards, leaflets, etc., are stuck in – a common practice in the 1950s and 1960s. In these cases, there are four creative steps to be distinguished: (1) the taking of the picture by the professional photographer, (2) its print and publication by the publisher, (3) its purchase by the tourist and (4) its inclusion in the album after the journey. The collage of private and professional pictures, printed products and handwritten commentaries, country and admission tickets, which is particularly typical of postwar photo albums, constitutes an extremely heterogeneous historical source.

How can the albums and their images be analyzed? Sometimes, methods from art history can be used in the analysis. Based on Erwin Panofsky's ideas, a three-step process of (1) exact iconographic description, (2) iconological classification and (3) semiotic and/or historical interpretation is useful.[22] The focus, however, is not on the individual photo as a piece of art but on a whole album page. While single pictures are often bought or shot in a hurry and are lacking the creative imagination of a piece of art, the album design often follows a dedicated creative idea and expresses a specific meaning. Furthermore, an album page often corresponds to a coherent topic or event like a celebration or a vacation.

Another helpful approach can be a quantitative content analysis.[23] In such a quantifying approach, the categories of themes and motifs used for encoding the pictures are necessarily formal. This works quite well for newspapers, leaflets or advertising.[24] With private photos, however, these abstract categories often cannot capture the private meaning of individual images. Nonetheless, a quantitative content analysis is helpful for determining the main themes and motifs in a given sample and for selecting individual images and album pages for more detailed qualitative analyses and interpretations.

The interpretation must understand the private photo album as an autobiographical source, compiled as a meaningful narration.[25] This meaning is a private one, of course, because the albums largely address a private audience from family and friends. As autobiographic sources, photo albums stand between diaries, memoirs and narrative interviews. They are less intimate and self-centered than diaries but have creative and biographical ambitions too. Taking pictures and fixing them into albums helps in the interpretation of one's own personal development and in finding autobiographic orientation through the album narration.[26] Compared with written memoirs, albums restrict themselves largely to the subjects of holidays and leisure. They are not to be published but do address a small public of relatives and friends, which – for the owner – is a highly important authority of recognition and appraisal.

Few photo albums cover the entire life span. More often, individual albums are only chapters of a multivolume visual autobiography. Usually, they are created a few weeks or months after the events being shown; thus the time interval between the experiences and their representation lies between the contemporary diary and the memoirs or interviews created decades later. Compared with biographical interviews, albums are non-reactive evidence, in which the researcher does not intervene as the interviewer necessarily does.

Analyzing the narrative structure of the album can give hints to the biographically relevant system of meaning. For this endeavor, we can adapt methods from the narrative interview analysis in oral history and qualitative social research: While a narrative interview consists of different text forms like the chronological telling of events, the static description of situations and the legitimizing argumentation,[27] in many photo albums we can find different picture categories like canonized patterns, unexpected events, daily routines or symbolic summaries. As in oral history, diary and memoir research, the main interest in the analysis of photo albums is in patterns of perception and interpretation, that is, the form of pictorial telling rather than the facts being told.

The history of the photo album

Becoming popular in the nineteenth century, private photo albums reached their creative and numerical climax in the second half of the twentieth century, before they almost vanished in the period of digitalization. Photo albums began to spread in the nineteenth century, especially in the private world of the emerging bourgeoisie. They obviously corresponded to the new middle-class wish to accumulate not only economic capital but also specialized scientific knowledge, cultural reputation – and family albums. Apart from private albums, there were also official company and product albums for representative reasons. The elaborate and preciously designed photo albums of the Krupp industrialist family, for example, clearly had mixed public and private functions.[28] Such albums were showpieces ready for presentation to visitors on the table of the salon.

In the twentieth century, the photo album saw a functional change. A medium once used for family or corporative representation became a tool for individual and autobiographical self-representation. Increasingly, it contained private snapshots and was therefore kept in drawers rather than on the table of the living room. Between the pages, interleaves with embossed patterns protected the images from dust but symbolically also functioned as an additional veil for the private life made partly visible in the albums.

In the interwar period, the rather strict arrangement of the pictures still followed the traditional patterns; photography was still expensive and constituted an important act for which everyone posed accordingly. More and more companies and public institutions now created photo albums to document their products and social or organizational achievements – partly for their own superiors, partly also to strengthen their employees' identification with the company. The tobacco company Reemtsma, for example, produced a company album in 1938 entitled 'Pictures from our Social Work'.[29]

The – mostly involuntary – journeys of the Second World War prompted many people in Europe to take photographs; German soldiers and company representatives produced albums, as did commanders of concentration camps but also Dutch or Czech forced laborers. The Starl Collection in the Munich Photo Museum contains countless photo albums of German soldiers.[30] Various exhibitions and studies have analyzed such private pictorial accounts of ordinary perpetrators in the Nazi army.[31] Executive staff of the Reemtsma tobacco company documented their business trips to new production sites in the occupied Soviet Union in a 'Crimean album'.[32]

The SS administrations in concentration camps such as Auschwitz, Ravensbrück or Sachsenhausen created photo albums.[33] These staged images of cleanliness and discipline in the camps served as a record of performance and efficiency for the commanders' superiors within the SS. Used repeatedly in exhibitions, publications and media, photos from these albums continue to shape our image of the Nazi camps to this day. Apart from this, some private photo albums of camp staff were discovered and analyzed in recent years: The Höcker album, for example, created by the last Auschwitz commander's adjutant, shows the banality of Sunday excursions and SS parties and gives a disturbing view on the mundane lives of ordinary men and mass murderers.[34]

After the Second World War, the photo albums became even more popular; as a result of the travel boom of the 'economic miracle', many families produced several new albums each year, which became increasingly imaginative and creative. Collages, drawings and witty comments complemented the increasing number of – now cheap – color photographs. The number, scope, variety and creativity of private photo albums flourished in the 1950s and 1960s. More than three-quarters of all pictures showed leisure time and holidays; the family albums became more and more travel albums. More and more families from the working class began

212 *Cord Pagenstecher*

to take pictures and create albums, too. The family photo album became a 'globally circulating form', being created and preserved in many countries around the world [Figure 11.1].[35]

Since the 1970s and 1980s, the photo album has gone into a decline: increasingly, private photos were stored in disorder in shoe boxes, cigar boxes or the paper envelopes of photo shops. The more photos were taken, the less time was taken for sorting, gluing and labelling. From the 1960s, slides became an inexpensive alternative, which corresponded to the viewing habits influenced by the new mass medium of television. The dramaturgy of a slide show on an evening with friends, of course, followed different patterns from designing and showing an album.[36]

Over the last decades, following the next technological development, after the only temporarily modern holiday videos, photography has now been completely digitized. The ubiquitous smartphone has indeed democratized photography on a world-wide level. Every day, more than one billion snapshots are being taken, many of them uploaded to internet platforms: in 2015, every day, 70 million photographs were posted on Instagram, 300 million on Facebook and possibly up to 700 million on Snapchat.[37]

Figure 11.1 Album page of a Berlin couple with photographs of the Großglockner-Hochalpenstraße, 1967

Source: Historical Archive on Tourism [HAT], Album Sal. 12/1967.

Transferring established cultural practices into new technologies, digital devices and platforms offer 'albums' or 'galleries' to organize and communicate their pictures and posts. How these 'albums' are really being used and what that can tell researchers, needs further analysis and is beyond the scope of this chapter. Researchers have studied the technological move from analogue to digital photography and the cultural move to social-media photography, revealing elements of change as well as continuity in the use and meaning of photographs and their 'albums'.[38] Obviously, the boundaries between the private and the public sphere get increasingly blurred. Furthermore, sharing has become more important than preservation, private photography is increasingly being used for instantaneous communication and much less for a long-term personal or family retrospective. Photo experts, as well as lifestyle journalists, started worrying: 'Are we breeding a 'lost generation' who won't have photo albums to capture their lives?'[39]

It is high time, then, to preserve private photo albums as a vanishing medium and to study them more thoroughly. The first of the following short case studies focuses on the private functions of the images, the second on the narrative structures of the albums.

Snapshots from the camp – a forced laborer's photo album

When researching the history of forced labor in Nazi Berlin, the existence of private photographs shot and preserved by the foreign workers in the German war industry was an unexpected discovery. But the collection of the Berlin History Workshop, built up in the late 1990s from survivors' letters and encounters, contains hundreds of private photos taken by forced laborers in wartime Berlin.[40] The civilian forced laborers could legally buy and develop films in German shops. Some of them had artistic ambitions: The Czech professional photographer Zdeněk Tmej who was conscripted to work for Breslau post office, created high-quality documentary photographs.[41] Most forced laborers, however, just took private snapshots of themselves, their comrades and their surroundings, many of them subsequently stored and preserved in photo albums. French, Dutch and Czech men from the urban middle classes took photos inside or outside of the barracks camps in their limited free time. Polish and Soviet forced laborers were not allowed to have a camera but also found opportunities to have themselves photographed in a photo studio or by fellow workers. Even prisoners of war, ghetto inmates and concentration camp prisoners illegally took secret photos, often in an attempt to document incredible atrocities.[42]

This case study draws on an album of a civilian Dutch forced laborer as an example of the genre.[43] Aart M. had to work in the spare parts warehouse of the Auto-Union plant in Berlin-Spandau from 1942 to 1945. As a Western European, the 22-year-old could leave the camp barracks after work and move around freely through the city, visit his brother-in-law in another workplace and make friends with female Ukrainian forced laborers. Commemorating the 50th anniversary of liberation, he returned to Berlin in 1995 and allowed the partial reproduction of his photo album.

There are over 100 pictures in the album, which cover the period from 1920 to 1960 in no chronological order, 50 of them regarding his stay in Berlin during the Second World War. The date of the album creation is unclear; Aart M. said, he had just found the pictures and glued them in before they were gone. In this compilation, his time as forced laborer is not isolated but integrated into his pictorial life-story.

Who took these pictures? As with many private pictures, the photographer of individual pictures is often unknown. In 19 of the 50 pictures examined here, Aart M. had himself photographed by comrades. On the other hand, he also took and gave pictures to other camp inmates in exchange for food or cigarettes.

What can be seen in the images? Of the 50 pictures, 35 show friends and acquaintances. Four pictures show leisure activities, five excursions, four the camp barracks and two are of other subjects. Except for a mesh wire fence, there is no sign of the camp being guarded. All pictures were taken during leisure time; not a single one shows a work situation. Essential spheres of the daily life of forced laborers, such as work, violence or resistance, are invisible. If it was already impossible or at least dangerous to take pictures during work, this was all the more true when 'organizing' food or witnessing punishments. Aart M. himself therefore doubted the value of his photographs for historical research: 'These are pictures of memories for me, this is nothing for you. The pictures would be good for the Nazi propaganda, what a good life the foreigners have'.

Forced laborers could hardly think of aesthetic, documentary or oppositional photography. As their privacy was permanently restricted or violated, pictures of 'beautiful' moments – a peaceful Sunday outing or a Christmas evening in the barrack – conveyed a special meaning. In blanking out the working sphere, forced laborers' photo albums are similar to any private photography in the world.

Yet, this private character and destination of the images was even more important to forced laborers. Often, they sent their photos home in letters to their family. Therefore, these pictures served as a sign of life for the parents or beloved ones who stayed at home. In order not to cause them any concern, the forced laborers presented themselves as well dressed and beautiful. This kind of embellished self-portrayal also served the purpose of psychological self-assertion. Anyone who was constantly treated as an inferior or even subhuman foreigner could counter this humiliation with an image as a sporty and smart man or an attractive, well-dressed woman. The Czechs proudly wore the Bohemian lion as their self-chosen identification symbol, while the Ukrainians often removed the obligatory, discriminating 'OST' badge for these photos. Conspicuously, the barrack inmates showed their food to the camera – perhaps a sign of joy at the special moment of a sufficient meal, perhaps an attempt to fake a sufficient diet to calm down the loved ones at home. Czechs and Dutchmen in particular often ironically staged tin bowls and other insignia of everyday camp life, probably also demonstrating their will to survive [Figure 11.2].

Most of the pictures were taken in the camp, in the barracks or in front of the barracks, but there are also tourist-like poses in front of Berlin sights. Apart from

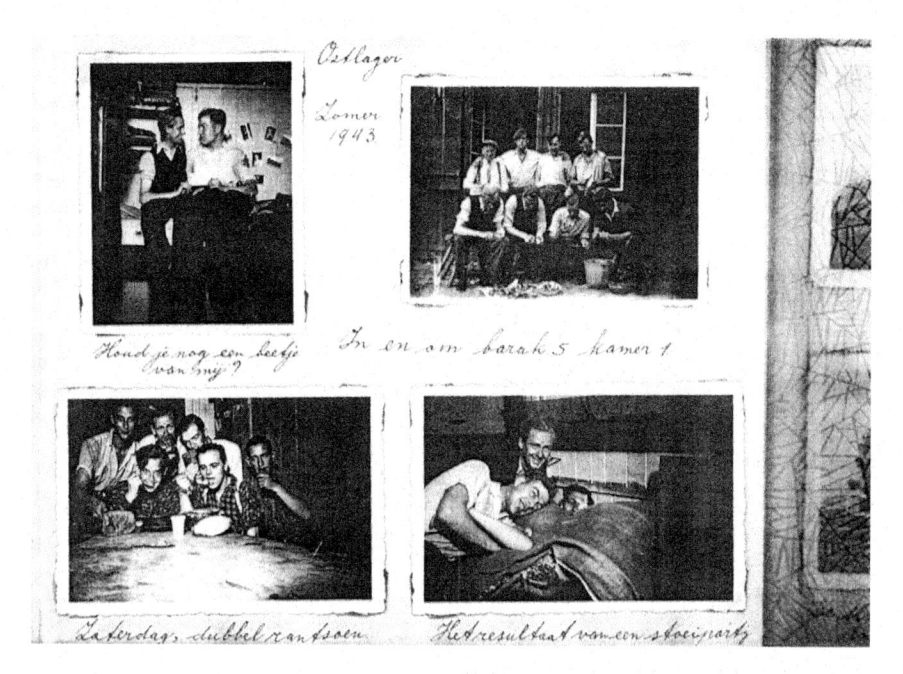

Figure 11.2 'Ostlager, Zomer 1943'. Page from Dutch forced laborer Aart M.'s album
Source: Archive Berlin History Workshop.

one snapshot of the family where Aart M.'s brother-in-law was accommodated, Germans are not visible anywhere. Many pictures show the Dutchman's mates from the same barrack. Sometimes, a hand-painted sign with place, room number and date retains the facts for memory. Often Ukrainian forced laborers from the same camp are also pictured, often with some Dutch men in the middle. In all group pictures – of men and women – there is intense physical contact through hugging or holding hands. A picture shows a Dutch-Ukrainian romantic couple; a childbirth in the Ukrainians' barracks was also an image captured by Aart M. in his album.

Some quieter pictures show Aart M. and his brother-in-law cooking or on excursions. Such a juxtaposition of domestic group pictures and individual activities can also be found in the pictures of soldiers' albums.

Sometimes, Aart M. captured the consequences of Allied air raids on German cities, although this was forbidden or at least sensitive even for Germans. A bombing raid in November 1943 left only the chimneys of his barrack; several photos of the ruin served as symbolic self-assurance that he had survived. Some other groups of forced laborers created albums after the war to commemorate their comrades killed in air raids on Berlin. Forced laborers had very mixed feelings about the daily bombings of Germany by American and British air forces. They

Figure 11.3 'Een gezellig zitje'. Dutch forced laborers, including Aart M. (2nd from left), on a Sunday in the barrack camp, summer 1944

Source: Archive Berlin History Workshop.

brought death and horror to Germans and foreigners alike, but they also marked the oncoming defeat of their German slaveholders. 'They were our liberators, but they killed us', Aart M. later described his conflicting feelings about the Allied bombers. Taking these pictures helped to overcome this dilemma.

Later, they also showed a kind of symbolic triumph about the destruction of German war industry: On his return journey on a US controlled train in spring 1945, Aart M. captured the 'totally destroyed Deutsche Volkswagen Werke in Fallersleben', as the album's caption says. When creating the album later, on a specific page he contrasted destroyed Hanover with his hometown Rotterdam, destroyed by the Germans in 1940.

At the end of his album, Aart M. stuck in a rather cozy photo from the Spandau camp with the signature 'Een gezellig zitje' (A social gathering). With this symbolic résumé, the album tries to give a positive conclusion to this review of years of a lost youth in wartime Germany [Figure 11.3].

Holiday albums – the postwar West German tourist gaze

The second case study is based on a series of private photo albums about postwar West German tourism. Of course, living conditions and pictorial motifs of German postwar tourists are extremely different from those of forced laborers under National Socialism. But certain pictorial patterns with various autobiographical or family related functions can be observed here too. In this case study, my focus will be on the narrative structure of the album. Building on methods from the narrative interview analysis I studied different picture categories in this album series, focusing on, (1) canonized patterns, (2) unexpected events, (3) daily routines and (4) symbolic summaries. Before discussing some examples of these categories, I will present my evidence and its biographical framework.

A Berlin-based baker and his wife – I will give them the pseudonyms Heinz and Elfriede Schmidt – had documented and described all their holiday journeys between 1942 and 1982 in 45 photo albums. The album series is available in the Historical Archive on Tourism at the Technical Universität Berlin.[44] Before their death, the childless couple donated their albums to the archive, which specializes in travel guides, tourist brochures and holiday photos.

The size of this series is big, but not exceptional: The big album collection at the Münchner Stadtmuseum includes several similar series.[45] During the travel boom in the postwar 'economic miracle', many German families created an album for every holiday. More than 80 percent of the pictures of the Berlin couple show – as with most photo albums – vacations and weekend trips; the workplace and the daily life at home are largely absent.

The albums were created shortly after each holiday, thus being a contemporary source that reflects their owners' selection, order and interpretation at the time. Furthermore, they are an anonymous source; because both spouses had died in the interim, I could not interview them and had to gather all information from the albums – which proved to be a methodologically challenging and time-consuming endeavor.

The pictures show an elderly couple without children from the urban lower-middle class. The Schmidts' travel biography started in the Nazi era with first hiking holidays in the Alps at the age of 30. Then there is a break – not during, but after the Second World War. Toward the end of the 1950s, their second era of travel started with weekend excursions at the age of 50, followed by long automobile journeys through the Alps and the whole of Central and Southern Europe. This biography reflects the general take-off of German mass tourism around 1960, marked by automobilization and travel abroad. After their retirement in the 1970s, the Schmidts adopted a stable rhythm with beach vacations in summer and a mountain holiday in autumn. Instead of travelling around, they now enjoyed relaxing vacations in one place, reflecting the general growing trend of beach tourism. Overall, their travel career was quite typical for the first generation of postwar tourists in West Germany.

Both spouses were using the camera (see Figure 11.1, middle: 'Who is snapping whom?'), thus the authorship of individual pictures is not always clear. Exceptionally, the traditional gender roles were not valid here. The Schmidts did not have great photographic ambitions; there are no lists about the exposure time or other technical details, which we find in other photo series. The albums, however, are designed lovingly: Pictures and other media are arranged in sequences or contrasting comparisons creating visual tension or telling small stories. The snapshots are surrounded by postcards, dried flowers, leaflets, maps, boat tickets or restaurant receipts. Like other postwar albums, this is a multimedial, heterogeneous source – beautiful, but difficult to analyze.

In addition to the captions, there are holiday chronicles typed on separate sheets of paper with a detailed documentation of travel routes, events, daily kilometer tallies, departure and arrival times, usage of gasoline and accommodation prices. These pedantic protocols provide much background information for image analysis but raise the question why this couple kept such an accurate record of their free time. A similar obsession with detailed travel documentation can be found in other albums or diaries, too, proudly proving how all organizational problems of traveling were mastered but also reflecting an internalized work ethic persisting even in holidays. Interpreted as a form of pictorial autobiographical narration, this album series includes the following types of images: canonized patterns, unexpected events, daily routines and symbolic summaries.

Picture type one: canonized patterns

As in many holiday albums, pictures of well-known tourist sights dominate. By sticking professional postcards in their private albums and by copying postcard and brochure images with their own snapshots, the Schmidts incorporated standardized perception patterns in their album's narration. In 1967, for example, a series of professional pictures integrated into the album showed the crossing of the Großglockner pass in the Austrian Alps, an episode that lasted only three hours but was definitely a climax in the story of their three-week holidays. A central picture that can be found in many leaflets and guidebooks showed the mountain peak together with the car-park above the glacier (see Figure 11.1, upper right). Next to this, the Schmidts put a very similar picture of their own, labelled 'This is how we saw it' (see Figure 11.1, upper left).

This re-photographing of pictures already known before the journey can be interpreted as an expression of canonized patterns of perception. With these photographic repetitions, tourists follow collective ideas, argue that they have seen everything 'worth seeing' and thus legitimize their travel style. These images reflect the prevailing models of the tourist gaze ('one must have seen this') and help in reproducing this standardized gaze themselves.[46]

Apart from tourist advertising, other elements of classic culture or popular advertising were being quoted too. With these quotations, the authors – just like the authors of written autobiographies – integrated their individual experiences into a widely shared body of knowledge. But, with snapshot albums being rather humorous or frivolous, these quotations tend to be somewhat ironic. The Schmidts captioned a picture of an elderly lady friend of theirs sitting on a small rock in a mountain creek as 'Lorelei', evoking parallels to Heinrich Heine's poem about a beautiful blonde sitting on Lorelei rock above the Rhine valley. In 1974, the Schmidts juxtaposed a professional, colorful and rather kitschy postcard of the Bavarian city Wasserburg with their own, less spectacular snapshot. The commentary read 'Poetry and Prose'. Our couple was well aware of and commented ironically on their tourist gaze being manipulated by the tourist industry and its embellished imagery. In their creative album design, the tourists playfully dealt with their role as individual travelers in the context of an industrially marketed mass tourism.

Picture type two: unexpected events

On the other hand, these albums tell us about moments when the tourists willingly or unwillingly left behind the tourist role and experienced something unexpected. These events might be small and funny: once, the Schmidts snapped a car-park guide moving around between the cars with a little scooter – just a little side-observation during a break on the road. The unexpected events might also suggest more exotic adventures: knowing it was not allowed, the Schmidts took pictures of veiled Muslim women in Montenegro. With some triumph about their – indeed rather invasive – behavior, they wrote 'Trouble ahead!' under the picture in the album. The events might also be weather catastrophes like storms or floodings. Increasingly, the Schmidts shot pictures of traffic accidents. Photos of other cars lying smashed at the side of the road became more and more frequent as the two travelers got older. These pictures seem to reflect their relief at having been spared from accidents themselves. Like a talisman, they warded off the motorists' daily danger by capturing it on celluloid. Overall, these stories of unexpected events often show amazement or even marvel at the unknown, unstaged world outside. In the albums, they are the pictures that differ the most from the standardized tourist gaze.

Picture type three: daily routines

A large part of the albums contains pictures with recurring everyday situations, giving even the holidays, defined as a different world, a kind of daily routine. With the caption 'Morning washing on the river Weser', a picture shows Ms. Schmidt in a negligee in the door of the bakery van that was being used as holiday camper in the 1950s. It was one of the first self-made photos in the whole series that was devoted to this rather unspectacular moment. Photos of a picnic site along the road, of the hotel or the restaurant abound in the album series. In 1975, the couple had themselves portrayed on the Italian Adriatic, enjoying an informal and relaxed beach life. The caption 'Siesta' was intended to show the tourists' rapid adaptation to the local way-of-life.

The frequency of such everyday images shows how important it is to document one's own travel experiences – independent of given tourist sights. Holidays not only involve visiting foreign places but also a daily practice shared as a couple or family. Its capturing, and re-visiting through viewing the albums together later on, strengthens family cohesion, which can easily get lost during everyday work periods. At the same time, the authors of the albums demonstrate a certain habitus: an improvised morning toilet proves independence from organized luxury and the tourist industry. Pictures of the cleaned car or the television back home demonstrate respectability and well-being. Pictures of the daily routine at home, however, are completely missing in this series.

Picture type four: symbolic summaries

Every album contains symbolic summaries, usually put at the start and the end of a holiday narration. Each vacation is introduced with a specifically designed title page framing this chapter of the narration with a certain atmosphere. The earlier tours around several countries were introduced by a road map with a marked route, often supplemented by the national flags of the countries crossed. In later years, contemplative nature photos and hand-drawn flowers gave the rather static Tyrol holidays a harmonic and peaceful setting.

Furthermore, most albums contain pictures of the moments of departure and return. In 1965 for example, the spouses snapped each other while cleaning the car before leaving home [Figure 11.4]. These pictures show typical '*rites de passage*' marking the entry into the world of vacation. The last stop of the journey, too, is always worth a photo, usually also featuring the car. Finally, the exact return time and sometimes the number of kilometres travelled is noted at the then end of the album. For the Berlin couple, the family car almost became a ritual object. The symbolically important acts of departure and return, like all passage rituals, included purifying ceremonies with this ritual object.

Figure 11.4 'Ready to go!!! Everything polished once more'. Album page about the start of holiday travel 1965

Source: Historical Archive on Tourism [HAT], Album Sal. 10/1965.

Conclusion

Private photo albums constitute a widespread and valuable historical source for studying different topics of nineteenth- and twentieth-century cultural and social history. While serving to demonstrate social status in the nineteenth century, they became an individual-biographical narration in the twentieth century, containing rather private snapshots not shown to everybody. Since photographs became cheaper, they were used in a playful, irreverent and individual way. Focusing on holidays and celebrations, in most albums the working sphere and everyday life are almost absent.

Private photo albums are an autobiographical source that needs qualitative methods open to individual interpretation. Approaches from different disciplines can be adapted including elements of quantitative content analysis or analyzing the narrative structure of the album design. Overall, we still need to elaborate more refined methods and techniques of visual history using pictorial evidence.

Notes

1 G. Batchen, 'Snapshots. Art history and the ethnographic turn', *Photographies*, 1.2, 2008, 121–42, p. 124.
2 B. Mary, *La Photo sur la Cheminée. Naissance d'un culte moderne*, Paris: Éditions Métailié, 1993.
3 Batchen, 'Snapshots', p. 121; Mette Sandbye, 'Looking at the family photo album: A resumed theoretical discussion of why and how', *Journal of Aesthetics & Culture*, 6.1, 25419, 2014, https://doi.org/10.3402/jac.v6.25419.
4 P. Bourdieu, *Un art moyen*, Paris: Ed. Minuit, 1965 (English: *Photography. A Middle-Brow Art*, Stanford: Stanford University Press 1996); R. Chalfen, *Snapshot: Versions of Life*, Bowling Green, OH: Bowling Green State Popular Press, 1987.
5 G. Jagschitz, 'Visual History', *Das audiovisuelle Archiv*, 29/30, 1991, pp. 23–51; C. Pagenstecher, *Der bundesdeutsche Tourismus. Ansätze zu einer Visual History: Urlaubsprospekte, Reiseführer, Fotoalben, 1950–1990*, Hamburg: Kovacs, 2nd edn. 2012; G. Paul (ed.), *Visual History. Ein Studienbuch*, Göttingen: Vandenhoeck & Ruprecht 2006; G. Paul (ed.), *Das Jahrhundert der Bilder, Vol. 1: 1900–1949, Vol. 2: 1949 bis heute*, Göttingen: Vandenhoeck & Ruprecht 2008/09; T. Starl, 'Die Bildwelt der Knipser. Eine empirische Untersuchung zur privaten Fotografie', *Fotogeschichte* 52, 1994, pp. 59–68; T. Starl, *Knipser. Die Bildgeschichte der privaten Fotografie in Deutschland und Österreich von 1880 bis 1980. Ausstellungskatalog*, München: Koehler und Amelang 1995; T. Starl, 'Zur Inventarisierung von Fotoalben', *Rundbrief Fotografie N.F.* 9, 1996, pp. 29–33; J. Steen, 'Fotoalbum und Lebensgeschichte', *Fotogeschichte* 10, 1983, pp. 55–67.
6 A. Kramer and A. Pelz, 'Einleitung', in: Anke Kramer and Annegret Pelz (eds), *Album. Organisationsform narrativer Kohärenz*, Göttingen: Vandenhoeck & Ruprecht 2013, pp. 7–23.
7 T. Starl, 'Zur Inventarisierung von Fotoalben', *Rundbrief Fotografie N.F.*, 9, 1996, pp. 29–33.
8 R. Herz, 'Gesammelte Fotografien und fotografierte Erinnerungen. Eine Geschichte des Fotoalbums an Beispielen aus dem Krupp-Archiv', in Klaus Tenfelde (ed.), *Bilder von Krupp. Fotografie und Geschichte im Industriezeitalter*, München: Beck 1994, pp. 241–67.
9 P. Jahn and U. Schmiegelt, *Foto-Feldpost. Geknipste Kriegserlebnisse 1939–1945. Ausstellungskatalog des Museums Berlin-Karlshorst*, Berlin: ElefantenPress, 2000;

P. Bopp, 'Images of violence in Wehrmacht Soldiers' private photo albums', in J. Martschukat and S. Niedermeier (eds), *Violence and Visibility in Modern History*, New York: Palgrave Macmillan, 2013, pp. 181–97; M. Umbach, 'Selfhood, place, and ideology in German photo albums, 1933–1945', *Central European History*, Cambridge University Press, 48.3, 2015, pp. 335–65.

10 B. Mandel, *Wunschbilder werden wahr gemacht. Aneignung von Urlaubswelt durch Fotosouvenirs am Beispiel deutscher Italientouristen der 50er und 60er Jahre*, Frankfurt a.M.: Lang 1996, p. 165ff.; Pagenstecher, *Der bundesdeutsche Tourismus*, pp. 268ff.

11 Sandbye, 'Looking at the family photo album', nn. 13 and 14; C. Cuevas-Wolf, 'Making the past present: GDR photo albums and amateur photographs', *Visual Resources*, 30.1, 2014, pp. 33–56; P. Pitt, 'Exploring subject positions and multiple temporalities through an Iranian migrant mother's family photograph albums', *Gender, Place & Culture*, 2014, pp. 1–17; B. Buggenhagen, 'A snapshot of happiness: Photo albums, respectability and economic uncertainty in Dakar', *Africa: The Journal of the International African Institute*, 84.1, 2014, pp. 78–100.

12 Sandbye, 'Looking at the family photo album'.

13 Pagenstecher, *Der bundesdeutsche Tourismus*, 68ff., pp. 264ff.

14 Ibid., pp. 255ff.

15 Sandbye, 'Looking at the family photo album'.

16 Pagenstecher, *Der bundesdeutsche Tourismus*, p. 256, p. 444

17 S. Niedermeier, 'Imperial narratives: Reading US soldiers' photo albums of the Philippine–American War', *Rethinking History*, 18.1, 2014, pp. 28–49.

18 Umbach, 'Selfhood, place, and ideology'.

19 Chalfen, *Snapshot*, p. 98.

20 Kramer and Pelz, 'Einleitung', p. 7.

21 M. Rutschky, 'Schneider. Sieben Seiten Lektüre eines anonymen Fotoalbums', *Fotogeschichte*, 27, 1988, pp. 40–54.

22 Pagenstecher, *Der bundesdeutsche Tourismus*, pp. 76ff., 280ff., 429ff.

23 T. Starl, 'Die Bildwelt der Knipser. Eine empirische Untersuchung zur privaten Fotografie', *Fotogeschichte* 52, 1994, 59–68, C. Pagenstecher, *Der bundesdeutsche Tourismus. Ansätze zu einer Visual History: Urlaubsprospekte, Reiseführer, Fotoalben, 1950–1990*, Hamburg: Kovacs, 2nd edn. 2012, pp. 79ff., 259ff.

24 C. Pagenstecher, *Der bundesdeutsche Tourismus*, pp. 319ff., 395ff., 410ff.

25 Ibid., pp. 268ff.

26 Starl, 'Die Bildwelt der Knipser', p. 59.

27 G. Rosenthal, *Erlebte und erzählte Lebensgeschichte. Gestalt und Struktur biographischer Selbstbeschreibungen*, Frankfurt/New York: Campus Verlag, 1995.

28 Herz, 'Gesammelte Fotografien und fotografierte Erinnerungen'.

29 S. Rahner, 'Soziales, Freizeit, Kultur', *Rauchzeichen. Fotoarchiv Reemtsma*, 2005, www.fotoarchiv-reemtsma.de/Themen/08_Soziales/index.html, last accessed 20.09.2019.

30 Starl, *Knipser. Die Bildgeschichte der privaten Fotografie*.

31 Jahn and Schmiegelt, *Foto-Feldpost*; Bopp, 'Images of violence'; Umbach, 'Selfhood, place, and ideology'.

32 R. Fröbe, A. Ehrlich, 'Reemtsma im Krieg: das Krim-Album', *Rauchzeichen. Fotoarchiv Reemtsma*, 2005, www.fotoarchiv-reemtsma.de/Themen/03_Krimalbum/index.html, last accessed 20.09.2019.

33 For example, I. Gutman and B. Gutterman, *The Auschwitz Album. The Story of a Transport*, edited by Y. Vashem in association with the Auschwitz Museum, 2002; G. Morsch (ed.), *Von der Sachsenburg nach Sachsenhausen. Bilder aus dem Fotoalbum eines KZ-Kommandanten*, Berlin: Metropol, 2007.

34 C. Busch, S. Hördler, R. Jan van Pelt (eds), *Das Höcker-Album. Auschwitz durch die Linse der SS*, Mainz: Philipp von Zabern Verlag, 2016.

35 Sandbye, 'Looking at the family photo album'; Buggenhagen, 'A snapshot of happiness'.

36 E. Fendl and K. Löffler, 'Die Reise im Zeitalter ihrer technischen Reproduzierbarkeit: am Beispiel Diaabend', in C. Cantauw (ed.), *Arbeit, Freizeit, Reisen. Die feinen*

Unterschiede im Alltag, Münster: Waxmann, 1995, pp. 55–68; Mandel, *Wunschbilder*, p. 205.
37 D. Miller, 'Photography in the Age of Snapchat', *Anthropology and Photography*, edited by The Royal Anthropological Institute of Great Britain and Ireland (RAI), 2015, www.therai.org.uk/images/stories/photography/AnthandPhotoVol1B.pdf, last accessed 05.05.18, p. 3.
38 Ibid.
39 T. Clark, 'The Vanishing Art of the Family Photo Album', *Time*, 04 September 2013, http://time.com/3801986/the-vanishing-art-of-the-family-photo-album/, last accessed 20.09.19; J. L. Smith, 'Are we breeding a "lost generation" who won't have photo albums to capture their lives?', *The Telegraph*, 5 November 2017, www.telegraph.co.uk/women/life/breeding-lost-generation-wont-have-photo-albums-capture-lives/, last accessed 20.09.19.
40 C. Pagenstecher, 'Privatfotos ehemaliger Zwangsarbeiterinnen und Zwangsarbeiter – eine Quellensammlung und ihre Forschungsrelevanz', Winifred Meyer and Klaus Neitmann (eds), *Zwangsarbeit während der NS-Zeit in Berlin und Brandenburg. Formen, Funktion und Rezeption*, Potsdam: Verlag für Berlin-Brandenburg, 2001, pp. 223–46.
41 C. Pagenstecher, 'Ein Fotograf der "seelischen Leere". Zdeněk Tmej und die Visual History der Zwangsarbeit', in *Im Totaleinsatz. Zwangsarbeit der tschechischen Hyphenation Be-völkerung für das Dritte Reich. Totálně nasazeni. Nucená práce českého obyvatelstva v období nacistické třetí říše*, Deutsch-Tschechischen Zukunftsfonds und dem Dokumentationszentrum NS-Zwangsarbeit Berlin-Schöneweide der Stiftung Topographie des Terrors, Redaktion: Martin Hořák, Prag/Berlin 2008, pp. 161–91.
42 G. Didi-Huberman, *Bilder trotz allem*, München: Fink, 2007.
43 Pagenstecher, 'Knipsen im Lager?', pp. 51–60.
44 Historisches Archiv zum Tourismus (HAT), http://hist-soz.de/hat/archiv.html, last accessed 20.09.2019.
45 Starl, *Knipser. Die Bildgeschichte der privaten Fotografie*.
46 J. Urry, *The Tourist Gaze. Leisure and Travel in Contemporary Societies*, London: Sage, 1990.

Further reading

Batchen, Geoffrey, 'Snapshots. Art history and the ethnographic turn', *Photographies*, 1.2, 2008, 121–42.
Bourdieu, Pierre, *Photography: A Middle-Brow Art*, Stanford: Stanford University Press, 1996 (orig. 1965).
Chalfen, Richard, *Snapshot: Versions of Life*, Bowling Green, OH: Bowling Green State Popular Press, 1987.
Pagenstecher, Cord, *Der bundesdeutsche Tourismus. Ansätze zu einer Visual History: Urlaubsprospekte, Reiseführer, Fotoalben, 1950–1990*, 2nd edn., Hamburg: Kovacs, 2012.
Paul, Gerhard (ed.), *Visual History: Ein Studienbuch*, Göttingen: Vandenhoeck & Ruprecht 2006.
Sandbye, Mette, 'Looking at the family photo album: A resumed theoretical discussion of why and how', *Journal of Aesthetics & Culture*, 6.1, 2014, doi:10.3402/jac.v6.25419.
Starl, Timm, *Knipser – Die Bildgeschichte der privaten Fotografie in Deutschland und Österreich von 1880 bis 1980. Ausstellungskatalog*, München: Koehler und Amelang, 1995.

12 Scrapbooks

A proliferation of meaning

Eloise Moss

In December 2012, a few months before completing my doctorate, I struck 'archives gold.' Visiting the Bishopsgate Institute Library and Archives near Spitalfields, East London, my main objective was to examine the diaries kept by Detective Frederick Porter Wensley (1865–1949). As the famous former head of the Criminal Investigation Department at Scotland Yard, home of the Metropolitan Police, Wensley had personally overseen the investigations and arrests of many of the criminals featured in my thesis, a history of burglary in London during the late-nineteenth and twentieth centuries.[1] I had already read and incorporated Wensley's autobiography, *Detective Days*: *The Record of Forty-Two Years' Service in the Criminal Investigation Department* (1931) into my research, so I was therefore fairly confident that the diaries themselves (the existence of which I had only recently become aware) would simply confirm points I had already made in the thesis about Wensley's work.[2] This was to be a nice day at the archives gathering a few extra footnotes, rather than a last-minute scramble for new material (or so I thought). However, the archivist, Stef Dickers – who has achieved his own renown among historians for his wonderful assistance and acquisitions of material relating to marginalised groups – recommended I also look at two volumes of bound scrapbooks kept by Wensley recording his career in the Force. These were a revelation. Presented with the two fat, dusty scrapbooks, stuffed full of newspaper clippings, photographs, and marginalia, and detailing a rich history of police work, criminality, and nuggets of Wensley's personal family life, I was confronted with a set of sources unlike anything I had ever encountered previously. An agglomeration of material collected over a lifetime, these books were neither wholly newspaper, nor photo album, nor diary. Furthermore, given their uniqueness, I had very little sense of how to go about analysing them – something I hope this chapter will rectify for future scholars.

By exploring the processes through which one can understand Wensley's scrapbooks, and by drawing on the expert guidance offered by other historians who have laid out a 'road map' to using these sources, this chapter is intended to offer a set of *starting-points* for analysing these unusual artefacts. I emphasise the term 'starting-point' because, as I have mentioned, every scrapbook is unique. Each manifests the interests and experiences of individuals, communities, and institutions via a set of 'scraps' – meaning ephemera that they alone had access to or sought out. 'Ephemera' is the most useful way to describe their contents, which might be textual (writings, both unpublished and published), visual (photographs, drawings/paintings, collage), or material (encompassing fabric and keepsakes of many kinds, including dried flowers and other items). The subjective interests of scrapbooks' author(s) informed the decision to draw the scraps into 'conversation' through juxtaposition on the page, a set of 'editorial' choices that could stem as much from personal preference as the expected needs of an audience, should a wider readership be desired (of which there was no guarantee, as I shall presently explain). As such, scrapbooks defy categorisation by genre, having no set of shared rules dictating their composition and style, nor necessarily following a pattern set earlier by other scrapbookers (or a 'pattern' at all). Even if individual scraps might be still be understood within the conventions of their origins (that is, treated in isolation; one can still analyse a newspaper cutting in relation to the content of the newspaper from whence it was taken), the context of the materials it is juxtaposed against in the scrapbook may well change its meaning in the eyes of the viewer. So how do we go about 'reading' them?

This chapter deploys an analysis of the Wensley scrapbooks as a connecting thread running through the essay. Alongside insights into other scrapbooks and scholars' readings of them, the analysis will show the many possible ways one could explore the significance of Wensley's scrapbooks, all equally having merit. As such, I do not intend to spend time here 'defending' my earlier analysis of the Wensley scrapbooks in my article 'Scrapbooking the Detective' published in the journal *Social History* in 2015, though I will revisit its arguments at key points.[3] Instead, as with every historical analysis, this chapter exposes how one can suggest alternative readings of the scrapbooks depending on the information one wishes to elicit, which indeed is what keeps our discipline interesting. I strongly suggest, though, that anyone wishing to analyse scrapbooks, whether student, professional academic, archivist, or family historian (or some combination of these, as is often the case) should also read Ellen Gruber Garvey's *Writing with Scissors: American Scrapbooks from the Civil War to the Harlem Renaissance* (2013).[4] Gruber Garvey's book represents a magnum opus on the ways in which historians can make full analytical use of scrapbooks, as well as the politics and fragility of their existence as sources, and I will return to her ideas several times throughout this chapter. For the title of this piece I have preferred, however, to deploy a phrase coined by historian Judith Walkowitz to describe the editorial selection of items on the Victorian newspaper page, the juxtaposition of which, she argues, served to create 'a proliferation of meaning' for readers.[5] This phrase seems best designed to describe the way that scrapbooks, on close and repeated scrutiny of their contents, also slowly unfurl a set of resonances between scraps powerfully to suggest a logic, argument, or set of concerns by their author(s). With training and a willingness to embrace inference, therefore, I propose they can become as legible as reading a newspaper page.

Pages: individually and collectively

Returning to my first encounter with the Wensley scrapbooks proves the unwritten rule for those embarking on archival research: always have a chat with the archivist, whose extraordinary knowledge of the collections in their charge often leads to invaluable suggestions of materials to consult that may not appear in the catalogue. Archivists' production of archives that may have some resonance, however tangential, with the topic proposed to them in initial enquiries can radically alter the direction of research, which has certainly happened to me more than once. So it was in the case of Wensley. Leafing through the scrapbook pages, I initially zeroed in on press cuttings and images that were relevant to the subject of my thesis [Figure 12.1].

The scrapbook page in Figure 12.1 features a cutting relating to Wensley's capture in 1908 of a burglar known as 'The Spider,' retold in one of a series of sensational newspaper articles Wensley wrote in 1933, riding the crest of a wave of publicity following the publication of his autobiography two years earlier. It confirmed the 'celebrity status' accorded certain burglars and the commercial nature of retelling stories about them, even decades after the crimes were committed, witnessed by their circulation in both national and local newspapers (such as the *Bristol Evening World*). At a basic level, this confirmed one of my key arguments relating to the existence of a 'pleasure culture of crime' surrounding burglary in this era, and the complicity of state, media, and market in cultivating representations of criminal 'masterminds' – anointing the Spider as 'the cleverest burglar in England,' for instance.[6] Yet a seeming-oddity of this scrapbook page was that

Figure 12.1 WENSLEY/3/2, Scrapbook with News Cuttings (1930–1947), p. 46
Source: Bishopsgate Library and Archives (henceforth BLA).

Wensley had snipped off the remainder of the article, leaving just the headline and images intact. Further, two other articles on the same page detailed Wensley's post-retirement invention of a device one could affix over a windscreen to prevent car theft, hardly in the same league as the canon of his more celebrated exploits as detective. Were these pasted beside each other at random, and why keep the text about the car-theft device and not the capture of the Spider?

Realising that the scrapbooks Stef had shown me were deserving of further scrutiny beyond the confines of my DPhil thesis, I began to consider 'reading' them as sources in their entirety, rather than taking a 'snippet view.' When teaching students how to write primary source analyses, the same questions always apply (not necessarily in this order):

1   Authorship. Who was the source written/created by? At what stage in their life/lives was it made? Can we draw on their professional and personal experiences, or broader social milieu, to better understand the source?
2   When was it created? What was going on at the same time, and did it coincide with any social/cultural/political/economic/technological developments or key events?
3   Is the source part of a broader genre? What methodological issues might need to be explored (such as factors relating to existing textual conventions, or memory, or the use of a particular technology) to better understand the source? Are there relevant theoretical texts that help with this?
4   Circulation. What did the author(s) intend the source to be used for, or among whom did they intend the source to be circulated, and what was the source's actual audience (if that information is available)? Who was the publisher (if there was one)?
5   Key themes of the source. In what ways does it speak to issues surrounding class, race, gender, or other theme with which its creator may have been concerned? Which do you (the student) think are most significant, and why?
6   Comparisons with other contemporary sources. What else was being written or disseminated at the time that may have influenced the source you are writing about, or that may contradict/confirm the ideas or perspective that the source propounds?

To this list, where scrapbooks are concerned, I would also add:

7   Intertextuality. The juxtaposition of different kinds of scraps makes scrapbooks inherently intertextual artefacts; 'intertextuality' meaning the way in which a single text must necessarily be read in relation to another, or more, for its meaning to be fully apprehended. Beyond the textual, scrapbooks' visual and material fragments add further layers of possible meaning, not all of which are expressed through language. As such, we must expand the definition of 'intertextual' to encompass 'texts' for which there are a range of subjective interpretations, requiring a certain comfort with drawing inferences based on logical deductions from what we also know about the conditions of

the scrapbook's creation (or educated guesses, depending on how comfortable you are with the analogy between historian and Sherlock Holmes). This gives us a broader, sometimes less tangible set of additional questions to ask. Is there a sensory quality to the messages a scrapbook is trying to communicate? What might be the emotional significance associated with scraps that may, in themselves, appear worthless? Do scrapbooks 'embody memory'?

Let's use these questions to decipher the Wensley scrapbooks. Born to a shoemaker and his wife in Taunton, Somerset, in 1865, the family had moved to London by 1881, presumably for work. After a brief stint as a telegraph messenger, at the age of twenty-two, Frederick Porter Wensley began his career in the police in 1887 as a lowly constable patrolling the poorer districts of the metropolis.[7] By quirk of fate, which might be regarded as both awful and fortuitous, the advent of Wensley's career coincided with some of the most notorious crimes in modern British history, when, the following year, a series of grotesque murders occurred in the very district with which his name was to become inextricably linked: the 1888 'Jack the Ripper' murders in Whitechapel. However, the earliest press cutting in Wensley's scrapbooks dates from around 1891, a couple of years after the Ripper murders, when the then Police Constable 'Fred' Wensley of 'L' (Lambeth) Division made the (with hindsight, sad) arrest of two 'homeless girls' for 'stealing a watch, a purse, and some clothing' from a domestic servant at the same Salvation Army Home in which they resided.[8] As the article (from an unknown publication, one of the few in the scrapbook not to be annotated), detailed, 'The magistrate marked the sheet: "I think the constable in the case displayed great intelligence and activity in arresting the prisoners,"' professional praise that would seem to account for the care taken to preserve it by Wensley. Indeed, the compliment was republished in the opening pages of Wensley's autobiography, suggesting a long-term commercial rationale for keeping it, as does the fact that Wensley's name appears in all six other news cuttings on the same page (and in the scrapbook pages that follow), always in connection with the successful prosecution of a case.[9]

Further research reinforces the notion that a celebratory strategy underpinned Wensley's scrapbooking habit from the outset, this time through an incident Wensley chose *not* to scrapbook. The 1891 cutting was not, in fact, the first time his police work had featured in the media. In 1888, a case of drunken and disorderly conduct in Southwark by Richard Morris, aged 53, made it into the *Daily News* when it was reported that in the course of arrest Morris began 'assaulting Police Constable Frederick Wensley, 153L, in the execution of his duty. . . . [Wensley] got him out of the [public] house, and prisoner refused to go away, and struck him over the left arm with a stick which he was carrying, and disabled him.'[10] The absence or 'silence' in relation to this incident in both scrapbooks and autobiography indicates it was a source of embarrassment for Wensley, a young officer at the time who should have been easily able to overpower a much older man. These initial insights into what the scrapbook tells us about Wensley, his psychology, and the masculine culture of his profession (the Victorian police force was an exclusively masculine body, and remained so until 1914) demonstrate what one can infer (1) by reading the scrapbook in isolation, and (2) by locating the scrapbook's contents in relation to other texts, including Wensley's autobiography.[11] As Gruber Garvey observes, 'For a scrapbook to be more fully understood, information needs to exist about its maker and his or her reason for creating it. If the scrapbook is separated from its maker's vision, the context is lost.'[12]

Yet such information does not always survive. Wensley was unusual for many reasons: his profession as a high-ranking detective, having been promoted through the ranks; the nature of the cases in which he was involved, including the Ripper murders and other famous cases such as the Thompson/Bywaters murder of 1922; and his post-retirement cultivation of a celebrity persona in the interwar media. As such, Wensley left the imprint of his existence across multiple corroborative texts with which one can compare his scrapbooks. Devoid of these, historians might still be able to accomplish some 'educated guesswork' about the scrapbooks' relationship to themes such as histories of masculinity, class, and celebrity by noticing the recurrence of these themes across all the press cuttings featured in the scrapbook (and that they all mention Wensley!). Few other scrapbooks are collections of cuttings relating directly to the author themselves, though. This was a feature of Wensley's celebrity shared only by the select few who likewise gained that status – the scrapbooks of celebrity photographer, artist, and theatre designer Cecil Beaton are another example.[13] That said, what one chooses to collect arguably has a bearing on the way one wishes to present one's personality and achievements, even sexual desires, to future generations. Since scrapbooks have historically offered a cheap, accessible, and democratised way of keeping and processing whatever 'scraps' appeared important to their authors, scrapbooks have survived that were created by figures as varied as 'nineteenth century doctors, plantation wives in Southern Carolina, and small-town Depression-era preteens.' The common thread between them, as Jason Vance writes, is the impulse to create and record in the first place:

> Each moment is represented through the ritualized collecting, organizing, and presenting of the information in a physical scrapbook. These scrapbooks become physical manifestations of memory and can be read as autobiographies that tell a story of a certain time, place, and idealized self through the use of recycled everyday objects.[14]

Recognising that shared impulse gives us, perhaps, the nearest means of placing scrapbooks in something we would understand as a 'genre.' Just as Wensley sought to preserve the evidence of his own life in his scrapbooks, so did many others, even without the ego-stroke of seeing their names feature in the media. Scrapbooking could ensure a kind of immortality. In 1902, the esteemed British photographer Henry Snowden Ward wrote a book on 'grangerising,' an activity closely linked to scrapbooking, whereby 'grangerisers' would cut out illustrations from books that were 'crumbling' and re-paste them into other books, as an act of 'extra-illustration.' The benefits, as Ward wrote, were not only conservation of the images:

> [t]here is no reason why any good piece of Grangerising should not become a valued British Museum unique; and there is no reason why any intelligent, reasonably educated person should not produce in his lifetime *one* volume, important enough to carry his name down to posterity, and with *very little cost* [original emphasis].[15]

This bears thinking about in relation to the history and nature of scrapbooking as an activity.

In an engaging and meticulously researched article entitled 'From scrapbook to Facebook,' Communication Studies scholar Katie Day Good traces a transnational chronology of scrapbooks' emergence as 'friendship books' (or *Stammbuch*) in sixteenth-century Germany to their digital transformation into the social media platform Facebook at the beginning of the twenty-first century.[16] Day Good's chronology intersects the evolution of scrapbooks alongside changing mass media, shifting from early records with annotations of acquaintances made alongside illustrations of travel, to the layering of texts and images with the expansion of print media and finally, the invention of photography in the nineteenth century. Throughout, these were intended as 'deeply social objects' for memorialising recent encounters and friendships alongside new experiences and ideas. As Day Good writes, 'today's social media practices are entrenched in a long history of habits and hobbies by which people interacted with media texts to both express themselves socially and, simultaneously, to document their lives.'[17] The point is echoed by historian Justin Fantauzzo, in his article about the way scrapbooking became an important practice for soldiers that had served in the Middle East during the First World War. Amassing materials to register their unique experience of warfare,

> Soldier photography and scrapbooks from the war in the Middle East remind us that the desire to capture, catalogue, and share life is anything but new. Seemingly strange, exotic lands, foreign peoples, and new experiences were all worth recording and sharing.[18]

Scrapbooks, therefore, can be analysed as statements of their creator(s)' existential 'worth' – both to themselves, to their friends and acquaintances, and at times, with an eye to history (particularly in relation to marginalised individuals and groups, as I explore presently).

Could one not make the same argument about photograph albums? At the risk of incurring the wrath of historians of photography, one can assert that scrapbooks leave more traces of the individual, being less deferential to the integrity of the materials within them when they conflict with the desire for meaning-making. For example, Wensley kept both a separate family photograph album and his scrapbooks, within the pages of which his treatment of photographs was very different

[Figure 12.2]. As Figure 12.2 shows, in the scrapbook Wensley was happy to crop images and layer them over illustrations, supplanting the latter with photographs that asserted his direct familiarity with the subjects of the press article in which they featured (two sisters rescued by Wensley and colleagues mid-way through being abducted and sold into prostitution in 1907). The cropping of the images is

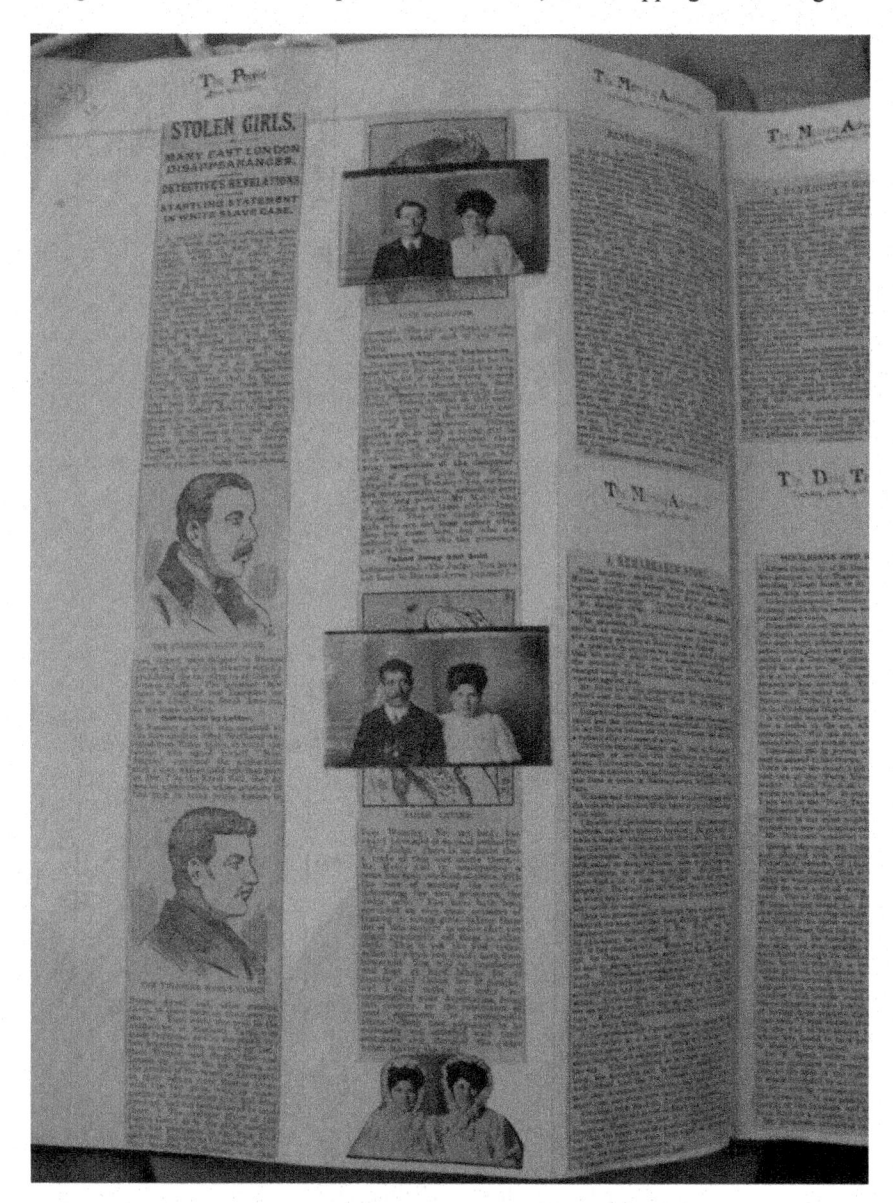

Figure 12.2 WENSLEY/3/1, Scrapbook with News Cuttings (*c*.1891–1929), p. 20
Source: BLA.

distinctive. In the top two photographs the women appear with their abductors, who posed as the sisters' husbands, and the intact frames with their opulent backgrounds suggest the money deployed to convince viewers of the respectability and legitimacy of these relationships. In the final image, situated beneath the account of their rescue, the two sisters appear returned to each other without the men, their physical proximity emphasised by Wensley having snipped around their outline, in turn highlighting matching frilly white bonnets that lend the image an almost heart-shaped innocence.

These little touches gesture at a complex form of dialogue less often found in photograph albums in quite the same manner, whereby narrative and image intersect deliberately to carefully explain to or remind the viewer of the context in which the photographs should be understood. This further gives viewers the sense that scrapbooks afford more direct access to the past, or at least, the creator's perception of it. In consequence, historian Sally Newman writes, scrapbooks can be more 'seductive' sources for scholars than most, accumulating evidence of their authors' tactile engagement with the ephemera inside that 'allowed me to indulge in the fantasy of seeing through these miniature portals into another time and place.'[19] We must, however, treat such feelings with caution, since our own sense of intimacy with these artefacts can lead scholars to 'identify' with scrapbook authors in a manner that can bely the complexity of their personalities or historically specific worldview.

Theoretical underpinnings

In attempting to develop a rationale for understanding historically what role scrapbooks have played in their creators' lives, and their significance to us today, scholars of these artefacts have drawn on the writings of nearly every well-known theorist familiar since the cultural turn. The way in which scrapbooks could be considered archives-in-microcosm has led to analogies with Jacques Derrida's observation that an archive is more than a set of materials; it is a set of practices, of selection, editing, and re-composition, channelled again through the work of the archivist (in their decision to acquire and conserve particular parts with more care than others), and then again reconstituted by the viewer(s), by their decision as to what aspects to omit, or include, in their scholarship. Hence the meaning of a scrapbook is constantly shifting between creator, archivist, and viewer, and is therefore just as slippery as any other primary source.[20] Other scholars have drawn on Pierre Bourdieu's ideas to assert scrapbooks as expressions of 'taste' and 'cultural capital,' which also bears similarity to the notion that they sustain a process through which to filter and comprehend a mass-mediated world in an act of 'textual poaching,' as propounded by philosopher Michel de Certeau.[21] On a more sinister note, Day Good suggests (with an eye to the ascent of social media) that scrapbooks were an early means of making us complicit in acts of self-surveillance, designed to reinforce existing power structures and ensure our compliance to social 'norms', especially when shared with others.[22]

From this, we can take away the point that the analysis of scrapbooks must necessarily be historicised against the development of the disparate media on which it drew at the time, and place, of its creation. Since many scrapbooks are an agglomeration of items their creators purchased – with all the politics of consumption (economic exclusion/inclusion along lines of race, class, and gender) that implies – Kristin Gilger's study of the scrapbooks collected by African American collector L.S. Alexander Gumby has also suggested scrapbooks could afford their authors an imaginative 'creative control' over the capitalist economy.[23] This evocation of scrapbooks as sites of resistance-through-reconfiguration of materials into a form that more closely reflects the author's values is a theme that recurs frequently in the scholarship on scrapbooks, reinforced by their democratic character. Finally, a focus on the way scrapbooks might serve to 'crystallise' particular memories has led historians to draw on the respective insights of Walter Benjamin and Pierre Nora. In the former case, Benjamin's notion that past habits of collecting might 'preserve' forms of memory with which viewers identify in the present, collapsing the two, is used as a reminder that scrapbooks can often seem to communicate the personality of their creators across time and space – and may well have been intended to do so.[24] By contrast, Pierre Nora's concept of '*les lieux de memoire*' – 'sites of memory' – has been applied to scrapbooks to explain their commemorative function.[25]

I suggest that the categorisation of scrapbooks into five common 'types' might offer a useful place to start thinking about whether a scrapbook was intended to function as a form of 'archive,' an act of self-fashioning, site of memory, or other model:

- Celebrity scrapbook (such as Wensley, Beaton);
- Personal scrapbook (maintained in private, possibly even hidden, with intended circulation limited to the creator and possibly, their family);
- Community scrapbook (local, knowledge-sharing function);
- Resistance Scrapbook (activists and marginalised groups);
- Institutional scrapbook (encouraged, inspired or commissioned by an institution, out of a desire for record-keeping or other form of commemoration).

As with any type of categorisation there will be natural crossover. Scrapbooks can be both personal and function as acts of resistance. Both functions are amply demonstrated in the scrapbooks of Monte Punshon (1882–1989), Australian actress, army officer, and diplomat, who, as historian Ruth Ford observes, scrapbooked images and texts about modern and eroticized versions of womanhood to explore lesbian desires that had to remain secret.[26] Wensley's scrapbook might arguably fit into a 'celebrity,' 'personal,' and 'institutional' frame of reference, given his police career. These categories are not meant to supply a set of definitive labels; the suggestions here are, as I asserted earlier, intended to act as starting-points for a more nuanced analysis that may well evolve several different, overlapping frameworks (or lines of argument) for understanding the significance of these artefacts. As with any primary source analysis, what appear to be the most significant features of a scrapbook to one historian might be entirely different from those argued for by another.

Let us examine two different ways to 'read' the Wensley scrapbooks. As I have indicated, the contents of the earliest pages of Wensley's scrapbooks strongly indicated a concern to preserve (or 'archive') those press cuttings that recorded his professional success. Hence, my own previous published work on the Wensley scrapbooks emphasized the detective's awareness of his growing celebrity, mediated via the press cuttings about himself he collected over the course of his career. Noting the 'intertextual' interaction between scrapbooked press cuttings and photographs of Wensley, and the rather triumphal tone of Wensley's autobiography, I suggested his scrapbooking habit was indicative of a strategic practice of record-keeping to inform his post-retirement plans (and income). Finally, I moved to argue that the items Wensley scrapbooked told us something important about his character and the way he regarded his (heroic) status and authority in relation to the police force, the organisation of which he progressively began to critique.

To return to the mystery of Figure 12.1, this analysis might be supported by the juxtaposition of cuttings on that page. Cutting carefully around the headline on his capture of 'The Spider,' Wensley's 'scissor-writing' also kept the image of himself and officers at the fingerprint department of Scotland Yard – housed in Wensley's own department, the C.I.D. – in focus. The record of his achievement spoke for itself (the size of the headline and images indicating the column inches he continued to attract); thus, following his retirement, Wensley's anti-car-thief invention articles, placed beside 'The Spider' article, indicate him wrestling to maintain that status and dialogue with his former profession, as well as his dissatisfaction with the clean-up rate of these crimes. A parallel process might be seen in the scrapbooks of Cecil Beaton. Besides scrapbooking materials relating to his own extremely successful career, Beaton similarly used scrapbooks to stamp his personal and professional imprint on the artistic sector in which he was pre-eminent.[27] Cutting-out and pasting magazine clippings of celebrities and fashionable figures, and re-posing them next to one another in artistic, humorous, and sometimes compromising positions, enabled Beaton to bring these figures 'into conversation' with one another and himself. Creating a tactile, homoerotic set of encounters through juxtaposition, as Dominic Janes examines, the scrapbooks distilled Beaton's 'imaginative process' into a 'camp aesthetic' that was later translated into major artworks and protest pieces utilizing collage.[28]

However, setting aside Wensley's autobiography, and picking up his family photograph album instead, one could, by contrast, argue that Wensley's personal life was the most significant thread running through his scrapbooks. Here I must recognise that my own positionality, as a historian of crime, may well have effaced an alternative exposition of Wensley's professional achievements being filtered through the lens of the masculine pride constituted by family responsibilities and paternal bonds that, as Julie-Marie Strange argues, defined Victorian working-class men's sense of self in the era Wensley grew to adulthood.[29] Pasted onto the front and back pages that bound the first scrapbook were photographs of and articles

Scrapbooks 235

about Wensley's family, including his father, his two sons (both of whom tragically died serving in the First World War), his daughter's wedding, and his grandchildren [Figure 12.3]. Additional press reports about the deaths of his sons were pasted in the centre of the volume.[30] Given their positioning, effectively book-ending the most significant era of Wensley's detective career and punctuating its 'heart,'

Figure 12.3 WENSLEY/3/1, back cover
Source: BLA.

one can hardly deny the significance of their overall juxtaposition in the broader scheme of the scrapbook's contents. This significance is further suggested by the interaction of scrapbook with photograph album, the major part of which consists of photographs of the graves of Wensley's two sons, pictures of the battlefields in France where they fought, and the visit to both sites of Wensley, his wife, and daughter Edith.[31] Hunting further in the Wensley archive at Bishopsgate reveals yet further traces of the enduring impact of the premature deaths of Wensley's sons and pride in their service; the collection includes the telegrams informing the family of their demise, mounted for hanging on the wall of their home.[32]

Again, comparable research into scrapbooking practices by those who had suffered the effects of war, like Wensley, supports this alternative reading. The aforementioned work by Fantauzzo on First World War soldiers' scrapbooks highlights, with reference to Pierre Nora, that some acted as 'spaces of private remembrance' of friends lost in the war and battlefields endured.[33] These were often private scrapbooks, not widely circulated (and indeed, Wensley's scrapbooks did not gain an audience outside his family until it was deposited at the Bishopsgate Institute in 2010).[34] Here was an example of scrapbooking serving a therapeutic purpose by 'cater[ing] to a soldier's psychological and emotional needs,' while also reaffirming masculine forms of status tied to fulfilling the military duties attached to citizenship in the Edwardian era – proof that one had been in the war, and not as a spectator.[35] This was another version of scrapbooking as an act of resistance, for, as Fantauzzo notes, the record of these (sometimes horrifying) experiences contradicted political efforts to commemorate the war as a collective memory shared by community and nation, rather than residing within personal experience.

Both analyses of the Wensley scrapbooks may be equally valid. Part of the difficulty in offering, with absolute certainty, a 'dominant' thematic analysis of scrapbooks lies in their narrative incoherence. Scrapbooks do not necessarily have a beginning or end. In Wensley's case, even his death did not quite spell the end of his scrapbooks, as his daughter continued adding in articles relating to him (including obituaries) and for several years post-mortem annotating existing scraps with information gleaned from her own research, also marking a temporary transference of 'authorship.' Thus, we could also read the scrapbooks as evidence of the relationship between father and daughter, and the forms of grief and devotion her labour signified if we adopt 'non-linear forms of reading' in Gilger's phrase.[36] Additionally, the global range of press articles relating to Wensley's career – stretching as far as America and Australia – strongly indicates that he employed a professional news cuttings service at some point to assist his collecting efforts.[37] There is no way of knowing whether this was to compensate for an interruption in his scrapbooking activities as his professional duties became more onerous (it is not uncommon for scholars to find that a scrapbook was discarded by its author for some years, then resumed again when circumstances permitted or with the waxing and waning of interest in the hobby).[38] It does, however, signal the level of fame and resources enjoyed by Wensley towards the end of his career, marking by the early 1930s a transition from working-class to upper-middle class social trappings.

The circulation of scrapbooks tells us a great deal about the creator(s) and their social worlds. This extends to the process of transition by a scrapbook from private to public ownership (such as the acquisition of the Wensley archives by the Bishopsgate Institute), likened by scholars to an act of 'publication' where scrapbooks are concerned.[39] The repository in which a scrapbook eventually finds its home offers another form of spatial juxtaposition, informing a viewer's initial encounter with these artefacts and shaping the potential meanings attached to it. The Bishopsgate Institute, for example, is well-known for its collections of archives by marginalised groups, including LGBTQ+ activists and civil rights campaigners, labour, socialist, and feminist history, as well as those of key figures relating to the history of London. In this context, the Wensley scrapbooks, and Wensley family archive, betoken a 'rags-to-riches' story stemming from Wensley's humble beginnings, as well as a slice of London's history of crime and policing. On this latter topic, they are complemented by a collection of oral history interviews conducted by famed historian Raphael Samuel with notorious East End criminal Arthur Harding, a 'contemporary' of Wensley's. On the other hand, as someone directly involved with a famous miscarriage of justice – the execution of Edith Thompson, on the grounds of letters sent to her lover, Freddie Bywaters, appearing to incite him to murder her husband – Wensley's presence in the archive sits uneasily beside the Bishopsgate's feminist history collections.[40]

Why do the Wensley scrapbooks still exist? The acquisition of a scrapbook by an archive is a choice based on the perceived significance of the scrapbook's contents, their resonance (or relevance) among the archive's other collections, the espoused 'politics' of an institution at a given historical moment, and the willingness or ability to commit resources to its conservation.[41] The 'celebrity' of a scrapbooker therefore undoubtedly helps ensure their survival. This means that many personal scrapbooks relating to everyday life have, in the past, either been lost, or remained undiscovered until some aspect of their life is considered worth recognising through the acquisition. Two examples particularly illustrate the perils of archive politics. The first is the fate of the scrapbooks kept by Philadelphia collector and civil rights activist William Henry Dorsey, whose archive of approximately 400 scrapbooks recording precious ephemera relating to African-American histories in the nineteenth century was deposited at Cheyney State College (formerly the Institute for Coloured Youth) in 1923. Subsequently, as Aston Gonzalez writes, they 'sat unused and effectively lost for decades until its rediscovery in the 1970s.'[42] Further context is supplied by Gruber Garvey, who outlines that the Dorsey scrapbooks were in existential danger 'until 1976, when they were found behind a wall in a massive office building, according to one account; hidden in storage according to another; or reclaimed from the bottom of a janitor's closet according to a third.'[43] Given their fate, it is unsurprising that, faced with the same choice in 1951, L.S. Alexander Gumby decided to donate his scrapbooks of what he termed 'Negroana' to Columbia University – 'a white institution' – since its comparative wealth guaranteed their preservation.[44]

In some circumstances, the survival of a scrapbook has rested entirely on the different aspect thrown upon its contents by the archive in which it is housed. As historian Helen Wickstead observes, the scrapbooks of nineteenth-century sexologist and anthropologist George Witt, situated in the British Museum, were for a long time 'treated more as an assortment of pornography rather than as works of serious scholarship.'[45] Forming a detailed archaeology and anthropology of sexuality and sexual practices in global cultures historically, fortunately, in recent decades the same scrapbooks have been recognised as 'among the world's most valuable resources for investigating the history of archaeologies of sexuality,' and even more crucially, necessary to 'unlock the relationships between objects, texts, and images among Witt's collections.'[46] No doubt their presence in the British Museum assisted in encouraging a reassessment (though as Wickstead points out, the pornographic features of the scrapbook are also worthy of scholarship). However, the aforementioned cases, including the Wensley scrapbooks, indicate the premium that is often placed on particular types of scrapbooks that have a more obvious educational or institutional dimension. As historian Jason Vance notes, 'just a fraction' of an incredibly important collection of scrapbooks created by librarians in Kentucky during the interwar years remain, now housed at the Franklin D. Roosevelt Presidential Library in New York. As Vance describes, these were scrapbooks designed to meet the demand for reading among rural Appalachian communities living along Pack Horse routes during the interwar years. Used to pool local knowledge about medical remedies and recipes, '[t]he resulting works not only met the demand for reading material along the Pack Horse Library routes but also became cultural artefacts of this time, place, and era in which they were created.'[47] Further, they functioned to promote literacy among their readers, partly due to the specific, digestible nature of scrapbooks which one could read in a 'non-linear way,' consuming only those scraps found interesting or relevant.[48] It would be difficult to argue that these scrapbooks were due any less preservation – or afterlife, through 'publication' in an archive – than Wensley's books.

Conclusion

Where once scrapbooks were treated uncritically as a 'hobby' deserving of little scholarly attention, there is now a healthy field of scholars examining and theorising these important artefacts. As this chapter has suggested, however, they remain a difficult source to define, given the way each scrapbook reflects the particular interests, materials, and social worlds of its creator(s). The Wensley scrapbooks illustrate how, with a wealth of other extant sources about the detective's life to hand with which to contextualise them, they can extensively enrich our understanding of both his professional and personal lives, as well as the broader social, cultural, political, and economic spaces he inhabited. Even without such additional information, the intricacies of how he juxtaposed images and text to suggest a particular narrative, and consistencies in his selection of materials with which to populate the scrapbook, offer a strong indicator of techniques scholars can use to effectively make scrapbooks legible. This chapter has, additionally, sought to suggest how my own exploration of the Wensley scrapbooks has developed over time, creating both a set of tools for those wishing to use scrapbooks for the first time, and providing what I hope is a transparent set of reflections on my own positionality in relation to the analysis featured in the original article I published using this material.

A final aim of this chapter has been to showcase the rich research on scrapbooks taking place globally, and how we might use these scholars' insights to better understand why certain scrapbooks survive and others do not, as well as the 'politics' of their acquisition by an archive (as noted, another important type of extra-textual juxtaposition where our analysis of these artefacts is concerned). Estimation of the 'worth' of a scrapbook tends to relate to its perceived lower economic and cultural value (or 'capital') versus published books, as well as a certain amount of earlier snobbery regarding the issue of 'discernment' in their contents given that they contain, well, scraps. Outside academia, it is often difficult for family historians who might be sheltering scrapbooks as a family heirloom to find the same ease of drawing connections between these 'personal' fragments of 'everyday' history, and the broader social, cultural, political, technological, and economic currents of change to which scrapbooks pertain. Hence scrapbooks' 'worth' can be grossly undervalued by those unfamiliar with the academic shift towards social history or 'history-from-below' and its impact on the field, as Family History scholars Anna Woodham *et. al.* have argued.[49] Yet, in the preservation of scrapbooks in families down the generations, as they suggest, '[t]here is clearly a great deal of expertise and experience in those who handle "unmanaged" heritage, regardless of whether the language of museums and archiving is used to describe those practices.'[50] One hopes that in the future, these efforts promise the discovery of yet more scrapbooks to confound our expectations in the archive.

Notes

1. E. Moss, *Night Raiders: Burglary and the Making of Modern Urban Life in London, 1860–1968*, Oxford: Oxford University Press, 2019.
2. F. P. Wensley, *Detective Days: A Record of Forty-Two Years' Service in the Criminal Investigation Department*, London: Cassell & Company, Ltd., 1931.
3. E. Moss, 'The scrapbooking detective: Frederick Porter Wensley and the limits of "celebrity" and "authority" in Inter-War Britain', *Social History*, 40.1, 2015, 58–81.
4. E. Gruber Garvey, *Writing with Scissors: American Scrapbooks from the Civil War to the Harlem Renaissance*, Oxford: Oxford University Press, 2013.
5. J. R. Walkowitz, *City of Dreadful Delight: Narratives of Sexual and Social Danger in Late Victorian London*, Chicago, IL: University of Chicago Press, 1992, p. 85.
6. E. Moss, '"How I had liked this villain! How I had admired him!": A.J. Raffles and the Burglar as British Icon, 1898–1939', *Journal of British Studies*, 53.1, 2014, 136–61; 'How we trapped "The Spider"', *Bristol Evening World*, 30 January 1933, cutting in BLA, WENSLEY 3/2, Scrapbook with News Cuttings (1930–1947), p. 46.
7. R. M. Morris, 'Wensley, Frederick Porter (1865–1949)', *Oxford Dictionary of National Biography*, 2010, https://doi.org/10.1093/ref:odnb/90014, last accessed 24.04.19.
8. BLA, WENSLEY 3/1, Scrapbook with news cuttings (*c*.1891–1929), 1. Although the annotation below this cutting is dated 1898, this appears to relate to the cutting that follows, with the first undated – since Wensley was promoted to Detective Sergeant by 1898.
9. Wensley, *Detective Days*, 6–7.
10. 'Southwark: Drunk or mad?' *Daily News*, 27 December 1888, 7.
11. H. Shpayer Makov, *The Ascent of the Detective: Police Sleuths in Victorian and Edwardian England*, Oxford: Oxford University Press, 2011, pp. 101–46; L. Jackson, *Women*

Police: Gender, Welfare and Surveillance in the Twentieth Century, Manchester: Manchester University Press, 2006.
12 Gruber Garvey, *Writing with Scissors*, p. 216.
13 D. Janes, 'Cecil Beaton, Richard Hamilton and the queer, transatlantic origins of pop art', *Visual Culture in Britain*, 16.3, 2015, 308–30, p. 314.
14 J. Vance, 'Librarians as authors, editors, and self-publishers: The information culture of the Kentucky Pack Horse Library scrapbooks', *Library and Information History*, 28.4, 2012, 289–308, p. 295.
15 H. Snowden Ward, *Grangerising, or Extra Illustrating*, London: Dawbarn and Ward, 1902, pp. 3–4.
16 K. Day Good, 'From scrapbook to Facebook: A history of personal media assemblage and archives', *New Media and Society*, 15.4, 2012, 557–73, p. 562.
17 Ibid., p. 559.
18 J. Fantauzzo, 'Picturing War: Soldier photography, private remembrance, and the First World War in Egypt, Sinai, and Palestine', *Journal of War and Culture Studies*, 10.3, 2017, 224–37, p. 235.
19 S. Newman, 'Sites of desire', *Australian Feminist Studies*, 25.64, 2010, 146–62, p. 153.
20 Ibid., p. 155.
21 Day Good, 'From scrapbook to Facebook', p. 565.
22 Ibid., p. 569.
23 K. Gilger, 'Otherwise lost or forgotten: Collecting black history in L.S. Alexander Gumby's "Negroana" scrapbooks', *African American Review*, 48.1/2, 2015, 111–26, p. 115; see, also: P. Wickham, 'Scrapbooks, soap dishes and screen dreams: Ephemera, everyday life and cinema history', *New Review of Film and Television Studies*, 8.3, 2010, 315–30; pp. 319–20.
24 C. Farago, '"Scraps as it were": Binding memories', *Journal of Victorian Culture*, 10.1, 2005, 111–26, pp. 114–22.
25 Newman, 'Sites of desire', p. 158; Fantauzzo, 'Picturing the war', p. 226.
26 R. Ford, 'Speculating on scrapbooks, sex, and desire', *Australian Historical Studies*, 27.106, 1996, 111–26; see, also: D. Janes, 'Frederick Rolfe's christmas cards: Popular culture and the construction of queerness in late Victorian Britain', *Early Popular Visual Culture*, 10.2, 2012, 105–24.
27 Janes, 'Cecil Beaton', p. 314.
28 Ibid., pp. 319–22.
29 J.-M. Strange, *Fatherhood and the British Working Class, 1865–1914*, Cambridge: Cambridge University Press, 2015.
30 BLA, WENSLEY/3/1, Scrapbook of newspaper cuttings, 1890–1929, inside and back covers, ff. 'NOP', 'QRS'.
31 BLA, WENSLEY/6/1 Photograph album (part of collection of family books), 1898–1933.
32 BLA, WENSLEY/4/7/6-10, Mounted copies of telegrams informing family of deaths, 1916.
33 Fantauzzo, 'Picturing war', p. 226.
34 'Wensley Family Archive', Archives Hub, https://archiveshub.jisc.ac.uk/data/gb372-wensley, last accessed 25.04.19.
35 Fantauzzo, 'Picturing war', p. 234.
36 Gilger, 'Otherwise lost or forgotten', p. 121.
37 Moss, 'Scrapbooking detective', p. 62, n. 16.
38 Farago, '"Scraps as it were"', p. 116.
39 Vance, 'Librarians as authors, editors, and self-publishers', p. 290.
40 For a fuller account of this case, see: L. Bland, 'The trials and tribulations of Edith Thompson: The capital crime of sexual incitement in 1920s England', *Journal of British Studies*, 47.3, 2008, 624–48.
41 A. R. Craft, D. Gwynn, and K. McCarty Smith, 'Uncovering social history: An interdepartmental approach to scrapbook digitization', *The American Archivist*, 79.1, 2016, 186–200.

42 A. Gonzalez, 'William Dorsey and the construction of an African American History Archive', *Social Dynamics: A Journal of African Studies*, 2019, 138–55, p. 153.
43 Gruber Garvey, *Writing with Scissors*, p. 225.
44 Ibid., p. 227.
45 H. Wickstead, 'Sex in the secret museum: Photographs from the British Museum's scrapbooks', *Photography and Culture*, 11.3, 2018, 351–66, p. 352.
46 Wickstead, 'Sex in the secret museum', p. 351.
47 Vance, 'Librarians as authors, editors, and self-publishers', p. 293.
48 Ibid., p. 305.
49 A. Woodham, L. King, L. Gloyn, V. Crewe, and F. Blair, 'We are what we keep: The "family archive", identity and public/private heritage', *Heritage and Society*, 10.3, 2017, 203–20, p. 217.
50 Ibid., p. 216.

Further reading

Day Good, Katie, 'From scrapbook to Facebook: A history of personal media assemblage and archives', *New Media and Society*, 15.4, 2012.
Delacruz, Elizabeth and Sandy Bales, 'Creating history, telling stories, and making special: Portfolios, scrapbooks, and sketchbooks', *Art Education*, 63.1, 33–9.
Gruber Garvey, Ellen, *Writing with Scissors: American Scrapbooks From the Civil War to the Harlem Renaissance*, Oxford: Oxford University Press, 2013.
Kuipers, Juliana M., 'Scrapbooks: Intrinsic value and material culture', *Journal of Archival Organization*, 2.3, 2004, 83–91.
Wickham, Phil, 'Scrapbooks, soap dishes and screen dreams: Ephemera, everyday life and cinema history', *New Review of Film and Television Studies*, 8.3, 2010, 315–30.

Index

archives 3, 13–14, 49, 62, 82, 113, 117–20, 128, 148, 161–2, 166, 172, 185–6, 199, 207–9, 217, 224, 226, 232, 233, 237–9; 'archives of the feet' 22, 49, 58, 68; digital 1, 3, 4, 6, 118, 120–1, 127, 147 *passim*, 167, 172, 185, 207
Aries, Philippe 48
art 116, 126, 187, 198; art-history 74, 169–70, 175, 184, 197, 209; art-works 1, 72, 79–80, 87, 88, 90–1, 100, 103, 106–7, 175, 196; sculpture 75, 93, 96; teaching 58
authenticity 8, 20, 32, 33, 36, 38–9, 72, 127, 135, 167, 172, 177; natural(ism) 22, 32, 54, 55, 57, 72, 87, 90, 136, 169

Beaton, Cecil 137, 139, 229, 233, 234
Benjamin, Walter 116, 233
bias 150, 155, 157, 161, 163
Bourdieu, Pierre 232
Braudel, Fernand 185
building 5, 6, 7, 10 *passim*, 32 *passim*, 49, 51, 52, 54, 56–8, 60, 68, 72, 73, 74, 75, 77, 88, 90, 95, 96, 97, 102, 140, 159, 161, 237

Certeau, Michel de 232
Classic FM 124–6
clothing 4, 5, 36, 132, 137, 168, 182 *passim*, 183–4, 185, 187, 197–9, 228
commemoration 42, 48, 50, 51, 53, 60, 61, 62, 69, 73, 76, 77, 81, 82, 213, 215, 233, 236; and public memory 60
connotation 70–1

dance 3, 23, 89, 90, 96, 97, 104, 122
Derrida, Jacques 232
design 11, 18, 20, 21, 23, 48 *passim*, 65 *passim*, 89, 90, 92, 93, 95, 98, 99, 101, 102, 106, 109, 136, 137, 169, 186, 187–8, 192, 193, 201, 209, 210, 212, 217, 219, 220, 221, 229
digitisation 1, 3, 34, 113, 115, 125, 127, 147 *passim*, 185, 207, 210, 212, 213; on-line 4, 6, 69; social media 33, 34, 35, 36, 42–5, 212, 230

economics 16, 17, 19, 20, 23, 32, 33, 34–6, 46, 49, 50, 54, 108, 115, 122, 147, 149, 150, 152, 153, 155, 156, 159, 170, 182, 184, 185, 188, 191, 192, 197, 199, 200, 210, 211, 217, 227, 233, 238, 239; commerce/ialism 53, 54, 69, 90, 95, 96, 102, 113, 114, 117–24, 125, 132, 150, 168, 169, 209, 226, 228; factories 73, 183, 192; technology 17, 33, 34, 37, 39, 45, 54, 59, 96, 114, 115, 117, 125, 162, 171, 183, 184, 191, 197, 201, 212–13, 227; trade 17, 151, 166, 168–9, 201
emotion 23, 87, 169, 208, 214; embarrassment 228; fear 142–3, 219; grief 48, 58, 69, 236; offence 102; romance 19, 22, 54, 139, 141, 186, 215
exhibition 10, 16, 23, 34, 37, 41, 119, 147, 196, 208, 211

fashion: clothing (*see* clothing); in fashion 103, 135, 191, 192, 194, 195, 234; out of fashion 1, 61
film 3, 4, 23, 95, 118, 119, 120, 124, 134, 135, 138, 195, 197, 198, 213

gaze 3, 4, 5–7, 58, 68, 78, 170, 216–19
gender 35, 40, 52, 53, 58, 68, 74–6, 77, 89, 118, 131–2, 135–6, 147, 182, 185, 187, 188, 191, 195, 197, 199, 200, 209, 213, 217, 227, 228–9, 234–5, 237
Georgism 17, 19

heritage 3, 4, 6, 10, 18–19, 20, 21, 22, 33, 34, 36, 38, 39–40, 66, 71, 73, 173, 175, 176, 178, 239; intangible 39–41, 42; organisations 32, 42, 43, 71, 77, 100, 119, 156, 157, 173

interview 1, 4, 34, 36, 65, 134, 210, 217, 237

Jagger, Mick 131

knowledge 3, 7, 14, 20, 23, 49, 73, 109, 117, 141, 148, 149, 174, 202, 210, 218, 226, 233; expertise 15, 21, 158, 224, 239; meaning 1, 4, 6, 37, 68, 70–3, 76, 78, 81, 82, 95, 103, 116, 131, 132, 167, 171, 173, 175, 176, 182–3, 184, 187, 195, 198, 200, 201, 202, 207, 208, 209, 210, 213, 214, 225, 227, 230, 232, 237; ontology 21–2, 151; paradigm 122, 127, 162; skill 3, 39, 128, 186, 193, 199

Lacan, Jacques 6
landmarks 72, 93
landscape 32 *passim*, 49, 51, 55–7, 60, 73, 81, 102, 167
law 17, 18, 20, 69, 98, 99–100, 138, 140, 142, 156, 182, 200; illegality 115, 124, 157, 200, 213; legality 51, 77, 108, 124, 132, 137, 139, 141, 156, 186, 200, 213
listening 1, 3, 5, 113 *passim*, 133
literature 10, 19, 23, 95, 100, 101, 102, 135, 148, 208, 218

maps 12–13, 14, 49, 68, 147, 150, 151, 152, 153, 155, 158, 218, 220
memory 51, 60, 62, 65, 69, 72, 73, 102, 121, 135, 208, 215, 227, 228, 229, 233, 236; historical memory 20, 65
music 3, 5, 10, 89, 91–2, 96, 102, 106, 109, 116, 143; classical 115, 122, 124–6; musicians 1, 3, 89, 92, 102, 107, 119; popular 114, 115–17, 121, 123–4, 125, 131, 132, 133; song 5, 23, 91–2, 101–2, 104, 105, 138

narrative 2, 4, 11, 12, 13, 19, 22, 32–4, 36–8, 40, 41, 45, 67, 72, 82, 91, 109, 135, 148, 162, 168, 173–4, 176, 177, 178, 183, 186, 195, 209–10, 213, 217, 221, 232, 236, 238; stories 11, 33, 43, 50, 61, 82, 89, 91, 103, 116, 121, 126, 134, 172, 175, 177, 214, 218, 229, 237

news 43, 91, 92, 115, 116, 118–19, 120, 127, 228, 236
newspapers/magazines 76, 78, 118, 123, 126, 136, 137, 138, 140, 171, 196, 198, 209, 224, 226, 228, 234

objects 10, 69, 147 *passim*, 166 *passim*, 182, 183, 186, 191, 194, 194, 220

performance 3–4, 5, 6, 7, 33–4, 36, 39, 45, 87 *passim*, 131 *passim*, 182, 202, 211; immersive 7, 41, 49, 71, 128
photography 1, 2, 7, 35, 36, 39, 43–4, 49, 80, 136, 137, 150, 170–1, 172, 174, 175, 185, 195–7, 200, 207 *passim*, 224, 229–32, 234, 236
pirate radio 113, 115, 123–4

radio 3, 113 *passim*, 132, 147
recording 1, 3, 5, 113, 117, 118, 119–20, 121, 123, 124, 127, 136, 138, 140
relics 174; data-relicts 2
restoration 4, 10, 14, 16, 20–1, 23, 38, 39, 41, 45, 103

sexuality 132, 135, 142, 234, 237
symbols 3, 17–18, 22, 32, 52–3, 58, 70–1, 77, 87, 92, 95, 96, 100, 106, 123, 143, 184, 187, 210, 211, 214, 215, 216, 217, 218, 220; allegory 89–90, 91, 96–100, 101–6, 107, 109; flags 17, 23, 41, 220

television 3, 4, 6, 34, 77, 113, 114, 121, 123, 125, 127, 131 *passim*, 212, 219
tourism 4, 6, 10, 18, 20, 21, 23, 32 *passim*, 65, 67, 71, 76, 81, 82, 90, 95, 97, 174, 175, 176, 178, 196, 211, 213, 219, 236
turns: cultural 185, 232; iconic 207; literary 2; material 147–8, 185; quantitative 148; spatial 2, 10, 151

de Vargas, Blas Infante Pérez 9
visitors 2, 4, 6, 19, 23, 32 *passim*, 65, 67, 71, 76, 78, 81, 82, 90, 95, 97, 174, 175, 176, 178, 196, 211, 213, 219, 236

World in Action 131